Cultural Chaos

D0544353

~y, FK9 4LA

Cultural Chaos explores the changing relationship between journalism and power in an increasingly globalised news culture. It examines the processes of cultural, geographic and political dissolution which are a feature of the post-Cold War era, in the context of global ideological realignment, rapid evolution in information and communication technologies, and an increasingly anarchic cultural marketplace. It investigates the impact of these trends on domestic and international journalism, and on political processes in democratic and authoritarian societies across the world. It also assesses the implications of these trends for media scholarship.

With examples drawn from media coverage of the war on terror and the 2003 invasion of Iraq, Hurricane Katrina and the London Underground bombings, students and teachers will find in *Cultural Chaos* an overview of the evolution of the sociology of journalism, a critical review of current sociological thinking within media studies, and an argument for revision and renewal of the paradigms which have dominated the field since the early twentieth century. Separate chapters are devoted to the rise of the blogosphere and satellite television news.

Written in a lively and accessible style, *Cultural Chaos* is essential reading for all those interested in the emerging globalised news culture of the twenty-first century.

Brian McNair is Professor of Journalism and Communication at the University of Strathclyde. His previous books include *An Introduction to Political Communication* (3rd Edition, 2003), *News and Journalism in the UK* (4th Edition, 2003), *Striptease Culture* (2002), *Journalism and Democracy* (2000), *The Sociology of Journalism* (1998) and *Glasnost, Perestroika and the Soviet Media* (1991).

Cultural Chaos

Journalism, news and power in
a globalised world

Brian McNair

 Routledge
Taylor & Francis Group

LONDON AND NEW YORK

First published 2006
by Routledge
2 Park Square, Milton Park, Abingdon, Oxon OX14 4RN

Simultaneously published in the USA and Canada
by Routledge
270 Madison Ave, New York, NY 10016

Routledge is an imprint of the Taylor & Francis Group, an informa business

Typeset in Baskerville by
Keystroke, Jacaranda Lodge, Wolverhampton
Printed and bound in Great Britain by
The Cromwell Press, Trowbridge, Wiltshire

British Library Cataloguing in Publication Data
A catalogue record for this book is available from the British Library

Library of Congress Cataloging in Publication Data
McNair, Brian, 1959–
    Cultural chaos : journalism, news, and power in a globalised
    world / Brian McNair.
        p. cm.
    Includes bibliographical references and index.
    1. Journalism–Social aspects. 2. Broadcast journalism.
    3. Government and the press. I. Title.
PN4749.M35 2006
302.23–dc22   2005029925

ISBN10: 0–415–33912–X (hbk)
ISBN10: 0–415–33913–8 (pbk)
ISBN10: 0–203–44872–3 (ebk)

ISBN13: 978–0–415–33912–4 (hbk)
ISBN13: 978–0–415–33913–1 (pbk)
ISBN13: 978–0–203–44872–4 (ebk)

Contents

Preface

This book is about the emerging relationship between journalism and power in a globalised world. It argues that changes in the political, economic, ideological and technological environments which shape globalised news culture are impacting on that relationship in ways that traditional media studies paradigms fail to acknowledge. In doing so it takes issue with two central strands in the critical orthodoxy which has dominated scholarly thinking about journalistic media.

The first I will call the *control (or dominance) paradigm*, to refer to that set of critical approaches which views capitalist culture, and journalism in particular, as a monstrous apparatus bearing down on passive populations of deluded, misguided or manipulated people. For all the variations on and refinements of that basic theme that have emerged in cultural theory since the early twentieth century, the idea of media as control mechanisms responsible for maintaining unjust social divisions remains core to materialist media sociology, and to critical commentary in general. This book, written though it is within a materialist framework, argues that the control paradigm is inadequate for the challenges facing media sociology in the twenty-first century, not because it was never valid, but because the world for which it seemed to offer powerful explanations of cultural phenomena has changed.[1] If theories of ideological domination and control made sense as an explanation for social order and political consensus in the twentieth century, they are less applicable to the ideologically realigned, hyper-adversarial, decentralised and demand-driven media environment of the twenty-first.

As an alternative way of seeing the relationship between journalistic media and power in contemporary societies, this book proposes a *chaos paradigm*. This approach shifts the analytic focus from the mechanisms of ideological control and domination to those of anarchy and disruption; to the possibilities allowed by an emerging *cultural chaos* for dissent, openness and diversity rather than closure, exclusivity and ideological homogeneity. The terminology and conceptual apparatus of chaos – a science developed in the late twentieth century to cope with the dynamics of non-linear systems in nature – are here applied to the turbulent flow of journalistic communication.

Adoption of a chaos paradigm, I shall argue, encourages the rejection of a second strand in the critical orthodoxy – *cultural pessimism*. This is the approach which asserts a process of backward evolution in capitalist culture, away from media outputs viewed as in one way or another good or worthy, and towards those defined as debased, vulgarised and dangerous. Cultural pessimism goes back at least as far as the first print media, was prominent in late-nineteenth-century commentary on the emerging popular journalism of that time, and was central to the arguments of Frankfurt School theorists such as Max Horkheimer and Theodor Adorno. Their 1944 work, *Dialectic of Enlightenment,* articulated a view of mass culture as a degraded, degenerate, 'barbaric' thing, manipulating the 'deceived masses' with barely less cynicism and sinister efficiency than the Nazi propaganda apparatus which had caused them to flee Europe.[2] They, like cultural pessimists before and since, did not associate media evolution with human progress, but implicated it in the manufacture of compliant, subordinate populations who, if they only knew what was good for them, would be consuming high cultural artefacts of quality and distinction as opposed to the commercialised trash offered by, for example, Hollywood cinema. 'This bloated pleasure apparatus', they wrote of the 1940s movie business, 'adds no dignity to men's lives . . . the example of movie stars encourages young people to experiment with sex and later leads to broken marriages' (1973: 221). The same or similar was true in their view of radio, maga-zines, popular newspapers and all other media which the mass culture critics, then as now, defined as degenerate, corrupt and inauthentic. Goodness knows what they would have made of *Big Brother* and internet porn, although it is reasonable to assume they would not have approved.

Since the 1940s cultural pessimism has remained authoritative and influential across the western critical tradition and in relation to every form of media output.[3] Political communication is said to be debased and dumbed down. Children are discussed as if they were zombies at the mercy of TV and computer screens. Adults are said to have their senses dulled by infotainment. The culture of contem-porary capitalism is not viewed as a liberating force, but as the new opium of the masses.[4] This book argues to the contrary that many things in the sphere of jour-nalistic communication are improving, as measured against normative standards of what our news media should be doing to and for the people who rely on them for information. There is much for the critic still to criticise, no doubt, but against the pervasive negativism that defines the critical scholarly consensus I want to advance a *pragmatic cultural optimism*, rooted in the recognition of what has changed for the better.

In making these arguments, *Cultural Chaos* develops ideas first sketched out in *The Sociology of Journalism* (1998) and *Journalism and Democracy* (2000), then in essays subsequently published in *Media, Culture & Society* (2003) and elsewhere. Those writings, and now this book, address recurring questions that have arisen in the course of my work since the late 1980s, when I saw at first hand how Mikhail Gorbachev's *glasnost* and his top-down attempt to reform the Soviet Union's moribund political and economic systems were complicated and ultimately over-whelmed by the influence of open communication within the country. Subsequent work on political communication in democratic societies has repeatedly provoked the sense that the premise of a close structural link between economic, cultural and socio-political power – what is called in media studies the *political economy model* –

fails to account for the complex dynamics of the twenty-first-century media system, or the unruliness of its journalistic outputs. If the desire of political elites in both democratic and authoritarian societies to control media remains as strong as it ever was, it is also true that putting those desires into practice has become more problematic than critical media sociology (with its focus on structure, hierarchy, dominance and control) has traditionally acknowledged.

If I adopt an optimistic stance it is also because, in thinking and writing about the sociology of sexual representation and gender politics over a number of years,[5] I have noted the potential of cultural capitalism to promote social progress (in so far as such trends as the advance of women's and gay rights, or the steady margin-alisation of racism within news and other media forms are deemed progressive). This recognition goes against the grain of media and cultural studies' generally pessimistic premises, which even now find it difficult to accept that the media in our time might be playing a positive socio-cultural role. This book presents a contribution to the case for a re-orientation of the sociological gaze towards a vantage point from which it can be recognised that, while not everything in our emerging globalised news culture is welcome, much more of it is than we media sociologists have been prepared to acknowledge.

Using this book

Students and their teachers will find this book a guide to much that has been written about the relationship between journalism and power in the last 30 years, as well as an overview of the rapidly evolving globalised news culture which forms the backdrop to their lives and studies. To my academic colleagues the book, and Part I in particular, presents a critique of some of the orthodoxies within which they currently teach and research the field. Beyond the academy, I hope the book may also be of interest to non-academic readers who are interested in the factors driving the evolution of journalism in the coming years and decades. For those readers I have kept technical jargon to a minimum and relegated it where possible to footnotes, my Foreword on the relevance of chaos science to media sociology, and Part I on 'Critiquing critical theory'.

Brian McNair
Glasgow, 2006

Acknowledgements

Financial support to undertake research in the United States, the United Kingdom and Australia was generously provided by the Carnegie Trust for the Universities of Scotland, the University of Stirling and the University of Strathclyde. A number of colleagues made constructively critical comments on the work as it evolved, and on the typescript as it neared completion. Special thanks go to Barbie Zelizer, Monroe Price, James W. Carey, Todd Gitlin and Danny Schechter in the United States; Catharine Lumby, David McKnight, Jessika Lofstedt, Simon Cottle, Hari Harindranath, Sally Young, John Hartley and Alan McKee in Australia; Jairo Lugo in Scotland. My thanks to all who contributed their time and advice, along with the customary qualification that responsibility for the views expressed herein is mine alone.

Foreword: a note on chaos

When Max Horkheimer and Theodor Adorno used the term *cultural chaos* in their 1944 essay 'The Culture Industry'[1] it was in the context of 'the loss of the support of religion, the dissolution of the last remains of precapitalism' (1973: 120). They associated this process with an industrial culture which 'now impresses the same stamp on everything' (ibid.),[2] and, as we have seen, were deeply pessimistic about the 'barbaric' consequences. Later in the twentieth century 'cultural chaos' was used by US Christian and conservative sects to describe the emergence of negative (as they perceived them) moral trends such as the growing acceptance of homosexuality in mainstream American culture. In August 1999 R. Albert Mohler Jr, president of the Southern Baptist Theological Seminary in Louisville, Kentucky, speaking on CNN's *Larry King Live* show, argued that 'the result of embracing the homosexual lifestyle is cultural chaos, the breakdown of our entire moral order'.[3] The webmasters for *Bushcountry.org* ('promoting the ideals of conservatism') used the term to describe the consequences of same-sex marriage in the USA.

Elsewhere, though, 'chaos' has come to have a less pejorative meaning. In the language of natural science 'chaos' is a descriptive term, devoid of negative moral connotations. Through the work of physicists, cosmologists, meteorologists and others we have come to understand that in the natural world chaos just *is*; a state of things which, if not universal, is commonplace. Defined by James Gleick as 'a science of process rather than state, of becoming rather than being' (1996: 5), the study of chaos can be summarised as the search for understanding of that category of non-linear systems in nature which had hitherto been excluded from Newtonian law-making by their apparent complexity, such as weather systems. If Newton's laws could predict the motion of planets moving around a star based on precise calculations of mass and velocity, or the depth of tidal waters on a beach decades into the future, there was nothing in the science based on that tradition which could predict tomorrow's weather with equivalent certainty. There were simply too many variables acting on weather systems for them to be reducible to deterministic laws of the Newtonian type. Such systems were chaotic or, as Edward Lorenz (1993) defined the term, 'sensitively dependent on interior changes in initial conditions'. The evolution of a chaotic system is determined not by linear laws (of gravity or thermodynamics for example) but by its pre-history, and the influence upon it of other, equally contingent systems. Chaotic systems are fundamentally unpredictable, although with sufficiently sophisticated mathematical tools they can be modelled.

From the 1950s scientists, armed for the first time with electronic computers capable of handling millions of individual measurements and calculations in a split second, applied themselves to unravelling these complexities. They were looking for patterns in the apparent unpredictability of weather; for warning of the sudden cascade of an avalanche or a mud slide; for underlying order amidst the chaos which seemed to characterise so many natural phenomena.[4]

Chaos has been recognised as a law of nature and the source of great beauty, as well as the cause of the destruction caused by hurricanes, earthquakes and volcanic eruptions. The mathematics of chaos have been applied to reveal the infinitely complex images of fractals, and to shed light on the process of biological evolution.[5] It has enhanced our understanding of how a complex universe works by revealing pattern within irregular structures such as clouds. It has alerted us to the possibilities of disorder and immanent collapse in apparently stable systems; to the certainty, as The Divine Comedy put it in their song of that name, of chance.[6] It has enabled better understanding of the processes which lead to phenomena as diverse as heart attacks, traffic jams and tropical storms.

This morally neutral sense is how I use *cultural chaos* in this book, to refer to the various disruptions accompanying the emergence of the globalised news culture of the twenty-first century. These signal a contemporary communication environment in which, as in nature, chaos creates as well as destroys, generating in the process enhanced possibilities for progressive cultural, political and social evolution, as well as trends towards social entropy and disorder. In that sense my usage is comparable to that of the 'chaos paradigm' attributed by Samuel Huntington to writings by Zbignew Brzezinski and Daniel Moynihan in the early 1990s, in which they referred to 'the breakdown of governmental authority; the break-up of states; the intensification of tribal, ethnic and religious conflicts; the spread of terrorism' (Huntington 1996: 35). My application of the terminology acknowledges all of that, while allowing for the possibility that the consequences of chaos (Part IV) can be both positive and negative.

In adapting the language of chaos to media sociology, I am aware of the dangers of importing a conceptual framework developed by the natural sciences into social science and humanities scholarship. These were exposed in Sokal and Bricmont's unsparing critique of what they characterise as 'postmodernism' (1998), but what is perhaps more accurately viewed as a relatively marginal, mainly French, subset of that strand of cultural studies which came to prominence in the late twentieth century, and acquired influence in some sectors of the English-speaking academy.[7] Baudrillard, Kristeva, the late Jacques Derrida and the rest do not intend their use of the jargon of natural science to be taken literally, one assumes, but the ponderous pseudo-scientificity of their writings, at least when translated into English, should not be permitted to exclude the possibility of productive intellectual synthesis between the spheres of natural science, social science and the humanities. Steven Johnson calls for scholarly work that 'tries to bridge the two worlds [of humanities and the sciences], that looks for connections rather than divisions' (2005: 209). My premise here is that the science of chaos offers a route into precisely the kind of 'conceptual bridge-building' Johnson proposes. Bridge-building between disciplines has, indeed, been a notable by-product of the focus on chaos within natural science, which has brought mathematicians together with physicists, epidemiologists with biologists, and so on. Why not employ it to the even greater divide which has long existed between natural science, social science and the humanities?[8]

There is resistance to this suggestion. Cohen and Stewart argue that 'there are no big areas of reductionist causality in social science' (1995: 182). For Sokal and Bricmont, the science of chaos can tell us little of value about social phenomena because 'human societies are complicated systems involving a vast number of variables, for which one is unable to write down any sensible equations. To speak of chaos for these systems does not take us much further than the intuition already contained in the popular wisdom' (1998: 136). Evolutionary biologist Richard Dawkins' review of the Sokal and Bricmont book shares its contempt for those 'intellectual imposters' such as Jean Baudrillard, whom Dawkins identifies as 'one of many to find chaos theory a useful tool for bamboozling readers' (2004: 59). For Dawkins, as for many others who revelled in Alan Sokal's hoax played on the American *Social Text* journal,[9] the use in social sciences and humanities writing of concepts drawn from natural science – not just chaos, but complexity, relativity, probability, quantum mechanics and others – is the last refuge of, if not the scoundrel, then those 'with nothing to say, but with strong ambitions to succeed in academic life' (ibid.: 55).

This is ironic, since Dawkins himself commits just such an act of allegedly inappropriate appropriation when he discusses the *meme* in *The Selfish Gene* (1989). With the concept of the meme, Dawkins suggests that the science that produced evolutionary biology and our modern-day understanding of genetics can be applied to the study of cultural evolution – the emergence, spread and adaptation of ideas, ideologies, fashion trends, religions. Dawkins does not mean his readers to view cultural evolution as exactly the same as biological evolution (there is no agreement, for example, on what unit of human communication a meme actually describes – is it a word, or an idea, or a worldview? Some dispute that there is such as thing as a meme at all, because, unlike a gene, it cannot be captured or measured in a laboratory context).[10] Dawkins merely wishes us to accept that there are parallels and analogies to be drawn between the two processes; that there are universal evolutionary principles which might apply to the abstract communicative creations of the human brain – *memotypes* – as much as to the concrete physical shapes of animals and plants (phenotypes); that human consciousness, and its intellectual products, are emergent properties of biological self-organisation, rather than the manifestations of divine creation or some other mechanism of intelligent design.[11]

Dawkins' essay on 'Viruses of the mind'[12] applies the memetic approach to religious ideas. The use of the term 'virus' to describe religious beliefs is also metaphorical, of course, though thought-provoking in its capacity to make us view the process of ideological 'contagion' (another concept appropriated from biology) in new and potentially fruitful ways. There is indeed, when one looks at it through the prism of Dawkins' viral paradigm, something contagious about the spread of religious ideas in general, and thus something to be gained from thinking about their comparative fitness for survival in a competitive ideological environment. That is the sense in which I propose a sociology of cultural chaos, where the concept of chaos is adapted from its technical usage in the discourse of natural science in order to facilitate a better understanding of how social processes (the public sphere of memes rather than the biosphere of genes) such as journalistic communication unfold and evolve. These processes – media effects on individuals, organisations and societies; the emergence of news stories and the aperiodic but cyclical nature of news agendas; the catastrophic potential of terrorist media spectaculars such as 9/11 – are fundamentally non-linear, and thus highly contingent. Like the strange attractors of chaos science,[13] they exhibit structure, but of an irregular kind. Communication systems are never in exactly the same place twice. We may discern patterns in the news cycle, but we know that, unlike the chaos-inspired plot of *Groundhog Day*, the same news story will never appear twice in exactly the same form.

In observing the essentially non-linear nature of communication systems, I am not suggesting that media sociology has much to gain from a crude application of the mathematics or physics of chaos. Nor do I dispute the long-held view of social scientists and humanities scholars that the objects of their intellectual labours are fundamentally different from those of physicists or astronomers. The worlds of social and natural science *are* distinct, epistemologically and methodologically. Natural scientists on the one hand have it harder than their colleagues in the social sciences and humanities, because the skills of top-flight mathematics and physics are difficult to master and at their peak the province of genius. They also have it easier, in that they can recreate and simulate many of the phenomena which interest them in vacuum chambers and particle accelerators. They can isolate, observe and experiment on them with a degree of empirical precision which sociologists or political scientists cannot match, testing hypotheses, formulating laws, and making predictions likely to be just as valid in one region of time and space as another. They generate statements which can be proved or disproved, and which allow empirically validated conclusions to be drawn.

These distinctions have been recognised and institutionalised over time. Intellectual barriers were long ago erected between natural and social science, as they have been between the various disciplines that make up natural and social science, between social science and humanities in general, and even, in my own field of communication, between such closely related areas as media sociology and cultural studies, many of whose practitioners treat each other as heretics to be despised and avoided at all costs. For good reasons and bad, disciplinary demarcation has been the norm for both natural and social science for centuries, further encouraged in recent times by the deepening specialisation of academic work and intensified professional competition for resources. That such compartmentalisation is now eroding in the natural scientific disciplines, not least because of the discoveries of chaos science,[14] can be viewed as one facet of the broader process of cultural dissolution described in Chapter 1 below, although it goes back at least as far as Marx's debt to Darwin, Einstein's theory of relativity, and the development of quantum mechanics. In the course of these advances, and especially through the work of Einstein and his successors, the importance of observer standpoint, uncertainty and probability to the workings of the natural world were recognised, fuelling a more general movement towards scientific and philosophical relativism which then leaked into the humanities and social sciences through the work of Thomas Kuhn and others.

This seems entirely appropriate. Social science, like the humanities, *necessarily* engages with complex, non-linear systems, and with phenomena shaped by multiple causal factors, including those arising from the workings of human emotion, perceptual relativism, subjectivity and cultural specificity. Social systems and processes are inherently non-linear. The problems of social science are inherently difficult to resolve by Newtonian cause-and-effect methodology, and more difficult to compute than any quantum solution. This is precisely what makes them suitable for the application of a chaos paradigm. What the science of chaos declares, after all, is that many natural processes are more like those we find in human society than Newton and his heirs could accept; that if important differences exist between natural and social systems, there are also more similarities than we realised.

Moreover, resistance to the adoption by social scientists and humanities scholarship of at least some of the elements of chaos science goes against the grain of two centuries of western intellectual development. Since Saint-Simon's invention of the 'science of man' and the emergence of positivism, and for all the epistemological and methodological challenges associated with doing so convincingly, we social *scientists* have always (as the appropriation of the word 'science' to describe the practice of such disciplines as sociology, political studies and economics itself gives away) sought the status and respect afforded the scientific. We have borrowed freely from the established natural sciences to develop theories and models of how the social world works, which, we hope, will be persuasive. Consequently, when the disciplines of natural science are seeking to incorporate the chaos paradigm into their theories of how the world works, it is entirely consistent with the history of social science that its practitioners should follow suit and abandon their reliance on the 'machine model'.

At times, let us concede, scholarly eagerness to engage with natural philosophy has tipped over into the arcane discourse of pseudo-science dissected by Sokal and Bricmont's taking apart of French post-structuralism and those influenced by it.[15] In the hands of some materialist thinkers, the authority and ideological power of scientific rhetoric has been used in the pursuit of political domination, to separate historical materialism, and later Marxism-Leninism, from mere ideology, and to win support for the notion of a *scientific* socialism (as opposed to lesser, non-scientific varieties). Louis Althusser's writings on Marx,[16] for example, largely comprise the attempt to demonstrate that the latter's 'epistemological break' with Ricardo, Smith, Malthus and other economic theorists of early capitalism, as set out most explicitly in *Theories of Surplus Value* (Marx 1969), amounted to a scientific leap analogous to the overthrow of the founding myths of Judaeo-Christian civilisation with a scientific theory of evolution. Just as Charles Darwin placed natural selection as the mechanism at the centre of the history of all organisms (deposing God and the myth of Creation), Marx (whose materialist dialectic was strongly influenced by Darwin's ideas) is argued by materialist sociologists to have revealed 'scientifically' the inner workings of the capitalist mode of production, and to have identified the motor force of human social evolution as the production and accumulation of material wealth, or capital.

Capitalism, which Marx is often said to have 'discovered', grew and spread like no previous mode of production because of its immense capacity for wealth creation. In time, though, and with all the inevitability of a natural scientific law, capitalism would disintegrate and be replaced by a higher mode of production, which he called communism.[17] Thus Marx turned the idealist Hegelian dialectic on its head to advance a 'scientific' theory of history as a process driven not by the actions of God on the world (what Hegel called the Absolute Spirit), but by economic forces of human origin (through the dialectical workings of which feudalism evolves into capitalism, which inevitably becomes communism). 'We recognise only one science, the science of history', wrote Marx and Engels in *The German Ideology* of 1845 (1976).

Lenin too, in the years of exile before he became a working revolutionary as the leader of Soviet Russia, wrote philosophical works promoting the scientificity of materialist thought, comparing it favourably with the bourgeois illusions under which his idealist philosophical contemporaries laboured.[18] In the materialist tradition, and especially its Marxist-Leninist variants as developed by Joseph Stalin, the communist parties of the Third International and later by western sociologists and philosophers such as Althusser, to be recognised as *scientific* was the Holy Grail of intellectual work, the distinguishing characteristic of Truth over Illusion, the ultimate riposte to the falsehoods of bourgeois ideology. The lingering impact of this view on materialist sociology has been a prolonged search for structures and laws of social motion which match in their applicability and solidity those observed at work in the physical universe. Such laws, once 'discovered', have repeatedly been used to justify the brutal dictatorships that killed millions of people in the Soviet Union in the decades during and after Lenin's death, and then again in Pol Pot's Kampuchea, Mao's China and Kim Il Jung's North Korea, to name the four most murderous laboratories of scientific socialism.

These perversions of the scientific method should not, however, prevent contemporary social scientists from arguing that to know the social world with the greatest possible accuracy is an entirely admirable aspiration. If natural science can move from mechanistic determinism and Newtonian linearity to the recognition of deterministic chaos, is it not reasonable to ask if social science might make the same journey? If the natural systems of the cosmos, the atmosphere and the oceans are now recognised as requiring a break with linear models, are not social systems in all their messy human-ness appropriate subjects for a similar approach? In asking that question, social science is merely doing what it has always done – learning lessons from the natural sciences.

Take, for example, the perennial problem of media effects, and the unending claims that this or that category of image – be it advertising, pornography, fictional screen violence, confrontational political journalism – is the cause of some unwelcome societal phenomenon or another (for example, and with respect to the categories of media message just listed, eating disorders, the rise in divorce, male violence, voter apathy). While confident assertions of cause and effect, stimulus and response are routinely made about the relationship between media messages and their reception, these have never, despite decades of trying, been verified to a standard which a physicist or a chemist would regard as reliable. Nor could they be. How can we know that the behaviours and attitudes observed in a given individual or group of individuals have been 'caused' by a media image, as opposed to any one of an unknowable, incalculable number of potential influences on an individual's personality and thought processes, which are as contingent as those driving any weather system? How can we know, without detailed micro-research of the type no social scientist will ever be sufficiently resourced to be able to carry out, what a particular media image means (and thus might cause an individual to think or do) to all the thousands, millions, or billions of individuals who might consume it, each in his or her unique environmental circumstances? In August 2005 the British government announced proposals to criminalise the consumption of violent pornography on the internet. Criticising the proposal in the *Guardian* newspaper, criminologist David Wilson noted that it 'seems based on the idea that viewing violent images produces violent acts. However, there is now 60 years' worth of research that suggests this simply isn't the case':

> We have yet to unravel the complex relationships between images, fantasy and action, and, crucially, which comes first . . . We know that the relationship between thinking, viewing and acting on that thinking is multifaceted and complex, and not at all as clear-cut and simple as has been presented. Look, for example, at motivation – in other words, where does the motivation to consume violent and pornographic images come from, and, crucially, is that motivation created by looking at violent and pornographic images, or does it already exist?[19]

To put it another way – advertising half-price sofas will generate a behavioural response in some consumers, but not all, and it is practically impossible to predict into which category a given individual will fall. As soon as one gets beyond the most simplistic of promotional communications to the more 'open' texts of journalism and art, the extent of media effects becomes insoluble within ways of thinking that assume that communication functions with a stimulus–response linearity. These are precisely the kinds of complex problems which, when encountered in the natural world, the science of chaos sets out to solve, or at least to understand more completely. If the motion of three bodies interacting in space is a problem of non-linear dynamics, the media effects problem is one of non-linear *cultural* dynamics.

John Gray has attacked contemporary social science and the positivist worldview in general (which he erroneously suggests are synonymous) for 'believing that [they] can establish universal laws of human behaviour, and thereby forecast the future development of mankind' (2003: 106). Of course, as he goes on to write, 'the behaviour of human beings cannot be predicted in this way'. Which is precisely the value of applying concepts drawn from the science of chaos to the phenomena of social life. The applicability of chaos and its related fields of enquiry to social science and the humanities is not that they might at some point in the future enable better prediction of what is currently unpredictable (although enhanced manageability of non-linear processes is already possible in such fields as emergency and traffic management), but that it permits a break with the systemic determinism which has traditionally framed the materialist perspective, and opens up new possibilities for thinking about such problems as media effects and the management of power.

As Roger Lewin has suggested, 'cultural evolution may be [an example] of an important general phenomenon' (1992) to which the study of chaos may be able to offer some valuable insights. It may be that in doing so, we are compelled to acknowledge that nothing is predictable, that all the best-laid plans are doomed to unravel in the chaos of events. Such a recognition will, however, of itself have implications for social actors of all kinds, and especially for how professional communicators, including journalists and their nemeses, the public relations specialists, do their work. It makes more transparent the idea that social processes *are* chaotic: contingent and unpredictable in their evolution, despite intense efforts to manage them by social actors; that power in a globalised, mediated world has become more fluid and fragile, no longer monopolised by ruling classes whose dominance is pre-determined by structural advantage.

In the context of globalised news culture, to talk about chaos is to argue that the journalistic environment, far from being an instrument or apparatus of social control by a dominant elite, has become more and more like the weather and the oceans in the age of global warming – turbulent, unpredictable, extreme. Like storm fronts, journalistic information flows around the world in globally con-nected streams of real-time data, forming stories which become news and then descend through the networked nodes of the world wide web to impact on national public spheres. Some stories, like some storms, blow themselves out harmlessly. Others, such as the Abu Ghraib prisoner-abuse scandal of 2004, 'get legs' and build to catastrophic political crises, despite the efforts of public relations and spin professionals to reassert elite control. Just as in meteorology, a complex of environ-mental variables, often undetectable to observers, determines whether or not a thunderstorm will develop into a twister over the Midwest plains and go on to wreak havoc to life and property. Similarly, a complex of contingent factors will determine if a particular event, firstly, achieves the status of a news story, and then becomes a significant factor in the news agenda before impacting on the political sphere. By thinking of this process as analogous to the phenomenon of chaos in nature, where cascades and tipping points regularly emerge to have unforeseen and catastrophic effects, we can ask: what are the conditions leading to such an outcome, and can they be acted upon or influenced by social actors?

Niklas Luhmann (1994) writes that 'sociology can strive to improve its instru-ments of description and to build a greater amount of controllable complexity into the self-description of society'. The chaos paradigm represents one approach to that effort. It draws on the related discipline of network theory, which is advancing understanding of the dynamics of data communication and message dissemination in a world wired up as never before. Duncan Watts observes that in an information environment globally connected by the communication technologies of satellites and computers, the dynamics of *social contagion* – the tendency of ideas, fashion fads or cultural trends (Dawkins' *memes*) to spread – are changing. 'When it comes to epidemics of disease, financial crises, political revolutions, social movements and dangerous ideas, we are all connected by short chains of influence' (Watts 2003: 301). Moreover, 'in connected systems, cause and effect are related in complicated and often quite misleading ways'. The study of communication networks, for Watts, 'can help us understand both the structure of connected systems and the way that different sorts of influences propagate through them' (ibid.: 303). The growth of a transnational communication network alters the dynamics by which events become news, news agendas are formed, and then impact on public debate and governmental decision-making.

Chaos and communication

Two insights produced by the science of chaos are applicable to media sociology. First, phenomena arising from the workings of non-linear systems are always *contingent*. Which is to say that they display what chaos scientists call sensitive dependence on the initial conditions of the system. Small variations in those initial conditions, such as the proverbial butterfly flapping its wings in a tropical rain forest, will be expressed through huge differences in outcome further down the line (producing a storm in London, for example, where otherwise only a light breeze might have been felt). The 'Butterfly effect', as its discoverer Edward Lorenz called it,[20] is how the world has come to understand the nature of chaos, although it is much more complex than that, since there are a very large number of butterflies flapping their hypothetical wings and impacting on the evolution of all non-linear systems, at all times. It is this fact which leads to their unpredictability. While we know with certainty that summer is warmer than winter, we cannot know, even a few days in advance, that rain will not fall on July 4.

As the butterfly analogy suggests, from contingency comes *interconnectedness*. M. Mitchell Waldrop writes that in chaotic systems

> everything is connected, and often with incredible sensitivity. Tiny pertur-bations [disturbances in the system] won't remain tiny. Under the right circumstances the slightest uncertainty can grow until the system's future becomes utterly unpredictable, or chaotic . . . Chaos theory tells you that the slightest uncertainty in your knowledge of the initial conditions will often grow inexorably. After a while, your predictions are nonsense.
>
> (Waldrop 1992: 66)

Miniscule variations are amplified as a system evolves, so that while the same laws of thermodynamics may be acting on two drops of water as they fall from a tap, the pattern of descent of each will quickly diverge, an idea entertainingly played out by Jeff Goldblum's scientist in Steven Spielberg's *Jurassic Park*, based on Michael Crichton's novel inspired by the implications of chaos for the management of complex, humanly fallible systems such as theme parks and genetic experimentation.[21]

The plot of *Jurassic Park* alerts us, if in dramatised Hollywood style, to the truism that the workings of many social systems – business organisations, government departments, societies and collectives of all kinds – are analogous to those of non-linear systems in nature. While subject to rules, regulations and laws intended to govern their operation, their evolution is highly contingent on (sensitive to) initial conditions over which no government or board of management can have absolute control. Outcomes are closely connected with, and affected by, not just initial conditions, but the evolution of other, equally contingent systems. They are thus inherently unpredictable. Small perturbations early in a system's evolution (the imprisonment or exiling of a dissident) can be amplified into huge social fractures (a political revolution). This is a process in which media are crucial, since the information alerting members of a society to phenomena on which they might act or have a view can only flow along whatever channels of communication exist in that society. In this sense, media organisations are the agents of cultural chaos. More media, moving more information further and faster, means a more chaotic communication environment, with corresponding implications for the acquisition and management of power in society.

Applications

Since the emergence of semiology as a 'science of signs', and through the emphasis placed by Stuart Hall and others on differential decoding, to more recent theories of the active audience, media sociologists have long worked with a chaotic model of communication, even if they have not tended to use the language of chaos science. That language has obvious applicability to the analysis of non-linear communication processes such as the rise and fall of stories on the news agenda, and the spread of moral panics and health scares, as well as the identification of the factors involved in policy formation,[22] decision-making and media management. Some news cycles are periodic and relatively predictable, such as those that form around election campaigns. Others are aperiodic, unstable and unpredictable, such as the news of the Asian tsunami of December 2004. Others still are periodic, but unpredictable, such as the 'silly season' which occurs in Britain and many other countries during the summer holiday season. This period marks the summer recess of Parliament and a frequent dearth of hard news (many reporters, like the rest of the population, being on vacation), leading to an eruption of quirky, minor news stories.

In making such distinctions, there are clear applications for a chaos paradigm in the study and practice of forms of persuasive communication such as public relations, which would not exist were it not for the volatility and turbulence of the communication flows unleashed by democratisation and the evolution of mass media in the twentieth century. PR can be viewed (and without making any assumptions about its effectiveness in particular cases) as a set of techniques for managing chaos, and for reducing uncertainty in the communication environment.

A chaos paradigm can be applied to the study of media effects, as noted above, and to media content, which can no longer be viewed, if it ever could, as the planned product of conspiratorial elites acting in unity. The chaos paradigm approaches content only *in context*, viewing it as the outcome of contingent processes which, though they may be influenced by quite simple underlying rules, are fundamentally unpredictable.

The creativity of chaos

One hypothesis of chaos science is that on the boundary between order and chaos – the Phase Transition – there is a zone within which creative, constructive things happen, such as the emergence of new biological species. This anarchy is one source of what we might call *progress* (or evolution). By extension to the sphere of materialist sociology, a world characterised by a vibrant cultural chaos (as opposed to elite-imposed order) is a world less likely to be vulnerable to control by dominant elites and ruling classes, be they communists, capitalists, Islamic fundamentalists or Christian conservatives; a world in which, in that state somewhere between order and chaos which best describes the times in which we live, top-down control is eroded, bottom-up creativity flourishes, and the struggle for human freedom can be advanced in new ways. A world governed by the non-linear dynamics of cultural chaos is, in short, a different world to that imagined by the materialist sociological tradition, with its assumptions of the ruling and the ruled over, of dominant and dominated, of superior and subordinate, of passive mass and active elite. It is a world, I suggest, in which a cautious, pragmatic optimism is, far from being naïvely utopian or Panglossially optimistic, quite reasonable.

Which is not to say that such a world cannot work to the political benefit, at least in the short term, of groups such as Al Qaida. The capacity to communicate at a global level of relatively small political entities, including those of extreme reactionary and fascistic views, is enhanced in an environment of cultural chaos. The growth of Islamic fundamentalist terror in the late twentieth century was in part a response to the accurate perception that globalised culture threatens authoritarian, patriarchal ideologies with the visible evidence it presents of the possibilities for individual freedom and well-being now provided by advanced capitalist societies (especially for women, ethnic minorities, homosexuals and other groups). That terror has in turn produced a backlash in the United States and other western societies which threatens to engulf the world in religiously inspired conflict. Not least among the aims of a sociology of cultural chaos will be to contribute to the prevention of that outcome.

1 Cultural chaos and the globalisation of journalism

As a student of the news media in the early 1980s it was necessary, if one wished to make empirically substantiated statements about news content, to take into account a finite number of national newspaper titles – in the UK, ten dailies, and another ten or so Sunday publications – and news bulletins on three television channels (BBC1, BBC2, ITV), amounting to perhaps two hours per day of TV news in total. Radio carried hourly bulletins and some current affairs, mainly on the BBC's Radio Four. Monitoring, archiving and analysing this material, as I had to do on becoming a postgraduate research student with the Glasgow University Media Group in 1982, was an expensive and time-consuming task, though satisfying in the feeling the exercise gave of inclusivity. Even after the arrival of a fourth terrestrial channel in January of that year, systematic content analysis of news output was still the realistic goal of a do-able research methodology. As late as 1991 one could still aspire to 'know' one's object of study – news content – in something approximating to its entirety.

Fast forward another decade, to September 11 2001. On that day, British viewers had access to coverage of events unfolding in New York not only on five terrestrial TV channels,[1] but also on three indigenously produced, dedicated 24-hour news services (BBC News 24, Sky News, ITV News), as well as the output of CNN, CNBC, Bloomberg and others available through subscription. There was also Radio Five Live, set up by the BBC in 1993 and dedicated to news and sport.

By then, too, there was the internet, providing hundreds of millions of people all over the world with round-the-clock access to online coverage from established titles such as the *Guardian* and the *New York Times*, as well as thousands of independent information and news-based web sites – not yet the 'blogosphere', as it has come to be known, but even in late 2001 a vast and growing network of online journalism. In 2002 the internet was estimated to contain some 533 petabytes of information (one petabyte = 10^{12} bits), including 7.5 terabytes of downloadable information, or the equivalent of the entire contents of the Library of Congress. Add to that an estimated 440 petabytes of annual emails, and the scale of online media was, even then, truly mind-boggling. It has expanded hugely in size since these estimates were made, and will continue to do so for the foreseeable future.[2]

The effect of these technological developments on the communication environment has been to increase exponentially the quantity of news and related forms of journalistic information which are available to the world's populations, whether they live in an advanced capitalist society, an emerging economic superpower such as India or China, an authoritarian Middle Eastern state, or a developing country in Africa. A graph depicting this expansion over a quarter of a century would begin in 1980, pre-CNN, with total journalistic information available at a low and steady level. This information would comprise national media outputs in print and broadcast form, a few global newspapers and transnational radio outlets such as the BBC's World Service. Thereafter the line would begin to rise as first CNN, then the BBC's World Service TV, News Corporation's Star, Bloomberg, CNBC, Al Jazeera and other transnational TV channels came on stream. By 2001 the quantity of news available had risen to infinity, from the perspective of the individual, since by then it was possible for any cable or satellite TV viewer, almost anywhere in the world, to watch TV news or surf online journalism sites for every hour in the day, and still not access more than a minute fraction of what was out there. The availability of news had reached saturation point.

Not only is there more news and journalism, but it circulates further and at much greater speed than ever before. The speed of news flow has increased, reducing the gap between an event's happening, its being noted and reported, analysed, discussed and acted upon. This acceleration is a function of the combined technologies of cable, computer and satellite, and of the highly networked nature of the global media environment, in which online journalists and bloggers who post an article or item in one part of the world immediately become part of a globally accessible system, their postings indexed, linked, signposted for others, rapidly becoming part of the common conversation of millions.

This book is about the impact of these trends on people and power, so let me begin here with a personal anecdote. I was on sabbatical study leave in the far north-east of Australia, 12,000 miles from my home in Scotland, when the first plane hit the World Trade Center on September 11 2001. It was approximately 10.45 p.m. in that geographically isolated part of the world, and my wife and I were eating pizza with a friend at a local restaurant. When we got home just after 11 o'clock I switched on CNN, as I often did at that time of night while 'down under', to enable me to keep up with events on the other side of the world. Like all those who were not in the immediate vicinity of the twin towers I missed the first strike, tuning in to the live TV coverage at a point when the north tower was already burning, but nobody as yet knew why. CNN's correspondents were speculating about the possible causes of the fire clearly visible on camera, but without firm information.

Along with the hundreds of millions of people by now following CNN and other broadcasters I witnessed the second strike as it happened a few moments later, and stayed with CNN throughout a night of journalistic confusion, panic and disbelief. As the realisation of what had happened grew and the towers fell, from that remote outpost in tropical Queensland I joined a global audience of spectators to an act of mass murder which would shape the course of world events for the foreseeable future, and which happened in real time, before the eyes of everyone on the planet with access to a television.

The sense of connection between my location in Australia, and events occuring 15,000 miles and 14 time zones away, was both exhilarating and unsettling. My feelings of anger, incapacity and impotence in the face of such an act were the same, I imagine, as those experienced by CNN correspondents narrating the drama from their Manhattan offices, although we were half a world apart. That sense of belonging to a new kind of global community was sharpened in the course of the Coalition invasion first of Afghanistan and then of Iraq when, like millions of others across the globe, I watched as live TV images showed Saddam's troops hunting frantically for a downed US airman in the River Tigris, or when Saddam's statue was pulled down on the day of 'victory' itself.

By coincidence I was again in far north Queensland watching CNN Asia when I received news of the July 7 suicide bomb attacks in London. Again, confusion and chaos reigned for several hours, in the TV studios as on the London streets, until the true nature of the events began to be clarified. The London bombings of July 2005, like the 9/11 attacks and their aftermath, were exceptional events that demonstrated in the most graphic way how growth in the quantity of journalistic and fact-based information in circulation, in conjunction with parallel trends in political culture and the media economy which I explore in the chapters below, are transforming the way individuals, institutions and societies relate to and interact with the world around them. The scale of that transformation suggests the need for what I have previously characterised as a new sociology of journalism, equipped to make sense of a different world to that in which the established paradigms of media sociology were formed. I characterise this re-orientation as a movement from a *control* to a *chaos* paradigm; a departure from the sociologist's traditional stress on the media's functionality for an unjust and unequal social order, towards greater recognition of their capacity for the disruption and interruption, even subversion of established authority structures.

The control paradigm stresses the importance of structure, stasis and hierarchy in the maintenance of an unjust social order. It is premised on economic determinacy, whereby ruling elites are presumed to be able to extend their control of economic resources to control of the cultural apparatuses of media, including the means of propaganda and public relations, leading to planned and predictable outcomes such as pro-elite media bias, dominant ideology, even 'brainwashing'. These outputs are then implicated in the maintenance of ideological control in the interests of dominant groups, whether these have been defined in terms of class, gender, ethnicity or some other criteria of stratification. The control–outcome–impact process is viewed as linear and mechanistic. It is, to use Malcolm Gladwell's phrase, a 'machine model' (2000) of the media–culture–society relationship.

By contrast, the chaos paradigm acknowledges the *desire* for control on the part of elites, while suggesting that the performance, or exercise of control, is increasingly interrupted and disrupted by unpredictable eruptions and bifurcations arising from the impact of economic, political, ideological and technological factors on communication processes. These lead to unplanned outcomes in media content – dissent from elite accounts of events rather than dominant ideology or bias; ideological competition rather than hegemony; increased volatility of news agendas;

and this routinely, rather than exceptionally. In September 2005 the random natural disaster of Hurricane Katrina unleashed a cascade of critical news coverage upon the administration of George W. Bush, setting in motion a chain of events with unpredictable political outcomes for the United States. This was a result not just of Katrina's destructive power (a naturally chaotic phenomenon) but of the 24-hour coverage that it generated, both in America and beyond. Body counts of ten and twenty thousand were reported in the first week of the crisis; grisly tales of looting, rape, murder and even cannibalism commandeered headlines. In the end, a few hundred died, and most of the atrocity stories turned out to be false. Before calm returned, however, the Bush administration was put on the defensive as never before since 2000.

The main argument of this book is to suggest that while the desire for control of the news agenda, and for definitional power in the journalistic construction of meaning, are powerful and ever-present, not least in a time of war and perceived global crisis, the capacity of elite groups to wield it effectively is more limited than it has been since the emergence of the first news media in the sixteenth century. To repeat, this is not an approach that seeks to deny the importance of control as a goal of elite groups in the political, military and economic spheres, or of social actors in general. Nor does it assume that the potential for control of cultural processes and information flows is entirely or forever lost.[3] We are living, after all, through an era in which religiously rather than class-inspired vanguardists – jihadists on the one hand, neo-conservatives and evangelical Christians on the other – are engaged in ferocious propaganda wars for global public opinion, using the full range of new information and communication technologies in their attempts to control and shape the global news agenda. As we shall see in Part IV, govern-ments of both the democratic and authoritarian type, as well as non-state actors like Al Qaida, constantly develop and refine their media management tools in the effort to assert control and/or restore order to turbulence in the globalised public sphere. The chaos paradigm acknowledges this, while questioning the extent to which communicative control can in contemporary conditions ever be more than an aspiration to which all social actors, whether resource-rich or -poor, must work with ever-decreasing guarantees of success. It views journalistic organisations and the professionals who staff them as more independent and disruptive of power in their communicative activity than their allotted role in critical media sociology (which is to act as agents of elite domination) has allowed. The chaos paradigm does not abolish the desire for control; it focuses on the shrinking media space available for securing it ideologically.

Cultural chaos in the era of dissolutions

The adoption of a chaos paradigm is a necessary response to what is emerging as a period of political, economic, ideological and cultural dissolution and realign-ment, unfolding globally across a range of axes and dimensions. The most visible aspect of this process, in relation to news and journalism, has been the technology-driven dissolution of the *spatial* boundaries which throughout human history have separated countries and continents. This has meant the narrowing of that distance from his or her mediated experience of remote events which was formerly imposed on the consumer of news by the passing of time. Our ancestors read or heard about events that had occurred in far-off places only long after the fact, a period of time determined by the level of technological development of the transport and communicative infrastructures which allowed information to be borne back from the point where things happened to the locations where they could be narrativised, packaged and disseminated as news. In the sixteenth and seventeenth centuries weeks passed between the battle and the news of it entering circulation. As the technologies of news gathering and distribution advanced that period shortened until, with the introduction of live broadcasting by satellite in the 1950s, it had shrunk to the time required for information to be electronically encoded and decoded, beamed to and from satellites in orbit, and for the carrier medium of light waves to cross the earth. For logistical reasons, journalists working in print and broadcast media still experienced delays in getting their news on air or into print of up to three days as recently as the 1970s and the Vietnam War. Only in the 1990s did conflict journalism become part of real-time news, and only in the post-9/11 conflict in Iraq did live reportage from the battlefield, with journalists embedded amongst front-line troops, become part of the routine experience of TV audiences around the world. We are not describing a revolution, then, but a long historical process, characterised by the gradual erosion of what Anthony Giddens has called *time–space distanciation* (1990), rather than a single event; a process of cultural evolution, but one that has accelerated in the half century or so since the first live global broadcast provided pictures of the 1953 coronation of Queen Elizabeth II to the world.

Giddens identifies a feature of modernity as the separation and regulation of time and space through 'disembedding mechanisms' such as money and media. These allow the extension of social relations across geographical space, while maintaining the physical separation of social actors. For Giddens the concept of 'high modernity' – what others might call *postmodernity*[4] – describes an era in which these separations are eroding through technology, and globalisation accelerates. The world has been 'shrinking', in this sense, for ever, or at least since the first communication media were invented. Drums and smoke signals, letters and morse code, newspapers, telegraph, radio and TV – each in turn brought human beings closer together, although decades and centuries separated the main technological leaps. What has changed with electronic media, and the invention of communication satellites and computers in particular, is the speed of this dissolution, and the abruptness with which we have been confronted with its results.[5] In 1990 Michael Gurevitch observed that the evolution of satellite communications technology had ushered in 'a qualitatively new stage in the globalisation of news' (1990: 179). Only four years later the launch of the world wide web produced another huge leap, of even greater cultural impact.

As with other aspects of technological progress, the rate of change has been exponential, facilitated in recent decades by the end of broadcast spectrum scarcity and the proliferation of dedicated news channels with transnational reach. Since the rise of CNN in the 1980s, the medium of rolling satellite TV news has made it possible to experience in real time, or 'live', events that are far away, so that news in this form has become something that is happening, rather than something that has happened. Images on a television screen are always a simulation of reality, of course, since what we see and hear through even the most advanced TV monitor can only ever be approximations of actual sights and sounds. But the immediacy and proximity of the illusion are real enough as we become spectators of, perhaps even feel ourselves to be participants in, events which in an earlier era would have been available only as verbal or written accounts days, weeks or months after their occurrence.

News is still what news always was: a socially constructed account of reality, rather than reality itself, composed of literary, verbal and pictorial elements which combine to form a journalistic narrative disseminated through print, broadcast or online media. No matter how 'live' the news is, and regardless of how raw and visceral the account of events being brought into our living rooms appears to be, it is still a mediated version of reality, what Niklas Luhmann (2000: 1) describes as 'a transcendental illusion'. But it is an illusion which, when we receive it, and when we extend to it our trust in its authority as a representation of the real, transports us from the relative isolation of our domestic environments, the parochialism of our streets and small towns, the crowded bustle of our big cities, to membership of virtual global communities, united in their access to *these* events, communally experienced at *this* moment, through global communication networks.

Since Anthony Giddens coined the term, the erosion of time–space distanciation has continued to the point where it would appear to have reached a limit defined by the speed of light itself.[6] CNN broke journalistic ground with its live coverage of the first Gulf War in 1991. Just ten years later we watched in awe as the twin towers collapsed before our eyes, and then followed Coalition military forces live into Afghanistan and Iraq. Many of my British readers will recall the unsettling experience of watching Sky News in April 2003, as a correspondent and camera crew followed British troops into a building where Iraqi soldiers were believed to be hiding. In the 4 a.m. darkness, illuminated only by ghostly-green night vision lights, we watched as the skirmish unfolded. At one point, a British soldier emerged from the building, his clothes in flames, and the camera rolled on while his comrades beat out the flames with their hands. At another location during the same invasion of Iraq (Mosul in the Kurdish north), a BBC camera crew led by foreign affairs editor John Simpson came under 'friendly fire' from a US fighter bomber. One of Simpson's crew was killed, and he himself was injured. The viewer back home in Britain was not watching as the bomb fell, but live coverage commenced moments after the attack, with a blood-smeared camera lens providing harrowing images of death, destruction and confusion.

John Gray remarks that the term *globalisation* 'really signifies no more than the widening and deepening connections that are being created throughout the world by new information and communication technologies that abolish or foreshorten time and distance' (Gray 2003: 112). If the economic and cultural effects of globalisation have been debated for some time now, and will be debated further in the chapters below, the psychological, emotional and sociological consequences of these deepening connections in the sphere of journalistic culture are not yet clear. Susan Moeller's *Compassion Fatigue* (1999), published before 9/11, articulated a widespread concern that through real-time news exposure to such human catastrophes as famine, flood and genocide, populations in advanced capitalist societies were losing their capacity to care, and belief in their ability to have any impact on events. Despite, or perhaps because of the application of news values which stress negativity and conflict, she wrote:

> TV audiences have in general very little understanding of events in the developing world or of major international institutions or relationships. This is in part the result of TV coverage which tends to focus on dramatic, violent and tragic images while giving very little context or explanation to the events which are being portrayed.
>
> (Moeller 1999: 17)

Not in itself an original critique of a system of mainstream news values that emphasises drama and conflict at the expense of exposition and background, the suggestion that we care less because we have become fatigued by the proximity of human suffering made possible through news media is even more relevant to the post-9/11 world, when we have not just the violence, the drama and the tragedy, but we have it in real time and around the clock. Can I be alone in feeling uncomfortable about watching live coverage of the September 11 attacks or the invasion of Iraq with the same sense of anticipation as I would apply to the World Cup finals or the Olympics? Whatever justification I may have made to myself for watching coverage of these events so obsessively (and of course they *were* important stories, so could easily be justified as a valid use of one's time), this was mass murder and war as entertainment.

Geographical separation does still matter, in so far as it offers physical and existential insulation from the horrifying reality which is so often the subject of satellite and online news media. We watch the twin towers falling in real time, in high definition, digitised sound and vision, but we cannot feel the pain of people burning or falling or choking to death. We cannot smell the smoke, or feel the vibration caused by bodies crashing to the ground. The horror we feel as viewers of real-time news is unprecedented for media audiences, but not comparable to that experienced by participants in the event, or by those present in the streets below. It is, indeed, more like the fear and exhilaration experienced by watching a movie on the big screen, but with an added viscerality contributed by the awareness that this scene, unlike a movie, *is really happening*, right now, to real people.

The unfolding chaos of the September 2004 school siege in Beslan, Ingushetia, was similarly distressing to those who watched live coverage of it on CNN and other real-time news channels. We knew that something terrible was happening, but never exactly what. We knew too, as on 9/11, that there was absolutely nothing we could do about it. The chaos of the situation on the ground was reflected in the inability of journalists to tell a story with anything like a conventional beginning, middle and end. There was a tragic conclusion to the event, in relation to which global TV viewers were passive spectators bearing horrified witness to an atrocity-in-motion. In this we shared precisely the emotions of journalists covering the story, and of politicians in Moscow or Washington wrestling with a chaotic situation, which was at the same time a global media event with potentially momentous political implications.

Different emotions are unleashed by the experience made possible by online media. On the internet, liveness is not so important as the fact that there is relatively little censorship of the information crossing national borders. In the era of cultural chaos, the internet becomes a weapon of war, used by insurgent organisations to disseminate images of terror into the homes of the enemy. The murders by decapitation of Daniel Pearl, Ken Bigley and many others were not broadcast live, but video recordings of the acts were uploaded onto internet sites, and provided to media organisations. British and American TV news organisations chose not to show these images in anything like their entirety, for reasons of taste and decency with which even the fiercest opponent of censorship can sympathise, but the know-ledge that they were available to be seen on the web – that they existed, out there in cyberspace – had a profoundly disturbing emotional impact. They brought geographically distant atrocity into the living room, from where it entered the collective imagination as the stuff of nightmares.

Thus we are permitted to be spectators of things which, before the invention of live broadcasting, satellite TV and the internet, we could have experienced only through the second-, third- or fourth-hand account of a print journalist, or an edited broadcast news bulletin. This has become possible not just because of the onward march of computer and satellite technology, but because of the miniaturisation of cameras, editing equipment and video-capable satellite phones. The potential for instantaneity has been supplemented by spontaneity, as journalists have become much more mobile in war zones and other newsworthy venues. The construction processes of journalistic selection and editing remain as important as ever, so that with real-time and online news we are still receiving an account, but without the sensation of separation in both time and space which necessarily accompanied the journalism of an earlier era.

Walls come tumbling down

It is clear that, while they remain in place, the relevance of *political* borders has been substantially weakened by the expansion of new information and communication technologies (NICTs). This is not to say that the nation-state itself is dissolving, or even decreasing in importance.[7] On the contrary, in the wake of the fall of the Soviet Union, and with the continuing impact of post-colonial independence movements in the developing world, the number of sovereign states recognised by the United Nations has steadily increased. The 2004 Athens Olympics saw 202 teams parade before the world, including sporting representatives of post-Taliban Afghanistan and post-Saddam Iraq. In advanced capitalist countries such as the United Kingdom, Spain and Italy strong, sometimes violent movements for 'national' independence persist. And notwithstanding the role of some media in dissolving geo-political barriers, most of what we consume as media is still national in origin and orientation. As McKenzie Wark (1999: 15) correctly observes, 'broadcasting, in particular, still creates powerful national zones which are unlikely to be dissipated by transnational media for some time yet.' As a rallying point for political action, then, national sovereignty is alive and kicking, while national identity remains a potent source of cultural inspiration.

But the sovereign nation-state is faced with the erosion of many of its traditional powers, not least among them the power of control over information crossing its borders and circulating within its territory. Whether in respect of news and journalism, pirated copies of movies and music, or the sexual transgressions contained in online pornography, the evolution of new information and communication technologies has substantially weakened the capacity of nation-states to police information flows. Despite continuing efforts by authoritarian states such as China, Cuba and Iran to hold the line, their cultural and ideological isolation has been reduced, and that of individuals within those countries to consume the cultural products of other countries (including journalism) enhanced. Umberto Eco has written, in respect of Europe, that 'we are in a historically new situation, unthinkable even fifty years ago. Short holidays or shopping trips regularly take us quite nonchalantly over borders that our fathers would only ever have crossed under arms'.[8] As tourists we bring our cultures with us, to places like Cuba and China as well as Tuscany and Mallorca. But culture also travels across borders through the globalised media, 'infecting' hitherto quarantined societies with the values of liberal capitalism. Monroe Price has asked if 'the nation-state can survive in a world in which the boundaries of culture, faith and imagination do not' (1995: 236). More than a decade later it is possible to answer that, yes, nation-states have survived, and will continue to do so, because the technology-driven dissolution of boundaries does not end national identity, so much as force it to engage with other, perhaps conflicting identities.

Paralleling the dissolution of political borders has been the process of ideological dissolution and realignment which has unfolded since the fall of the Berlin Wall in November 1989, and the demise of the Soviet Union shortly thereafter in 1991. Prior to that point, for the 70 years or so since the Bolshevik Revolution of 1917, and interrupted only by the 1939–45 war which saw a one-off strategic east–west alliance against the common threat of fascism, the majority of the world's nations were grouped into one or other of two politico-ideological blocs – capitalism on the one hand, state socialism on the other. That distinction no longer has relevance beyond the borders of a handful of decaying 'socialist' states. The new global ideological divides, as 9/11 jarred us into realising, are those between secularism and religion, modernity and medievalism, democracy and authoritarianism. Ideology has not ended, any more than history has, but the defining bi-polarity of the twentieth century has dissolved, and with it the frameworks within which journalists in that period tended to make sense of events both global and domestic.

Socio-cultural dissolution

Within nation-states we have seen the dissolution of many long-established social and cultural boundaries, often with hugely disruptive consequences for elite political actors.[9] On the one hand, new technologies have spawned a proliferation of communication channels along which news flows faster and more freely than at any previous time in human history. On the other, that news is increasingly irreverent of and lacking in reserve towards elites. If political scandal (or any other kind) is not unique to the late twentieth and early twenty-first centuries,[10] the speed with which scandalous information spreads and reproduces certainly is, fuelled by the commercial imperative of news organisations to compete with one another in being first with the story. The public–private distinction which has traditionally maintained a separation between news coverage of the affairs of state and the affairs of statesmen (for men they usually are)[11] has been eroded.

The presidency of Bill Clinton was the most extreme example to date of this phenomenon, with its drawn-out sagas of alleged corruption and sexual infidelity, live videotaped testimonies about sexual intimacy, and best-selling autobiographies (from both the President and Mrs Clinton), not to mention the media feeding-frenzy around Monica Lewinsky herself. We live in what I have previously described as a culture of emotional striptease and confession (McNair 2002), where 'we' extends to the previously insulated elites of the political, business and entertainment worlds. 'The personal is political' has become true in a way that the feminists who coined the slogan could never have imagined, and the affairs of the private sphere have become an increasingly important part of the business of the public sphere.[12]

Associated with this process has been a related erosion of the distinction between high and low in journalistic culture, that view which automatically defines tabloid journalism as trash, and broadsheet newspapers (or their TV equivalents) as 'quality'. In the academic sphere, writers such as John Hartley (1996) and Catharine Lumby (1999) have defended the radical, even revolutionary virtues of popular journalism. More recently, Steven Johnson's *Everything Bad Is Good for You* (2005) dares to suggest that reality TV – a hybrid of observational documentary, game show and soap opera – can legitimately be evaluated, not as the freak show or manifestation of cultural degeneracy described in most critical commentary on the subject, but as complex, individually empowering television. Here and elsewhere, taste hierarchies used to police cultural consumption are eroding.

Accompanying these dissolutions, stratificatory distinctions between social classes, between white and black, homosexual and heterosexual, masculine and feminine – boundaries which have directed the unequal allocation of economic and political resources for centuries – have also been challenged. The quasi-journalistic forms of reality TV, for example, are spaces where the ordinary become celebrities, and celebrities are reduced to the level of the ordinary. *Big Brother* in the UK and elsewhere has been a valuable platform, even as the streets of British cities were inflamed by race riots, for primetime displays of multiculturalism and multi-ethnicity.[13]

In the arena of 'straight' news, journalists have repeatedly broken high-profile stories about racism (the Trent Lott revelations of 2004; the Stephen Lawrence story in the UK), sexism (the Clinton–Lewinsky scandal), and the rights (and wrongs) of homosexuals. If in the past coverage of celebrity homosexuality would have been framed in overtly homophobic terms almost everywhere in the media, the gayness of such stars as George Michael and Elton John, once acknowledged, has often become the vehicle for an expanded and largely non-judgemental public discussion of homosexuality. While homophobic and other reactionary eruptions occur from time to time, not least because of the ascendant religious conservatism of the era in which we live, even tabloids such as the UK *Sun* have grown up and learnt to live with the presence of gay men and women in most walks of life. Elsewhere, as in coverage of some UK footballers' domestic violence and racist attitudes, the journalism of celebrity has often propelled the erosion – what I prefer to call the *progressive dissolution* – of oppressive taboos and discriminatory moral standards.

Although this trend dates back to the 1960s and the rise of gay rights and feminism, it too has accelerated amidst a media environment of daytime TV, therapy culture and reality TV.[14] In journalism the normative separation of the public and private spheres has narrowed, as the business of politics has become more personalised, and the worlds of entertainment, government, business and other spheres have merged. John B. Thompson observes that 'as recently as the early 1960s it was common practice for journalists to refrain from probing and publicising the private lives of public figures' (2000: 82). As Seymour Hersh's account of the JFK-era White House revealed, the hyperactive sex life of the glamorous President Kennedy was an open secret to the political journalists of the time, some of whom were present at more than one of his White House sex sessions (Hersh 1997). Kennedy's sexual promiscuity remained hidden from the American people as a whole until well after his death, however. That it would do so now, in the era of the internet and real-time TV news, is inconceivable.

The hybridisation of journalism

Dissolving, too, are boundaries between journalism and not-journalism, between information and entertainment, objectivity and subjectivity, truth and lies. Dan Schiller was right to note that as new media technology advances, 'boundaries between news, entertainment, public relations and advertising, always fluid historically, are now becoming almost invisible' (1986: 21). For Schiller this was a negative trend, associated with the growth of what critics have called 'info-tainment', meaning news and journalism in which the normatively approved delivery of 'rational' information is sacrificed in the name of audience- and profit-friendly entertainment. It is also a prescient forecast of how reality, as mediated through real-time news and the internet, indeed becomes a kind of entertainment, stimulating and perhaps terrifying in its consumption, but compelling at the same time.

Technology has contributed not just to the globalisation of news culture, but the dissolution of the boundary between truth and lies which journalists have jealously guarded since the seventeenth century. The activities of Stephen Glass,

Jayson Blair and others, often exposed by online media, have made audiences aware of the extent to which the digitisation of newsroom practices make ethical lapses in journalism – fabrication and plagiarism in those cases – easier to inflict on established media, and even on publications of record such as the *New York Times* and the *New Republic*.

A related facet of the current 'crisis of objectivity' is the status of honestly arrived at information disseminated through the expanding universe of online journalism and web-blogs. As more and more information becomes available to users of the internet, it becomes more and more difficult to evaluate reliably the quality of that information. Hamilton and Jenner's discussion of 'the new foreign correspondence' notes that 'internet international news provided by untrained and unsupervised journalists can flood public discussion with error, rumour, and disinformation that is often difficult to sort out from the authentic and factual' (2003: 137). In the age of the internet the production of international news has been diversified, decentralised and democratised, in so far as both its production and consumption have become much more accessible to the averagely resourced individual. But with the explosion in the quantity of information flowing around the world, the consumer's ability to discriminate between truth and falsity, honesty and deceit, accuracy and error, has inevitably been reduced.

At the same time the journalistic ethic of objectivity, and with it a large degree of the public's trust in the veracity of news output, has been destabilised with the development of portable technologies and the recognition of the inevitability of subjectivity by many of the most popular of today's journalists, such as Michael Moore, Nick Broomfield and Louis Theroux. If this trend began with the New Journalism movement of the 1960s in the United States, first-person journalism has now become the stuff of prime-time TV and mainstream multiplex cinema. To an even greater extent than in the gonzo journalism of the late Hunter Thompson, the huge popularity of first-person documentaries in the early years of the twenty-first century reflected a cultural environment of fluidity and uncertainty, a world where there is acknowledged to be no absolute truth, just a plurality of vantage points, of which the *auteur*'s is only one. Of course, that *auteur* wants us, the audience, to accept his or her viewpoint as the most accurate, perceptive and valid. But a feature of many of these journalistic narratives is the stress they put on the possibility of alternative interpretations of events. These transparently subjective forms of journalism have been made possible not just by the current vogue for personalised, confessional journalism, but by the advent of new technologies such as lightweight digital cameras and affordable editing software, which make possible unprecedented levels of editorial self-reliance and information-gathering autonomy.[15]

Optimism, pessimism, agnosticism

Whether we consider the dimensions of time and space, the political lines which correspond to state borders, the stratifications traditionally associated with class, ethnic and sexual identities, the formal categories of genre separating journalism from not-journalism, or the taste and aesthetic hierarchies handed down over centuries to police the consumption of different categories of journalistic information, the tendency to cultural dissolution is emerging as a general characteristic of human societies in the twenty-first century.

Some observers are optimistic about this trend, both for the prospects of good government in liberal democracies, and for the long-term future of authoritarian societies around the world. In their introduction to *Global Journalism* (2006), Wilkins and Lacy identify the 'optimistic perspective' of those 'who rejoice in the security and progress promised by the age of enlightenment', and who believe that we are in the midst of 'a continuation of the Enlightenment project of historical progress, where technology, democracy, free markets and the deterritorialising dynamism they make possible lead to a cosmopolitan planet where traditional identities and practices lose significance'.

Others take the opposite view, seeing the future as containing more, not less, of what critical commentators often call *cultural imperialism*, and the consolidation of western, especially American, domination over a reluctant planet. Daya Thussu observes that globalisation and 'the growing flow of consumerist messages through Western-owned or inspired television has been seen by some as evidence of a new cultural imperialism' (2005: 158). For Ed Herman and Robert McChesney (1997), leading exponents of this view, globalised media are 'the missionaries of capitalism', making the world safe not for freedom and democracy but for Mickey Mouse, Ronald McDonald and Rupert Murdoch. McChesney argues that the global media are 'ultimately politically conservative, because the media giants are significant beneficiaries of the current social structure around the world' (2003: 34). From this perspective the trends are towards reinforcement rather than erosion of Anglo-American domination of the world (a domination which is seen as counter to global social progress).[16]

Another strand of critical thinking associates media evolution with an ongoing cultural degeneration, often characterised as the 'dumbing down', 'Americanisation', 'commercialisation', 'tabloidisation' or, more recently, 'McDonaldisation' of journalism.[17] This process, even when it is not being interpreted as the result of a conscious strategy by a ruling class bent on world domination, is nonetheless argued to contribute to the exercise of elite control in so far as it dulls mass sensibilities, narcoticises individuals, and makes them more amenable to the dull compulsions of life in a capitalist society. In 1986, for example, before the Challenger disaster and just as Ted Turner's CNN was beginning to hint at its journalistic potential, Dan Schiller wrote that

> new technology is grooming the citizenry for yet another dismal shift downmarket. Global trivialisation, round-the-clock happy talk, total commercialisation and downright manipulation are its strange fruit. Mass news . . . now engenders systemic ignorance.

> (Schiller 1986: 21)

By 'systemic ignorance' he meant public unawareness of many of the things that were undoubtedly wrong with advanced capitalist societies, especially their inequalities and injustices, both in domestic and overseas territories. The same presumption of mass ignorance appears in a more recent work, Hanno Hardt's *Myths for the Masses*, in which he writes that 'while mass communication has multiplied experience of the world – or increased empirical knowledge – it has failed to equip individuals with an intellectual disposition – or rational knowledge – to approach the complexity of the world with confidence' (2004: 2).

Historically and sociologically decontextualised as they are, such statements continue to be made by critical media scholars who view current trends in communication from within the broad framework of cultural pessimism contested in my earlier study of *Journalism and Democracy* (McNair 2000).[18] Critical anxiety – what some have termed 'the lament' – is here focused not merely on the perceived concrete evils of globalised capitalism, but on a more amorphous, existential fear of the consequences on the human psyche of the media environment we now inhabit. Zygmunt Bauman remarks that 'one of the most consequential effects of the new situation is the endemic porosity and frailty of all boundaries' (2002: 13), adding that 'in this global planetary space, we can no longer draw a boundary behind which one can feel fully and truly secure' (ibid.: 12). With echoes of Horkheimer and Adorno's critique of mass culture (see Preface), Todd Gitlin complains about 'the travesty of human existence' brought on by the 'media unlimited' which provide the title for his 2002 book,[19] and argues that modern life has become too fast and too cluttered for comfort. Siva Vaidhyanathan exemplifies contemporary cultural pessimism with his argument that the United States operates a strategy of 'remote control'[20] of global cultural policy. He contrasts something called 'free culture' (good) with the 'torrent' of information (bad), joining Gitlin and other critical scholars in seeing largely negative outcomes from the globalisation of media. Vaidhyanathan, like his co-pessimists, adopts the familiar critical strategy of contrasting inauthentic trash with authentic, worthy journalism. From this perspective the globalisation of media and culture is merely another stage in the proliferation of elite power, and thus to be resisted.

Adopting a more agnostic stance close to the starting point of this book, the authors of a recent study of Jürgen Habermas's work assess the German sociologist's view of the contemporary public sphere in the following terms:

> Late-modern society is characterised by dominant discourses, world views and forms of understanding which are put under pressure [as] new, more unconstrained patterns of communication emerge . . . and are in constant competition. The public sphere has become anarchistic . . . it is vulnerable to perversions and communication disturbances . . . it is a medium for unlimited communication.
>
> (Eriksen and Weigard 2003: 189)

Indeed it is, and 'anarchy', like chaos, can be creative as well as destructive, a force for both good and ill in the evolution of human societies. In seeking to better understand what it means for the journalism–power relationship, I do not seek to replace the technological dystopianism of the critical orthodoxy with a utopian optimism, but to elaborate an analytical framework which is more empathetic to the complex and often paradoxical social realities of the age.

Ien Eng observed some years ago, without adopting a notably optimistic or pessimistic position, that if 'chaos' is not yet 'the order of the day . . . any sense of order, certainty and security – of structure and progress – has become provisional, partial and circumstantial' (1998). Boyd-Barrett and Rantanen suggest, in terms that nicely capture one of the features of contemporary news culture I wish to highlight, that 'globalisation is in its very essence a process of dialectic, not least between the local, national, regional and global, a process of conflict and struggle both among the agencies of globalisation and the alleged subjects of globalisation' (1998: 6).

This is true of globalised culture in general, and of journalistic forms in particular. Videos broadcast by Al Jazeera of hostages being beheaded can have effects on US and UK domestic policy, just as Al Jazeera's coverage of the Israeli–Palestine conflict will impact on the 'Arab street'. Events in the two spheres are connected by technology with a closeness never before seen in the history of human affairs, their consequences constantly leaking into and through each other, bypassing the traditional mechanisms of elite control. Through real-time news an overseas war becomes an active part of a domestic policy process, which feeds back into the fighting of the war, which feeds back into the domestic political sphere, and so on until, for reasons which are not always or immediately apparent, the story fades from the news and the public's agenda.

In stressing the fluid, interactive nature of relations between these spheres – between the real, and the representation of the real through journalism – the chaos paradigm seeks to better understand the dynamics of their connectedness, to view them and their interaction (and then the impact of that interaction on public opinion and political behaviour amongst populations) as holistic and organic, rather than structured, ordered processes achieved through the manipulation of cultural apparatuses by dominant elites engaged in efforts at mass manipulation.

History repeating: crisis or utopia?

James Curran's *Media and Power* (2002) reminds us that the debates now gathering pace around trends in national and global media echo those of earlier phases in communication history, where a similar division into optimistic/pessimistic, utopian/dystopian camps was apparent. Well over a century ago, as the 1871 Education Act encouraged the emergence of a literate mass public in Britain, Matthew Arnold and others were expressing deep anxiety about the disruptive impact of mass media and popular journalism – the 'New Journalism', as it was called – on the quality of cultural life in capitalism. Similar underpinnings of cultural pessimism, which I have previously characterised as an elite-defined crisis of mass representation in culture (McNair 2000), shaped the work of the Frankfurt School, whose members, responding to the horrors of Nazism, saw cultural degeneration and media-led oppression wherever they looked in mass society. In *Dialectic of Enlightenment*, Horkheimer and Adorno complain that

> modern communications media have an isolating effect . . . The lying words
> of the radio announcer [today we might substitute TV for radio] become firmly
> imprinted on the brain and prevent men from speaking to each other; the
> advertising slogans for Pepsi-Cola sound out above the collapse of continents.
>
> (Horkheimer and Adorno 1973: 221)

My preface quoted their views on how movie stars 'encourage young people to experiment with sex', leading among other evils to broken marriages. With some minor changes, these words could have been written at any time in the subsequent 60 years. More than two decades ago Elizabeth Eisenstein noted the tendency of commentators to see 'cultural crises' in the introduction of successive waves of communication technology, from scribal (written) culture through print and electronic (Eisenstein 1983). A similar 'crisis' accompanied the rise of the VCR in the 1980s, and the internet in the 1990s, when anxieties about cyberporn and chat rooms led to attempts to impose various forms of censorship on the new medium, such as the failed Communications Decency Act of 1996 in the United States.

There is thus a sense of familiarity about the current scholarly concern with the social consequences of what I am calling cultural chaos; an awareness that, discourses of the new notwithstanding, we have been this way before, and are engaged in what might be viewed as merely the latest round in a recurring pattern of attack and defence, optimism and pessimism, hope and despair. Armand Mattelart's essay on the information society makes this explicit when he argues that talk of a new communication revolution represents the latest wave of 'redemptive discourse' on the liberatory effects of communication technology, a discourse which goes back to the seventeenth century. Each new generation, observes Mattelart, 'revived the discourse of salvation, the promise of universal concord, decentralised democracy, social justice and general prosperity' (2003: 23). Each was disappointed, just as the optimists of the internet age are destined to be.

It will take a century or so before we know if Mattelart is right. But let me make two points here. First, the implication of Mattelart's argument, that there cannot be a real democracy or authentic social justice in the future because it has not been achieved in the past, exemplifies the pessimism, even fatalism of the critical perspective. And second, Mattelart's blithe assertion that nothing of substance has changed in centuries of capitalist evolution is simply wrong. As the next chapter describes, capitalism has achieved huge advances in the living standards of the average human being, as measured in increased access to consumer goods, public services, leisure time. There is more social justice, and more democracy, in most of the capitalist countries of the world, than existed 100, 200 or 300 years ago. People have access to more media and more culture. It may be true, as some social surveys have argued, that we do not *feel* any happier than the people of seventeenth-century Europe, but that is an existential rather than a sociological question.

Contemporary debates about the social impacts of an evolving media environment cannot be dismissed as merely cyclical, but reflect a qualitatively different set of political, technological and cultural circumstances. History may indeed be repeating, in so far as intellectual anxieties about the cultural consequences of, say, confessional talk shows and reality TV echo those that accompanied the rise of *Tit-Bits* and other popular newspapers in the late nineteenth century, or in the way that contemporary concerns about cyberporn and violent computer games remind us of debates around comics and music hall a century ago, or the moral panic about 'video nasties' in the 1980s. But history is also repeating in the politically more significant sense that the democratising consequences of the emergence of print culture in early modern Europe may be viewed as an analogue of what is happening now with the internet and real-time satellite TV on a planetary scale.

If indeed it is happening (and I shall argue below that it is), the scale of the democratic transformation being effected by globalised news culture in the early years of the twenty-first century has the potential to be greater than that achieved by print at the end of the sixteenth, if only because it is global rather than national, with political and cultural effects which transcend nation-state borders. If, as is accepted by most media historians, the invention of print facilitated the great bourgeois revolutions in the United Kingdom, America and France, and was central to the processes of democratisation set in motion by those revolutions, it is neither naïve nor utopian to speculate that the recent expansion of global news culture, delivered through the proliferation of channels provided by the internet and satellite television, can facilitate democratic progress at the global level.

Cultural chaos and critical theory

In focusing on the problematics of communicative chaos and competition, rather than media sociology's traditional concern with ideological dominance and control, my aim in this book is to add to the ongoing renewal of a body of theory which risks terminal marginalisation if it is unable to adapt to the distinctive *material* conditions of the times; to assist in the development within media studies of a new critical language. In this respect I am endorsing Slavoj Žižek's view that what once constituted the intellectual left (and media sociologists will tend to place themselves in that category) needs 'to reinvent its whole project'.[21] As Chapter 5 argues, one of the defining features of our post-Cold War, ideologically realigned times is that there is no longer a 'left' in the traditional sense of that term (and by implication no 'right', either, notwithstanding the fact that many continue to define themselves in those terms). There are still ideological struggles to be fought, but they are not those which shaped the century and a half between the publication of Marx and Engels' *Communist Manifesto* and the fall of the Berlin Wall.

Critical media studies has yet to acknowledge that much of significance has changed in the media–power–society relationship since Horkheimer and Adorno wrote their *Dialectic*. This is the context in which journalist Anthony Andrews has observed, with particular reference to the left-of-centre anti-war movement in the UK but in terms that could be applied with equal relevance to 'critical theory' in the academy, that 'the desire to appear more radical-than-thou, to be more marginal, to be more against' has 'prevented the kind of rigorous thinking that might lead to new ideas on the left'.[22] McKenzie Wark argues that the left are in danger of becoming leftovers – a residual and resistant force without a positive and progressive culture of change . . . Much of the agenda of the left seems either to be about resisting change completely or accomodating to it in ways that preserve the interests of certain constituencies'

(Wark 1999: 278)[23]

As the fall of the Berlin Wall and the dissolution of the Soviet Union fade into history, it is time for materialist media sociology to review its key assumptions. That process is essential, indeed, if the materialist approach is to regain its relevance in the years and decades to come. Manuel Castells has observed that 'in the twentieth century, philosophers tried to change the world. In the twenty-first century, it is time for them to interpret it differently' (2000: 390).[24] Kevin Williams's overview of the current state of media studies calls for 'new theories, new ways of conceptualising and explaining the role of the media as well as making sense of the changes for the individual and society' (2003: 1), while Cees Hamelink has suggested that 'if the field could accept that contradiction and chaos are indeed the very characteristics of reality, it could liberate itself from traditional epistemological constraints and begin to take the future seriously' (1998: 65). The following should be read in that spirit.

Part I

Critiquing critical theory

2 Materialism and the media

In both classical and critical sociology, from Comte to Parsons, culture and the media institutions which lie at its heart have tended to be regarded in their collective functioning as a control mechanism, a stabilising device meant, as Zygmunt Bauman expresses it, 'to keep things in a steady shape' (2002: 27). From the perspective of mainstream American sociology, and other strands in the administrative tradition, this stabilisation has been positively evaluated as a necessary, integrative function of the media, which has contributed substantially to the prevention of disorder and social breakdown. From Niklas Luhmann's 'systems theoretical standpoint' (2000: 1) the media constitute one of a society's 'recursively stabilised functional mechanisms', constructing reality in terms which its individual members can know, understand and identify with. 'Whatever we know about our society', he notes, 'or indeed about the world in which we live, we know through the mass media'. In so far as societies need a set of shared values and commonly agreed conventions to bind their members together, it is the media system which ensures their social circulation. In addition, as what Luhmann calls an 'autopoetic' system, the media are the main means by which a society talks to and regulates itself, identifying its problems, airing them for public debate, communicating the outcomes of these debates. In both respects the media are functional for social stability and order.

From the perspective of materialist sociology, on the other hand, culture's controlling function is interpreted negatively, since it is perceived to operate on behalf not of the people as a whole, of society in general, but in the interests of a privileged minority within a divided, stratified society. That minority may be called a ruling class, or patriarchy, or dominant elite, or establishment, but is always imagined as a group that employs the media of communication to strengthen and perpetuate its control and dominance of society. Habermas observes of Marx that he 'denounced public opinion as false consciousness . . . [hiding] before itself its own true character as a mask of bourgeois class interests' (1989, 124). And public opinion was a construction of the media. For Marx, and the materialist tradition that he inspired, the media are functional not just for social order, but for the maintenance of elite dominance and social control amidst systemic inequality, injustice and exploitation.

In his *Critique of Information*, Scott Lash summarises this approach – what I am calling the *control* paradigm – thus: 'the media are weapons of bourgeois ideology through which the dominant class can enforce a system of beliefs on the subordinate social classes that will reinforce the domination of the dominant classes' (Lash 2002: 67). Expressed in this form, the argument appears simplistic and crude, although Lash's characterisation is by no means an inaccurate statement of its main elements – dominance, enforcement, subordination, control of the many by the messages produced by the media, in the interests of the few.[1] And simplistic or not, this approach remains central to contemporary media sociology. Simon Cottle describes the control paradigm (without himself endorsing it) in the following terms: 'the news media routinely access and privilege elite "definitions of reality". These serve ruling hegemonic interests, legitimise social inequality and/or thwart access to participatory democracy' (Cottle 2003: 5). John Fiske argues that the 'dominant discourses, those that occupy the mainstream, serve dominant social interests' (1996: 5). More recently, critical theorist Hanno Hardt defined mass communication as 'a politicised process which serves the dominant ideology . . . conceived to secure the prospect of social control' (2004: 90). In the international arena Mowlana *et al.* assert that the media 'function as major proponents and defenders of the status quo' (1992: 30). The suggestion that communication could play a progressive role in the evolution of human society is dismissed (by Hardt, for example, in the work cited above) as 'customary dreams'.

Adherence to the control paradigm is often accompanied by a critical view of media content as fundamentally biased in favour of dominant elites. Hanno Hardt, again, exemplifies this tendency when he makes a statement such as: 'working-class life rarely makes it into the media, either as a dramatic performance or a news item' (2004: 102). For this author, mass communication is no more than 'an ideologically predetermined performance for the purpose of commercial gain rather than public enlightenment' (ibid.: 51).[2]

Closing the logical circle, the continuing presence of social stability in advanced capitalist societies is attributed in whole or part to the flaws identified in media content, and cited as evidence not just of agency, but also of the success of ruling-group strategies of control. The control paradigm thus tends to come packaged with a view of the audience as a passive, manipulable mass, the victims of 'brainwashing under freedom', as Noam Chomsky and others have termed it, and vulnerable to the ideological effects of 'propaganda' by a ruling class or national security state united in its desire and ability to control the masses. One recent study of journalism in Britain and the US identifies a 'hierarchy of access embedded in dominant news values'.[3] On the way in which people are represented in news media, the study concludes that:

> citizens are passive observers of a world constructed and defined by those more powerful than themselves. While they are allowed to express basic emotions about the world, these representations offer no room for citizens to express political opinions and offer solutions to problems.

The terminology varies, but the model of top-down dominance and control forms the foundation on which critical media sociology was built in the twentieth century, and on which it largely continues to rest.

The development and enduring appeal of the control paradigm reflect a desire to understand the causes underlying what materialist sociologists rightly perceive to be a universal historical truth: that all human societies for which evidence exists, past and present, have been structured around social relations of domination, exercised by one or both of two mechanisms. The first, depressingly familiar, is violence: straightforward brute force, wielded by institutions such as police and armies in the name of charismatic individuals, corporations, parties or gods. We have seen it in Saddam Hussein's Iraq (and, some would argue, in the invasion of March 2003 which removed him), but violence has also been used as a tool for imposing order on democratic societies, when governing elites have determined that the risks of permitting social protest outweigh the benefits of being seen to be tolerant of dissent.

A second, more typical strategy of control in advanced capitalist societies is the mobilisation of popular consent to elite domination, a collective consent (or hegemony, as Antonio Gramsci described it from his fascist prison cell in 1920s Italy) made possible by the more or less directed activities of cultural institutions – what the French philosopher Louis Althusser termed in the 1970s *ideological apparatuses*, referring to the churches, education systems and media, as well as the less formal structure of the nuclear family (through which the child learns the pre-vailing norms and conventions of his or her social surroundings). Whatever we call them, these institutions have been necessary because all human societies have been organised along hierarchical, more or less exploitative lines, along which political and economic resources have been divided unequally between master and slave, lord and serf, capitalist and proletarian, men and women, white and black, gay and straight, Christian and Jew, Sunni and Shia, Catholic and Protestant, Hutu and Tutsi. Most of these divisions have been functional for the elites whose members have dominated their respective societies (the power of men over women in patriarchy, for example, has clearly provided the former with significant socio-economic and other benefits over many millennia; a belief in the scientific basis of racism was an essential prerequisite for the practice of slavery in self-avowedly Christian societies). Class, gender and ethnic divisions, and even divisions based on belief or lifestyle, such as those that define religious groups and groups dis-tinguished by their sexual orientation, have almost always had real economic and political consequences for those affected.

Wherever they exist, these divisions have been rationalised through various forms of legitimising ideology – the doctrine of primogeniture and the divine right of kings, in the case of feudalism and the despotic monarchies; the proclaimed virtues of hard work and entrepreneurship in capitalism; religious sectarianism in twentieth-century Northern Ireland; sexism throughout patriarchal history; nationalism in the Balkan wars of the 1990s. The Nazis' murder of millions of Jews in the name of the Aryan 'race' was echoed in the Hutu genocide against Rwanda's Tutsis, or the Serbs' 'cleansing' of Bosnian Muslims, Al Qaida's doctrine of holy war against Jews and Infidels, or the Janjaweed militia men's murders of Sudanese Africans in Darfur in 2004.

The criteria on which distinctions are made between the dominating and the dominated have varied between societies according to local conditions, so that if anti-semitism and white-on-black racism have been a feature of western societies since at least the time of Shakespeare, black-on-black, black-on-brown or yellow-on-black racisms have characterised Africa and Asia for just as long. Indeed, these are now well established in western multicultural societies such as Britain and Australia, where a citizen of Asian descent is just as likely to resent the presence of an African asylum-seeker in his or her neighbourhood as any white person (and for broadly the same reasons). The content of the distinctions changes over time, then, but division and the inequalities which flow from it have been ever-present features of human social organisation, as has been the need for control of the disadvantaged by those who stand to benefit from that division. As Althusser argued of capitalism:

> The reproduction of labour power requires a reproduction of its submission to the rules of the established order, a reproduction of submission to the ruling ideology for the workers, and a reproduction of the ability to manipulate the ruling ideology correctly for the agents of exploitation.
>
> (Althusser 1971: 128)

Similar formulations have been advanced to explain the role of patriarchal ideology in reproducing the nuclear family, or of racist ideas in the maintenance of systems of ethnic discrimination.

But control is never imposed without challenge. Often in the face of great cruelty and repression, from Spartacus and the slave revolts to the pro-democracy students of Tiananmen Square, human beings have demonstrated an instinctive tendency to resist the domination of others. Exploited and oppressed people have always sought improvement in their fortunes, through individual or collective action, and by whatever legal or illegal means are available to them. Correspondingly, domination of the exploited, and control over their lives sufficient to prevent effective resistance, has been the necessary governing strategy of all ruling elites since the great empires of ancient Greece and Rome. Some have adopted slaughter, massacre and pogrom as their tools. Others have preferred more subtle, ideological means of securing social and political order.

And it is precisely the longevity and success of capitalism, when seen alongside the persistence of obvious inequality, injustice and oppression in even the most affluent and humane of capitalist societies, which has encouraged the persistence of a *control paradigm* in materialist media sociology. In so far as that sociology assumes, following Marx and Engels, that capitalist societies harbour tendencies to instability, disintegration and collapse, it must account for stability, integration and the fact that the system remains intact. In doing so it must identify the cultural mechanisms by which dominant ideology (i.e., the belief systems and values consistent with the existing hierarchical structure of a society) is reproduced and order maintained, despite presumed resistance and pressure for change from the exploited masses below.

Order achieved through the application of brute force, as in Pinochet's Chile or Saddam's Iraq, requires little explanation. Consent, on the other hand, where it is present, tends to be viewed from within the control paradigm as signalling the prevalence of some form or other of false consciousness. The stability of advanced capitalism – or the absence of sufficient opposition to make it unstable – is interpreted from this perspective not as the result of its economic and other achievements as a mode of production, but as a consequence of the manufacture not merely of consent but of propaganda, brainwashing, or some other form of wrong thinking. The apparent fact of popular consent to capitalism's rule, or at least acquiescence in the broad status quo, is attributed by critical theorists to the persuasive power of the ideological control mechanisms wielded by a society's ruling class, rather than rational acceptance of the policies or the governments themselves.

Marx and the media

This hypothesis is derived directly from Marx's and Engels' writings on the function of communication within capitalism, from which we can infer their view that the means of communication have a triple function.

- First, communication is an essential lubricant for the circulation of capital, allowing information about commodity prices to flow when and where it is needed. In the late twentieth century, indeed, the infrastructure to support such flows became a strategic economic as well as a military asset, leading among other things to the development of the internet as a means of securing information from hostile attack.
- Second, information of all kinds, and financially significant information in particular, becomes from an early stage in its history an integral part of the capitalist system of commodity production. The specialist news channel Bloomberg made its owner into a billionaire (and when Michael Bloomberg became mayor of New York in 2002, the richest man ever to hold elected office in the United States) by making the supply of financial information its unique selling proposition. Reuters is an older media company which grew rich after the invention of the telegraph made possible the efficient supply of niche market financial data, as well as journalistic commentary on and analysis of that information. Journalism in all its forms has evolved into one of the most economically important cultural commodities of the twenty-first century, employing millions and generating billions of dollars in revenue.
- Third, information is an ideological instrument of control. The means of intellectual production, Marx and Engels asserted in *The German Ideology*, tend to be concentrated in the hands of those who own the material wealth of a society, and to be used by the latter as a means of maintaining their position:

> The ideas of the ruling class are in every epoch the ruling ideas, i.e. the class which is the ruling material force of society, is at the same time its ruling

intellectual force. The class which has the means of material production at its disposal has control at the same time over the means of mental production, so that thereby, generally speaking, the ideas of those who lack the means of mental production are subject to it. The ruling ideas are nothing more than the ideal expression of the dominant material relations . . . grasped as ideas.

(Marx and Engels 1976: 59)

This implies a conscious, and generally successful effort to control the thinking of those non-ruling groups in society, with the media – 'the means of intellectual production' – acting as instruments of control. That observation is the starting point for all variants of the control paradigm, which have differed only in their theorisation and understanding of how control is exercised.

The final sentence of the above passage also suggests a concept of ideology as false consciousness, of 'innocent' Illusion juxtaposed with Reality and Truth. Truth and ideology – the latter conceived as the conscious, but quite probably false perception of reality – are different things. One is true, the other merely the 'visible, external movement'[4] of a truth which resides elsewhere, available only to the enlightened (materialist) scholar. Dominant ideology, in whatever sphere of culture and intellectual activity it emerges, expresses dominant class interests, as defined by the material conditions of existence of the dominant class. By definition, therefore, these ideas cannot reflect the best interests of the subordinate classes in a society.

Antonio Gramsci's concept of *hegemony*, where ruling ideas are accepted voluntarily by a society as a whole, is also a form of false consciousness. As Stuart Hall puts it, hegemony works 'by ideology':

This means that the definitions of reality favourable to the dominant class fractions, and institutionalised in the spheres of civil life and the state, come to constitute the primary 'lived reality' as such for the subordinate classes.

(Hall 1977: 333)

These dominant groups 'strive and to a degree succeed in framing all competing definitions of reality within their range'. Notwithstanding the qualification in that sentence, and the attempts to develop increasingly sophisticated theories of ideology in the twentieth century, materialist sociology has assumed ruling-class 'success' in its strivings to contain 'all' opposition within intepretative frameworks consistent with the maintenance of an exploitative and unjust capitalism. The survival of capitalism is the best proof that ideology works, since without its controlling influence the system would collapse.

At a time when Marx's ideas still retained huge influence amongst media sociologists, Marshall McLuhan suggested that historical materialism ignored the impact on capitalist production relations of material wealth and intellectual communication. Marx and his followers had 'reckoned without understanding the dynamics of the new media of communication' (McLuhan and Zingrone 1997:

172). The editor of a collection of Marx and Engels' writings on 'the communication question' dismissed McLuhan's assertion as 'a mundane bit of nonsense' and 'a gross distortion' (De la Haye 1983: 10), insisting that the great Germans had indeed considered the impact of an evolving communication infrastructure both on capitalism as a global system, and as 'factors in the formation of a new social personality, that is, new sensibilities, new interests, new ways of relating to the world' (ibid.: 29). And as we have seen, for Marx and Engels the means of communication had ideological as well as economic applications in capitalism; reproductive as well as productive functions. This hardly refutes McLuhan's charge, however. Nor need it, for us to retain the core of a materialist framework.

Marx's life and work, and in particular the theory of politico-economic and intellectual domination which was at the heart of his political philosophy, were developed in capitalism's infancy, and before the coming of electronic media. Marx appreciated the communicative power of the telegraph, and of the printed media, a power which could be used both by ruling elites and subordinate groups (for much of his life he earned his living as a journalist, and founded several radical periodicals to exploit the revolutionary fervour of mid-nineteenth-century Europe). But he could not have imagined television, or satellite communications, or the internet. Nor did he live to see universal suffrage, or consumer society, or globalisation. That being so, it would be surprising if his theory of ideological dominance developed in the nineteenth century could have applicability to the twenty-first without revision to reflect the changes that capitalism has undergone in the intervening time.

Marx and Engels, strongly influenced by Charles Darwin's work,[5] adopted an evolutionary approach to the study of human societies; a variation of social Darwinism in which it was hypothesised that one mode of production – primitive communism, slavery, feudalism – was gradually transformed into another, more progressive and economically efficient mode. Relations of production, and the forms of exploitation associated with them, changed over time, but the wealth of society as a whole always increased. Socio-economic evolution generated, over time and on aggregate, higher standards of living for the majority, even if the distribution of wealth was uneven and the tendencies of the dominant economic classes were always towards self-enrichment. To this extent, Marx and Engels never disputed that capitalism was an economic improvement on feudalism, and that the introduction of this mode of production amounted to social and economic progress. In the *Manifesto* they wrote that capitalism had rescued 'a considerable part of the population from the idiocy of rural life'. The bourgeoisie, they wrote, 'by the rapid improvement of all instruments of production, by the immensely facilitated means of communication, draws all, even the most barbarian, nations into civilization' (Marx and Engels 1998: 39). This was qualified progress, however, achieved at the cost of ruthless exploitation of the type exemplified by child labour, 14-hour working days, and below subsistence wages. The gradual pauperisation of the proletariat made necessary by the drive for profit would eventually, they believed, expose the contradictions of the capitalist mode of production and burst the system asunder, ushering in the classless era of communism. Capitalism, in its blind efficiency and relentless drive towards greater profit, would crash and burn before giving birth to a higher mode of production in which inequalities and hierarchies would be banished. The harsh conditions of working-class life which Marx and Engels observed in mid-nineteenth-century Britain and Europe made it inconceivable to them that the system could evolve peacefully, sustainably and sufficiently to make revolution unnecessary.

In *Capital*, however, Marx allows that successful capitalism is consistent with a 'quantitative reduction in the amount of unpaid labour the worker has to supply' (1973: 43) over time. In other words, capital can be accumulated at the same time as the workers find their conditions and remuneration levels – which reflect the intensity of their exploitation – improving. As capitalism evolves, and the production process becomes more technology-intensive, allowing more surplus value to be produced from the application of less direct labour power, there is at least the theoretical potential for the workers' material conditions of life to improve at the same time as profits rise and capital accumulates. And indeed, that is what has happened in the advanced capitalist societies. In 2003 it was reported that average incomes in Britain were 300 per cent higher in real terms than they had been in 1950. Globally, hundreds of millions of people have seen major improvements in their material standards of living during the same period, and if large parts of the world remain in shameful poverty and deprivation, whether as a result of unfair trading practices, the rapaciousness of unrestrained overseas capital, or corruption and incompetence on the part of local governing elites, it is a fact that more people have more wealth today than at any previous point in human history, and that this trend is set to continue. In 2004 the World Bank estimated that world poverty would reduce by a further 50 per cent over the next ten years. Much of this reduction, should it transpire, will be a consequence of the fact that China and India are currently experiencing unprecedented growth rates, promising rapid improvements in material well-being for billions of people.

Marx writes of the limits on exploitation of the worker as being not merely physical (how many hours a person can work before collapsing from exhaustion) but moral: 'The worker needs time in which to satisfy his intellectual and social requirements, and the extent and number of these requirements is conditioned by the general level of civilisation' (Marx 1973: 343). Over time 'the extent and number of these requirements' increases. Social expectations rise, and to the extent that they are met, the exploitative tendencies of capital are constrained by the very success of the system in developing democratic and cultural institutions, facilitated of course by a constantly advancing technological base. One thinks, for example, of the automated car manufacturing plant, in which ten workers may produce as many cars in 2005 as 100 workers achieved in 1955, or 1,000 in 1915. This is possible because much of the process is automated, and although the intensity of exploitation of those ten workers is many times greater than that of their predecessors, they do not experience it as such, as they enjoy their relatively high wages and a clean, air-conditioned, statutorily regulated working environment. With their increased leisure time they develop new tastes and pursuits, which are in turn passed on to subsequent generations, where the cycle begins again, and from a higher base.

Marx also argues in *Capital* that 'the accumulation of wealth at one pole is at the same time the accumulation of misery on the side of the class that produces its own product as capital' (ibid.). But the theory of progressive immiseration of the proletariat takes no account of the political impact of social and cultural factors feeding back into the system, which effectively force up the cost of labour-power to the capitalist. To put it simply, as the proletariat becomes better educated, better organised, better able to know what it wants and to campaign for its demands – processes in which the media and cultural institutions are crucial – collective expectations rise. Consequently the price paid by the capitalist (and by the system as a whole, through the collective provision of welfare, education, health and other public goods and services) has to increase in order to secure labour-power. These improvements are not volunteered by the system, which will always tend to exploit its wage labour to the maximum extent possible within prevailing conditions, but are extracted from it only through struggle.

Despite periodic shocks such as the global depression of the 1920s, or the restructuring of British capitalism unleashed by the Thatcher government in the 1980s, both of which produced mass unemployment and social unrest, the historical trend has been for capitalism to deliver higher levels of social wealth over time. The idea that mass pauperisation is an inevitable outcome of capitalist production, while it may have reflected the realities of nineteenth-century capitalism in western Europe (and twenty-first-century capitalism in much of the developing world) is by Marx's own assertion no more true than the prediction that a ball thrown in the air will inevitably come back to earth. It will certainly tend to fall, but a hand in the way will stop its descent. Likewise, the absolute (as opposed to relative) pauperisation of the proletariat can be, and increasingly has been prevented by the legal and political interventions made expedient by the establishment of democratic government, as well as by the rapid technological progress made possible by capitalism's very ruthlessness. Increasing exploitation, and the relative pauperisation of the proletariat, coexist with increases in the absolute standards of living of the majority under advanced capitalism. For all its flaws and imperfections, capitalism has proven to be the most productive form of socio-economic organisation yet developed by human beings, next to which twentieth-century competitors such as the centralised economies of the state socialist era seem like short-lived mutations.[6]

Just as Marx and Engels' historical materialism was strongly influenced by Darwinian ideas, so the application of evolutionary principles to human social development can help account for this outcome. Evolutionary theory predicts that those organisms that survive will be those best adapted to their environments, and that an ability to adapt (equivalent to a tolerance for environmental change) will lead to better performance. Paul Ormerod, author of *Why Most Things Fail* (2005), argues that

> the Soviet Union is, par excellence, an example of a social and economic system that failed. Its rigidly planned economy was able to develop a primitive industrial economy based on iron and steel, and fight a war in the 1940s. But

it was completely unable to adapt to the more fluid environment of the [late] 20th century and became extinct.[7]

In conditions where the capacity to maintain cultural isolation was eroding (see Chapter 10), the USSR's inflexibility and lack of correctional mechanisms led it to break apart. Capitalism's adaptability, on the other hand, has until now allowed it to evolve in such a manner as to avoid the systemic collapse predicted by Marx and Engels in the *Manifesto*. Commentator Andrew Sullivan observes that 'open societies – because they can disseminate information more efficiently than police states – can also self-correct more swiftly'.[8]

Capitalism's fundamentals as a socio-economic mode of production remain as Marx described them in *Capital*. What changed (or, more precisely, what was not apparent to Marx and Engels in the mid to late nineteenth century) was the system's capacity for self-regulation and self-correction in the face of social pressure, much of it inspired by Marx and the socialist movement he came to personify. It is in the spirit of the materialist dialectic to note that the most far-reaching political impact of Marxism may have been to provide, by theorising the catastrophic consequences of not doing so, an incentive for the more brutal elements of the capitalist class to be reined in, regulated and required to enter into progressive socio-economic compromises with the working class.

The history of capitalism is analogous to that of a complex organism, then, evolving in competition with other organisms (in Marx's terms, other modes of production). That human societies are comparable to biological structures in their workings is not a new idea,[9] but its significance can perhaps begin to be appreciated only now, when evolution is established as scientific (the resurgence of creationism in the west notwithstanding), and the evidence of the twentieth century can be taken into account. That evidence suggests that those forms of society that can adapt best (and fastest) to their changing environment will survive. Capitalism has proven to be, if far from perfect, the best model of socio-economic organisation thus developed by human beings, not for reasons of superior morality or ethics (advanced capitalism has achieved its current level of sophistication only after centuries of precisely the same forms of brutality seen in many parts of the developing world today), but simply because the political (democracy), economic (competitive markets) and cultural (freedom) conditions of its existence have permitted the greatest advances in human productivity and material wealth, alongside the greatest improvements in human well-being for the greatest number. Of all the surviving 'socialist' states that came into being in the twentieth century, only China has prospects of significant economic and social progress in the twenty-first, and this only because it has constructed underneath its nominally socialist ideological superstructure an aggressively capitalist economic base with which it can compete in global markets.[10]

The implication of this analysis for Marx's original hypothesis is to necessitate revision of its conclusion that capitalism, though a necessary and objectively progressive stage in human evolution, is so oppressive and inhuman that it must be transitory, and that it is destined to be replaced by an egalitarian, nonhierarchical society of the type outlined in the 1848 *Manifesto*. Subsequent experience has shown that, on the contrary, capitalism evolves in a generally progressive direction, and that mutations such as fascism, or the type of authoritarian state which prevailed in 1980s Latin America (many of which were assisted by the United States government as part of its global war against communism) are unsustainable in the long term. In democratic political conditions, and in the presence of global communication networks able to disseminate models of best practice in the economic, political and cultural spheres, capitalist evolution tends to be in the direction not merely of increased economic productivity, but towards a deepening humanitarianism and improved quality of life, as measured by improving levels of income, education and longevity.

Capitalism, when democratisation and cultural commodification are relatively advanced, becomes of necessity more adaptable, flexible and reflective of the life needs of those who toil within it. For this reason, capitalism can no longer be viewed as a stage in the long march to a communist utopia (nor even to a more concrete, but still superior socialist alternative). Instead, and within any conceivable scenario of human progress in the decades and centuries to come, capitalism – defined as a competitive, market-based system – looks more and more like a stable evolutionary outcome. Capitalism is not the 'end of history', as Francis Fukuyama misleadingly described the post-Cold War era (1992), but simply that form of socioeconomic organisation which has been demonstrated to be the most successful in producing the greatest material improvements for the greatest number of people on the planet. Capitalism has not produced enough for everybody (though with sufficient political will it could), and its unequal relations of distribution mean that too many receive less from it than they deserve or need. But by comparison with a decade, or a century or a millennium ago, capitalism produces much more wealth than it once did, and certainly more than the state socialist alternative was ever able to generate, or the global Islamic theocracy pursued by Al Qaida could conceivably aspire to.

Capitalism and critical theory

The scale of this social change presents a fundamental challenge to the premise on which all variants of the control paradigm are founded. To assert the employment of media as ideological instruments presumes, on the one hand, a need for control to support hierarchical structures and elite dominance in the face of mass inequality and exploitation; and on the other, the availability of an alternative, without which there would be no need to suppress through false consciousness the perception amongst the masses that there is something to be gained by replacing or removing ruling elites. As Jon Simons notes, the dominant ideology thesis rests on a logic 'according to which if people were able to make a genuinely enlightened, substantively rational democratic choice, they would not accept capitalist domination' (2003: 171).

In his end-of-millennium essay *Hooking Up* (2000), Tom Wolfe argued that the United States had, by the millennial turn, achieved the socio-economic position idealised by utopian socialists from Marx onwards, a world in which 'the working man [and woman] would have the political and personal freedom, the free time and the wherewithal to express himself in any way he saw fit and to unleash his full potential'.[11] Wolfe had plenty of criticisms to make of the 'lurid carnival' that market forces and individualism had delivered to contemporary America, but his accurate identification of the material progress experienced by the majority of working people has an important sociological implication. Ideological control is not required in advanced capitalism, because consent is freely given (if not without complaint).[12]

Pessimists protest that the wealth created by capitalism continues to be divided unequally amongst the members of capitalist societies. As Manuel Castells' prophetic study of the information society observes, 'the average living conditions of the world's population have improved steadily' since the 1970s (2000: 78), although distribution of wealth has remained unequal. 'The assent of informational, global capitalism', he suggests, 'is characterised by simultaneous economic development and underdevelopment, social inclusion and social exclusion' (ibid.: 82). True, and no less disturbing for the fact that it is precisely capitalism's encouragement of differential rewards – its capacity to reward effort and entrepreneurship – that guarantees its immense productivity. What is also true is that no other industrialised system has achieved more equality, or more wealth, and certainly never both at the same time.

Among the many cherished ideas of Marxist intellectuals undermined by the fall of the Soviet Union was that human beings are not by nature greedy or acquisitive, and that these are artificial qualities created by capitalism's encouragement of 'bourgeois' individuality. On the contrary, post-1991 revelations showed that even after 70 years of 'socialism' in the USSR, severe inequality and elite economic privilege (the *nomenklatura*), not to mention endemic corruption and exploitation of the workers, as well as widespread racism and sexism, were as deeply ingrained as in any capitalist system. This was true of all actually existing socialist societies, including those that functioned as aspirational models for the left, such as Cuba, where child prostitution flourishes and gay men are routinely imprisoned. In the 1990s, following the trauma of the Tiananmen Square massacre, the communist government of the People's Republic of China acknowledged this truth and abandoned what remained of its socialist economics (if not authoritarian politics) to get on with the serious business of becoming the twenty-first-century's leading global power, a goal which it should achieve by around 2020.

Where poverty and exploitation of the type described in the classic works of historical materialism continue to exist, they do so in the absence of advanced capitalism (as in much of the developing world, where Dickensian conditions still apply), or against the background of local violation of its steadily improving standards on working conditions, human rights, environmental protection and the like. Capitalism in the developed world, however, while remaining founded on the same social relations of exploitation as those accurately dissected by Marx and Engels 150 years ago, is experienced by the majority of its inhabitants as a successful economic system, or at the very least one in which there are opportunities for success sufficient to justify individual and collective compliance with the system. The capitalist may be rich, but so is the worker, relatively speaking, and getting richer. There is poverty, but it too is relative.

These facts are accepted even by the most vocal critics of contemporary capitalism. Commentator George Monbiot concedes a 'massive redistribution [of wealth]' after the New Deal and the Second World War which 'raised the living standards of the working class' in the west. 'Ours', he writes, 'are the most fortunate generations that ever lived'. He agrees with the view of the *Spectator* magazine that 'we live in the happiest, healthiest and most peaceful era in human history'.[13] Marxist historian Eric Hobsbawm reflected at the turn of the century that throughout the world, 'the majority of people are better off', and that the greatest improvements in living standards have been in capitalist societies. 'There is no precedent for this in the history of mankind. In developed countries, even the poorest and the most abandoned live immeasurably better than their grandparents did' (2000: 86). The proletariat of advanced, twenty-first-century capitalism is self-evidently not the pauperised mass of the mid-nineteenth century, working for subsistence-level wages in brutally exploitative, unregulated conditions. Rather, they are a home-owning, share-owning, overseas holiday-making class of relatively empowered and well-informed individuals who, if still proletarian in the technical sense defined by Marx in *Capital* (i.e., wage-labourers, dependent on the sale of their labour power for their income), are increasingly difficult to associate with the call to arms – 'Workers of the world, unite! You have nothing to lose but your chains' – of the *Communist Manifesto*.

Given all of that, can the control paradigm, as I have termed it, retain its usefulness in the advanced capitalist societies of the twenty-first century?

3   From control to chaos

In conditions of relative mass affluence and consistently rising living standards, do we need an explanation for social stability that focuses on the persuasive, even 'coercive' role of the media (Rushkoff 1998), as opposed to the rational interests of people in the real world?[1]

Critical scholars will reply: yes, we do, continuing to frame their media analyses around three premises:

- the reproduction of capitalist societies requires ideological control;
- the media are a key ideological apparatus in the control of ruling elites;
- the media are effective in generating variants of false consciousness, not least in time of war and global crisis.

Coverage of the post-September 11 'war on terror' and the Coalition invasion of Iraq in 2003, for example, has been accused of pro-western, pro-American, pro-UK government bias by a succession of recent studies conducted within a control paradigm, including *War and the Media* (Thussu and Freedman 2003) and *Tell Me Lies: Propaganda and media distortion in the attack on Iraq* (Miller 2004). In the latter collection Des Freedman accuses the UK media of 'amplifying and echoing government lies, distortion and misrepresentation' in their coverage of Iraq (Miller 2004: 63), adding that in both the UK and US, 'most media outlets supported the war and failed systematically to challenge the arguments for an invasion or to expose the brutality and consequences of the war'. Notwithstanding the ferocious criticisms of the BBC which came first from Downing Street and then the Hutton Inquiry in 2003,[2] researchers at Cardiff University concluded that it was the most 'pro-war' of any UK broadcaster,[3] and that 'far from revealing an anti-war BBC [as had been asserted by sources close to prime minister Tony Blair], our findings tend to give credence to those who criticised the BBC for being too sympathetic to the government's pro-war stance'. Greg Philo and Mike Berry of the Glasgow Media Group have asserted pro-Israeli bias in British broadcast news coverage of the Israeli–Palestinian conflict (Philo and Berry 2004). In the UK, they assert, 'much of what the TV news audience hears is dominated by the official Israeli perspective' (ibid.: 225). Israeli views are given 'preferential treatment' over those of the Palestinians by the BBC (ibid.: 199), 'part of a consistent pattern on TV news in which Israeli perspectives tended to be highlighted and sometimes endorsed by journalists'.

From control . . .

I shall return to these claims below. Before doing so, I observe that in its assertion that the masses are being fed from above information that is in some sense wrong or illusory, the control model assumes a media system which is demonstrably at the disposal and direction of ruling elites; an *ideological state apparatus*, as Althusser called it; a *propaganda apparatus* of a national security state, as Chomsky and Herman put it in their still-influential works of the 1970s (1979a, 1979b), to which many contemporary variants of the control model owe an obvious debt. Herman and Broadhead's *Demonstration Elections*, an analysis of US media coverage of Latin America, is presented by its authors as 'a case study of how the mass media of the Free World function as a propaganda system' (1988: xi).

The common theme running through these approaches is that media are structurally linked to the dominant groups in society by economic, political and cultural connections. The western media are 'ideological institutions' with the capacity to 'falsify, obscure and interpret the facts in the interests of those who dominate the economy and political system' (Chomsky and Herman 1979a: xi). News is manufactured, as is public consent to the nefarious activities of the national security state. The media do not produce journalism, but 'thought control' (Chomsky 1989) and 'systemic ignorance' (Schiller 1986). Commonality of class interest is the tie that binds in this alleged conspiracy, linking industrial, military and political elites in pursuit of pro-systemic, anti-opposition propaganda.

Control is founded in:

- *economics*, above all, through private ownership of media capital, or in the power to allocate scarce advertising revenues, or in the control of the public relations and promotional industries. As a result of these economic factors, 'news coverage in the mass media will reflect the narrow values and interests of corporate owners' (D. Chomsky 1999: 597);
- *technological constraints* on access to and production of media, which are capital-intensive and thus exclusive of the vast majority of relatively resource-poor individuals;
- the influence of *political factors*, manifest in the various forms of state censorship and regulation of information, from official secrecy laws to informal 'flak' to news management and spin techniques, to which journalistic media are subject;
- and finally, the *cultural* power of the dominant *ideology*, internalised or imposed from above, which drives such elements of news production as news values and interpretative frameworks.

These are the key 'filters' guaranteeing the desired outcomes in US media coverage of both foreign and domestic affairs, and thus securing the reproduction of the system without the need for overt censorship of the type relied upon by authoritarian societies such as the old Soviet Union. As a result of their operation, Chomsky and Herman assert:

> Fundamental criticism that openly rejects the basic premises of the propaganda system, especially the assumption of the essential justice and decency of any major foreign venture, may be granted token appearance as an oddity in the mass media, but is generally confined to journals and pamphlets that are guaranteed to reach no more than a tiny fraction of the population. Exceptions to this generalisation are rare and unusual.
>
> (Chomsky and Herman 1979a: 23)

In the second volume of the *Political Economy* they insist that 'the system of brainwashing under freedom' is sustained by

> the Big Distortion and negligible grant of access to non-establishment points of view; all rendered more effective by the illusion of equal access and the free flow of ideas. US dissenters can produce their Samizdat freely, and stay out of jail, but they do not reach the general public or the Free Press except on an episodic basis.
>
> (Chomsky and Herman 1979b: 300)

In Parts II and III I shall make the case that, three decades later and in a transformed environmental context the propaganda model, and contemporary applications of the control paradigm in general, fail to account for the unruliness and ideological fluidity of media outputs, or to understand the complexity of the processes which produce them. I will argue that, far from being control mechanisms at the disposal of elites, these same four filters – economic, political, ideological and technological – act as catalysts for a democratising cultural chaos. Before doing so, however, it should be acknowledged that Chomsky and Herman's articulation of the control model reflects the context of the Cold War times that inspired it. In their observations about media content (if not necessarily in their conspiratorial explanations as to why content was the way it was), they had a point. Media content during the Cold War did reflect the rigid ideological polarity of the capitalist–communist divide, and the high degree of elite and political consensus which existed around the notion of the Soviet threat. At the same time the high costs of access to print and broadcast media favoured big capital, and pushed alternative voices to the margins of print and broadcast media. Dissidence was legal and available, as Chomsky and Herman conceded, but restricted by economic realities (which were in turn a function of a particular stage of development of communication technology) mainly to the fringes of academia, political activism and the artistic avant garde. The vibrant counter-cultural capitalism of the twenty-first century (see Chapter 6) had still to develop. Feminism, gay rights, environmentalism, anti-globalisation – all were peripheral to mainstream political culture in the western world, where they existed at all. This was a world still in the grip of decades-long geo-strategic division and the ideological stasis suggested by the term 'Cold War', in which there were limited opportunities for political actors to present alternative or oppositional arguments.

Mainstream media coverage did not create these conditions, by brainwashing or any other means, but it did reflect and communicate them. The control model *worked*, in so far as it was consistent with features of media content such as the journalistic preference for stories about Soviet dissidents rather than Brazilian, or about Polish human rights abuses rather than Chilean, or the differential coverage of the Soviet shooting down of a Korean airliner as against that of an Iranian jet by the US navy in 1988.[4] Even at the height of the Cold War, however, amidst the rhetoric of 'evil empires' and 'Soviet barbarism' favoured by Ronald Reagan and Margaret Thatcher, and even amongst many sociologists who shared the materialist assumptions of the model, formulations such as 'brainwashing under freedom' and the 'propaganda system' were recognised as flawed, for reasons which apply with much greater force to contemporary versions of the control model.

Over-generalisation and exaggeration

First, they exaggerated and decontextualised the bias of media content. They over-generalised from the content of a few, some or even many media organisations and understated the relative importance and cultural weight of exceptions. Even before the era of Michael Moore, the suggestion that 'fundamental criticism' of American policy was 'rare', 'unusual' or tokenistic could only be sustained by the avoidance or dismissal of celebrated eruptions of media controversy such as the Watergate affair of the early 1970s, or the later, highly elite-critical phase of coverage of the Vietnam War. This major conflict, more deadly and protracted for both soldiers and civilians than anything yet seen in the Middle East was, after an initial period of journalist acceptance of official accounts of events, reported within what Dan Hallin has defined as the 'sphere of legitimate controversy' (1986), contributing substantially to a political climate in which a humiliating US withdrawal from Vietnam became necessary.

Beyond the sphere of straight news, the savagely satirical political journalism of the late Hunter Thompson was at its best and most influential in the 1970s and 1980s, anticipating and then embellishing Watergate with scabrous denunciations of the Nixon presidency and the Republican establishment. In cinema Oliver Stone's *Salvador*, made at the height of the Reagan presidency, and ferociously critical of US foreign policy in central America, was a mainstream commercial product, starring a well-known Republican-supporting actor (James Wood) in a drama based on actual events. Two decades before Michael Moore's polemical critiques of the US government stormed the book and movie best-seller charts Oliver Stone's angry movies were doing something similar (see too his *JFK*, with its florid allegations of an assassination conspiracy involving Lyndon Johnson).

In response to such eruptions of dissent, the propaganda model's explanation for bias – a ruling-class conspiracy in which the media were consciously and enthusiastically implicated – was viewed by some materialist sociologists as crude and simplistic. In the mid-1990s Michael Schudson described it as 'misleading and mischievous' (1995: 4) in its conclusion (as he characterises it) that 'every apparent sign of debate or controversy [is] merely a cover for a deeper uniformity of views'. There was indeed a 'deeper uniformity of views' around in the 1970s, structured by a decades-old Cold War and an associated ideological consensus. This frame-work was not imposed Soviet-style on the media, however (even Chomsky and Herman did not dispute that point), so much as internalised by its professional core. The belief in a communist threat was real, if illusory, because American and western politics had been premised on that notion since 1945 (just as Soviet media were locked into an opposing worldview). When that belief dissolved following the end of the Cold War, so did patterns of media coverage which used it as an interpretative framework for making sense of the world (see Chapter 5).

Naïvety and moral drift

Others accused Chomsky and Herman of excessive moral relativism in their efforts to prove 'brainwashing under freedom', as when they portrayed critical US coverage of the Pol Pot genocide in Cambodia as propaganda, accusing journalists of 'a highly selective culling of facts and much outright lying' (1979b: 295). Capitalist media had exaggerated the extent of human rights abuses in a communist state, they argued, just as those of 'our side' in Central and South America had been downplayed. After the Vietnamese liberation of the country in 1979, and the full revelation of what had occurred under Pol Pot, this argument, their critics countered, betrayed a naïve refusal to accept that the nominally socialist Khmer Rouge could in fact be engaged in systematic mass murder. Francis Wheen's recent polemic on the rise of what he provocatively calls 'mumbo jumbo' quotes as an example of this moral drift Chomsky's assertion in a 1980 book that 'the positive side of the Khmer Rouge picture has been virtually edited out [by the western media]', while 'the negative side has been presented to a mass audience in a barrage with few historical parallels, apart from wartime propaganda' (cited in Wheen 2004: 303).

Content out of context

A comparable naïvety can be observed in contemporary articulations of the control model. Philo and Berry's *Bad News from Israel* (2004), for example, criticises UK broadcasters for using the term 'murder' to describe Palestinian attacks on Israelis. The 'freedom fighter or terrorist' debate is of course a long-standing one, and has improved awareness and understanding within both journalistic and public circles about the sensitivities of language use. But just as, post-Cold War, no one seriously defends the virtues of the Pol Pot regime, post-9/11 the argument that acts of terrorism carried out against civilians can be justified by any national liberation, religious or ideological cause has been discredited as amoral and nihilistic. I argue in Chapter 5 that one consequence of the ideological realignment set in motion by the end of the capitalist–communist division has been the universalisation (or de-ideologisation) of concepts such as freedom and democracy. As part of that process, I suggest there, we have seen the assertion of the idea that murder is murder, be it the act of Chechen rebels against school children in Beslan, the Real IRA against Saturday afternoon shoppers in Omagh, young British Muslims bombing their fellow citizens on the London underground, or Palestinian teenagers blowing up Israeli pensioners and night clubbers. In the 1970s many western intellectuals defended the legitimacy of the Red Brigades and other terrorist groups, including that of the Palestine Liberation Organisation (PLO). Right up to the end of the Provisional IRA's armed struggle there were many on both the left and right of the political spectrum in the UK and USA who defended its right to kill civilians in the name of Irish nationalism. Today there is close to zero tolerance for terror as a political tactic.

In this context the broadcasters' use of the term 'murder' to describe acts of terror against civilians, and the failure of the media to be more sympathetic to the Palestinian side in recent times can be argued to be the result not of producers' bias as between Israelis and Palestinians, but of changing public perceptions of the conflict, shaped also by the positions and strategies adopted by key protagonists. Yasser Arafat's decision to support Saddam Hussein during the 1991 Gulf War, for example, had a major negative impact on global perceptions of the legitimacy of the Palestinian cause, with which he had become so personally identified. So too has the well-documented corruption of the Palestinian authority after it was granted governing powers in Gaza, the violent vigilantism of many of its radical Islamist affiliates, and the PLO's involvement in and ambivalent attitude to the activities of suicide bombers in Israel. Philo and Berry devote less than a paragraph in a book of 315 pages to the significant fact that the Palestinians had taken Saddam's side in 1991. This error of judgement, they concede, 'lost much of the political capital' (2004: 67) built up by the PLO over many years, but then ignore the impact of this development on later media coverage of the conflict.

Neither do they consider the significance of the increased Islamicisation of the Israeli–Palestinian dispute, and the fact that it is now conducted by many Palestinian groups and their supporters amidst the same extreme form of anti-Semitism which fuels global jihad. The PLO's political capital and media sympathy peaked in the 1980s, when it was perceived as a secular, national liberation movement more akin to the ANC than Al Qaida. Today it is tainted with fanatical and reactionary religiosity, which inevitably alters the way it is perceived by media and audiences alike. The justice of that changed perception is for the reader to judge. It is, however, an essential contextualising factor when assessing the degree and direction of 'bias' in western media coverage of the Israeli–Palestinian conflict. To imply, as Philo and Berry do, that if only western news audiences were more attuned to the justifications for suicide bombing they would be less critical of the Palestinian campaign, and that the media are thus complicit in maintaining a generalised ignorance about the conflict, ignores the changing ideological environment within which the conflict is reported.

To take another example of content analysed out of context, Philo and Berry assert that UK TV news coverage of the beginning of the second Palestinian *intifada* in September 2000 downplayed the role of Ariel Sharon's provocative walk in the

Temple Mount in East Jerusalem. 'Ariel Sharon was not named in many bulletins and his significance as a figure to the Palestinians was not explained' (Philo and Berry 2004: 227). The authors concede that he *was* named in at least two BBC and ITV bulletins, but then shift the ground to assert that 'there is nothing on the role of Sharon or his history. Without this it is not easy to understand why the Palestinians are so angry' (ibid.: 131).

If I may challenge this reading of the news with one of my own: I clearly recall watching coverage of these events on British television at the time, and emerging with the definite impression that the renewed violence was indeed the fault of Ariel Sharon and his deliberately inciteful act of invading a sacred Muslim place. I remember feeling anger and frustration at another reckless twist in the cycle of violence, and sympathy with the position of the Palestinians. I was not taking notes, and cannot recall which bulletins on which channel contained this information, but I know the impact it had on my interpretation of events. If my response can be taken as representative (and why should it not?), then it was at least possible to infer from the coverage that the Israelis, or some elements within the Israeli political establishment, were responsible for the violence which triggered the second intifada. Neither I nor Philo and Berry can say with confidence how likely such an inference would have been amongst the millions of TV viewers who saw one or more of those bulletins. But if I, as one of those viewers, concluded that Ariel Sharon had triggered the second intifada with his Temple Mount provocation, it is only reasonable to assume that many others must have done so too. *Bad News from Israel*, however, makes its case as if BBC viewers were not aware of, and never accessed, the vast quantities of more detailed journalism available elsewhere in the broadcast media, in the press and online.

In general, argue Philo and Berry, 'there is a dearth of in-depth, analytic and explanatory material included in news reports' (ibid.: 244). As a result, we are deprived of what Philo calls a 'sensible' debate on the Israel–Palestine conflict.[5] Taken out of context, and with the erroneous assumption that it is the only journalism people consume, a prime-time news bulletin may well be considered lacking in the historical background required to understand complex issues. But it was always thus. Peak-time TV news bulletins, argued the BBC's head of news and current affairs Roger Mosey in reply to the Philo/Berry findings, cannot be expected to provide detailed history lessons in one of the longest-running and most contentious territorial disputes of the day.

> Television is still the dominant medium of our age, and 36 million people a week watch BBC news. But if you printed a transcript of the Ten O'Clock News [the BBC's flagship bulletin], it would still not fill one page of a [broadsheet] newspaper: it is, inevitably, a brief digest of the day's events with as much analysis as we can manage. For the complete background you may need to go to a website or a newspaper or a book.[6]

Or to current affairs television, on the BBC and other UK channels, which has regularly explored the background not just to the Arab–Israeli conflict but to the war on terror and the invasion of Iraq. Here, we might cite a single evening of Channel 4's current affairs output, February 28 2005, which was dedicated to a series of programmes exploring the alleged use of torture by British and American forces against suspected terrorists and insurgents. This came just a few days after extensive news reportage of the conviction of British troops for abusing Iraqi prisoners during the post-invasion occupation of the country in 2003. In August 2005 Channel 4 broadcast *The Cult of the Suicide Bomber*, a three-part series which included interviews with captured suicide bombers in Israeli prisons, as well as the families and associates of 'martyrs'. The documentary's author, a former CIA operative, set out precisely the kind of background and historical context which allowed the viewer, even if he or she did not end up endorsing suicide bombing as a political tactic, to better understand its roots and motivations. In September 2005 BBC4 ran an hour-long debate on *The Future of Islam* which brought together a wide range of Muslim opinion. One could cite many more examples of explanatory, contextualising broadcast journalism to which audiences in the UK have had access. As for TV news itself, the withdrawal of Israeli settlements from Gaza in September 2005 was accompanied by several reports about Israeli settler abuse and intimidation of Palestinians.

Explaining exceptions

Critical media scholars, while asserting the control function of the media in capitalist societies, have always recognised the capacity of alternative outlets to challenge established authority, and sought to incorporate these into their models. As a rule, however, where journalistic accounts have not obviously supported the presumed interests of elite groups, they have been interpreted from within the control paradigm as marginal to the workings of a capitalism presumed a priori to be so exploitative and unequal that it could not exist or reproduce itself without an ideologically biased media. Chomsky and Herman's works are explicit on this point, as we have seen, asserting that there is no 'serious ideological contestation' in the capitalist media, and that exceptions to the rule of pro-systemic media bias are precisely that.[7] One contemporary Chomskyan concedes that there is 'some scope for dissent in the mainstream media although this is without doubt limited' (Miller 2004: 95). The implication that 'unlimited' dissent is possible in any media system, that it ever has been in the past or could be in the future, is of course meaningless. The pertinent issue is that of how *much* dissent a system permits.

Capitalism, for the reasons suggested in Chapter 2 (and detailed in Parts II and III below), has evolved into providing the most open and receptive space for dissenting voices of any form of society in human history. This dissent includes the virulent anti-Bush polemics of Michael Moore and many other best-selling critical authors, not least Noam Chomsky himself, as well as strident works of popular anti-capitalism and anti-consumerism such as *The Corporation* (Jennifer Abbott, 2004) and *Super Size Me* (Morgan Spurlock, 2003). By contrast, capitalism's only serious competitor system in the twentieth century, state socialism, was noted (and still is in Cuba, North Korea and China) for its violent suppression of dissent.

Whether by stressing its limits, however, or by asserting the illusory nature of media freedom in capitalism, advocates of the control paradigm tend to dismiss mainstream media criticism of governing elites, even when it appears at a time of warfare and in conditions of global emergency, as less far-reaching than, from their perspective it ought to be, and less damaging to dominant interests than it seems – i.e., not representative of how the media work in capitalism. As Hanno Hardt puts it in *Myths for the Masses*, 'there is no free press – or freedom of expression – in a society of captive audiences' (2004: 51).

Brainwashing under freedom

Not only is media freedom illusory within the critical framework, but it is also the cover for and cause of 'brainwashing'. To this one must respond, repeating the point about effects made in Chapter 1, that even if it is accepted that elites do exercise effective control over media content, the impact of that content on audiences is far from straightforward. Chomsky and Herman themselves stress that their propaganda model makes no claims about the effects of the propaganda produced by the national security state, although frequent references to 'the system of brainwashing under freedom' (1979b: 300) and 'manufacturing consent' (the title of one of Chomsky's books) might be viewed as having one's critical cake and eating it too. David Miller, while advancing the propaganda model, acknowledges with respect to the Iraq debate that many people, indeed 'a large majority saw through many of the lies and opposed the war' (2004: 95). And he is at least partly right, as the huge anti-war demonstrations of 2003 showed. How this significant minority (*not* the majority – 42 per cent of the UK public opposed the war on the eve of invasion)[8] overcame the brainwashing and propaganda to which critical media scholars asserted they had been subject from the outset was not explained.

In promoting contradictory arguments of this kind, critics illustrate the complexity of the media effects problem, and the practical difficulty of reliably demonstrating connections between a particular news story and a particular political outcome. The alleged biases in mainstream media messages have had little discernible effect on populations, one way or the other. Forty-eight per cent of US voters did not vote for George W. Bush in November 2004, despite a critical consensus that the US media are hopelessly biased towards him. Only 22 per cent of the UK population voted for New Labour in 2005, despite the allegations of bias cited at the top of this chapter. Tony Blair's government was re-elected not because of any media bias in its favour, but as a consequence of an imperfect electoral system, and in the face of sustained media criticism of its Iraq policy right up to polling day in May 2005 (see Chapter 4).

Bias in the eye of the beholder

Observing the debate about media bias more than two decades ago, American sociologist Jeffrey Alexander noted that only those members of those communities directly associated with the particular medium consider the reporting to be accurate; it is regarded as biased by all other groups, which in turn have their own version of the facts supplied by their own 'client' mediums.

(Alexander 1981: 26)

This observation still resonates a quarter of a century later. Bias is in the eye of the beholder, and the accusation of bias can nearly always be restated as an ideologically rooted dispute over the correct emphasis and interpretation to be placed on the available facts. Both left and right criticise the media. Indeed, they often both accuse the same media outlet, even the same news item, of bias against their particular reading of events. On the one hand, we have the left-intellectual critique of BBC and mainstream media bias over coverage of the Middle East. On the other, we have 'neo-con' commentator Andrew Sullivan complaining about the left-wing bias of the same US and British media, and blaming 'media bias on the march' for the alleged marginalisation of conservative viewpoints,[9] a criticism echoed in the lobbying of conservative media monitoring organisations such as Fairpress. On the one hand, we have governments in Britain and Australia accusing their public service broadcasters of anti-government bias[10] and unacceptable even-handedness in coverage of the invasion of Iraq; on the other, critical media scholars denounce these same organisations for pro-government favouritism.

All these critical voices cannot be right, clearly, but are any? Yes and no, all and none. The perception of bias is predetermined by the ideological assumptions one takes to the media content under consideration. The bias debate is in fact excellent proof of the relativism of Truth so often identified as a characteristic of postmodernity. Claims of bias are usually interpretative, subjective, decontextualised readings of what news is telling us, superimposing the already formed opinions of the critic on the presumed intentions of the journalist. When the Australian government accused its public service broadcaster, ABC, of bias for reporting setbacks in the invasion of Iraq (see Chapter 4), this reflected its genuine failure to understand why its good intentions in that country were not recognised by the media, especially the media funded by Australian taxpayers' money. On the other hand, anti-war activists in Australia, as in other Coalition countries, were enraged by what they saw as the broadcasters' inability or unwillingness to report their opposition to the war, or to adequately cover alternative approaches to solving the problem of Saddam Hussein. The British and US governments had a similar problem with the broadcasters' tendency to report every sand storm, every reported attack by the Republican guards on Coalition forces as they advanced on Baghdad in March 2003, as evidence of looming disaster and the onset of a Vietnam-style quagmire. Others, as we have seen, interpreted this same coverage as biased towards government 'lies, distortions and misrepresentations'.

. . . to relative autonomy: refining the control paradigm

The obvious limitations of the propaganda model and its contemporary variants have been widely acknowledged by critical media scholars. Materialist accounts deriving from the work of Antonio Gramsci and others, including those that have sought to reconcile the control paradigm with the still carefully guarded political independence of British and European public service broadcasting, have adopted a less instrumentalist approach. This acknowledges that elite control of the media is not absolute, and that there is a *relative autonomy* for the cultural superstructure (and mass media in particular) in relation to the economic base of a society. The late Ian Connell attacked the simplistic notion that the media in a country like Britain function as 'the ideological executive of the ruling class' (Connell 1983: 69), and that 'there is a tight and necessary correspondence between market forces and decisions on the one hand, and the nature of the media's ideological output'. Hall, Connell and Curti elsewhere characterised assertions of such correspondence as a 'conspiracy thesis' (1976), seeking to modify it with a model of *hegemonic* media control. This may be summed up as control without the appearance (or awareness) of control. Hegemony can be summarised as an ideological environment in which the members of a society as a whole consent to the maintenance of a system which it is not in their interests to support, not because guns are being held to their heads, or because they are duped by blatant propaganda, but because they internalise the values and beliefs of dominant groups as their own.

Though distinct from the propaganda model, this approach is still firmly within the control paradigm, in so far as it implies the dominance of the mass by an elite conscious of its dominance, and equipped to reproduce itself as an elite. That it does so by sleight of hand rather than overt propaganda or brute force – persuading the masses to embrace notions such as 'freedom of choice' and 'consumer sovereignty' which are not in their 'objective' class interests – does not make it any less founded on the premise that elite control is needed to explain the survival of capitalism.

The concept of autonomy became necessary in materialist accounts of the ideological role of the media after the Second World War, when the emergence of a relatively luxurious consumerism in advanced capitalist societies required revision of the crude base–superstructure approach which had hitherto prevailed. Media organisations were recognised to enjoy a certain amount of independence in respect of elite groups, while being *determined in the last instance* by the economic needs of capital, and the reproductive requirements of the capitalist mode of production viewed more broadly. The conditions of ideological reproduction of a fundamentally exploitative system would always assert themselves in the end, however, implying a deep structural conservatism on the part of the media. Observable failures of control – Woodward and Bernstein's exposure of the Watergate scandal, for example – had to be explained in terms which could be presented as compatible with materialist assumptions about the exercise of power in advanced capitalism. In Britain, for example, Ralph Miliband argued that 'impartiality and objectivity are quite artificial', operating only 'in regard to political formulations which are part of a basic, underlying consensus' (1972: 200).

The idea of media independence as a necessary legitimising device was influential on the work of Philip Schlesinger and others, although always interpreted as essentially ideological in itself. In their study of *Televising Terrorism* (1983), Schlesinger and his colleagues observed that 'presentations of terrorism on British television are a good deal more diverse and complex than simple assumptions about terrorism's relation to the state and to dominant ideology predict' (Schlesinger *et al.* 1983: 22). Control was still asserted, however, albeit through an ideological mechanism – impartiality – designed to give the impression that there was none. American scholars, observing the unruliness of their media with respect to the war in Vietnam, described 'arenas' or 'spheres' of 'legitimate controversy' (Hallin 1986; Schudson 1995), by means of which dissent was managed and contained. In a 1989 essay, Michael Schudson observed that 'the media are formally disconnected from other ruling agencies because they must attend as much to their own legitimation as to furthering the legitimation of the capitalist system as a whole' (1989: 270). But for all that the promotion of journalistic independence in the media marketplace was acknowledged within this framework as a source of 'relative autonomy', the underlying premise continued to be that, appearances notwithstanding, the media are connected to the 'ruling agencies' in ways that compromise their independence, and are themselves, if only 'in the last instance', agents of the ruling class.

Efforts to identify and account for the relatively autonomous ideological control mechanisms operative in capitalist societies have driven theoretical development in media and journalism studies for decades, and continue to define the default position of the field. In 1989 the journal *Media, Culture & Society* rehearsed the 'gatekeeper versus propaganda models' debate in articles by Philip Schlesinger and Michael Schudson which sought to reconcile materialist sociology with the evidence of a more diverse and dissenting media output than the propaganda model permitted. For Schudson, even before the fall of the Berlin Wall had signalled the end of the Cold War, it was apparent that 'the abilities of a capitalist class to manipulate opinion and maintain a closed system of discourse are limited; ideology in contemporary capitalism is "contested" territory' (ibid., 269). By way of an alternative explanation, Schudson suggested what he described as a 'social organisation' approach, placing emphasis on the notion that journalism is 'socially-constructed, elaborated in the interaction of the news-making players with one another' (ibid.: 275). This was not a convincing alternative to the propaganda model, since it could not rule out that in the process of social interaction 'dominant' ideas and values would be imposed on or inserted into news accounts. This approach did not deny the control paradigm, so much as relocate the mechanisms of control and dominance away from the ruling-class conspiracies observed by Chomsky and Herman to the more fluid interactions of media professionals going about their business. Chomsky was justified in replying that this attempt to explain control without the appearance of control was so woolly as to be meaningless.

The sociology of sources

In the same edition of *Media, Culture & Society*, Philip Schlesinger presented another challenge to the propaganda model, rooted in the growing awareness amongst both media sociologists and political actors of the growing importance of public relations, lobbying, terrorist spectaculars, non-violent direct action, and other activities designed to manage and shape the news agenda. Developing the argument of his 'Rethinking the Sociology of Journalism' essay (1989a), Schlesinger attacked the media-centrism of the propaganda model, arguing for greater attention to be paid to how news output is shaped by the 'source strategies' of social actors (1989b). For Schlesinger, the dominance of any ideological position was to be viewed as an 'achievement rather than a wholly structurally determined outcome'. There was still determination by structure, but in the context of relatively open competition for access to media and influence on the journalistic processes of meaning definition. This introduced a welcome measure of uncertainty and unpredictability into accounts of how class power translated into media output. Contrary to Chomsky and Herman's confident assertion that their propaganda model accurately predicted media content in coverage of issues such as human rights, terrorism and foreign policy, Schlesinger argued that 'the range of effective voices in the public sphere is an outcome of battles over information management in society in its broadest sense. Recognising this, we [media sociologists] need to develop further our understanding of the conditions of success and failure in the development of information strategies by official and non-official sources' (ibid.: 288).

This statement of the rationale for a sociology of sources was influential in media studies, although many scholars subsumed it back into the control paradigm by branding public relations and 'promotional culture' in general as themselves tools in the ideological apparatus of the capitalist system. Douglas Rushkoff's *Coercion* (1998) is a polemic against the ideological effects of corporate PR and marketing which, as his title suggests, are viewed as 'coercive' forms of communication in the control of compliant populations. In this manner public relations and its linked professions came to be viewed within critical media sociology as an industry of dishonest persuasion, an infrastructure of propaganda. There is now an extensive critical literature on public relations, which develops the Habermasian notion of PR as a degeneration and corruption of the public sphere, a communicative practice which has interfered with the delivery of rational communication as required by normative democratic theory. Within the control paradigm, public relations is perceived to have usurped the free flow of information between politician and citizen, and to have distorted reality itself in favour of private interests, which have used it as a means of translating their economic dominance into intellectual, ideological and cultural dominance. If the materialist claim as set out by Marx and Engels in *The German Ideology* was principally one about ideological control through ownership of the media, in the twentieth century the thesis was extended to the assertion of control of the means by which media, and thus publics, could be influenced by capital and its representatives.

As with the control paradigm in general, there is a historical basis for this argument. Public relations is not just about communicative entrepreneurship, as its practitioners might claim, but about resources, and these resources like others are unequally distributed in capitalist societies. I and others have noted the role of public relations in the American anti-communist campaigns of the twentieth century fought by big business and government, as well as in the conduct of Cold War, anti-trade union campaigns, and in the conduct of military operations from Vietnam to the Falklands and the Middle East, up to and including the 2003 invasion of Iraq. Although the effort to persuade and manipulate through communication long predates the twentieth century and the democratic era, the modern practice of public relations first emerges in the context of ideological struggles between big US capital and the unions in the pre-First World War years, intensified by the rise of the Bolsheviks and the systemic socialist alternative to capitalism promoted internationally by the Soviet communists.

The growth of public relations as an industry was fuelled in large part by the early twentieth-century's demand for anti-communist propaganda, as well as pro-war propaganda in the context of the First World War (during which Bolshevik and socialist-inspired opposition was deemed a significant threat by both UK and US governments). Public relations continued to be used for overtly propagandistic purposes throughout the decades of the east–west conflict, until Mikhail Gorbachev's uniquely (for a Soviet leader) skilful use of PR techniques after 1985 hastened the end of the Cold War and facilitated the global ideological realignment described in Chapter 5 below. In these cases, and many more recent examples, the controlling power of public relations has been seen to reside in the ability of its practitioners to cover up, manufacture or 'spin' information in various ways, thus deceiving populations without their being aware of that deceit.

While clearly an advance on crude propaganda models, the sociology of sources, like all perspectives reliant on the concept of relative autonomy, continues to presume a controlling relationship between elite goups and the media, in the last instance. They allow that dissenting media voices are on a longer leash, and have more room to move around the field of ideological contestation, but they remain tethered. They are necessary attempts to improve and refine the control paradigm, and have achieved much in making a materialist sociology of journalism more empathetic to the complexities of the actual social world. They remain inadequate to a full understanding of those complexities, however, in so far as they continue to conceive of the capitalist mode of production as a system maintained in its injustices and inequalities by ideological control apparatuses such as the media, and the 'ruling agencies' that control them, rather than the contingent interaction of political, ideological, economic and technological factors. However autonomous and independent from elites critical theorists may allow them to be, media institutions are still conceptualised as frames, or supporting structures for a pyramidic edifice in which control flows downwards from elite to mass, the latter duped or hegemonised into acceptance of an unjust and hierarchical system which, for all its glitz and gloss, does not and never can work in their interests. Without the presence of these apparatuses, it is implied, the system would collapse, or perhaps, with the input of radical/critical ideas transmitted through other, alternative media, mutate into something better (if not socialism, for the construction of which there is now a credible template, then some more just and humane form of capitalism).

. . . to chaos

In contrast to the economic determinism of the control model, a chaos paradigm assumes multi-causality. It stresses contingency[11] (sensitive dependence on initial conditions) at all phases of the communication process, including *production*, or content outcomes; *consumption*, or intepretative outcomes (meanings); and *social action*, or effects on individual and collective behaviour.[12]

Production and content

The chaos paradigm implies an *ecological* or *environmental* model of media production, in which causes of content are present somewhere in the fog of events but difficult to separate and disentangle in specific cases. These factors of journalistic production are:

- *political* – the impact on professional practices and ethics of extra-media political actors, and of evolving political culture;
- *ideological* – the cultural power of ideas acting on media production processes;
- *economic* – the impact on media content of the cultural marketplace;
- *technological* – the possibilities allowed by a given state of technological development.

For adherents to the *control paradigm*, these factors of production act in a conservative direction. News is 'manufactured' by committees of the powerful. Features of media content (such as 'dominant ideology') are explained by the actions of dominant groups on media organisations (exercised through economic control, political pressure, or other mechanisms). Media content produces systemic ignorance.

A *chaos model*, on the other hand, approaches features of content such as plurality of opinion and dissent not as aberrations but as the manifestations of external environmental factors working on the journalistic production process; the unplanned outcomes of a combination of many factors and forces, acting independently of one another. News, from this perspective, is not an agent of ideological imposition, but a product of the interaction of all the environmental factors within which it is formed. If the environment changes, so does content, irrespective of the desires of dominant groups. Its content and meanings cannot be reduced to the influence of one factor or another (economics, for example, or political pressures) but can be understood only in the context of events in their totality. Communication is in these terms a complex adaptive system, always evolving, its content always contingent on what has gone before, as in the process where a moral panic or a health scare such as the MMR vaccination alarm of 2002 develops uncontrollably (see Chapter 12). Such systems, and their contents, are the outcome of the communicative activity of networks of agents, independent of but interacting with each other, in the absence of central co-ordination.

The chaos model thus stresses unpredictability of outcome in media production processes, a consequent uncertainty around the quantity and quality of information flow, the importance of feedback loops, and enhanced volatility in the management of both communication and power. From this perspective news is not manufactured (neither, therefore, is consent), nor is it 'constructed'. Nor does it just happen. It *emerges* from the interacting elements of the communication environment which prevails in a given media space. These spaces contain many social actors striving to manufacture and shape the news, but none has any guarantee of success. Yes, there are patterns and structures in the news cycle which aspiring agenda-setters can seek to harness. Particular dates in the calendar may confer newsworthiness on a specific action, such as a terrorist bombing on an anniversary. Quiet periods in the news cycle, such as the summer months or the Christmas holiday, are opportunities for social actors to seek to inject their stories into the news agenda. News values can be studied, as can the styles and personae of particular outlets, with a view to analysing which kinds of information are likely to attract their attention. But just as no amount of meteorological data-gathering can make the weather entirely predictable, so no social actor, be he president, prime minister or pope, can predict with certainty what tomorrow's news will contain.

Consumption and meanings

Where the control model stresses such effects as brainwashing and ideological domination, the chaos model asserts the fundamental unpredictability of media effects, and the importance of context in assessing the range of potential meanings to be drawn from media messages. Impacts are never to be inferred from content alone, far less predicted, but only from *content in context* – the environmental context within which media consumption takes place, and which is unique for each individual consumer of the media message. Two consumers of the same media message will quickly diverge in their readings of its meanings, because those readings are contingent on their individual backgrounds.

In this sense, at the level of impacts, the chaos paradigm incorporates that view of the media–society relationship pioneered by semiology – that there is no linear causality in the relationship between media content and broader social phenomena. That relationship is fundamentally unknowable. As a consequence, while control of public communication remains an aspiration of political actors, there is a practically infinite range of outcomes to which those efforts may lead, and a high likelihood of failure in any attempt to ensure 'dominant decoding'. Effective elite control of how media messages are received is the holy grail at the heart of cultural chaos – always aspired to, occasionally glimpsed, but never certain. No actor can know in advance what spin will be put on an event by the media and then the public, or what impact news coverage, from the individual news item to the totality of journalistic discourse about a particular event, will have on the life of a society.

Social action and effects

Contingency again comes into play when we consider the relationship between meaning and action in the communication process. What is the connection between what messages mean to those who receive them, and behavioural outcomes? We can never know for sure, except in quite limited circumstances, and then only after the fact. News coverage of a street riot may produce further rioting amongst some of those who witness it, as has been documented in the past in relation to Northern Ireland and Los Angeles. UK media coverage of the alleged risk of autism associated with the MMR vaccine in 2002 (see Chapter 12) caused some parents to withdraw their children from the vaccination programme, but not others. TV news coverage of the devastation caused by Hurricane Katrina, and journalistic criticism of the administration's slow response, brought President Bush hurrying down to Louisiana. These are clear, unambiguous effects of messages which people have received from their news media, and they are present at both national and international levels. Journalism can be effective in alerting us to events, and may have consequences in so far as follow-on action is possible. Are the streets under the control of law enforcement agencies, for example, or free for looters to do what they will? Is there an alternative to MMR available for those parents who have been scared off by the news coverage? Was President Bush high or low in the polls when natural disaster struck out of nowhere to make him look weak and complacent?

A chaos paradigm recognises that media messages do not impact on reality as an external influence in isolation, but become *part* of what reality is, and that the two elements are inseparable for analytic purposes. Journalism, from this perspective, is not just an account of reality, but an essential component of it. Events happen, are reported, and that reportage may feed back into events, changing their evolutionary paths. Politicians react to news coverage of their policy pronouncements; figures in authority respond to leaks and exposés; public figures, campaigning groups, terrorist organisations design their activities to generate a particular kind of media coverage. Journalists build accounts of that design, and those reactions, into their reportage, and so on in an endless loop. As opposed to the linear model of top-down cause-and-effect, the chaos paradigm implies a non-linear model of constant feedback and adaptation as the news cycle evolves, each iteration of the cycle determined by what has gone before, the future of the system contingent on its past, and the evolution of other, interacting cycles. In this environment there is loss of control, dilution of authority, and expanded opportunity for disruption of elite power.

Conclusion

These characteristics of journalism are not new to the twenty-first century. My argument here is that in the period since the end of the Cold War they have become more pronounced, creating a communication environment which can be characterised as qualitatively different – and necessarily more chaotic – than any confronted by social actors (and media sociologists) before. In Parts II and III I make the case for that claim in more detail, under the headings of, respectively: politics (Chapter 4), ideology (Chapter 5), the economics of the cultural marketplace (Chapter 6), and new information and communication technologies, or NICTs (Chapters 7 and 8).

Part II

The political economy of chaos

4 The politics of chaos: democracy, media and the decline of deference

Five interconnected trends in the political sphere have generated the conditions for a paradigm shift from control to chaos. They are:

* global democratisation;
* the associated rise in the importance of public opinion at both global and domestic levels as a factor in political decision-making;
* the associated rise of public relations as a factor in shaping public opinion;
* declining journalistic and public deference towards political elites;
* the increasing adversarialism of journalism, as a response to all of the above, and also to intensifying competitive pressures on news media (see Chapter 6).

Global democratisation

In 1900, lest we forget, there were on the planet precisely *no* democratic countries (I define democracy as universal suffrage in competitive multi-party elections). In Britain, the United States and other countries with restricted parliamentary systems (25 in total at the turn of that century), women were excluded from the vote, as in America were African-Americans and other ethnic minorities. Women obtained democratic rights in France and Italy only after the Second World War, and as late as 1950 only 22 countries were fully democratic, accounting between them for less than one-third of the world's population.

By the end of the century, with the demise of the Soviet Union and its one-party partner states in the Warsaw Pact, 120 countries of a possible 192 were classified as democratic by the think tank Freedom House,[1] representing nearly two-thirds of the world's population. Notable additions to the list included South Africa in 1994, the Baltic countries (Estonia, Latvia, Lithuania) and most of the countries of Central and Eastern Europe following the end of the Cold War, as well as Russia itself after the failed coup attempt of August 1991. These were joined by the countries created by the break-up of Yugoslavia. Latin America, having been notorious for its proliferation of brutal authoritarian regimes during the Cold War, had by 2005 'experienced an unprecedented period of political stability and consolidation of democratic regimes', with Cuba the only country in that region not to have an elected government (Alves 2005: 181).

These new democracies, like their more established forebears in the advanced capitalist world, were imperfect, struggling to overcome the effects of decades of authoritarian rule by Marxist-Leninist parties, as African and Asian countries were struggling with the legacies of colonialism. Freedom House distinguished between 'free' and 'partly free' societies, the latter characterised by 'some restrictions on political rights and civil liberties, often in a context of corruption, weak rule of law, ethnic strife, or civil war'. In Russia, and some of the former Soviet republics (Belarus, for example, and Ukraine, where presidential elections in November 2004 were widely condemned for their fraudulent nature), the establishment of formal democratic rights went hand in hand with the continuing effects of what Russians in the post-Soviet era called 'the genetic memory of Stalinism', inhibiting the development of a fully functioning civil society and democratic politics. About 21 per cent of the world's population were estimated to live in 'partly free' democracies as of 2003.

As of 2003 there were judged to be only 89 'liberal' democracies, defined by Freedom House as countries that are 'free and respectful of basic human rights and the rule of law'. Eighty-nine, however, is better than none at all, and the long-term global trend is clearly towards further extension of democratic principles to countries where ruling elites are presently resistant to them. In 2004–05 there were 'revolutions' in Ukraine, Georgia and Kirghizia which, if less than fully satisfactory in their outcomes, undoubtedly signalled the desire for democracy on the part of populations previously denied it. Protests in Uzbekistan in May 2005 led to massacres of civilians by government forces, reminding us that in many countries the path to democracy remains a difficult one.

Democratisation was also occurring at the local level. Within nation-states, and within multi-nation-states such as the United Kingdom and Spain, the trend in recent years has been towards greater democracy, as measured by constitutional reforms designed to make government more representative and accountable. In the UK since the election of a Labour government in 1997, parliaments or assemblies have been established for the devolved government of Scotland, Northern Ireland and Wales, with elected mayoralties in London and other cities. Notwithstanding the substantial 'No' vote in the referendum for a local assembly in the north-east of England in November 2004, and the 'No' vote in several countries' referenda for a European constitution in 2005, the trend is towards greater regionalism and more localised government, while the European Union has expanded to include some 30 of the sovereign states created in the wake of the fall of communism. In December 2004 Ukraine became the latest of the former Soviet republics to fully commit to a democratic transition and eventual entry into the European union.

The media and democracy

Since the appearance of the first periodical publications in late sixteenth- and early seventeenth-century Europe the process of democratisation has gone hand in hand with the expansion of the media, one set of institutions legitimising and generally reinforcing the work of the other. Following the invention of print in the late fifteenth century, the journalistic media quickly evolved into organisational and propaganda instruments of the bourgeois revolutions which drove the transition from feudalism to capitalism in Europe and North America, agitating against (and sometimes for) decaying aristocratic regimes and in favour of constitutional, democratically elected assemblies. The precursors of modern newspapers, or *newsbooks*, became significant social actors, as opposed to mere purveyors of information, against the background of the English Revolution and the Civil War of 1642–46, in the course of which they also became partisan cheerleaders for competing factions. As feudal societies fragmented and censorship declined, newsbooks were at the heart of an expanding 'public sphere of political debate' (Raymond 1996), a role which duly became normative in mature capitalist societies anxious to avoid a return to despotism and dictatorship. By the late eighteenth century journalists had become what Martin Conboy describes as 'radical propagandists . . . able to articulate a particular moment in the aspirations of the people to be involved in political affairs' (2000: 37). At that time such aspirations were still far from being realised, of course, and 'the people' remained a minority elite of wealthy, educated men. However, as mass education and literacy became a reality, and restrictions on democratic procedures were gradually removed, the news media developed an ethic of campaigning for and promoting progressive change, albeit within the constraints imposed by a capitalist system still relatively red in tooth and claw.

Not only did journalism facilitate public debate in emerging bourgeois democracies, for societies with recent experience of absolute monarchy the media were required to monitor the use and potential abuse of political power, to act as watchdogs or a fourth estate over political and other elites, and to exercise critical scrutiny over their activities. In Thomas McCarthy's words:

> [I]n its clash with the arcane and bureaucratic practices of the absolutist state, the emergent bourgeois gradually replaced a public sphere in which the ruler's power was merely represented before the people with a sphere in which state authority was publicly monitored through informed and critical discourse by the people.
>
> (Cited in Habermas 1989: xi)

From recognition of the need for institutions able to engage in this 'informed and critical discourse' emerged the liberal normative principle of journalistic independence from political power, and press 'freedom' in the form elaborated in John Milton's *Aeropagitica* of 1644. Political rights and media freedom were thus linked as constituents of liberal capitalism, and have remained inseparable in democratic theory ever since. When the fourth estate encounters the abuse of elite power, normative standards demand that journalists move from the work of mere reportage, interpretation and commentary to exposure, criticism and advocacy, thereby becoming political actors in their own right. To this extent, as James Curran observes, 'democratisation was enormously strengthened by the development of modern mass media' (2002: 4). Ithiel de Sola Pool puts it more strongly, in his assertion that 'the printing press was without doubt the foundation of modern democracy' (1983: 251).

Curran's observation is made in the context of a broader critique of liberal cultural history, which questions the contribution to democracy made by the media in practice. When first established in the revolutionary conditions of the seventeenth century, the journalistic principles of critical scrutiny and adversarialism were rooted in the harsh reality of late feudal history and bloody civil war, viewed as essential by a rising class (the bourgeoisie) in its struggle to prevent the return to power of another, declining one (the aristocracy). During the course of this process, however, and after the successful establishment of democracies in Europe and North America, the newly ascendant bourgeoisie found itself having to defend the young capitalist system from a further wave of reform from below. While the aristocrats of early modern Europe were either banished, beheaded or incorporated into constitutional monarchies, depending on local circumstances, the emerging proletariat and lower middle classes, still without citizenship rights and brutally exploited by unrestrained market economics, were becoming restive and revolutionary in their turn. In that context the capitalist media, once agents of revolution against an oppressive absolutist despotism, shifted to a more consolidatory, conservative stance. Horkheimer and Adorno argued in 1944 that 'the instrument by which the bourgeoisie came to power, the liberation of forces, universal freedom, self-determination – in short, the Enlightenment, itself turned against the [liberal] bourgeoisie once, as a system of domination, it had recourse to suppression' (1973: 93).

From the time of the English Revolution the vast majority of media organisations were pro-capital, pro-system and conservative. They were also anti-anti-capital, responding to radical and socialist social movements as threats, and seeking to act as ideological controls on populations who might be vulnerable to persuasion of the merits of an alternative to capitalism. These control mechanisms were economic (the constraints imposed by proprietorial demands, as well as the barriers to entry into media production formed by high capital costs), cultural (journalistic reproduction, voluntarily or under peer pressure, of dominant, pro-systemic values) and political (state censorship). The British radical press of the late eighteenth and early nineteenth centuries, which sought to pursue a progressive social agenda, was defeated by the price rises caused by government-imposed stamp duties and then by the competition provided by an increasingly commercialised popular press, as much as by the decline of the revolutionary movements across Europe after 1848 or the reformist concessions of the British state. James Curran quotes the manager of the London *Times*, testifying to the parliamentary committee which deliberated on the future of the stamp duty system, that '[the production of] newspapers should be limited to a few hands, and be in the hands of parties who are great capitalists' (Curran 2002: 91). And so it transpired for most of the nineteenth and twentieth centuries, encouraging a critical scholarly view of the media as structurally biased towards the ruling elites of capitalism, from the first jingoistic tabloids to the 'Tory' press of the Thatcher era.

That efforts to establish the press as instruments of social control dampened down working-class radicalism in the nineteenth and twentieth centuries is far from self-evident. As Chapter 2 argued, the absence of significant social upheaval, far less the socialist revolutions anticipated by Marx and Engels in countries such as Britain and the United States, cannot be assumed to be the consequence of anything communicated by the media. Rising living standards and rational consent are just as persuasive as explanations for order in advanced capitalism as media bias. Even if one assumes that the media did act as ideological control mechanisms, and that they were indeed effective in preventing the socialist transformation of capitalist societies, by the end of the twentieth century and the effective marginalisation of any viable alternative to the capitalist mode of production as currently configured, the 'capitalist' media had moved to occupy a different position in the democratic political process.

I will characterise this shift as a deepening of the media's normative functions in respect of the bourgeois revolutions and the maintenance of liberal democracy – i.e., those involved in the monitoring and scrutinising of political power *in general*, as opposed to bourgeois power in particular; facilitating political debate, and disseminating to the people as a whole the information about political issues required for them to make meaningful (*because* they are informed) political choices. Until well into the twentieth century, democracy, free media and the public sphere idealised by Habermas were institutions restricted to wealthy male elites drawn mainly from what John Keane characterises as 'the educated bourgeoisie, the aristocracy, state officialdom and crafts people who had the money to pay for reading material, and the desire and leisure and physical space to pursue it' (1991: 30). With universal suffrage on the one hand, and the critical scrutiny of a vastly expanded mass media system on the other, and in conditions where the long-term stability of the capitalist system is not threatened by a systemic rival, the features of democracy so regularly criticised as lacking authenticity by materialist thinkers – as one of Noam Chomsky's 'necessary illusions' – are transforming into something more in conformity with normative expectations.

'Media freedom' in capitalism is still bounded by the requirements of pro-systematicity. In the absence of a systemic alternative to capitalism, however, those structural limits are now wider than they have ever been, threatened mainly by events such as 9/11, which permit concepts such as 'homeland security' and the 'war on terror' to be invoked over and above media freedom, both in western countries such as the USA and the UK, and in places like Russia and Uzbekistan, where Chechen and other terrorist groups are regularly cited as the justification for restricting media freedom. Even in these cases, however, such restrictions require to be defended before both domestic and global publics as deviations from normative standards, to be corrected at some point in the future when 'terrorism' is defeated. Everywhere else the adversarial principles associated with liberal pluralism and the fourth estate which emerged in the course of the English, French and American revolutions have become steadily more entrenched in the professional ethic of political journalism.

Different countries apply these principles in different ways, and have different conventions in, for example, the degree of media criticism of executive power which is permitted, but the normative importance of a watchdog media is now accepted in every society that aspires to be democratic. Journalistic media have acquired the characteristics of what Luhmann calls 'a function system' (2000: 22) or, in other terms, 'an autopoetic, self-reproducing system', autonomous from political and economic structures. The ideology of liberal journalism has come to form the basis for a state of affairs in which 'the mass media keep society on its toes. They generate a constantly renewed willingness to be prepared for surprises, disruptions even' (ibid.).

To put it another way, the media in an era of globalised (and globalising) democracy are freer to do their normatively ordained democratic work than at any time since the bourgeois revolutions themselves. In the twenty-first century journalists are liberated to assert with greater sincerity and determination their democratic function within capitalism, and to fight for it in places where it is not yet consolidated, such as post-Soviet Russia, Zimbabwe or the Middle East, where a fiercely independent, anti-American Arab-language news channel such as Al Jazeera has no hesitation in defining its role in traditionally liberal democratic terms (see Chapter 7). In the first two of those cases, the adversarial role of the journalist is advanced against political forces whose abuses of power are rooted in Marxist principles (now abandoned by ruling elites in Russia, of course, but still lingering in political culture, especially at a local level). In the Middle East, on the other hand, Al Jazeera's appeal for tolerance of its independent editorial stance is directed not just at a US administration which is uncomfortable with its reportage of the war in Iraq, but at the authoritarian regimes of the region, few of which are yet ready or able to embrace the critical scrutiny aspired to by Al Jazeera's staff.

Al Jazeera's stance demonstrates that the struggle for a journalism free of political constraints – the demand for a liberal journalism of intellectual, economic and political independence as invented by the early radical bourgeoisie in its struggle with feudal autocracy – lies at the heart of political struggle and public debate, from Africa to Latin America. In the latter, as Rosental Calmon Alves observes, 'during the democratisation period, journalism has evolved throughout the region toward an independent and aggressive style, more attuned with the role of the free press as a fundamental tool with the checks and balances necessary for a working democracy' (Alves 2005: 181). The ideological qualifications that once surrounded the notion of free media have been supplanted by the enthusiastic assertion of liberal journalistic principles across the world, and across the political spectrum.

The commodification of news

Chapter 6 addresses the cultural marketplace in more detail. Here, let me anticipate that discussion by noting that the democratic function of exercising critical scrutiny over elites, the journalistic propensity to surprise and disrupt power noted by Luhmann, is heightened by the commercialisation of the media which, while producing conservatism and pro-elite bias in many journalistic organisations past and present, has also encouraged a more vigorous adversarialism over time. Martin Conboy notes that critical political journalism was popular in seventeenth-century England (2004), and it has remained so. In the competitive news marketplace of the twenty-first century, as outlets proliferate and chase audiences, effective critical scrutiny of political elites becomes a marketing tool which distinguishes one news organisation from another, leading to incidents such as the *Daily Mirror*'s exposé (later exposed as fraudulent) of British troop 'abuses' of Iraqi prisoners, the feeding frenzy of the Monica Lewinsky affair, and other scandals. The visible display of freedom and independence has commercial value for media organisations. Normative and economic imperatives reinforce each other.

One can see this in the branding strategies of CNN, the BBC and Fox News as well as in the case of a new global provider such as Al Jazeera. Al Jazeera's critical scrutiny of governing elites in the Arab countries has proved hugely popular with audiences unused to encountering it in Arab-language media, and genuinely problematic for those elites, many of whom have sought to close the channel down or constrain its activities in their countries.[2] If Al Jazeera survives it will be because its brand of independent, critical journalism is sufficiently popular to connect with an expanding Arab middle class and attract advertising revenue. Al Jazeera is a commodity as much as a democratic asset in a region of emerging and transitional democracies, and its commercial value to advertisers may turn out to be the best guarantee of its continuing editorial independence from the conservative political forces that would shut it down if they could.

Public opinion, public relations

The steady expansion of democratic institutions since the nineteenth century, and the establishment of genuinely universal suffrage as a basic democratic principle in recent times, alongside the growth in adversarial journalistic media, has made governing elites in capitalist societies necessarily more responsive to mass opinion and feelings (or, at least, sensitive to the need to be *seen* to be responsive) than was the case, for example, in Tudor England, or is the case in Saudi Arabia today. The implications of this for the exercise of political power were noted by Walter Lippmann in 1922, when he wrote that 'the significant revolution of modern times is not industrial or economic or political, but the revolution taking place in the art of creating consent among the governed' (quoted in McNair 2003b). Lippmann was expressing the sense, clearly evident even then, that mass democracy and mass media were evolving in parallel, each reinforcing the other, and in combination demanding respect for public opinion from political elites, no matter how reluctant they may have been to extend it.

Inseparable from the huge expansion of mass media in the twentieth century is the proliferation of opportunities for political actors, both elite and non-elite, to intervene in and impact upon media content. More media, in the context of more democracy, means that what people think, and in particular what they think as a result of consuming media, becomes of greater importance, other things remaining equal. Political actors henceforth have an incentive to ensure that they are presented favourably in the media, and that any negative coverage is minimised. The result has been an explosion in the managed use of media for planned political communication; of *source strategies*, employed by the full range of political actors, from presidents to popes, and terrorists to trade unions. The Phillis review set up by the UK Labour government in the wake of the Gilligan/Kelly affair of 2003 argued that:

> In the current media climate, with many more outlets for news, an adversarial relationship between the media and the government, and the cult of the celebrity fuelling a focus on personalities in all walks of life, press and media relationships are crucial for all ministers.[3]

As the previous chapter noted, elites in politics, business and the military have led the development of professional public relations techniques since the First World War and the anti-socialist campaigns of the early twentieth century. But as Philip Schlesinger pointed out in 1989, effective source tactics are also available to subordinate social actors, who have been able at times to shape the mainstream media agenda. My own doctoral research on UK media coverage of the 1980s nuclear debate included analysis of the efforts of the Campaign for Nuclear Disarmament (CND) to command the news agenda through the organisation of spectacular demonstrations and protests. Sometimes these events were newsworthy because of their size (hundreds of thousands of people marched in London, as well as other western capitals, to protest about the introduction of Cruise missiles, Trident submarines and other then-controversial weapons systems). Sometimes their newsworthiness was a product of their organisers' clever use of symbolism to generate media-friendly happenings, such as the human chain which was formed around a number of key UK nuclear bases over Easter weekend 1983. These forms of spectacular non-violent action were designed to attract journalistic attention, and succeeded, forcing political responses (if not policy reversals) from the Conservative government of the time (McNair 1988).

Media-focused source strategies were also adopted in the 1980s by environmental campaign groups such as Greenpeace, whose symbolic protests frequently made it into the news and contributed substantially to the emergence of 'the environment' as an issue in the late 1980s and 1990s. Terrorist groups such as the IRA and ETA had long used violent spectaculars such as bombings, assassinations and kidnappings to attract media attention, and Al Qaida brought terrorist PR to a new level with the 9/11 attacks. Never before has a small, relatively resource-poor group demonstrated such a capacity to shape the news agenda, form global public opinion, and influence the decision-making of superpowers.

Whether violent or non-violent, progressive or reactionary, subordinate source strategies have frequently transformed the political environment by putting issues on the agenda which had not been there before, or compelling governments to act (or be seen to act) in ways that they would not otherwise have done. We can never say how the environmental debate would have developed without the consciousness-raising impact of Greenpeace and other groups. Nor can we say whether the Good Friday Agreement would have been signed in 1998 without the preceding three decades of violent spectaculars by the IRA and its loyalist co-terrorists in Northern Ireland. Without a doubt, however, media campaigns of this type – public relations by any other name – became in the late twentieth century a key front in the intensifying battle for public and government attention. To the extent that subordinate source activities were designed and implemented by skilful communicative entrepreneurs (as they were in the case of the IRA, Greenpeace and Al Qaida), knowledgeable about how to capture and control the news agenda, they could compete in the public sphere with much more luxuriously resourced government communication and propaganda apparatuses. As Simon Cottle observes in his introduction to *News, Public Relations and Power*, 'in today's promotional times, we can no longer assume that dominant social interests have it all their own way' (2003: 9).

Conversely, a failure to deploy the techniques of news management effectively can lead to 'bias' of the type identified in Philo and Berry's analysis of UK media coverage of the Israel–Palestine conflict (2004). As they point out in a chapter entitled 'Why Does It Happen?', 'one reason for this disparity [an alleged preference for the Israeli viewpoint] was the more efficient public relations machine which the Israelis operated to supply information to journalists' (ibid.: 247). That Israeli perspectives dominate British TV, they note, is 'in part the result of a very well developed system of lobbying and public relations' (ibid.: 251). They quote an Israel-based US journalist's view that:

> Palestinian spokesmen are their own worst enemy. They often come across as boorish, the message is often incoherent . . . Arafat [the interview took place before the PLO chairman's death] is a one man show, he is almost always incoherent.
>
> (Ibid.: 246)

This view is shared by Arab observers, some of whom have acknowledged that at the same time as Arafat and the PLO leaders were failing to get their message across, Israeli government sources were communicating their positions effectively and consistently to the world's media. According to the editor-in-chief of Saudi-based 24-hour news channel Al Arabiya:

> The Israelis always have 24/7 round-the-clock spokesmen and their hours are listed. The Arab governments never had anything like that. Unless you knew the minister personally and could see him or call him up, you couldn't even get an answer from an Arab government spokesman that was quotable. And if you did, it came too late and almost never got used.[4]

Of alleged anti-Arab bias in the western media this Arab journalist argues that in many cases 'there was no bias at all, simply lack of access'.

Spin and anti-spin: the journalism of political process

As noted in the previous chapter, the rise of public relations in the twentieth century has been viewed within the control paradigm as a source of the degeneration of political culture. Political discourse, from this perspective, has become manufactured and inauthentic, dishonest and propagandistic, just another elite instrument for controlling the subordinate masses. A substantial body of critical media scholarship has since been devoted to the exposure and denunciation of public relations and spin as it has been applied to a range of political debates. This body of work has performed a useful function in documenting the rise of public relations as an industry, and the abuses to which it can be put, while ignoring the dialectical nature of the relationship between public relations and the media. If one sees this relationship as evolutionary and adaptive, and one set of communication professionals (the journalistic fourth estate) as locked in a communicative arms race with another set (the PR practitioners, or fifth estate), then it becomes possible to observe and welcome the emergence of a deconstructive, meta-discursive journalism which scrutinises planned processes of media management in ways that are good for democracy.

The effort to manufacture consent through public relations and other forms of media management remains key for political actors, but it has been rendered transparent (and thus subverted) by the forensic analysis of spin undertaken by political journalists. If the communicative work we know today as spin is not new, it has become a newly visible element of the political environment, subject to constant commentary and critique everywhere in the political media. In the era of mediated democracy, politics is packaged, as Bob Franklin correctly asserts (2004), but the quality of the packaging is a matter of journalistic debate and public knowledge, a factor for public consideration alongside questions of policy and 'substance'. PR has become the subject of political journalism, as much as its master.

In the era of spin, an increasingly important facet of the journalist's adversarial role has been the exposure and dissection of spin; the critical analysis of spin as well as the views and behaviour of the political actors behind it. Hitherto secret and elusive processes of planned political communication have been rendered transparent by journalists who see it as part of their democratic role to report on the processes of political communication as much as the substantive messages. Spin has generated anti-spin, or *process journalism*, as journalists have become more aware of what PR is, how it works, and why it is important, passing that knowledge on to their audiences. The practice of public relations can no longer be viewed only as a corruption of authentic political communication by controlling elites (although it can still be that). It has become the subject of that communication in its journalistic form, through the deconstructive, demystificatory sub-category of political journalism I have called the 'demonology of spin' (McNair 2004).

Within the pessimistic paradigm of control, process journalism has been condemned as a derogation of the media's watchdog role, reflecting the ascendancy of 'style' over 'substance', and of 'process' over policy. It is naïve, however, to suggest that in contemporary conditions there can be a complete journalistic analysis of policy and the substance of government without consideration of the presentational and communicative context. Presentation was always important, even if we didn't realise it until the current generation of political journalists became aware of spin and its role in the political process, and decided that we, the public, ought to know about it too. As the report of the Phillis review on governmental communication put it in 2004:

> The response of the media to a rigorous and proactive news management strategy has been to match claim with counter-claim in a challenging and adversarial way, making it difficult for any accurate communication of real achievement to pass unchallenged.[5]

As a result, complained the UK editor of *Die Zeit*, 'the politicians are losing control over the political agenda. The much-maligned spin doctor was an attempt to win back the initiative. It failed a long time ago'.[6] Others would dispute this assessment, arguing that spin remains too powerful. Far from being present at *The Death of Spin*, as one recent volume describes it (Pitcher 2003), adherents to the dominance paradigm remain convinced that public relations is a key mechanism of elite control, from the battlefields of Iraq and Afghanistan to the corridors of Whitehall and the White House. The truth lies in between, behind the fog of an intensifying war for control of the news agenda which is fought by subordinate social actors with as much chance of success as their better-resourced opponents.

However one judges the current health of spin as a communicative practice, there can be no dispute with the argument that to assert political control over journalistic media in an era of mature democracy is far from easy, and increasingly requires potentially damaging government–media confrontation of the type which led to the death of David Kelly and the setting up of the Hutton Inquiry in the summer of 2003, and which is itself likely to become, as Hutton did, part of an ongoing journalistic narrative of lies, deceit and betrayal. The BBC may have been cowed by the findings of Lord Hutton's inquiry when they were published in January 2004,[7] leading to the loss of the BBC's chairman and director general, but it won most of the arguments. When one considers the admonitory tone of so much media coverage of the affair, it was arguably the government which emerged from the Gilligan/Kelly scandal with the greatest damage done to its reputation. Those events, indeed, marked a watershed in the politics of spin, hastening first the resignation of Alistair Campbell, then forcing a review of the Blair government's information policies in the form of the aforementioned commission on governmental communication chaired by Bob Phillis.

The decline of deference

Reinforcing and intensifying the above trends has been another – the decline of public (and journalistic) deference towards elite groups. In the UK as recently as the 1950s around one-third of the population still believed in the literal truth of the doctrine of the divine right of kings, that is, that the power of the monarchy was ordained by God. Today the royal family is still revered by some, but for most UK citizens coverage of its doings has been subsumed into the same celebrity culture which gives us Posh and Becks of 'Beckingham Palace'.

The reasons for this trend are complex. One might speculate that in the British case, the role of the ordinary people in the defeat of fascism (and the election of the first Labour government in 1945) produced a sense of popular power and agency which simply had not existed before the Second World War, when class and status hierarchies were much more strictly policed. Some blame the media for what they portray as a negative cultural trend, in so far as the irreverent scrutiny of elite behaviour which has been one manifestation of declining social deference is a media phenomenon, with the journalism of scandal fuelled by the competitive pressures towards heightened adversarialism discussed above. From this viewpoint the rot set in for the British royal family when in 1969 the Queen permitted the BBC to make an intimate documentary with unprecedented access to royal palaces and practices. For some American observers, the processes which led to the sexually explicit feeding frenzy of the Clinton–Lewinsky scandal in 1998/99 began with Watergate, and the subsequent mythologising of muck-raking, elite-subversive journalism as the normatively preferred mode.

It is not possible to conclude a cause and effect relationship here (and it would go against the grain of the chaos paradigm to suggest that it was), nor is it necessary for our present discussion. Suffice to note that changed public expectations of what is possible and appropriate in media coverage of elite behaviour have produced both pressure on, and the space for journalists to confront, scrutinise and expose elite behaviour and actions, in government as in the worlds of entertainment, sport and celebrity in general.

This not just a British or American phenomenon, moreover. French media coverage of the scandal affecting Nicolas Sarkozy and his wife Cecilia in August 2005 suggested that this most elite-deferential of political cultures was at last opening up under the same pressures which gave us sleaze journalism in the UK and Monicagate in the US. Journalistic expectations were also changing in the Middle East, where medieval-style deference towards elites until recently held sway. Naomi Sakr observes that since its formation in 1996, Al Jazeera has 'rejected entrenched pan-Arab codes of journalistic submissiveness' (2005b: 89), and agrees with the conclusion of local observers that this has had a progressive demonstration effect on its Arab-language competitor media (see Chapter 7 below).

Mediated access

A contributing factor in the decline of public deference towards elites is another trend in the political environment – the rise of public participation broadcasting. Alongside the expansion of formal democratic institutions, advanced capitalist societies have evolved political cultures of public debate with elites, exercised through what I have described elsewhere as *mediated access* (McNair et al.: 2003). As opposed to the limited (and shrinking) availability of non-mediated forms of access to politicians (doorstep encounters during election campaigns, attendance at rallies), mediated access takes the form of non-elite participation in radio phone-ins, talk shows and studio debates of the type exemplified by BBC television's *Question Time*, or Tony Blair's pre-Iraqi war appearances on live TV. In few other democratic countries does the executive branch of government submit to direct scrutiny of the kind permitted by Tony Blair during his time in office since 1997, but in most, significant forms of mediated access have developed.

In the United States, talk radio is now recognised as an important channel of public participation in political debate. Australia too has talk radio, as well as TV formats which echo some of those pioneered in the UK, though without the high-level executive participation which has become routine in Britain. In authoritarian political cultures, too, mediated access and public participation programme formats have increasingly been adopted as symbols of the democratisation of political culture, from the pioneering interactive styles of political debate to the entertainment-oriented Arab versions of western-originating shows such as *Pop Idol* and *Big Brother*. As with its adoption of a less deferential journalistic style, Al Jazeera's use of debate and audience participation formats in its political coverage has been influential on the programming of other Arab TV stations such as Al Arabiya (Sakr 2005b).

All over the world, if to varying degrees determined by the conditions prevailing in specific political cultures, formal democratic procedures are complemented by new forms of mediated elite accountability. These can be characterised, adapting Habermas' (1989) assertion that the public sphere has been refeudalised by private interests and degenerate political communication, as a 'defeudalisation' of the public sphere, with the citizenry constituted not just as spectators of power, but as participants in deliberative democratic processes. Expectations of elite accessibility (extending to Clintonesque revelations of personal impropriety or unethical conduct) have changed, and while the political establishments of different democratic countries have responded to this new reality in different ways, none can safely ignore it.

This trend has attracted critical commentary from both left and right of the spectrum. Commentators of both radical and conservative persuasion have expressed anxiety about the alleged degradation of the public sphere represented by mediated access. Critical scholars such as Pierre Bourdieu (1998) have interpreted it as a vindication of Habermas's pessimism about the future evolution of the public sphere, seeing it as market-driven and emblematic of a 'crisis of public communication' (Blumler and Gurevitch 1995). Those who defend public participation, including this writer, do so on the grounds that it is a logical and welcome extension of the democratic process in a media age (Lumby 1999; McKee 2004), which affords citizens unprecedented opportunities to engage with political elites, or to break into the public sphere with dissenting political opinions.[8]

A feature of the 2005 UK general election, as of the 1997 and 2001 campaigns before it, was the extent to which senior politicians made themselves available on public participation access programmes such as ITV's *Ask the Leader*, BBC1's *Question Time*, and radio shows such as *Today*. On an edition of *Question Time* broadcast one week before the 2005 British general election, Blair appeared live to answer hostile questions on Iraq from a studio audience. On this occasion a perspiring, visibly uncomfortable Blair experienced once again what he had voluntarily submitted to on many occasions since 1997 – the anger of a public fully aware of the accusation that he had lied to them and their elected representatives, or had at least told less than the full truth about the reasons for his decision to go to war two years previously. When the results of the election were announced on May 6, few doubted that this issue, and the intense scrutiny afforded it by the political media, had been a key factor in reducing New Labour's House of Commons majority to 66.

From adversarialism to hyper-adversarialism

Declining public and journalistic deference have increased the quantity and intensity of critical elite scrutiny in the mainstream media. In Britain, forensic scrutiny of the performance of the Blair government since September 11 has been the default position of both print and broadcast media coverage. After the London underground bombings of July 2005 the media contained many articles blaming the Blair government. Broadcast news and current affairs outlets such as *Newsnight* and *Panorama* carried interviews with some of the most radical Muslims in the country, who were frank in their refusal to condemn the suicide attackers, and in their belief that the murders were heroic acts of martyrdom which the British people had brought on themselves.

When in April 2005, on the eve of the general election, prime minister Tony Blair was forced to release the text of legal advice received by him from the UK's attorney general on the legality of the invasion of Iraq, it included the latter's view that a 'reasonable' case could be made for the decision to go to war. The 1998 UK–US action on Kosovo, and the bombing of Iraq that year in Operation Desert Fox had, he noted, both been based on 'no more than reasonably arguable' cases. The main difference between 1998 and 2003, and the reason for the much more contentious status of the Iraq intervention, was in his view: 'that on previous occasions when military action was taken on the basis of a reasonably arguable case, the degree of public and parliamentary scrutiny was nothing as great as it is today'.

Where previous generations of political elite had been able to take greater risks with military and foreign policy, because there were fewer, more deferential media and thus more manageable political environments, Tony Blair's Labour government faced constant critical scrutiny from a hyperactive fourth estate which harried its policy on Iraq from the outset. Mainstream media criticism of governing elites, far from being exceptional, had become routine. As a result, both the UK and American governments criticised what they suggested was the inappropriate degree of media criticism of their policies on Iraq, as did the Australian government of John Howard's Liberal Party. In March 2003 the Australian minister of communication published a dossier exposing what he claimed to be a record of consistent media criticism of the Coalition invasion of Iraq. The dossier provided some 68 examples of alleged anti-Coalition 'bias' by journalists of the Australian

Broadcasting Corporation (ABC). The following is typical of the document's tone.

Day 20 (of the invasion) – Wednesday 9 April, 2003 – 08:00:23

The death overnight of three journalists led [ABC correspondent] Linda Mottram to make a furious attack on the United States: '. . . the chances of independent reporting of the events on the ground have suffered a *body blow* overnight, and it's raised new questions about how the Coalition has *attempted to shape* reporting on this war'. [his emphasis]

What was the basis?

Well apparently the following remarks by Brigadier General Vince Brookes: 'What we can be certain of, though, is that this Coalition does not target journalists and so anything that has happened as a result of our fire or other fires would always be considered as an accident.'

This led Linda Mottram to sign off with: 'Brigadier General Vince Brookes with a sense of how the US military would prefer reporters in Iraq to work. And it should be noted that the key buildings that were attacked overnight, the coordinates and locations of these buildings have been given to the Pentagon some time back.'

Given that the remarks in question are logical and given that they contain no indication of how the US military would prefer reporters in Iraq to work, Linda Mottram seemed clearly determined to read something sinister into the deaths of journalists, whatever the evidence. In fact her last comment, on its face, seeks to give the impression that the targeting of journalists may have been a deliberate Pentagon strategy.[9]

Similar accusations of bias and knee-jerk negativism were made against British and American news organisations by government sources and their media supporters during the invasion of Iraq. The US Fairpress organisation accused the US media of painting a 'falsely bleak picture' of the conflict.[10] In the UK senior Labour minister John Reid attacked the BBC during the invasion phase of the Iraqi crisis, as did anonymous 'sources close to the prime minister'. While it is tempting to dismiss such accusations as predictable official defensiveness under pressure, there is evidence that media coverage of government policy *was* highly critical before, during and after the invasion of Iraq, in both print and broadcast media, and even in traditionally conservative newspapers such as the *Daily Telegraph* and *Daily Mail*. Chapter 3 noted that media bias is always in the eye of the beholder, but that there was at least some substance in the claims of Reid and others is supported by Tumber and Palmer's book-length study of the content of media coverage of the crisis (their sample included the BBC and four press outlets). This concluded that:

In the reporting of the pre-invasion phase there was a high degree of scepticism about the process . . . The BBC was sensitive to the need to reflect opposition to US policy as well as support for it. The scepticism took the form both of reporting opposition to the policy and of sceptical analysis of the process of policy formulation and implementation. Active campaigning against the policy was also prominent in left-wing press titles. In summary, there was no consensus in UK media about the reasons for going to war.

The reporting of the post-invasion phase has also been predominantly sceptical. This takes the form of a dominant focus on bad news regarding the situation inside Iraq and of an intensely sceptical – not to say aggressive – reporting of the UK government's justification for going to war.

(Tumber and Palmer 2004: 162)

During the invasion phase itself, both UK and US media focused on the looming quagmire likely to be caused by anything from desert sand storms to phantom armoured columns of Republican Guards roaring out of Baghdad. One observer notes that 'the European press in particular viewed the [Iraqi] war through a prism that highlighted the human costs, difficulties and risks' (Snow, 2004: 60).

Negative stories in the period during which this book was being written (negative from the point of view of political elites in Britain and America, that is) have included accusations of murder, torture and abuse of prisoners by Coalition troops, substantiated by voluminous photographic evidence; cover-up over the causes and conduct of war; allegations of inappropriate relationships between the Bush family and the Saudi ruling elite, from *Vanity Fair*'s lengthy exposé of November 2003 to Michael Moore's *Fahrenheit 9/11*; suggestions that 'poodle' Tony Blair had ceded control of British national interests to the US neo-cons; that he had deceived Parliament, broken international law and ridden roughshod over popular opposition.

Over a period of years the efforts of governments on both sides of the Atlantic to control media coverage of the reasons for war in Iraq, to set the terms of the debate around such issues as weapons of mass destruction, the ethics of regime change, or the performance of the Coalition after Saddam Hussein's eviction from office, have been singularly unsuccessful, to the extent that they have themselves frequently become the story, as in coverage of the Hutton and Butler inquiries of 2003 and 2004 respectively. In the US several extensively reported commissions on the events of 9/11 and its aftermath produced comparably critical coverage of the executive. Where Fox News has adopted a patriotic pro-war editorial stance – in June 2004, for example, at the height of the scandal, Fox News repeatedly and defiantly referred to the Abu Ghraib torture pictures as evidence of 'misbehaviour' by US troops, brandishing this formula in response to what the channel's managers would see as the liberal bias of the network news providers – other voices were heavily critical. The *New York Times* of June 13 2004 contained the following letter from Marta Bacon of Austin, Texas, responding to the administration's employment of war veterans to defend the Abu Ghraib abuses:

Why is it that these [veterans] who say they fought for freedom, democracy, justice and the so-called American Way failed to be the first to voice outrage when some of their own undermine and soil the supposedly noble fight? Cruelty can be so easy; justice and humanity are so hard. We are all sullied by Abu Ghraib and any evil done in our name.

Jacqueline Gens of Brattleboro, Vermont wrote in the same newspaper that 'wheeling out elderly soldiers in uniform as a defence of these acts is an embarassment to our military at best – hollow patriotism at worst'. In August 2005 US anti-war protester Cindy Sheehan was being described on British TV news as 'the most talked about woman in America',[11] following her lengthy and much-reported protest at the gates of the White House. In the aftermath of Hurricane Katrina in September 2005 many commentators observed that, almost regardless of the media's intentions:

> One of the great surprises of the Katrina catastrophe is that reporters on the ground have flatly contradicted the sunny, upbeat cluelessness emanating from the White House. You could last week often see Bush or some equally dissociative upper echelon idiot proclaiming one thing about the Katrina nightmare on the left half of a split-TV screen, even as visual evidence directly refuted their words on the right.[12]

So routine has journalistic criticism of political elites on both sides of the Atlantic become that within the ranks of established journalistic commentators, as well as many academics (including those who elsewhere argue for journalism's controlling function), the most vocal criticisms of the media in recent times have concerned their negativism and wilfully destructive attitude towards authority. In the late 1990s, and before the explosion of the Clinton–Lewinsky scandal into public view, American journalist James Fallows coined the term *hyper-adversarialism* to describe a media environment of intense, gladiatorial hostility towards governing elites (1996).[13] In Britain, commentators such as academic Steven Barnett and journalist Polly Toynbee condemned respectively 'the hounding of politicians by a cynical and corrosive media',[14] and the fact that 'journalism of left and right converges in an anarchic zone of vitriol where elected politicians are always contemptible, their policies not just wrong but their motives all self-interest.'[15] Barnett added:

> The time has come to point an accusing finger at the increasingly hostile and irresponsible tenor of political journalism and to ask whether it is contributing to a progressive loss of faith in the democratic system itself . . . the hounding of politicians by a cynical and corrosive media [is] a disaster for democracy. We have entered a new and destructive era in political journalism: the age of contempt.[16]

John Lloyd's (2004) book-length attack on the British media developed this argument, prompting a major debate in the pages of the *Guardian* newspaper about the appropriate relationship of the media to the political class. There the late Anthony

Sampson argued that 'journalists have gained power hugely, and become much more assertive, aggressive and moralising in confronting other forms of power'.[17]

The thrust of these analyses is correct, as one example selected at random from this writer's own viewing of British TV news illustrates. On the edition of BBC2's *Newsnight* current affairs magazine broadcast on November 12 2004, presenter Kirsty Wark referred to Tony Blair's White House meeting with George W. Bush as a 'love-in', and asked, in a deeply sarcastic tone suggesting that we already knew the answer to her question: 'Will the PM come home with some sort of reward for being George W's best friend?' Her casual presumption that the British prime minister is in a submissive, subordinate relationship to the US president is typical of the style of political journalism criticised by Barnett, Lloyd and others. Under the combined pressure of professional ethics and practices, market forces and public expectations, the traditional adversarialism of the fourth estate in liberal capitalism has matured, some might say mutated, into a confrontational stance which at one extreme verges on nihilism. Political journalism is said by one leading journalist to have become:

> obsessed with the processes of government, but incurious about any complex problem that cannot be blamed upon some hapless minister. Intense circulation wars have created a vicious press pack which ultimately might make the country ungovernable.[18]

The highly adversarial mediated access which characterised the 2005 general election campaign re-energised the long-running debate about the role and limits of such scrutiny in a healthy democracy. While practitioners such as John Humphrys of BBC Radio 4's *Today* show once again defended their critical role as watchdogs over power,[19] critics blamed hyper-adversarialism for declining voter turnouts.

The question of how much critical scrutiny is consistent with good government in a highly mediated democracy is a subjective matter, impossible to resolve once and for all to everyone's satisfaction. From the perspective afforded by the chaos paradigm, the preference must be for more rather than less scrutiny, even if that means upsetting the occasional prime minister or president. Such opportunities cannot of themselves be expected to solve the problems of democratic legitimacy and low electoral turnouts afflicting Britain and other advanced capitalist countries in the early twenty-first century (although they can provide a platform for the expression of popular discontent about the political process), nor need they have a measurable impact on short-term policy formation (although political elites do monitor access media as indicators of public opinion). They do, however, create a political environment of substantially greater volatility and uncertainty than was faced by previous generations of the governing elite.

As Tony Blair looked at his party's election results on May 6 2005, having been repeatedly called a liar and worse by audiences on TV, radio and the hustings over his policy on Iraq, he would have known that he had at least made himself accessible to the worst that the British public could throw at him. If one function of the public sphere is to render power transparent before the people, then this environment of mediated access and hyper-adversarial, attack journalism, of deconstructive process journalism, for all its excesses, represents a progressive evolution of our political culture, to be encouraged rather than reined in. Where political elites and their supporters in the commentary media view casual put-downs such as that of Kirsty Wark quoted above as 'anti-war bias' or even 'corrosive cynicism', a pro-democracy perspective welcomes any and all scrutiny of a controversial war, especially at a time when politicians, as they always do when fighting wars, were seeking to pressurise media organisations. Better from the democratic perspective to have an excess of critical elite scrutiny on an issue of such importance than a deficit.

5 Cultural chaos and the end of ideology

Another cause of the paradigm shift from control to chaos is the collapse of the ideological dividing lines which structured both domestic and global politics in the twentieth century. Since the end of the Cold War, which I will date to the collapse of the Berlin Wall in 1989, the bi-polarities of left and right, capitalism and communism, east and west, have given way to a more fluid ideological conjuncture. That trend has led in turn to the dissolution of one of the key interpretative frameworks which formerly structured mainstream journalism in capitalist societies.

The end of ideology and the left–right divide

For 70 years or more, from the Bolshevik Revolution of 1917 to the 'velvet revolutions' of the late 1980s, capitalism evolved alongside a systemic socialist alternative, equipped with a coherent ideological system.[1] Until *glasnost* and *perestroika* exposed the unpalatable realities of Soviet power, past and present (McNair 1991), western capitalism still had a rival model of social organisation with claims to present a viable alternative to the exploitation and injustice of the free market system. Marxism-Leninism as practised in the Warsaw Pact countries of Eastern and Central Europe, parts of Asia and Africa, Latin America and Cuba remained for many a flawed, but essentially well-intentioned, progressive approach to socio-economic organisation. Maoist China, nominally socialist but divergent from the ideological path of the USSR and its allies, still had ahead of it the massacre at Tiananmen Square and the rapid transition to the hybrid but hugely successful form of free-market capitalism which will see it become the world's second largest economy by 2015. Yugoslavia was still a 'socialist' country, not yet broken into warring ethnic tribes.

During these years western capitalism was often a reactionary, oppressive influence on the planet, as in the Central and South American wars of the 1970s and 1980s. American government support for neo-fascist death squads engaged in indiscriminate slaughter against peasant populations, or for despots such as Pinochet against democratically elected governments, was by any objective standard reactionary. It was also, in most cases, driven by anti-communist ideology. On the other side of the ideological divide, the Soviet Union made alliances of an equally unpalatable character, supporting any corrupt Third World dictator willing to lend his name, and his country, to the Marxist-Leninist cause. And just as the US media were often silent on human rights abuses by US-supported regimes, so were the Soviet media towards the abuses of *their* ideologically favoured governments, as of their own. Throughout the Cold War, political and cultural elites on both sides routinely put geo-strategic interests before any consideration of human rights or socio-economic progress.

After the fall of the Berlin Wall, however, and then the formal dissolution of the Soviet Union in 1991, and encouraged by the international Coalition which formed to eject Saddam Hussein from Kuwait, a 'new world order' began to take shape. With the end of Soviet power, and the discrediting of the ideology of Marxism-Leninism which had sustained it for 70 years, it was no longer possible to present something called 'socialism' as an alternative to capitalism. The great structuring bi-polarity of the post-Second World War years had ended. In its place? Global capitalism, faced with the far from finished task of internal reform (though not revolution) within its leading economies, and with overcoming resistance to its values overseas. Castells observes that 'the end of Soviet communism, and the hurried adaptation of Chinese communism to global capitalism, has left a new brand of leaner, meaner capitalism alone at last in its planetary reach' (2000: 2). 'Suddenly', notes former British communist Martin Jacques, 'capitalism became the only show in town, both in Europe and globally.'[2]

Although the process of ideological realignment accelerated after the end of the Cold War, it can with the benefit of hindsight be seen to have begun before that with the rise of new social movements based on sexual and other forms of identity politics, as well as consumerism and environmentalism. These were not class-based issues, and could not be addressed within the terms of conventional left–right debate. The Soviet Union and its allies were worse polluters of the environment, and less concerned about workers' rights and health, than the most rapacious of capitalist corporations. Western environmentalists were not always left-wing in the conventional sense, often representing the interests of wealthy rural populations against the perceived encroachment of the urban masses. Feminism was rejected by traditional socialism as a bourgeois deviation, and Soviet feminists were treated as dissidents. Contemporary 'socialist' societies such as China, Cuba and Zimbabwe were and remain among the most homophobic and patriarchal on the planet.

Even before the fall of the Berlin Wall, therefore, the relevance of left–right politics and ideology to people's lives was eroding. John B. Thompson noted the late twentieth-century's decline of ideology and its political impact:

> Traditional class-based party politics, with its sharply opposed belief systems and its strong contrast between left and right, has not disappeared, but it has been significantly weakened by the social transformations of the post-war period.

> (Thompson 2000: 112)

For Italian commentator Antonio Polito:

> Left and Right have become indistinguishable. The only way to mark out a division in the politics of [the twenty-first century] will be between progressives and conservatives. The former promote competition as the modern means to assert individual talent under conditions of equal access to the social contest. The latter wish to maintain the status quo of corporations and privileges, including those of working-class aristocracies and their trade unions.
>
> (Cited in Hobsbawm 2000: 111)

For Martin Jacques, 'the left has disintegrated' throughout Europe, and become 'but a rump of its former self', for two reasons:

> The first is the loss of agency, the decline of the industrial working class and its consequent erosion as a meaningful and effective political force. The second reason is the collapse of communism.[3]

By 1991 and the winding up of the Soviet state, the east–west, capitalist–communist confrontation which had structured ideological struggle since the Second World War had been replaced by confrontations of a nationalist, ethnic and religious nature, which necessarily forged new alliances. In a *New York Times* article published to coincide with the publication of his book in praise of globalisation, *The World Is Flat* (2005), Thomas Friedman noted that the fall of the Berlin Wall 'had, for the first time, 'allowed us to think of the world as a single space',[4] rather than an environment divided into hostile opposing camps.

William Lance Bennett has argued that 'with the expansion of globalisation and the death of rival socialist systems, neo-liberalism has been proclaimed the reigning idea system by leading political, economic and media elites in most nations' (2003: 144). This is not the End of Ideology, however, in the sense intended by Daniel Bell in his 1960 book of that name (2000), any more than the fall of the Berlin Wall signalled the End of History (Fukuyama 1992). It is the end of a particular *phase* in history, defined by the particular ideological conflict (left–right; socialist–capitalist; east–west) which had dominated the twentieth century and shaped its critical paradigms (including those that have dominated media sociology). In the terms of chaos science, it is a phase transition from a twentieth-century stability bounded by left–right bi-polarity to a twenty-first-century instability in which the contours of ideological struggle are less clear. Struggle continues, but organised less around class issues than of competing notions of modernity and modernisation, morality and ethics.

In the vanguard of this new struggle, Islamic fundamentalism seeks to replace the Marxist-Leninist alternative to capitalism with that of a global theocracy, or *umma* (community) (Hiro 2002). Since 9/11 the key ideological division at the global level has been between this fundamentalism and all other belief systems, including not just atheisms of various types, but all non-Islamic religions, and even moderate Muslims, to all of which Islamic fundamentalism is violently opposed.[5] Although the jihadists lack the military-industrial capacities of the Nazis in the 1930s, they have much in common with the latter, being profoundly anti-Semitic, homophobic, and adhering to a cult of violence which explicitly dehumanises all those with whom it differs ideologically.[6] In this context, the ideological environment of the early twenty-first century is closer to that of the fascist era (when advocates of 'left' and 'right' ideas were necessarily united against a common enemy which detested them both with equal fervour) than it is to that of the Cold War.

With some anachronistic exceptions, such as the ongoing Maoist insurgency in Nepal, the ideological terrain of the post-Cold War era is not shaped by confrontations between 'bourgeois' and 'proletarian', or communism and capitalism, but between modernity and medievalism, between dictatorship and democracy, between ethnic or religiously defined groups, and between corruption and competence in government. These are not necessarily *class* struggles, far less Marxist (although, as in the case of Al Qaida, wealthy Islamic revolutionaries may co-opt the poor from the 'Arab street' to fight their jihad), where the aim is to replace capitalism with a secular socialism. They constitute, by the statements of their leaders, nothing short of efforts to halt the forward march of human social evolution in its tracks. Samuel Huntington's essential point about the contemporary 'clash of civilisations' (1996), made before 9/11, is valid – the great struggle of the new century is not between capitalist and socialist worldviews, but between modernity and the reactionary religious zealotry of fundamentalist Islam.[7]

Ideology and the control paradigm

The intellectual environment in which the founding texts of materialist media sociology were written, and by which the control paradigm was shaped, was dominated first by support of or opposition to totalitarianisms of left (Bolshevism) and right (fascism), and then, after the Second World War, by left–right, capitalist–socialist ideological divisions. Historical materialism, rooted in a Marxian-socialist worldview, spoke to the need for human progress, and in the theory of ideological control which took centre-stage in media sociology offered an explanation as to why it was not happening in advanced capitalist societies. Its founders, Marx and Engels, were Germans who lived for much of their lives in England at the height of the Industrial Revolution, and wrote their greatest works on the basis of observations made about British capitalism. For all its later adoption by revolutionaries in less developed countries, historical materialism was an intellectual product of advanced, Western European capitalism, where it had immense appeal amongst left intellectuals and activists until the very end of the Cold War era. Martin Jacques has observed that:

> [while] the mainstream labour movement in this country [the United Kingdom] never subscribed to its tenets, both the social democratic and communist traditions shared, in different ways, the vision of a better society based on collectivist principles. For over a century, European politics was defined by the struggle between capitalism and socialism.[8]

As for politics, so for media scholarship which, if rarely explicitly pro-Soviet, was derived from the same historical materialism which drove Marx and Engels, then Lenin and the Bolsheviks, and a corresponding belief in the innate instability of capitalism, with its internal contradictions, injustices and inequalities. The hold of the dominance paradigm on the intellectual left within advanced capitalism reflected the political primacy of class division at both the nation-state and global levels, the geo-strategic balance of class forces, and the sense that there was something better to come.

This intellectual environment has to be set against the existence until very recently of only a limited number of media channels disseminating news, analysis and commentary to relatively passive publics (in so far as they consumed, but could not produce or interact with media in the manner taken for granted by today's net-savvy citizens). The world in which the founding texts of media sociology were written was a world of relative information scarcity, of top-down information flow and capital-intensive, industrial media. It was a world in which what the BBC said, or didn't say, mattered much more than in the multi-channel environment of today, where no news organisation, no matter how prestigious, exists in isolation, but must compete for attention alongside hundreds of other sources (see Chapters 7 and 8).

Even before the collapse of the USSR, or the coming of the internet, Nicholas Abercrombie and his colleagues challenged the dominant ideology thesis with the argument that 'the existence of a postmodern culture (defined by these authors as 'the fragmentation and diversification of modern cultures by the forces of consumerism and global markets') means that by definition there cannot be a single, dominant, or coherent ideology' (Abercrombie *et al.* 1990: 250). Around the same time Fredrick Jameson declared that 'ideology is now over, not because class struggle has ended and no-one has anything ideological to fight about, but rather because conscious ideologies and political opinions have ceased to be functional in perpetuating and reproducing the system' (1991: 398). He added:

> [I]f the ideas of a ruling class were once the dominant (or hegemonic) ideology of bourgeois society, the advanced capitalist countries today are now a field of stylistic and discursive heterogeneity without a norm. Faceless masters continue to influence the economic strategies which constrain our existences, but they no longer need to impose their speech, or are henceforth unable to.
>
> (Ibid.: 117)

Ideology was not 'over', of course, but for these observers the materialist concept of a dominant ideology functioning as a control mechanism over the passive proletariats of capitalism could no longer be taken seriously as an explanation for social stability. With the end of the Cold War, the ideological bi-polarity which had structured global and much of domestic politics in Britain and other western countries for decades had begun to erode. Dominant ideology, such as it was, had ceased to dominate advanced capitalist societies, replaced by a more fluid set of values and beliefs in which left and right were no longer so easily identifiable.[9]

The global struggle between capitalism and socialism was over, as was the ideological configuration which reflected it, and which had led concepts such as freedom and democracy to be viewed from within the control paradigm as 'necessary illusions' (Chomsky 1989).

The consequences of this ideological shift were first seen in the Gulf War of 1991, which united western powers such as the US and the UK alongside Arab countries, the Soviet Union and China, in common pursuit of an aggressor state and its despotic leader. Twelve years later, as the invasion of Iraq loomed, that very visible manifestation of a new world order had fragmented, but the decoupling of concepts such as freedom and democracy from their Cold War connotations remained a feature of public discourse. For example, merely because the war on terror and the subsequent push for democratisation in the Middle East were sponsored by a right-wing Republican administration, displaying a scary religious fanaticism of its own, this did not mean that it could be dismissed as US 'propaganda'. By 2005 many commentators in Britain and the US who had been opponents of the Bush–Blair strategy from the outset were acknowledging the beneficial consequences of the invasion of Iraq and the downfall of Saddam Hussein, and accepting that it could have positive consequences for democratisation in the Middle East. The execution of the invasion and subsequent occupation was messy, it was generally accepted, and major mistakes were made. War crimes and human rights abuses were committed, with or without official complicity, in Abu Ghraib, Camp Breadbasket and elsewhere. But in the final analysis the removal of Saddam was deemed a progressive act, whether or not it came at the hands of a Republican US president or a British Labour prime minister (the alliance of Blair and Bush, indeed, exemplifies the environment of ideological dissolution we are discussing in this chapter).

In 2005 many commentators observed a domino effect of democratisation rippling out from post-Saddam Iraq to the rest of the Middle East and the 320 million Arabs still governed by despotic regimes. Observing the Lebanese elections of May 2005, Saad Eddin Ibrahim of the American University of Cairo wrote in the Australian press that 'social transformations under way in the Middle East are leading towards democracy'. Ibrahim attributed this trend, at least in part, to the US-led interventions in Afghanistan and Iraq:

> Whatever one thinks of American military intervention, one must concede that it has altered the region's dynamics. Domestic opposition forces, while distancing themselves from the US, have been markedly emboldened in Lebanon, Egypt, Saudi Arabia and elsewhere. Something about the past few months feels new and irreversible. Too many people in too many places are defying their oppressors and taking risks for freedom.[10]

Professor Tom Melia of Georgetown University argued that

> You don't have to be an enthusiast for Bush to know that many of his critics were wrong. Making democracy a strategic goal for American interests in the world doesn't sound so wacky any more.[11]

In the *Guardian* of March 2 2005, anti-war critic Jonathan Freedland conceded that, although the invasion of Iraq was not the only factor promoting democratisation in the Middle East, it had 'changed the calculus in the region' and set off 'a benign chain reaction'.[12] In response, he argued further, opponents of Bush and Blair should acknowledge that the invasion of Iraq had enabled a series of 'potentially welcome side effects', and that:

> The call for freedom throughout the Arab and Muslim world is a sound and just one. Put starkly, we cannot let ourselves fall into the trap of opposing democracy in the Middle East simply because Bush and Blair are calling for it. Sometimes your enemy's enemy is not your friend.

Even the left-wing warrior Walid Jumblatt, veteran leader of the Lebanese Druze community and no friend of the Bush administration, recognised that the growing pressure for democratic reform, not just in Lebanon but everywhere in the Middle East, was 'a process of change [which] has started because of the American invasion of Iraq'.[13] Whether this process would be good or bad for western strategic interests was not entirely certain, given the likelihood of fundamentalist Islamist success in elections in the Middle East, but that pressures for democratic reform were building even in hitherto rigidly authoritarian states such as Saudi Arabia was beyond dispute.[14] British journalist David Hirst noted in April 2005 that while democratisation in the Middle East, such as it was, had been a product of colonial-style intervention by the US and Britain in Iraq, it was at the same time a genuine goal of reformers in Syria, Egypt and other authoritarian states. Whatever the ultimate motivations of western powers in promoting democracy, Hirst argued, the goal was a valid one. Thus, strategic western interests and the goals of social progress were converging. Resistance to western 'imperialism' by Arab nationalists (and thus, presumably, by western critics of their governments' imperialist policies) had become 'little more than a rhetorical tool to suppress democracy'.[15]

Within advanced capitalist societies we see a similar decoupling and redefinition of hitherto ideologically-charged terms. The ritual murder of Theo Van Gogh in Amsterdam in November 2004 by an Islamic fundamentalist angered by his film about the abusive treatment of women in Muslim societies sparked debate in Holland about the limits of multiculturalism and the implications of large-scale Islamic immigration, debates which have been paralleled in Britain, Australia and France. This was a debate in which feminists and supporters of gay rights found themselves on the same side as racists opposed to immigration per se. Anti-war leftists, meanwhile, found themselves marching alongside Islamic fundamentalists dedicated, among other things, to the rolling back of a century of social progress on such issues as women's equality. In this environment those who would once have regarded themselves as being on the left supported wars pursued by distinctly right-wing US presidents, in opposition to others on the left who regarded such groups as the Shia Mehdi army of radical cleric Moqtada al-Sadr as 'freedom fighters'. The categories of left and right (in the diminishing arenas where they are still used) could no longer be assumed to equate to progressive and conservative (or revolutionary and reactionary).[16] In Britain, leftist journalists such as David Aaronovitch, John Lloyd and Anthony Andrews found themselves occupying much of the same terrain as the hated 'neo-cons' and neo-imperialists in the Bush administration.[17] Marxist intellectuals such as Norman Geras declared that they 'didn't agree with the left liberal consensus on the war'[18] (see Chapter 8). In the United States former-Trotskyist Christopher Hitchens defended the invasion as a progressive act.[19]

The shifting fault lines of geo-strategic division have thus impacted on the ideological connotations of terms such as 'democracy' and 'freedom'. When there were competing ideologically rooted definitions of these terms to choose from, based on rival theories of social organisation, something called 'bourgeois' or western democracy could be credibly challenged, if never (as it turned out) successfully replaced. With the fall of the Soviet Union and the end of the Cold War that choice evaporated. Freedom has become simply freedom. Democracy is now simply democracy. Both words signify universal political goals signed up to by Christian and Muslim, left and right, east and west, and north and south. Which is not to say that the term is not used cynically to mask or excuse abuses of power by political elites all over the world, or that Islamic democracy as it develops may not take a different form to that seen in the advanced capitalist world, An important task of a critical media (and a critical media scholarship) continues to be to exercise scrutiny over abuses of the rhetoric of democracy. But opposition to democracy, as a concept or as a policy goal, can no longer be credibly based on the fact that George W. Bush supports it, or on the assertion that there is a better alternative mode of governance out there, be it the 'workers' democracy' used to legitimise Stalinist-era dictatorship in the state socialist world, or the concept of 'Islamic democracy' often used to legitimise the religious fascism of the twenty-first century.

Ideological bi-polarity and the media: from consensus to dissensus

That there is a relationship between ideological bi-polarity and media content has been a lynchpin of critical media sociology. Daniel Hallin's study of US news coverage of the Vietnam War argues that it was framed in 'Cold War terms', in that phrases such as 'the swiftly encroaching Communist menace' were deployed not as attributed statements, opinions or judgements, but as 'a sort of baseline reality' (Hallin 1986: 53). During this period there existed 'a tight consensus on the nature of world politics and the American role in it; none brought into question the premise that the preservation of an anti-Communist Vietnam was indeed a legitimate goal of American policy' (ibid.: 50). As Hess and Kalb (2003: 1) note more recently:

> For a generation, until the collapse of the Soviet Union, American news organisations [and those of other western countries] reported the world largely through the prism of the Cold War . . . the East–West conflict was a useful framing device.

The exposé of double standards in US reportage of Soviet dissidents and central American death squads presented in Chomsky and Herman's *Political Economy of Human Rights* (1979) resonated at a time when this 'prism' was still in place. Their analysis of the filters through which US news came to be produced was undertaken against the backdrop of central American death squads, and the kinds of scenarios depicted in Oliver Stone's *Salvador* (which dramatised the brutal murder of four American nuns with, if not the active complicity of the CIA, at least its passive acceptance). In the face of the limited coverage of such atrocities to be found in the mainstream media, it was indeed striking that the activities of Soviet dissidents (Andrei Sakharov, for example, and Anatoly Scharansky) could receive so much more attention in the American press than that received by the deaths of tens of thousands of civilians in Chile and Paraguay.[20]

There was, however, no brainwashing, and no conspiracy to brainwash, so much as a generalised elite consensus around the nature of the Threat, and the primacy of the east–west, communist–capitalist division. As the cultural arm of that elite, and in the context of a much less decentralised media system than exists today, mainstream journalists in the 1970s and 1980s had a convenient script to follow when framing news about foreign policy and international affairs. This script had good guys and bad guys, and clear narrative threads which conformed to the Americans' sense of moral superiority, and also suited its business interests overseas. Journalists, as *Vanity Fair* noted in August 2005, 'prefer packaging conflicts as if they followed the classical unities of drama with a linear beginning, middle, end and coda'.[21] Cold War-era conflicts had those story-telling qualities and, with very few exceptions in the mainstream media, that is how they were reported, not just in the US but in Britain (McNair 1988).

With ideological dissolution and de-alignment, however, it became more difficult to fit the messiness of events and their media coverage into the interpretative frameworks of the Cold War era. Since the 1988 massacres of Armenians by Azeris in the (at the time) Soviet region of Nagorno-Karabakh, the main conflicts on which western journalists have been called upon to report are ethnic, nationalist and religious in nature, having nothing or little to do with the ideological divides of the Cold War. In some cases they represent the resurgence of conflicts long suppressed by the superpower stand-off. In others they have been an unforeseen consequence of manoeuvres by one or other of the USA, the USSR or the lesser colonial powers – the first Gulf War; the ethnic conflicts in the former Soviet Union and Yugoslavia; the Rwandan genocide; territorial disputes between India and Pakistan. And then, of course, Islamic fundamentalism in the Middle East and Africa, as exemplified by the debacle afflicting US forces in Somalia. The rise of Islamic fundamentalism began in the mountains of Afghanistan, with Mujahidin fighters funded by the CIA and the Saudi Arabians, then and since key allies of the USA in the Middle East.

These conflicts had to be made sense of, if they were to be made sense of at all, in terms very different from those used by media organisations during the Cold War. The ideological assumptions which had guided journalists since the Second World War no longer applied. Journalists were rudderless, and thus more likely to move beyond the 'limits of legitimate controversy', precisely because no one knew what those limits were any more. *Die Zeit* editor Jürgen Kronig observes that 'after the end of the great ideological divide, politics is more often than not complex, not easy to understand, and more difficult to report'.[22] James Woolcott observes that conflicts such as that in Iraq 'refuse to follow the playbook', marking instead 'new co-ordinates in chaos'.[23] Cultural chaos has replaced the ideologically structured order of the Cold War, and journalists no longer reproduce the 'propaganda' of the 'national security state' with anything like the predictability of the 1970s and 1980s. The ideological bi-polarity of the Cold War had, by defining the limits of legitimate controversy or *consensus*, acted as a cultural policing mechanism for journalists on both sides of the geo-strategic divide. When it ended, so did the need for cultural policing. Consensus was replaced by *dissensus*.

Given the declining deference and heightened adversarialism of public and political journalists described in the previous chapter, the erosion of a consensual interpretative framework for making sense of foreign events permitted news media to report them with greater flexibility and less concern for what might once have been the propaganda of governing elites (who were themselves confused and rudderless in the new environment). These elements combined to create a much more open journalistic terrain. An example. On Friday May 13 2005, as the protesting people of Andizhan in Uzbekistan were being mown down in their hundreds by the regime's soldiers, BBC1's peak-time 10 o'clock news bulletin led with the story, referring in unambiguous terms to Uzbekistan as a 'dictatorship' with a long record of flawed human rights. Another report spoke of a 'cruel, authoritarian regime'. In terms that were clearly disapproving, the fact that the US government had turned a blind eye to these abuses for strategic reasons to do with the war on terror was stressed repeatedly by the BBC: not qualified as an opinion, but as an objective fact without which the full significance of the story could not be appreciated.

This example, drawn at random from peak-time UK TV news, illustrates how, in the wake of the collapse of Soviet power and the eroding credibility of its associated ideological frameworks on the global stage, we see the emergence of a media free, or free-*er*, to engage in the democratically important work of critical elite scrutiny. Criticism stops being dissensual and dissonant, and becomes routine. Hallin's 'sphere of legitimate controversy' widens, because it is no longer bounded by the imposition or internalisation of a Cold War mindset. Elites in the political, military and media spheres are as uncertain, ideologically speaking, as everyone else. From the relatively tight ideological control encouraged by a world frozen into two rigid and defensive blocs, we enter the turbulence of a world falling back into obscure, murderous conflicts of the premodern type, fuelled by religious and ethnic intolerance, legitimised by competing nationalisms and definitions of morality, and communicated by new information and communication technologies. Instead of Dominant Ideology, we see competition between a variety of ideological strands associated with particular political factions within capitalist public spheres, such as American neo-conservatism, or New Labour's 'Third Way'. Of course there is still propaganda, in the sense of intentionally partisan news. But if a channel such as Fox News is overtly patriotic in its coverage of the war in Iraq, then the US networks, CNN, the *New York Times* and others are deeply sceptical, often critical, as are many of the media in European countries and Australasia.

Saddam, Al Qaida and the war on terror: images of the enemy revisited?

Ideological dissolution and realignment notwithstanding, since the start of the war on terror an attempt has been made by some critical media scholars to revive the control paradigm by suggesting that 'terror' in general, and Iraq and Saddam Hussein in particular, have replaced the Soviet threat as a convenient, if exaggerated, enemy. There is, clearly, a sense in which US and British government claims about the threat posed to the world by Saddam Hussein, and in particular the now-notorious claim that he possessed weapons of mass destruction (WMD) poised to strike at his enemies within 45 minutes, remind one of the rhetoric and imagery used to colour the Soviet threat 20 years before (McNair 1988). Threat inflation, selective use of dubious intelligence, apocalyptic warnings of imminent catastrophe if the enemy were left to his own devices – all these techniques were used by Ronald Reagan and Margaret Thatcher in their time to justify development and deployment of new weapons like Cruise missiles and Trident submarines. Stock footage of the Soviet military marching through Red Square in 1980s was echoed in similar images of Saddam's army parading its (illusory) might in Baghdad two decades later.

But there is a significant difference between the two periods. The concept of the Soviet threat referred to a real superpower, with real nuclear weapons, offering a real ideological and political alternative to capitalism at the global level. The threat may have been exaggerated, not least by the Soviets themselves, but that it existed was a matter of elite and popular consensus for decades, not least because it was endorsed by the mainstream western media. The mythology of the Soviet threat was hegemonic.

The nature of the Iraqi threat, on the other hand, if inflated by the leaders of the US–UK Coalition in order to secure public support for military intervention, was subject to critical media scrutiny from the moment invasion began to look likely in early 2002 and fell securely into the 'sphere of legitimate controversy'.[24] Journalistic consensus around the reality of the Iraqi 'threat' lacked the solidity of their belief in the Soviet threat, not just because of the existence of a faster, more expansive, more competitive and globalised news culture constantly interrogating it, but because there was no longer a simple left–right structure to the public debate. Long before the Andrew Gilligan story for Radio 4 about the 'sexed-up' WMD dossier, journalists were reporting the fact that much of the case against Saddam Hussein had been plagiarised from an old PhD thesis. A week after the publication of the second WMD dossier in February 2003, 'it was revealed to be a mish-mash of intelligence reports, student work and publicly available briefings by Jane's Intelligence Review'.[25]

The limits of mainstream media debate had expanded beyond what was possible in the 1970s and 1980s, when just about every country in the world (and most journalists) were obliged to choose between two opposing camps, armed to the teeth and ready to commit mutual suicide if need be.

Since the invasion, as the previous chapter noted, media 'scepticism' towards US and UK policy in Iraq has been routine (Tumber and Palmer 2004). Illustration of this point comes in the context of a recent, highly acclaimed documentary, widely seen around the world, despite challenging the concept of the war on terror at its core. Adam Curtis's three-part film *The Power of Nightmares*, broadcast by the BBC in the UK and in several other countries thereafter, asserts that the 'war on terror' is founded on a myth, and that Al Qaida does not exist in the form conventionally understood. The threat posed by Osama Bin Laden, and by Islamic fundamentalism in general, is argued to have been exaggerated by neo-conservative think-tanks such as the Project for a New American Century, nostalgic for the loss of the Evil Empire and anxious for a new rationale for American global domination beyond the Cold War. From this perspective, coverage of the 'war on terror' represents business as usual for US–British imperialism and the media that prop it up with pro-systemic propaganda.

Curtis does not dispute that there exists a planned campaign against the west, and non-Islamist views in general, which has led to spectaculars such as 9/11, the Bali bombings, the Madrid massacre and the London bombings of July 2005, as well as individual assassinations of prominent 'infidels' such as Theo Van Gogh in the Netherlands. He argues merely that the threat has been mythologised for elite convenience, and that the war on terror is a cover for less worthy motives than defeating Islamic extremism. It is a provocative thesis, and not without some substance. Al Qaida, Curtis shows in his film, is not an army, nor even a tight-knit organisation such as the IRA, but a loose network of tech-savvy religious extremists who have established themselves as a global political force out of all proportion to their economic and military power. Al Qaida have killed fewer than 4,000 civilians in terrorist attacks since Osama Bin Laden's declaration of jihad in 1999. The Nazis killed 27 million in Soviet Russia alone between 1941 and 1945. There is, in short, no 'global terror network' capable of world domination.[26]

Curtis is also correct to show how western elites have been both hypocritical and opportunistic in their response to 9/11, reversing their previous tolerance for and encouragement of Mujahidin fighters in Afghanistan, for example,[27] and backing for Saddam Hussein in his war with Iran, to portray these forces as suddenly a global threat. Curtis's film performs a valuable service in pointing out both the true nature of Al Qaida, and the (ab)uses to which an exaggerated view of the threat it poses can be put. His error, however, is to suggest that the process by which we have come to believe what we believe about Bin Laden and Al Qaida is planned by the sinister ideologues of US neo-conservatism. On the contrary, the rise of Al Qaida into global media and public consciousness is a direct and unplanned consequence of cultural chaos.

Western governments have been heavily criticised for underestimating the Al Qaida threat until it was too late, and blamed for encouraging Islamic funda-mentalism as a weapon against Soviet power during the Cold War. They, as was made evident by the oft-replayed footage of George W. Bush stunned into inaction by the news of the World Trade Center attacks just as he was about to address a class of school kids, were just as much taken by surprise as their citizens, and have been on the defensive ever since. Michael Moore's *Fahrenheit 9/11* justifiably makes much both of the Bush administration's lack of preparedness on the eve of September 11, and the Bush family's close links with the Saudi royal family.

Unlike the Soviet threat of the Cold War era, then, fear of Al Qaida and belief in the war on terror has not been created by the conspiratorial actions of western governments, but by its opposite – the short-sighted support of many of those governments for a militant religious movement which was deemed to be anti-Soviet (my enemy's enemy is my friend), and their subsequent inattentiveness to the emergence of that movement as a threat to western interests after the withdrawal of the Soviets from Afghanistan. Post 9/11 the power of Al Qaida, such as it has been, is almost entirely media-generated, arising from the automatic, unthinking response of a globalised news culture to violent spectaculars which, though horrifying and deadly, bear no comparison in their destructiveness to the atrocities committed by the Axis powers in the 1930s and 1940s, or to the potential threat posed by a genuine superpower such as the Soviet Union in the post-Second World War period. Because the twenty-first-century media were able to report 9/11 in the way they did – intensively, round-the-clock, with few firm facts to go on – they established in the minds of their audiences, which included political leaders, the existence of a 'global terror network'. This then fuelled policy in the US, the UK and elsewhere, from the invasions of Afghanistan and Iraq to the Patriot Act and the proposed introduction of identity cards in the UK. The existence of a global media network, and a globalised public sphere (see Chapter 10), made possible and then amplified the symbolic power of the Al Qaida actions.

The chain of post-9/11 events cannot be explained in terms of left versus right, or Democrat/Labour versus Republican/Conservative, or in terms of ruling elites imposing dominant ideologies on subordinate masses. After 9/11 many of the actions and pronouncements of Bush and Blair may reasonably be interpreted as attempts to control and manage public opinion, and of course there have been attempts to exploit the fear of Al Qaida for narrow political gain. But these efforts at control are constantly blown off course by media-generated bifurcations of various kinds, such as the scandal of Abu Ghraib, the extended forensic scrutiny of the Blair government by the Hutton Inquiry, and a host of US Senate inquiries into the intelligence and security failures which led to September 11. If journalists ever were the ideological agents of a ruling capitalist class, the dissolution of traditional ideological divisions has freed them from that role, at least for the time being.

6 Cultural capitalism and the commodification of dissent

The economic drivers of cultural chaos arise from two evolutionary trends in the capitalist mode of production. The first, discussed in Chapter 2, is towards greater productivity within the capitalist system as a whole, notwithstanding the persistence of social relations of exploitation within the production process, and the unequal distribution of wealth both within the nation-state and internationally. This trend challenges a key premise of the control paradigm – that ideological control through the inducement of false consciousness in the minds of the masses, as opposed to their informed consent, is required to explain the reproduction of capitalism over time.

Second, and the subject of this chapter, is the evolution of news and other journalistic forms as cultural commodities, to the point at which producers have an economic incentive to 'surprise and disrupt' elites, as Luhmann puts it, by being the first to report stories such as Abu Ghraib (or the shooting by US troops of unarmed prisoners in Falluja in November 2004, covered on the front page of newspapers all over the world) quickly, and with as much objectivity as they can manage.

The perverse logic of cultural capitalism

Chapter 2 argued that capitalism's economic success can be reconciled with a materialist theoretical framework if it is accepted that capitalism contains the seeds not, as Marx and Engels believed, of its own destruction, but (in conditions of mass democracy, and in the era of mass media) of its auto-reform and progressive humanisation; its self-correction and improvement, as measured by standard economic and quality of life indicators. Just as the mechanism of self-destruction of capitalism, for Marx, was the blind application of the profit motive and the merciless extraction of surplus-value from the worker, so the mechanism of self-improvement and self-correction is also the profit motive, and in particular the need to sell cultural commodities. In contemporary conditions, these commodities have to succeed (sell) in a competitive market of relatively empowered, relatively knowledgeable citizen-consumers, who are in a position to exercise choice and who do not respond well to being patronised.

Critical media sociology is most passionate when condemning the evils of commercialisation and the commodification of journalism. Herman and McChesney typify the style of attack when they note that, because they 'represent narrow class interests', commercial media organisations present 'a clear and present danger to citizens' participation in public affairs, understanding of public issues, and thus to the effective working of democracy' (1997: 1). 'The very logic of private media market control and behaviour', they continue, 'is antithetical to the cultivation and nurture of the public sphere' (ibid.: 7). The media, however, have always been mainly commercial entities, producing content for profit by capitalists. There have been markets, more or less free, since the birth of capitalism, not least in the cultural sphere. Indeed, with the exception of UK-type public service broadcasting, and a few isolated examples of publicly subsidised or party-run media, almost all the products of the capitalist culture industries since the invention of the printing press have circulated in commodity form. Even system-dissenting media, be they Trotskyist newspapers or books by Naomi Klein, have survived largely on their ability to sell copies at a price capable of producing a profit.

The example of Klein's *No Logo* (2000) demonstrates that cultural commodities are distinct from other kinds in that the act of their consumption has ideological consequences which, through the mechanisms of consumer choice and democratic participation, impact on the wider commodity system, creating a virtual cycle in which profits are made at the same time as radical and even subversive ideas are disseminated. Cultural commodities generate political and ideological feedback, and open up opportunities for further (commercial) production and distribution of radical ideas. Madonna's music and videos were a triumphantly commercial phenomenon, as well as a political statement about women's sexuality at the end of the twentieth century. Following on his record-breaking documentary *Bowling for Columbine*, Michael Moore's *Fahrenheit 9/11* was one of the cinematic hits of 2004 in the United States, as well as being a trenchant assault on the Bush administration and American foreign and economic policy in general. In contemporary cultural capitalism, commercial viability and political radicalism coexist, as Jeremy Rifkin observes in *Age of Access*:

> Counter-cultural trends have become particularly appealing targets for expropriation by marketers . . . By identifying products and services with controversial cultural issues, companies evoke the rebellious anti-establishment spirit in their customers and make the purchases stand for symbolic acts of personal commitment to the causes they invoke.
>
> (Rifkin 2000: 174)

To this extent, the circulation of cultural commodities becomes at one and the same time a source of profit, a mechanism of systemic self-regulation, and a means of promoting progressive social change. At a certain point in feminist history, for example, and well before Madonna made her first record, women began to matter economically to the smooth reproduction of capital. Always important to the reproduction of labour power, and thus worshipped in patriarchal culture as mothers and lovers, during and after the Second World War they emerged as a key group of industrial workers, and then increasingly important consumers, compelling respect and attention from a still-patriarchal system. In satisfying the demands of women as consumers, capitalism thereby hastened the progressive evolution of patriarchy as a system of stratification, to the point that by the twenty-first century, only eight decades after women first achieved the vote in Britain and the United States, overt displays of sexism were politically and culturally taboo in public life and in the mainstream media (the defiantly pre-feminist sexism of lad mags and a character such as Sid the Sexist in *Viz* magazine fall, I have argued elsewhere, into the category of postmodern irony, indicative of feminism's success rather than its failure [McNair 2002]).[1]

The same *commodification of social progress* has been seen in relation to racism and homophobia. Notwithstanding the debate about the persistence of ethnically based inequality in America unleashed by Hurricane Katrina in September 2005, the rise of the black middle class and the ascendancy of black subcultural forms such as hip-hop are oft-noted trends in the west. Whether in the rise of Colin Powell and Condoleezza Rice in the political sphere, or Kanye West and Missy Elliot in the cultural, the direction of change in America (and in comparable countries such as the UK) is clear.

Observing the mainstreaming of homosexuality, Andrew Sullivan, an 'out' gay conservative, states that the gay rights movement in America has been 'perhaps the most tangible social revolution of the last twenty years of conservative ascendancy', and wonders about the meaning of this 'paradoxical confluence'[2] of 'cultural conservatism simultaneous with gay revolution'. There is no paradox, however. There *is* cultural conservatism (as there is still racism in society), and since 2000 it has been established in the White House. But the gay rights movement in America, as in Britain, Australia and many other advanced capitalist societies, has, like feminism, become integrated into mainstream culture by virtue of its economic power, and its associated demand for goods and services. As Sullivan puts it, 'what happened was neither right nor left'. What it *was* was good business. The sexual citizenship enjoyed by women and practising homosexuals in the western world today has been facilitated not least by the media marketplace, which is blind to sexual preference as long as the money is right. In socialist Cuba, by contrast, or the quasi-medieval feudalisms favoured by Islamic fundamentalism, homosexuality, like feminism, is still regarded by the state as a crime, subject to severe punishment up to and including death.

In this sense the erosion of what might once, and quite recently, have been dominant ideas (be they racist, sexist, or class-ist) can be a process entirely consistent with the normal workings of the cultural marketplace, with the only constraint being on ideas that are incompatible with capitalism (and neither feminism, nor anti-racism, nor gay rights have been anything but good for capitalist economies, since they improve the available human resource). Far from being held back by the commercialisation of the media, social and political progress have been its by-product. The market provides a highly efficient mechanism for the circulation of dissenting, progressive ideas in commodity form.[3]

Critical media sociology has resisted this conclusion, preferring to see apparent advances in the representation of women or ethnic minorities (to cite two categories of media image traditionally criticised as inadequate) as either tokenistic or illusory, in that the appearance of progress is really the cover for something else. John Fiske's *Media Matters* labours to make its case that US media coverage of the O.J. Simpson trial, which ended in a controversial acquittal due to revelations of police racism, 'contributed to racial antagonism' (Fiske 1996: 274) and promoted 'essential racism'. That is one reading of the story. An alternative is that by highlighting institutional racism in the LAPD, and making that racism the justification for the acquittal of an accused man generally regarded as guilty (and later convicted in a civil case), coverage put racial antagonism high on the US media and public agenda, where it was extensively debated for months and years afterwards. Coverage of the Stephen Lawrence murder had a similar impact on UK debates about racism, leading to ground-breaking investigative journalism such as the BBC's *The Secret Policeman*, in which an undercover reporter produced evidence of overt racism at a police training college.

There is similar resistance to the idea that images of women in mainstream culture have altered for the better. The recent *Women and Journalism* (Chambers *et al.* 2004) argues that, notwithstanding the obvious increase in the number and status of women working in the news media, journalism is still sexist. These authors concede the emergence of women as an economic force, but then suggest that this has

> sanctioned the rise of a whole new feminine, but covertly anti-feminist, journalistic form in the twenty-first century, in which it is now permissible for women to expose their own and other women's personal insecurities and vulgar habits, sexual conquests and defeats, and abuses of substances and people.
>
> (Chambers *et al.* 2004: 214)

Why such content should be judged 'anti-feminist' was not made explicit by these authors. As I and others have argued, however, the feminisation of the public sphere through such formats as daytime talk shows, reality TV, lifestyle and makover strands, and entertainment formats such as *Footballers' Wives* and *Desperate Housewives*, can be viewed as a progressive evolution rather than a 'vulgar' dumbing down or cultural degeneration (Lumby 1999). From this perspective, the emergence of women into mainstream political, economic and social life has been reflected in, rather than constrained by, popular culture. The market has been the vehicle for the dissemination and articulation of a diverse, popular feminism.

The commodification of the counter-culture

Competitive market pressures impose constraints on the content of mainstream media, clearly, but commercial considerations also determine that there is a market – a *counter-cultural marketplace* – for dissent. Political dissidence sells like never before, as the career of Michael Moore demonstrates most clearly. His best-selling books, and two successful documentary films, confirm the observation that 'the culture industry doesn't mind dissent – as long as it produces a profit'.[4] In Moore's view, as reported in that most upmarket and consumer-oriented of media outlets, *Vanity Fair*, 'the reason I survive doing what I do with these large media conglomerates whose heads aren't necessarily in agreement with me politically is I make them a lot of money'.[5]

Within weeks of its release on more than 700 US screens – the biggest opening for a documentary ever in the United States – Moore's *Fahrenheit 9/11* had become the surprise hit of the summer of 2004, earning $200 million at the box office and an estimated $50 million for Moore personally.[6] This success followed on a highly effective promotional campaign (which included turning up at Cannes and winning the Palme D'Or from a predictably anti-Bush French jury – this was the year of 'freedom fries' and 'cheese-eating surrender monkeys'), during which Moore claimed that he was a victim of censorship because the Disney corporation which produced his film subsequently refused to distribute it. Moore provided a master class in the art of making counter-culture commodities work in the capitalist media marketplace by turning his low-budget, anti-government polemic into a box office smash eclipsed in that pre-election summer only by *Spider-Man 2*.

The mainstream ascendancy of Moore's films and books (only the most commercially successful of a wave of successful counter-cultural commodities which accompanied the era of George W. Bush and the war on terror, including Morgan Spurlock's *Super Size Me* [2004] and Jennifer Abbott's *The Corporation* [2003])[7] illustrates the loosening connection between control of the media, which clearly remains in the hands of big media capital, and control of the message, as well as the *meaning* of the message. Joel Bakan's book, on which the film of *The Corporation* is based, is published by Free Press, a subsidiary of VIACOM corporation. Its commercial success leads Bakan to remark that 'I think the market for our film and the book and the other critical stuff shows that people are actually really interested in engaging with critical ideas'.[8] Robert Greenwald's *Outfoxed* (2004) was a successful documentary critique of News Corporation's Fox News network,[9] joining a plethora of counter-cultural commodities dedicated to debunking so-called Big Media.

People have always been interested in dissent and debate, of course. Radical newspapers flourished in both Britain and America in the late eighteenth and early nineteenth centuries (Conboy 2004). The success of *The Corporation* and other counter-culture products shows that the twenty-first-century media market has more space than any in history for outlets for quite radical, even anti-systemic debate. If the McDonald's corporation is viewed by many critical theorists as an evil empire, and the exemplification of all that is wrong with global capitalism in the twenty-first century, it is one which *Super Size Me* brought to heel with a low-budget movie, shot on video for less than $200,000, which played to packed houses all over the world and made some $150 million in cinema and rental receipts. Spurlock's critique of Big Capital, like those of Moore, Klein, Chomsky and many others, was not censored, or marginalised, or dismissed, but became on the contrary a successful counter-cultural commodity, a lucrative brand of dissidence in a cultural marketplace which cares not what you say, as long as there is someone prepared to pay to hear you say it.

This is also true of the press. Francis Wheen's book-length essay on *How Mumbo-Jumbo Conquered the World* (2004) cites an article written for the *Guardian* by UK-based journalist Seamus Milne, two days after 9/11. In it he blames the American people, including those killed in the World Trade Center buildings that morning, for the atrocity inflicted upon them by Al Qaida. By their 'unabashed national egotism and arrogance', argues Milne, and their failure to address 'the injustices and inequalities' that in his view motivated the bombers, they had gotten more or less what they deserved, 'once again reaping a dragon's teeth harvest they themselves sowed'.[10] A contributor to the usually genteel *London Review of Books* declared in an essay a few days later that 'however tactfully you dress it up, the United States had it coming. World bullies, even if their heart is in the right place, will in the end pay the price'.[11] Such dissent from the general sense of horror at innocent lives cruelly snuffed out appeared in many media outlets throughout the western world, not least in the United States. When they did they were criticised by other commentators, as in the case of Susan Sontag's *New Yorker* article defending the 'courage' of the September 11 terrorists.[12] But they appeared, and in high profile, in mainstream media. There was no censorship and no constraints on what might be said.

In the 1960s Umberto Eco declared that the future of the revolution (in the days when the idea of socialist revolution could still be taken seriously) was not dependent on the Bolshevik model of seizure of the means of intellectual production – on storming the radio and TV stations and replacing them with progressive propaganda apparatuses – but on influencing the reception of the message by audiences (Eco 1986). Eco championed the subversive power of semiotics, and analysed the implications of differential decoding for a materialist theory of ideological control. Half a century later we can develop this idea to argue, with due respect to Marshall McLuhan, that the medium is *not* the message.

The medium, whether it is controlled by Silvio Berlusconi, Rupert Murdoch, or the heirs of Walt Disney, is merely the carrier of messages which, once released into the cultural marketplace and the maze of new information and communication technologies described in Chapters 7 and 8, exhibit viral characteristics. For reasons that are not always obvious or predictable, they replicate and spread, and as long as they make money for cultural capital, they are free to flow around an expanded, interconnected sphere of communication. Some, like the films of Michael Moore, are explicitly 'radical', system-critical messages. Others mutate and come to mean things that their makers may not have intended or foreseen. They interact with the political and ideological environments in ways that no media baron can entirely control. News stories set off political crises; radical movies and books dominate significant portions of the media agenda, sometimes forcing change on governments and corporations. *Super Size Me* embarrassed McDonald's into launching healthier fast-food lines; Jamie Oliver's 2005 Channel 4 series on the deficiencies of British school meals provoked policy responses in the direction of healthier eating for kids.

Fox News reflects the views of its proprietor-in-chief, no doubt, but itself becomes the subject of best-selling books, a film (*Outfoxed*) and a mainstream critical discourse about news bias within which News Corp has to operate, like it or not. To adapt the materialist slogan – those who control the means of production control also the means of intellectual production, but not the content of what those means produce, nor the meanings derived from that content by individuals in societies increasingly informed by a globalised public sphere. The link between economic base and cultural superstructure is weakened. New information and communication technologies (see Chapters 7 and 8) have not ended the concentration of media ownership in the hands of a few big corporations, but they have enabled an environment in which the latter are obliged in their own self-interest to share the public sphere with an increasingly diverse range of editorial viewpoints and voices.

Some resist. And in the post-9/11 era of resurgent neo-conservatism there are examples of advertisements being pulled from controversial publications, and crude attempts to reimpose an earlier model of moral and political censorship even in countries such as the USA. These have a tendency to backfire on the would-be censors, however, as they inevitably become part of the media agenda. When two News Corporation newspapers refused to carry advertisements for *Outfoxed*, the resulting publicity helped promote the film better than any paid advertising could. The Disney corporation did indeed pull out of its agreement to distribute *Fahrenheit 9/11*, as Michael Moore alleged in the months leading up to its release by another distributor. But the publicity which its shrewd director generated from that decision merely increased the film's commercial power. 'Censorship' became part of the film's unique selling proposition.

As we have seen, the response of critical media scholarship to a phenomenon like the mainstream commercial success of a counter-cultural text such as *Fahrenheit 9/11* is to dismiss it as tokenism. Like the Chomskyan response to an elite-critical news item, an elite- or system-critical film commodity such as *Fahrenheit 9/11*, or Moore's chart-topping book, *Stupid White Men*, which by June 2003 had sold 500,000 copies in the UK alone, tends to be neutralised in the terms laid out by Horkheimer and Adorno more than six decades ago in their *Dialectic of Enlightenment*. These writers, expressing the deep pessimism of the Frankfurt School, believed that the capitalist culture industry 'made up such a totalising system that it was literally impossible to rebel against it. This complex not only anticipated the urge to revolt but would sell you something to satisfy'.[13] In cultural capitalism, they insisted, 'departures from the norm' of mass cultural, pro-systemic uniformity are to be regarded as 'calculated mutations which serve all the more strongly to confirm the validity of the system' (Horkheimer and Adorno 1973: 129). Such an analysis assumes that it is only these 'calculated mutations', and the totalitarian mind control they allegedly permit, which can explain social order and apparent mass consent to the capitalist system.

A somewhat different strain of cultural pessimism runs through Naomi Klein's best-selling *No Logo* (2000), a work which, like Michael Moore's books and films, went to the top of the charts (and became a leading counter-cultural brand) by condemning the commodity economy within which it flourished. Acknowledging the growth in the 1990s of 'cultural diversity' and 'identity politics' (ibid.: 113), Klein condemned them as evidence not of social progress but the ascendancy of an all-pervasive promotional culture in which branding is king. Contrary to what the feminists, gay rights activists and ethnic minority activists thought they were doing by fighting for access to cultural resources and political rights all these years, Klein argued that 'identity politics weren't fighting the system, or even subverting it. When it came to the vast new industry of corporate branding, they were feeding it.'

She was right on that latter point, if not in the conclusion that identity politics is thus devalued. It is true, as I have suggested, that social progress in sexual and ethnic politics, as well as in related spheres of identity politics such as disability rights, has been achieved in large part through the communicative, distributive channels of the cultural marketplace, and the growing power of women, gays and other once marginalised and suppressed communities to influence those channels through economic pressure. That, indeed, is precisely my point in this chapter. Access to cultural commodities, and the participation of previously excluded social groups in mainstream culture, has been an index of political success and social progress, if not a sufficient end in itself. Before there could be a Pink Dollar or Pound there had to be a gay liberation movement, endowing homosexual men and women with sufficient confidence to 'come out' and demand the same range of consumer goods and lifestyle accessories as straight people. Before there could be a globally successful hip-hop music scene there had to be a black power movement with a worked-out critique of mainstream, white-dominated culture. When progress has been achieved, however, by one marginalised group or another, that group has often found the cultural marketplace a fertile arena for the articulation of identity and the realisation of previously suppressed lifestyles. The producers of cultural commodities, conversely, have found members of these groups an increasingly lucrative source of business.

From Adorno to Klein, then, the pessimistic perspective has viewed mass access to and participation in culture as incorporation into a commercial system which is by definition antithetical to what they define as 'genuine' human progress; equivalent to the corruption of authentic cultures by mass-marketed forms, and the illusory façade of a global village where, in reality, 'the economic divide is widening and cultural choices narrowing' (ibid.: xvii). In cultural capitalism, from this perspective, rebellion and dissent are commodified and integrated in such a way that the system is not threatened, but shored up. This is a coherent position if one assumes that capitalism (and its associated phenomena, such as consumerism) is decadent and doomed to be replaced by a superior mode of socio-economic and cultural production. If so, shoring up the system can be viewed as a conservative media function. When, on the other hand, it is recognised that capitalism is here to stay, and that the critical task is to reform and humanise rather than replace it, the capacity of the media to channel dissidence and diversity becomes a valuable political tool in the progressive project.

At the end of the century of Stalin and Hitler, it is notable that while they and the totalitarian systems they built have long gone, liberal democracy, consumer capitalism and mass culture have indeed been shored up, with or without the help of counter-cultural commodities. And when one considers the alternatives, would we have had it any other way? In the context of the 1940s when *Dialectic of Enlightenment* was written (an atmosphere of creeping, aggressive totalitarianism which also produced Orwell's *Animal Farm* and *1984*), mass culture pessimism can be understood. To accept it today means acceptance of the view that there is a realistic alternative to capitalism available; that capitalism was and has remained oppressive in its nature; and that dissenting, ideologically subversive cultural commodities can never actually *change* the system for the better, as opposed to merely masking or putting Band-Aids on its wounds. The pragmatic optimism implied by a chaos paradigm, on the other hand, acknowledges the status of capitalism (for the reasons of self-interest in profit maximisation outlined above) as a fundamentally progressive system in economic, political and social terms, and that the contemporary media marketplace now provides an important mechanism for the ongoing internal reform and humanisation of the system. The concrete evidence of global socio-economic progress, democratisation and the exercise of critical media scrutiny leading to progressive change on a number of fronts can easily support a reading of capitalism's capacity for change which acknowledges more than tokenism, and a view of critical cultural commodities as more than distractions.

Why should it be so? Simply because the accumulated weight of historical, political and cultural experience means that contemporary capitalism contains within it many individuals who, far from being brainwashed or seduced into submission to a dominant ideology which is opposed to their own interests (if such a thing as a dominant ideology can be discerned from the diversity and chaos of contemporary media coverage), are fully aware of the flaws of the system, who may even be prepared to demonstrate for change at G8 meetings, but who recognise that it remains the best, if not the only, game in town. They are affluent, many of them, and young, with historically unprecedented reserves of disposable income. In their desire to have their dissent recognised and validated they form a valuable market for the cultural commodities of symbolic dissidence.

The circulation of these commodities may, as in the case of *Fahrenheit 9/11*, have a real influence on the political environment. One observer notes that

> *Fahrenheit 9/11* was woeful journalism. But that didn't deter the public. A report by the activist organisation MoveOn.com estimated that 44 per cent of all US voters would have seen the film by the time of the presidential election – and a third of those would have been self-identified Bush voters.[14]

Michael Moore's film did not prevent the re-election of George W. Bush. It may indeed have contributed to the victory by angering and mobilising the Republican vote. Moore himself believes that his film 'prevented a Bush landslide',[15] while one senior Democratic campaigner in 2004 attributes the high turnout that November to 'the fact that the other side [the Republicans] would not allow their president to be trashed by Michael Moore'.[16]

I have already noted the difficulty of demonstrating media effects, and no one can say for sure if *Fahrenheit 9/11* helped or hindered the fortunes of the Bush campaign in 2004. The key point here is that the critical message contained in the film was freely available to all who wished to access it. The competitive logic of cultural capitalism placed it at the heart of the mainstream media marketplace, regardless of the well-documented wishes of the Bush administration, the Disney corporation, or any other elite faction in the United States. Although Disney did withdraw from a commercial deal to distribute the film, reportedly because of its dependence on the goodwill of the governing elite in the state of Florida (led at this time by the president's brother, Jeb Bush), *Fahrenheit 9/11* was quickly picked up by another distribution company, going on to become the most commercially successful documentary feature film in history.

The commodification of news

Commodified social progress – progress driven by the cultural marketplace of ideas and images, dialectically interacting with socio-economic change – is also occurring in the context of the evolution of global news culture. What we today call journalism was one of the first cultural commodities, developed in the early modern period to facilitate the communication of knowledge about price fluctuations in foreign markets, the intrigues of court politics, the progress of foreign wars and other matters about which the powerful of those times wished to be informed, and for which they were willing to pay. The printing shop performed an important cultural function in early modern Europe by 'bringing together intellectual and commercial activities which reinforced each other' (Eisenstein 1983: 68). The correspondent was the communication professional whose business it was to package information in usable form, first through hand-written letters, then newspapers and on down through successive technological revolutions to the multi-skilled 'information architect' of today.

As a commodity in a capitalist system, journalism had to compete with other journalisms in the expanding media marketplace. Thus evolved the standards of objectivity, accuracy and independence which still define liberal journalism today, and which allow journalistic organisations to brand themselves as producers of 'quality' in a marketplace of superficially similar products. If the reporting of news had a *use-value* (to use Marxian language), the *objective* reporting of news produced *exchange-value* (the price commodities can achieve in the market). Not only was accurate and fair reportage deemed a political requirement of journalists in a democracy (see Chapter 4), but by the late nineteenth century it had become a marketing necessity, without which the purveyors of news were unable to persuade potential customers of their worth. And as a branding tool, objectivity has never been more important to the selling of journalism as it is in the crowded communication environment of the twenty-first century.

So what is objectivity? Of what is it made, and how do these elements contrive in contemporary conditions to generate an expanded media space for the expression of dissent?

Above all, objectivity means independence, and a relationship between journalism and power which permits critical scrutiny of elites. In an earlier era, when there were many fewer media outlets, much less transnational in their reach, imposing elite control on coverage of events was less of a challenge (if never risk-free). Before the Clinton–Lewinsky affair more than supported his case, Michael Schudson observed that in the 1990s 'the American press is unusually aggressive among Western news institutions in pursuing scandal' (1995: 5). Watergate became a scandal and Richard Nixon was ousted from office only after years of dogged investigation by Woodward and Bernstein. Exposure of sexual misdemeanours of the type which afflicted Bill Clinton in the late 1990s were never permitted by the US media establishment to affect John F. Kennedy's saintly reputation. But in a global media market of many news providers, where immediacy and exclusivity are selling points for the journalistic commodity, competitive realities determine that an organisation's reputation for independence is also a key branding tool. Bad news will out, therefore, irrespective of whose elite interests are damaged by it.

In the UK too 'fierce competition among British news organisations fosters aggressive reporting with a political edge' (Seib 2004: 37).[17] In both Britain and America

> competition often pushes the media toward the least common denominator of news reporting, other competitive pressures push news institutions not to miss a hot story – at least, not when it has reached a certain level of notice and notoriety. And a 'hot story' is not necessarily one that pleases the powers-that-be.
>
> (Schudson 1995: 5)

Schudson cites My Lai, Watergate and Iran-Contra. Contemporary news audiences will be more familiar with Abu Ghraib, the Clinton–Lewinsky scandal, and the WMD dossier allegedly 'sexed-up' by the British government in order to prepare people and Parliament for war with Iraq. In the global news market of the twenty-first century critical, revelatory journalism is not a luxury dispensed at the whim of proprietors but a marketing necessity, as is the visible demonstration of reliability, objectivity, authority, independence and diversity. Sabato *et al.* argue of the US media that

> competition from new and alternative news sources [means that] mainstream news outlets no longer serve as almost exclusive gatekeepers of information about those who hold or seek elected office. At the same time, evolving public standards and increasing competitive pressures for a shrinking news audience are changing the ways editors and producers determine when and how to delve into the private lives of political figures.
>
> (Sabato *et al.* 2000: 2)

The importance of a reputation for adversarialism, independence and objectivity can be seen in the recent wave of high-profile scandals affecting US media. The plagiarism and fabrications of the *New York Times*'s Jayson Blair and the *New Republic*'s Stephen Glass present two examples where embarrassing lapses have seriously damaged leading journalistic organisations.[18] In January 2005 NBC's network news management dismissed several journalistic and editorial staff for their role in the transmission of an election news story alleging that President Bush had falsified his military service record. In 2004 the BBC was criticised by the Hutton Inquiry for its sloppy editorial management of the Andrew Gilligan/WMD story.[19] Whatever their place on the political or ideological spectrum, news organisations must be seen to be objective if they are to compete in the information marketplace. All serious players in the news business, regardless of proprietorial bias, have no choice but to be seen to be making at least an effort. When they fail, as in the case of the *NYT* and the *New Republic*, or NBC, the failures themselves become major news stories with potentially damaging commercial implications. Even Fox News in the United States, universally recognised as the most overtly biased of US real-time news outlets (they prefer the term 'patriotic'), chooses to brand its product as 'real news, fair and balanced'.[20]

I referred above to the fact that in June 2004 Fox News repeatedly referred to the torture of Iraqi prisoners in Abu Ghraib as 'allegations of misbehaviour'. While the rest of the world's media were talking about torture and abuses of human rights hardly less barbaric than those committed in the same prison by Saddam Hussein's regime itself, this phrase was a deliberate gesture of defiance, employed in the full knowledge of the responses it would generate amongst supporters and critics alike. Such deliberately tendentious terminology could not have been used by Fox News's sister channel in the UK, Sky News, which exists and must compete effectively in an environment defined by the impartiality ethic of public service broadcasting. This constrains it from adopting the gung-ho patriotism of Fox News in the US, where public service journalism is marginalised and the practice of overtly opinionated attack journalism was long-established on radio before it migrated to television.[21]

Outside the US, in a world where Al Jazeera communicates its take on events to hundreds of millions of Arab viewers, western-based outlets aiming to compete in the global marketplace cannot be satisfied with propaganda of the type once disseminated by Radio Free Europe into the former Soviet Union, even if that is what proprietors might wish them to produce. For a profit-hungry, commercially focused, globally targeted news media, speed and exclusivity are hugely important, and a scoop is a scoop, even if it involves American newspapers and satellite channels telling the world about US troop abuses of Iraqi prisoners, or British massacres of civilians in Basra.

Commercial factors are also key to the success of Al Jazeera in the transnational satellite news market. An Arab audience researcher argues that 'the primary factor in the transformation of the [Arab] media is that today we have a market-driven media'.[22] The desires of some, both in the west and in the Middle East, to suppress the channel's fiercely independent stance[23] are countered by the desire of its growing ranks of commercial backers to reach an audience of Arab viewers – an 'Arab street' which has grown used to independent journalism. In April 2005 it was again being reported that the government of Qatar was investigating the possibilities of privatising Al Jazeera. According to the *Guardian* newspaper, consultants Ernst & Young had been employed 'to look into possible privatisation models'.[24] The piece reported what had long been true – that hostility to Al Jazeera's editorial approach from the US administration on the one hand, and local Arab regimes on the other, was driving efforts to neutralise the channel by turning it into a commercially motivated operation, dependent on advertising from the Saudis and other conservative governments. As this book went to press, the long-term financial structure of Al Jazeera was unresolved, although it seemed reasonable to speculate that the same popular pressures which make banning and violence ineffective as control tactics would hamper efforts to privatise the radicalism out of it. If Al Jazeera's independent editorial stance, radically pro-Islamic as it is, is genuinely popular, the cultural marketplace will ensure its delivery in one form or another. From this perspective the privatisation of Al Jazeera, were it to happen, could strengthen rather than weaken its independence.

Ownership and control

In the twenty-first century, media organisations and their outputs are no longer instruments to be used as megaphones by private interests.[25] Precisely because, and to the extent that journalism is a commodity, it succeeds or fails in the market-place by delivering what consumers, rather than proprietors, expect and want. In respect of major news media, the demand among large sections of the market is for accuracy, independence and objectivity. Where the BBC news brand is built around the concept of impartiality, private news media combine objectivity (if they wish to be taken seriously as organs of record) with advocacy and partisanship. This too, is what consumers want, though not usually at the expense of believ-ability. The fact that in a pluralistic media market there are advocates of many different positions on the issues of the day, and that most if not all of these will also claim to embody the virtues of objectivity, illustrates the fact that truth – or at least the true interpretation to be derived from the known facts – is, indeed, relative. Far from being a postmodern affectation, to note this relativism is simply to acknow-ledge the possibility that different observational positions imply different interpretations of phenomena, and that more than one of these interpretations may be 'true' at the same time.

None of which is to dispute that private control of media organisations has been a feature of capitalist societies since the invention of print, and will continue to be so; merely that it does not necessarily lead directly to control of content, far less to control of how that content is interpreted (and thus will affect) those who receive it. Such control is an easier connection to make in the case of some media outlets than others, and in the context of some countries, for example modern day Italy, where the ruling elite, led by prime minister Silvio Berlusconi, as of this writing owned the greater part of the country's print and broadcast media, and showed little hesitation in using it for political ends.[26] In Russia too, the transition from authoritarianism to democracy has been accompanied by crude, if broadly successful attempts by both the Yeltsin and Putin governments to secure editorial control of both state-owned and private media outlets (Zassoursky 2003).

Neither Russia nor Italy can be regarded as typical of advanced capitalist societies, however: the first because it is still in the process of democratic transition after 70 years of Communist Party control of the media; the second because it has since the Second World War supported a uniquely partisan media, within which even the Italian Communist Party, even at the height of the Cold War, controlled major newspapers and broadcast channels. More common, at least in Europe, is the situation prevailing in Britain, where a plurality of private media outlets coexist with a public service system, and the stance of political journalism is perceived by many commentators to be one of 'corrosive cynicism' fuelled by competitive pressures.

In America, where there is no tradition of public service media (excluding the charitable status PBS), private media dominate, although their proprietors do not necessarily see themselves as propaganda outlets for a national security state. For every Fox News Channel, with its overtly pro-Bush, pro-Republican, patriotic stance after 9/11, there is an NBC, or a *New York Times* presenting an anti-Bush editorial line. Notwithstanding the overt patriotism displayed by many US media in the immediate aftermath of 9/11 (Zelizer and Allan 2002), and the generally pro-systemic framework within which the great majority of media report the news, there has been no shortage of critical elite scrutiny in American journalists' coverage of politics in recent years. Nor has there been a shortage of criticism of media bias. Early 2005 saw a series of scandals in the US regarding what might be called 'cash-for-columns'. At least three columnists were accused of accepting payment from government agencies at the same time as they were writing favourably (without declaring an interest) about government initiatives. The furore surrounding these allegations, and the Bush administration's hasty denial of any wrongdoing, confirmed that even in the post-9/11 USA, there are clear limits to the partisanship of the press.[27]

Conclusion

There is a meaningful (rather than tokenistic) plurality of voices within contemporary cultural capitalism. If the majority of these fall short of advocating the end of capitalism as we know it, or revolutionary socialism NOW, it is beyond dispute that the system can accommodate and give mainstream visibility to a more diverse, broader range of opinion, ranging from the anti-globalisation chic of a Naomi Klein to the more politicised output of such as John Pilger and Tariq Ali in the UK, and Noam Chomsky himself in the US. This has happened because of, and not despite, the commodification of culture. It is the unplanned and unforeseen consequence of counter-cultural capitalism.

Part III

The infrastructure of chaos

7 Mapping the global public sphere, I: transnational satellite news

On its own, the transformed political economy of journalism discussed in Chapters 4–6 would justify some revision of materialist assumptions about how the media relate to power in capitalism. Their impact is amplified, however, by the recent introduction of new information and communication technologies (NICTs)[1] based on satellite, cable, computers, and the combination of all three in the form of the internet. From the launch of Cable News Network (CNN) in 1980 to the more recent emergence of the blogosphere, these new means of communication have amplified the anarchic, disruptive tendencies of journalism, at the same time as problematising the status of traditional print and broadcast news media.

On the one hand, NICTs have dramatically expanded the quantity of information of all kinds, and journalism in particular, which is in circulation at any given time. While the proliferation of news outlets within nation-states has been going on for many years (with respect to the UK, the provision of free-to-air terrestrial TV news increased from about one hour to five hours per day between 1982 and 1997 [McNair, 2003c]), this expansion has now become exponential, as well as transnational in scope. The development of NICTs has permitted the construction of an expanded infrastructure of communication comprising, in addition to the 'old' media of print and terrestrial broadcasting on TV and radio, the internet and a proliferation of dedicated news channels on satellite TV, operating transnationally or globally. Some of the transnational TV news providers – CNN and the BBC are the best known, but Bloomberg, CNBC and now Al Jazeera are also in the market, as is News Corp with Star TV – customise their services to better fit the local conditions of the geographical region covered by their 'footprint' (BBC America, for example, Star in China, CNN Asia, or CNBC Pakistan) but market themselves, and are recognised as global news brands, with global influence. At the time of writing there were six 24-hour or 'real-time' TV news providers with transnational reach, joining a smaller number of radio news channels, many of which, like the BBC World Service and Radio Free Europe/Radio Liberty, have been in existence for many decades.

The internet, meanwhile, has expanded from its marginal beginnings as a military and academic tool[2] to become the first truly global news medium (global in that, given the absence of governmental blocking devices and the availability of a networked computer terminal, any website is accessible anywhere on the planet).

On the internet, global really does mean global, since local and national news-papers, or TV and radio stations which use video-streaming technology, their reach once bounded by geography, now have the possibility of access through online editions to audiences located anywhere in the world.

Newspapers have long been exported overseas, of course, to expatriate com-munities, holiday makers, business travellers and others with a use for news from home. The *Financial Times*, *Wall Street Journal* and *International Herald Tribune* have been marketed as global newspapers to the business community for decades.[3] From my own home town of Glasgow in Scotland, the *Daily Record* has been despatched, like 'tattie scones' and Old Firm football scores, to the sizeable Scottish diasporas in Canada, Australia, New Zealand and the USA. Irish newspapers are sold in Boston, the UK *Sun* in Spanish beach resorts to British tourists, and so on.

These titles, like most other newspapers that wish to survive and prosper in the twenty-first century, now produce online versions to complement print editions. The *FT.com*, for example, has 78,000 subscribers to its pay site, and records nearly four million 'unique users' of its free pages each month.[4] Before the internet, the logistics of air and sea travel necessarily imposed time lags in the distribution of newspapers beyond the borders of the home market, and access required a conscious decision by the overseas reader to go to a newsagent and purchase, usually at a cost greater than that of the newspaper or periodical in the domestic market. For the time being at least, online access to most, if not all of these organisations' online sites is free (organisations make their money by advertising, or through the valuable marketing data which subscribers may be required to provide), and requires very little investment of time as long as one has access to a computer wired up to the internet. Crucially, for our purposes, the online reader of a title such as the Edinburgh-based *Scotland On Sunday* has access to the news at precisely the same moment as his or her co-user back in the old country, as indeed does every other web user on the planet who wishes to take advantage of that fact, regardless of where he or she lives. From the perspective of news consumption, the reader of an online newspaper in Sydney is in precisely the same position as one in Toronto or Dublin – part of a global community of readers, existing physi-cally in different time zones but, in this aspect of their lives at least, unconstrained by the separations of time and space.

The combined impact of these developments in communication technology is to have brought into being, within a decade, a cultural environment in which literally billions of people, in dozens of countries, have immediate, 'always on' access to hundreds of thousands of news media. This access is not universal and, in keeping with the historic divide between the information-rich and information-poor which has existed within countries, and between them, is unevenly distributed in a pattern that reflects broader social inequalities of wealth, education and status. But just as telephones, TVs and VCRs became globally available technologies much more quickly than some observers had predicted in the late twentieth century, the spread of transnational news media by satellite, cable or online means is rapid and irreversible, not least in developing countries such as India and China.

In 1999 commentator Jon Pavlik observed that 'one thing is certain: tomorrow's audiences will have access to much more news and information than any previous generation' (Pavlik 1999: 59). Tomorrow has arrived, with significant implications for the relationship between media, their audiences, and the management of elite power. Not only is that relationship now shaped by very different political, economic and ideological contexts from those that prevailed during the Cold War (see Chapters 4 and 5 above). It is also shaped by a highly volatile cultural marketplace (see Chapter 6) and is conducted within a dramatically altered information and communication environment – a multichannel, multimedia environment of unprecedented complexity and connectedness, as different from the Cold War era of the late twentieth century as that period in turn was from the coffee house culture of early modern Europe.

Global communication and the cultural imperialism thesis

From the pessimistic perspective of the control paradigm, this is not necessarily good news. Traditionally, materialist media sociology has analysed the impact of the globalisation of communication technology within a framework of perceived western (essentially Anglo-American) dominance. Yves de la Haye's anthology of Marx and Engels' writings on communication states that 'at the present time, communication technology and the social effects which it engenders are among the principal supportive and regenerative elements of bourgeois ideology' (De la Haye 1983: 10). In the work of Ed Herman and Robert McChesney (1997), US and British media organisations have been viewed as 'missionaries of capitalism', controlling transnational flows of news and other forms of communication to the rest of the world. In an extension of Lenin's 1916 thesis on *Imperialism: The highest stage of capitalism* (1978), which analysed capital flows and the centralisation (or globalisation) of economic assets even then proceeding apace, the flow of information has been characterised as top-down, north–south, east–west, rich–poor, with little genuinely free exchange of cultural goods or communicative interaction. In the second half of the twentieth century, and especially during the Cold War, the intention and effect of this communicative domination came to be viewed as a *cultural* imperialism, functional for but distinct from the economic imperialism dissected by Lenin.

Cultural imperialism was characterised not just by Lenin's heirs in the Soviet Union and other communist states but by many of the developing countries as a threat to their value systems and social orders. Authentic national cultures, it was argued within the cultural imperialism thesis, were threatened by alien values and beliefs imposed from outside, embodied in global brands such as Coca-Cola, McDonald's and Disney. With the support of the United Nations' cultural agency, UNESCO, and in contradistinction to the concept of the New World Information and Communication Order (NWICO) as set out in the McBride Report of 1980,[5] Anglo-American cultural exports were increasingly viewed as invasive, predatory and destructive of local cultures. In accordance with the presumption of the control paradigm that, in so far as they exhibit compliance with the status quo, audiences are best viewed as passive victims of media messages imposed from above, the evident global popularity of Disney and the rest, from Saudi Arabia to the Philippines, was interpreted not just by local ruling elites but by critical media scholars as symptomatic of false consciousness and Anglo-American brainwashing – the product of a cynical seduction of vulnerable populations by transnational media corporations bent on global domination.

Anglo-American news media in particular were attacked for their imperial ideological role, and for interpreting the problems and conflicts of the world from the self-interested perspective of the USA and its allies (Tunstall and Machin 1999). In a typical articulation of the cultural imperialism thesis, one writer asserted in the late 1990s that 'the cultural product of the international television news agencies serves to perpetuate a western hegemony hostile to developing nations' (Paterson 1998: 95). Others have condemned what they perceive to be the global 'implantation of the commercial model of communication' (Herman and McChesney, 1997). In these authors' view, capitalism and its export to the developing world, including the export of cultural commodities, is presumed from the outset to be, with some qualifications, a very bad thing.[6]

This view – the expression of the control paradigm at the global level – along with the concept of the NWICO which emerged from it, has increasingly been recognised as flawed (Downing 1996). Resistance to cultural imports from the US or the UK, or indeed from Australia or Latin America, is now more readily acknowledged to have been rarely, if ever, an expression of popular opinion so much as, at best, a reflection of local elite anxieties about the loss of control over cultural life, and at worst an excuse for the cover-up of corruption and human rights abuses.[7] All over the world people have embraced the products of western culture with enthusiasm. In the Soviet Union, where this author lived for nearly a year at the beginning of Gorbachev's *glasnost* campaign, the great majority of ordinary people welcomed with enthusiasm the access to western products which the process of *perestroika* opened up. Indeed, the first copies of Beatles records in the state book shops, the first McDonald's in Pushkin Square, the first Irish theme pubs and the first tabloid newspapers on sale at metro stations, were received as evidence of progress in late Soviet Russia. Cultural imports were not forced on people by an external imperialist force, but only with great reluctance permitted entry by the Soviet authorities in response to popular pressure, and as an incentive for people to embrace the reform process.[8]

Armand Mattelart, one of the twentieth-century's leading proponents of the cultural imperialism thesis, acknowledges in a recent book that the campaign for a NWICO by the state socialist and developing countries in fact 'provided many [of those countries] with an easy way to clear themselves of any responsibility for the lack of transparency and freedom of the press in the third world' (2003: 12). Most of these countries were ruled by authoritarian regimes, which permitted no mechanisms for the free and open expression of public opinion. After the collapse of Soviet power and the beginning of democratic transitions across Europe, those political parties which *did* express concern about foreign cultural imports, as in post-

Soviet Russia, tended to be on the far right of the political spectrum, associated in that case with anti-Semitism as well as an open admiration for the achievements of Hitler and Stalin. In Russia, protests against Anglo-American cultural imperial- ism were often accompanied by the assertion of extreme Russian nationalism, linking communists and fascists in what became known as the 'red–brown' alliance (McNair 1994). In the post-Soviet case, as in many others (the authoritarian Islamic states of the Middle East, for example), accusations of 'cultural imperialism' were often orchestrated by the representatives of deeply reactionary political tendencies, and with the benefit of hindsight can be recognised as a convenient cloak for local regimes to justify tight control over their news and other media. It was, of course, precisely the inadequacies of these local media, not least in the sphere of news, which pushed audiences eager to know what was going on in the world towards CNN and the BBC, and which would eventually lead to the rise of independent non-Anglo, non-American media such as Al Jazeera (see below).

At the height of the cultural imperialism thesis's popularity in the 1970s and 1980s, as was noted above, much transnational journalism *was* harnessed to the propaganda needs, not just of the Anglo-American 'empire', but of all those states involved in the seven decades-long struggle between capitalism and communism which dominated the twentieth century. America in the west, the Soviet Union in the east, and their allies and proxies around the world such as Britain, France, China and Cuba operated their own transnational media in the same way, and for the same reasons, that they deployed military power around the world – to assert their place in the global balance of power. Until the breach of the Berlin Wall in November 1989 the American government, through its US Information Agency (USIA), funded the broadcasts of the overtly propagandist Radio Liberty and Radio Free Europe to countries behind the Iron Curtain. The USSR for its part had Radio Moscow and the TASS news agency, performing a similar service for the developing world, and even to the advanced capitalist countries of the west, where communists and other 'fellow travellers' would seek out Soviet-produced news as an alternative to what was assumed to be western propaganda.

In this sharply polarised era only the BBC World Service, founded in 1926 as the British state's cultural diplomatic arm, aspired to serve the international com- munity with journalism which embodied the values of impartiality and objectivity associated with the BBC in its home market. And notwithstanding the sociological critique of the concept of impartiality developed by materialist media scholars, in general it was successful in meeting this aspiration. In 1991, following the attempted coup by communist hardliners in Moscow, Soviet president Mikhail Gorbachev famously claimed that, while under house arrest on the Black Sea, he listened to the BBC World Service coverage of the crisis because it was the only source of news he could trust. Throughout the world, during and after the Cold War, the BBC enjoyed a reputation for reliability and credibility never equalled by US-funded outlets, and to this day remains a model for how transnational broadcasters should seek to communicate with overseas audiences.

During this period, then, roughly coterminous with the Cold War, transnational or global news culture comprised a small number of radio channels, of which the great majority were elements of or affiliated and aligned to competing state-controlled propaganda apparatuses dedicated to ideological and psychological warfare. In addition to transnational radio broadcasters, there were a handful of privately owned global newspapers and periodicals; titles which, from their bases in New York, London or Paris, focused their coverage on international issues and were distributed to a variety of countries. Like the periodicals which serviced the nascent public spheres of early modern Europe, these global newspapers were elite media, accessed by relatively small numbers of relatively privileged readers. In the communist countries they were available as perks to ruling party loyalists, and eagerly read as a more reliable source of news about world events than the party-approved outlets such as the Soviet *Pravda* or Cuban *Granma*.

In developing or 'Third World' countries they were too expensive for the great majority of ordinary people engaged in the struggle for subsistence, and were restricted to the wealthier sectors of society, in business and politics. They had influence, which was managed in a carefully controlled fashion. Where, on rare occasions, a particular story or subject matter threatened to destabilise local elites, or challenged local cultural tastes and moral codes in a manner deemed threatening by those elites, they were censored or banned. The Saudi authorities, for example, have famously blacked out the more explicit images contained in copies of *Playboy* magazine imported into the country. The BBC's Arabic-language service, from which Al Jazeera emerged in the late 1990s, was banned by the Saudis for broadcasting news deemed unhelpful by the regime.

The beginning of the end of this highly ideologised, restricted access system was signalled with the launch in 1980 of Cable Network News, owned by the Atlanta-based entrepreneur Ted Turner. Much has been written about the formation of CNN, its early struggle for acceptance and profitability in the domestic US media market, and its subsequent expansion into overseas broadcasting markets, first as a service principally used by business travellers in their hotel rooms, then by a more general audience across the world, with services increasingly tailored to specific markets (CNN Asia, CNN Europe, etc.).[9]

CNN's emergence and, by the late 1980s, domination of the transnational satellite news business was punctuated by a series of events which, not least through their coverage by CNN, became global in their reach and significance. The Challenger disaster of 1986, at which CNN cameras were present, was watched live by viewers of CNN both within and outside of the US (organisations such as the BBC and ITN took live feeds from CNN, including prominent display of the company logo), giving the deaths of seven astronauts an immediacy and poignancy which undoubtedly enhanced the global impact of the event. With this and other spectacular stories CNN's capacity for 24-hour coverage revealed its unique use value, and established the channel as a new kind of news medium, an 'always on' service uniquely placed to respond to the unpredictable and unforeseen, capturing the confusion of contemporaneously unfolding events and transforming them into journalistic narratives. By being there when events like the Challenger disaster occurred, and making attractive footage available to the network news and print media (which began to publish CNN stills on their front pages), CNN made them more newsworthy than they might otherwise have been. Moreover, by making live pictures of life and death happenings possible, CNN changed the very definition of news, as Roger Ailes famously put it, from something that *has happened* at some time in the past, to something that *is happening*, right now. News on 'real-time' satellite and cable became a *flow* medium, rather than a medium of record; a turbulent river of journalistic data into which one dipped one's toes from time to time, and especially at times of great drama, from the Challenger disaster through the first Gulf War in 1991 up to the greatest drama of them all in the history of real-time news thus far, the attacks on the World Trade Center of September 11 2001. Real-time news was non-linear in form and content, as opposed to the narrative regularity of traditional news bulletins.

The notion of news as a flow medium expresses not only the 'always on', ever-present quality of the real-time satellite provider, but its extended reach. With a combination of communication satellites, cables and computers CNN was able to flow – one might also say leak – across nation-state boundaries into a relatively unpoliced transnational communication space. Part IV considers the broader implications of this dissolution for authoritarian and democratic societies respectively, but here we note that it made possible, for the first time, a multinational news audience, geographically separated but able to access news coverage of events communally. To put it another way, real-time satellite news brought into being a global public, accessing a common news source.

CNN took some time to achieve profitability after its 1980 launch, and executives in other media organisations took some time to recognise the implications for their businesses of its eventual success. When they did, however, CNN began to be joined by competitors for the transnational news audience. First out of the blocks was the BBC, which in 1988 announced its intention to launch a global television news service, utilising the reputation of its domestic news and current affairs and the accumulated experience and resource base of its External Services and World Service divisions. Where CNN was deemed in these years by the then-head of the World Service to be 'terribly American oriented',[10] as well as 'localised' and 'small towney', the BBC's World Service Television (WSTV) would seek to exploit the global reputation of the corporation's long-established radio output, making that reputation the basis of its claim to be a competitor to the US-based pioneer. As the World Service head put it in a 1991 speech, just as WSTV was going on air:

> Who could be content to leave the domination of this immensely powerful sector of the global information market – international network news – to one company and one nation, the United States? Now there are two players in this market, BBC World Service and CNN.
>
> (John Tusa, quoted in McNair [2003c]: 137)

In due course WSTV became BBC World. BBC World was joined in 1997 by a domestic 24-hour service, BBC News 24, to compete with Sky News, News Corporation's UK-targeted real-time news channel which had been established on the Luxembourg-based Astra satellite in 1989. News Corporation, in turn, followed the BBC into the global news market by establishing Star TV on satellites with footprints in Asia and the Middle East. An Australian/New Zealand version of Sky News was launched in 2004. In 1999 News Corporation launched Fox News as a competitor to CNN in the domestic US market,[11] and BBC America was established in 2002. Other real-time TV channels emerging in the 1990s and early 2000s included CNBC, run by the NBC network news provider, and Bloomberg News, which specialised in financial news (and whose multi-billionaire owner, Michael Bloomberg, became the richest person ever to hold elected office in the United States when he became mayor of New York in 2002). In 2004 Bloomberg News employed over 1,500 people in and outside of the USA, providing specialist financial news to paying customers, and servicing ten TV news networks globally. In Europe there were several attempts to launch transnational satellite TV, though with mixed success (Chalaby 2005).

Since 1980, and especially as countries like Great Britain have been opened up to satellite and cable TV, coverage of successive events – the TWA hijacking of 1985; the Challenger disaster; the US bombing of Libya in 1986; the first Gulf War of 1991; NATO's 1999 intervention in Kosovo; the 2003 invasion of Iraq – has propelled CNN and its growing number of competitors ever more visibly into the consciousness, and the domestic viewing environments, of more and more people, a process facilitated by the spread of digital TV. With expansion and competition has come greater niche marketing, with CNN International (CNNI) branching off into a multitude of regional services such as CNN Asia. By 2005 BBC World was reaching 258 million people in 200 countries, alongside the 43 languages utilised by the World Service radio as it broadcasts to some 146 million people. CNBC India was established in 2004, joining CNBC Arabiya. CNBC Pakistan was launched in May 2005.

Average audiences for these services are small, and likely to remain so by comparison with audiences for free-to-air terrestrial TV news, but increase dramatically when events of global significance occur. In the weeks after the invasion of Iraq in March 2003, Sky News UK audience share rose by 820 per cent, or from 0.9 to 8.29 per cent in multi-channel homes. Over the same period the BBC News 24 audience rose by 500 per cent, from 0.65 to 3.2 per cent, while ITV News increased its audience share by 400 per cent on a much lower base (from 0.2 to 0.9 per cent). In the days following the Asian tsunami disaster of Boxing Day 2004, audiences for all the UK's real-time news channels (RTNs) increased substantially. In the pattern seen since the launch of CNN in 1980, dramatic international events have driven the rise of RTN channels, whether domestic or transnational. Audience peaks around specific events – 33 million UK TV viewers watched BBC News 24 on September 11 2001 – have punctuated steadily rising average viewing figures. Though still low, and unlikely to increase greatly, since few TV viewers have the time or inclination to do more than sample the unceasing flow of information which RTN channels provide, these figures reveal populations for whom the availability of real-time news is gradually becoming a taken-for-granted fact of cultural life. RTNs are especially valued at times of international crisis, and an important background element in what Hargreaves and Thomas

(2002) call 'the ambience' of contemporary televisual news culture. Their potential influence rises steadily, even if the vast majority of TV viewers still did not, as of this writing, watch 24-hour channels routinely. Transnational television news, that is to say, is a more important source of information for populations across the world than average viewing figures might suggest on their own.

Not only has digitalisation made more channels available to more viewers, it also allows viewers in the UK to subscribe to channels made for the domestic US market, and vice versa. I, as a digital subscriber, can watch Fox News and MSNBC from home in Glasgow, although these services are produced for an exclusively US audience. In this sense the real-time TV news market can be divided into two distinct categories: the truly transnational providers, such as CNNI and BBC World, which provide tailored news services for audiences around the world (although no single service is fully 'global', the brand clearly is); and domestic 24-hour news channels such as Fox News, MSNBC (USA) and Sky News (UK), which digitalisation is now making available to audiences to whom they are not specifically addressed. Viewers in the United States can watch a variety of Arab-language news channels produced in the Middle East for Arab-speaking audiences.

Precisely which channels viewers in a given country can tune into will of course depend on their access to the necessary delivery technologies, as well as linguistic capability. The transnational news market has been, and remains principally an English-speaking domain, reflecting the dominance of English as the global lingua franca, and the common currency of cultural globalisation. English has emerged, for good or ill, as the language that most people speak, or are prepared to learn, if they wish to communicate across borders. While it is true that more people speak Mandarin or Spanish as a first language than do English, these have not achieved the universal status enjoyed by the latter, and it seems unlikely that they will in the foreseeable future.

But if the prevalence of English in transnational TV news is a fact of cultural life in the early twenty-first century (the situation is different on the internet, as the next chapter notes), it is one that has long been recognised as rendering news broadcasters vulnerable to the charge of cultural chauvinism. Organisations such as the BBC, therefore, in the effort to build their reputation as truly global, rather than parochially British news providers, have for many years operated services in other languages, including Arabic, on both radio and television.

The end of Anglo-American domination – Al Jazeera

Before its closure due to Saudi government pressure in 1996, the BBC's UK-based Arab-language news service had generated a pool of broadcast talent schooled in the liberal journalistic tradition for which the corporation is renowned. On the invitation and with the resources of the relatively progressive emir of Qatar, Sheikh Hamad Bin Khalifa Al Thani, these personnel transferred to that country where they established Al Jazeera, the first locally produced Arab-language real-time news channel with transnational reach and global influence. Al Jazeera was 'the child of a benign leader who sees that it is the way to open up democracy'.[12] It was also a product of the rise of CNN, and the perceived impact of that channel's coverage of the first Gulf War in 1991. CNN's ground-breaking but US and western-oriented stance in that conflict suggested the need for an Arab-language competitor, capable of providing the same kind of 24-hour rolling coverage. With the availability of the BBC's Arabic staff after 1996, the conditions were right for Al Jazeera's launch.

Established as part of the oil-rich emir's broader campaign of democratisation and liberalisation in Qatar, Al Jazeera was relatively well resourced from the start, with an operating budget of $175 million in 2004.[13] The name means 'island' or 'peninsula', and was selected not least as a gesture of defiance to the Wahabbi sect in Saudi Arabia, who had traditionally monopolised the use of the term. By comparison with their austere authoritarianism, the emir of Qatar was a liberal, allied to the US but still of necessity attentive to the threat from Islamic fundamentalism. For this reason, Al Jazeera was permitted from the outset to adopt a pro-Islamic, pro-Arab, anti-Israeli and even anti-western editorial standpoint, to act as a partisan cheerleader for Arab identity and interests in an environment hitherto dominated by western journalistic voices. But the channel was more than just an outlet for anti-western propaganda. While criticism of the Qatari regime itself was prohibited (or at least absent) from Al Jazeera's programmes, criticism of other Arab regimes was permitted, and a culture of debate, dissent and what Mohamed Zayani (2005) calls 'accountability' was permitted to flourish for the first time in Arab-language TV.

Arab journalists who had worked for the BBC had internalised and now wanted to pursue on their own terms the corporation's journalistic approach of aspiring to independence, objectivity, accuracy and reliability. From the start, however, and especially after the 9/11 events, Al Jazeera's independence fuelled an anti-American editorial position, leading to major problems later on, such as the 'accidental' US airforce bombing of its Baghdad bureau during the March 2003 invasion. Al Jazeera's anti-Americanism, and its more or less overt sympathy with Islamic fundamentalism (it routinely referred to Al Qaida and Palestinian suicide bombers as 'martyrs') was genuine, as well as popular with many in its audience. The emir, however, was hostile to Al Qaida, and considered himself a moderate in Middle Eastern terms. He, unlike the Saudis, allowed his country to be used as a base for US air strikes on Iraq during the 2003 invasion. From this perspective, his sponsoring of Al Jazeera enabled the emir to have what one observer called

> pro-American positions and even to have a policy that [was] more cooperative with Israel than otherwise might have been possible. It gives them the cover, the credentials, the democratic appeal, the reach, the influence that mitigates the anger on their hosting of US troops.[14]

S. Abdallah Schleiffer defines the paradox of Al Jazeera's emergence at the instigation of a pro-American regime:

It was Al Jazeera's talk shows and sometimes its reporting which more than any particular pan-Arab politician stirred anti-Americanism in the region, while Qatar built a military base to host the very US/Coalition Central Command that directed the invasion of Iraq.[15]

Al Jazeera's editorial stance permitted the emir's regime to straddle the thin line between being viewed as an American puppet on the one hand, and a supporter of authentic Arab identity on the other. By February 2003 *Vanity Fair* was describing the channel as 'the most subversive media experiment in the world'. At that time its estimated viewing audience was 35 million people. Following the invasion of Iraq in March and April of that year, those figures were estimated to be up to around 50 million. Just as the 1991 Gulf War had made CNN essential viewing for politicians and publics around the world, the 2003 invasion of Iraq, and the subsequent occupation of the country by a US-led Coalition, pushed Al Jazeera to the forefront of the global media, allowing the channel to support 50 correspondents in 30 countries. It was the preferred source of news in the Persian Gulf, including Saudi Arabia, Jordan and Kuwait, with substantial audiences also in Lebanon and Syria. For one local observer it had 'put an end to the western monopoly on both the global production of news and the global dissemination of information' (Zayani 2005: 29).

In June 2005 Al Jazeera announced a 'bouquet' of new services, including an English-language news channel (still pending as this book went to press). This expansion was accompanied by a moderation in its anti-Americanism, and an attempt to develop more sophisticated editorial standards. As already noted, many of the founders of Al Jazeera came from the BBC, and expressed allegiance to its journalistic ethos. Since its launch the channel's managers have stressed their objectivity and reliability, one senior editor claiming with pride that 'Al Jazeera is more loyal to television's cardinal craft of field reporting than the BBC, CNN or the US networks'.[16] Most observers, however, including many Arabs well disposed to the channel, found Al Jazeera to be crude and confrontational in its coverage, dominated by 'talk show shouting matches between fundamentalists and secularist militants'.[17] Criticising the channel's approach to Al Qaida, one observer complained that 'we hardly learned anything on Al Jazeera about the terrorist operations that al Qaida undertook in the Arab world before turning its attention to the West'.[18] Noting the channel's readiness to give credibility to conspiracy theories such as the anti-Semitic 'blood libel', this commentator continued:

> The viewer who turned on Al Jazeera might immediately have formed the opinion that the bombing of the World Trade Towers had never happened, or that the United States had carried out the crime because it could not find anything else in the world to destroy.

Even after Bin Laden had confessed to Al Qaida's role in the 9/11 plot, Arab observers conceded, Al Jazeera had sought to absolve Arabs of blame, and instead to scapegoat 'Zionism' and US 'imperialism'.

More damagingly for those who worked on the channel, in showing uncut video footage of dead and mutilated US casualties in Iraq, Al Jazeera came to be seen by the Bush administration as an appendage of the insurgency there, a participant in rather than a mere reporter of the invasion and the subsequent war against the mixture of Baathist remnants and foreign Al Qaida operatives who made up the main resistance to the US and its allies. As a result (and official US denials that such incidents were intentional were widely dismissed), Al Jazeera offices were bombed, as had occurred in Afghanistan during the liberation of that country from the Taliban, its journalists killed, and its ability to function on the ground severely restricted.

Whether through choice (to improve the quality of the brand in the global news market) or necessity (to stay on the air), Al Jazeera's managers have subsequently modified their approach to coverage of the Middle East. Since 2004, as part of a process of international consolidation and expansion, and with the assistance of such facilities as a centre for training and development of its staff, Al Jazeera has sought to strengthen its ability to report diverse views in a manner consistent with liberal pluralistic norms, and has softened its support for Islamic fundamentalism by giving greater access to moderate Islamic as well as western views and voices. As Schleiffer put it in late 2004, a 'sense of self-criticism and a readiness to more consciously embrace professionalism now pervades the highest levels of Al Jazeera's editorial management',[19] as it seeks to position the channel as the leading 'Arab media service with a global orientation'.

Arab sats: beyond Al Jazeera

If Al Jazeera was the first to do so successfully, it is no longer the only Arab-language transnational news channel with aspirations to compete alongside the leading global brands such as CNN and the BBC. For decades before Al Jazeera broke the mould, Arab TV news had either been dependent on local authoritarian regimes, heavily censored and propagandistic, or produced overseas, such as MBC (Middle East Broadcasting Centre) headquartered in London, and the BBC's Arabic-language service. CNN was reaching the Arab world by the late 1980s, and during the first Gulf War of 1991 was received in Egypt and Saudi Arabia (the latter with censorship). In response to CNN's growing influence, the Saudi government financed three Arab-language satellite media distribution systems: MBC, launched in September 1991, ART (Arab Radio and Television, a global platform with twenty non-news channels), and Orbit, based in Rome and which distributed over 40 TV and radio channels, including Orbit News, a composite of NBC, CBS and ABC, and transmissions of Sky News and CNBC. Orbit also commissioned the BBC to produce an Arab-language TV service, which lasted only a year before falling foul of the Saudi censor.[20]

With the growing success of Al Jazeera, and to counter the threat it posed to the credibility of other Arab-language broadcasters, and ultimately to the stability of the Middle East's authoritarian regimes (see Chapters 9 and 10), competing services were launched or developed by the governments of several countries and their business allies. In this sense, the explosion of the Arab-language news media since the late 1990s has been both a political necessity and a consequence of the expanding marketplace for news in the Middle East. MBC News, for example – packaged as 'the CNN of the Arab world' – moved from its base in London to Dubai's Media City in late 2001, launching the 24-hour Al Arabiya news channel in 2002. The channel, funded by a consortium of Lebanese and Kuwaiti business interests, was targeted by suicide bombers in Iraq in 2004, reflecting the insurgents' anger at the channel's coverage of the occupation.

In addition to the relaunched MBC News, Al Jazeera also faced competition from the Lebanon-based LBC-al Hayat, the Hezbollah-sponsored Al Manar, and Abu Dhabi TV. Between them these channels and Al Jazeera claimed by late 2003 to be reaching between 70 and 80 per cent of the Arab audience in the Middle East.[21] Targeted at a more restricted audience in post-Saddam Iraq, Al Fayha began broadcasting from the United Arab Emirates in July 2004, as did Al Alam out of Iran, finding the majority of its audience in the Shia-dominated south of the country. By 2005 one observer could report that 'the Middle Eastern media world is essentially and almost exclusively managed and financed by Arab citizens' (Le Pottier 2005: 114).

Al Jazeera's success was also reflected in what most observers recognised to be positive change in the content of domestic news in the Middle East. For one observer, 'competition for pan-Arab audiences has forced key Arab satellite channels to shed the image conjured up by the state-owned media'.[22] In January 2004 the Saudi government launched Al Ikhbariya, a 12-hour per day news service expressly intended as 'an attempt to win over Saudi viewers who often complain that the country's television news is bland and boring'.[23] Throughout the region, if to varying degrees, Al Jazeera had a clear demonstration effect on the quality of broadcast journalism, obliging a less authoritarian approach from regimes used to tight control over the information environment.

Beyond the Middle East

Since 9/11 the focus of attention amongst observers of transnational news culture has been the Middle East, not least because political developments in that region have fuelled particularly rapid change in the information environment there, amounting to what one writer characterises as 'a media explosion in the Arab world'.[24] Elsewhere in the world, however, a similar process of erosion of what was once fairly characterised as Anglo-American domination of the news market is underway. Hamilton and Jenner observe that 'technology-driven changes are reshaping international news flows by lowering the economic barriers of entry to publishing and broadcasting and encouraging the proliferation of nontraditional international news sources' (2003: 132). In 2004 it was reported that the Indian 24-hour news organisation NDTV, broadcasting one channel in English and the other in Hindi, had pushed the Murdoch-owned Star TV into fourth place in India's ratings charts. NDTV was just one of dozens of successful news channels then operating in India, exploiting the more favourable structure of costs made possible by cable and the falling cost of technology. NDTV's head of operations, Prannoy Ray, gave examples of these cost reductions in a newspaper interview:

> Five years ago, to rent space on a satellite annually would cost you $3 million. Today it costs just $300,000. Cameras cost you one tenth of the price now. The same with editing suites. You are looking at a 75 per cent to 90 per cent drop in the cost of starting a news channel.[25]

These trends, and they apply also to Latin America, southeast Asia and Africa, encourage a greater measure of sensitivity to local conditions from the hitherto dominant global broadcasters. CNN, for example, has undertaken extensive research on the informational needs and cultural sensitivities of its Indian audience, recognising the threat to its market share posed by channels such as NDTV. In China and elsewhere News Corporation's Star TV must take greater care than ever to satisfy the demands not just of local political elites, but local audiences presented with unprecedented choice in their consumption of TV news. It need hardly be added that this development has had less to do with good intentions on the part of media executives than harsh competitive reality. Increasingly it is good business to supply audiences around the world with cultural products of a type they can embrace and identify with. Large and rapidly growing cultural marketplaces such as India and China cannot be ignored by big media corporations, if they wish to remain big in the twenty-first century.

Conclusion

With the evolution of real-time satellite news, the concept of cultural imperialism so crucial to the control paradigm is, if not yet wholly redundant, losing its critical force. As Jean Chalaby puts it, 'the cultural imperialism thesis has too many shortcomings to deal adequately with the complex reality of the contemporary international television market' (2005: 9). On the basis of his study of the ASEAN countries, William Atkins has argued that

> it is necessary to move beyond the perennial debates about media imperialism and national sovereignty, which do not effectively accommodate the inter-nationalised forces of media capitalism. These forces no longer reside in cultural-imperial monoliths in New York, Los Angeles or London, but rather straddle continents and markets, bound through mergers, joint ventures, subsidiaries and a transnational media culture.
>
> (Atkins 2002: 6)

Noting the growing exportation of TV programming from India, and the fact that Indian programmes have become 'part of a global cultural experience', Daya Thussu acknowledges that such trends 'raise questions about the assumptions of the cultural imperialism paradigm' (quoted in Chalaby, ed., 2005: 9). On the one hand, channels such as Al Jazeera are challenging the traditional global dominance of Anglo-American news providers, not just in their local areas but in Europe, America and Australia. On the other, because of the proliferation of local RTN broadcasters taking advantage of improving cost structures, the big global news brands are obliged to localise their products. If CNN or the BBC continues to dominate the global news market in the years and decades to come, it will not be for lack of competition. In satellite news, as in other NICT sectors such as mobile telephony, the global information gap is narrowing.

8 Mapping the global public sphere II: online journalism and the blogosphere

Astonishing as it is to contemplate, given the ease with which we have become used to its contemporary ubiquity, the other main artery of an emerging globalised news culture, the world wide web or internet, was still little more than a decade old as this book went to press. The launch of Netscape's Mosaic – the first free browser – in October 1994 is generally accepted as marking the 'beginning' of the internet as a mass medium. Before that breakthrough, and for the two-and-a-half decades going back to the establishment of ARPANET by the US Defense Department in 1968, the global network of computers linked by satellite and cable now known as the internet was primarily the tool of the military and the academy, used by the former as a safeguard against nuclear attack and by the latter for data-gathering and sharing. After Netscape brought its user-friendly interface to the mass market, the internet began its exponential growth to the point where, by early 2005, more than 70 million Americans reported using it daily,[1] including 35 million who used it for news. More than 50 per cent of British households had access to the internet by the summer of 2003,[2] and this figure has continued to increase.

In the Scandinavian and southeast Asian countries internet access was equally, if not more, widespread. In China the internet has spread rapidly, albeit in restricted (censored) form, with the qualified support of the Communist Party. Here, as in other countries, the development of the internet as a communication medium started in the universities. Chinese academics began to connect to the internet in the late 1980s, but after the Tiananmen Square massacre in 1989 development ceased until 1994, when it again began to move forward. Internet access was granted to ordinary Chinese, though with legal constraints on content and usage (see Chapter 10). Development has proceeded rapidly in the intervening years, with a proliferation of official and unofficial sites.[3] In 2003 internet access in China was estimated to have reached the 300 million mark, with a further half billion regular users anticipated by 2008. As of 2004 it was estimated by Nielsen/ NetRatings that some 100 million Chinese were logging on to the top four internet portals each week. China's online population was already larger than Europe's, 400 per cent bigger than that of the UK and, if these rates of growth continued, set to overtake the USA in number of regular users by 2007.[4]

The internet and journalism

When my *Sociology of Journalism* was published in 1998, online journalism was still in its infancy, with the number of sites devoted to news and related materials counted in the hundreds. Pioneer online publications such as *Slate* and *Salon* were just emerging, professionally produced and well resourced by companies such as Microsoft. As too were more amateurish online gossip columns such as the *Drudge Report*, which famously broke the news of the Clinton–Lewinsky scandal and thereby demonstrated the anarchic, subversive potential of online news for the first time. If the San Francisco earthquake of 1994 was the first 'scoop' to be broken by a website rather than a newspaper or TV bulletin, Matt Drudge's revelation of the president's alleged dealings with a White House intern was the first occasion on which a web-based news outlet set the agenda for the media as a whole.

These two strands of online journalism established early on a fundamental distinction in the evolution of online news media: that between established professionalism and iconoclastic amateurism. Or, to put it another way, the distinction between, on the one hand, journalism aspiring to the ethics and standards espoused by print and broadcast news media for centuries and, on the other, journalism (though many disputed that it could even be described as such) founded on alternative principles having less to do with the values of objectivity and reliability than with subjectivity, immediacy, and independence from, even rejection of, established journalistic institutions. These new voices, and the tension between 'new' and 'old' journalistic media which they inevitably encouraged, would feature strongly in the evolution of the internet and online news media as they developed from the late 1990s, and produced four categories of online actor:

1   *Professional-institutional actors*, including the BBC, CNN, Al Jazeera and other transnational satellite broadcasters; the websites of newspapers and national broadcasters; and the web sites of internet-only journalistic organisations, such as *Slate*;
2   *Professional-individual actors*, such as Andrew Sullivan, Glenn Reynolds, the Baghdad Blogger, and a few others, numbering in the hundreds at most (I refer here only to English-language outlets);
3   *Non-professional-institutional actors*, including government agencies, NGOs, political parties, campaigning and lobby groups, and terrorist organisations such as Al Qaida and the proliferation of web-savvy Islamic groups that support them;
4   *Non-professional-individual actors*, or private bloggers, numbering in their millions.

To begin with, journalism on the internet was dominated by professional sites, some created in order to take advantage of the new medium, others spinning off from established print and broadcast news brands. *FT.com*, the *Guardian Unlimited*, *CNN.com*, *BBC Online*, as the best designed and most successful of online news sites, demonstrated in the late 1990s what quickly became clear after the initial flurry of pessimistic 'death of print' speculation about the impact of the net on the established media. The best way for an established news organisation to deal with the emergence of the net as a mass medium was not to deny its importance, nor to ignore it and hope it might be a passing fad, but to incorporate it into the organisation, making it a complement rather than a competitor to print and broadcast outlets. This was best effected by transforming the producers of news from being either print or broadcast into *multimedia organisations* operating on both 'old' and 'new' platforms, employing 'information architects', as the fashionable jargon of the time called the new breed of multi-skilled, multi-tasked journalistic professional.

It took some time for this lesson to be learned, and even Rupert Murdoch was driven to acknowledge the commercial implications of the emerging online environment only in April 2005, when he delivered a speech making clear his view that the ongoing, steady decline of print media circulations presented both a threat and an opportunity to news organisations. The digital revolution, he argued, 'is a fast-developing reality we should grasp as a huge opportunity to improve our journalism and expend our reach'.[5] News Corporation implemented its chairman's view in July 2005 when it announced the purchase for $580 million of *MySpace.com*, described as 'the world's fastest-growing social networking portal'.[6]

At the time of writing there are few serious news organisations operating at local, national or transnational level anywhere in the world, whether rooted in print or broadcast media, that do not have an online presence. To maintain a website had by the early twenty-first century become a standard marker of a news organisation's ability to keep up with the pace of industrial and technological change. While web-only publications generated mainly original content, online editions of established news outlets relied heavily, as they continue to do, on the content produced for newspapers and/or broadcast bulletins, while exploiting the interactivity of the internet with links to other online information sources. Many organisations, such as the *Guardian*, had designated online editors.

For newspapers, integrating their copy with the internet was a relatively simple task, involving the straightforward conversion of articles and other editorial content into web pages. For broadcasters, the development of broadband and video-streaming technology facilitated the archiving of programmes for time-shifting, the making available online of hourly bulletins and even live transmissions, all of ever-improving audio-visual quality. This writer spent rather too much of late December 2004 accessing online coverage of the Asian tsunami disaster with one eye, while catching 24-hour TV news on the BBC News 24 and Sky News with the other.

As time passed, online news sites acquired growing editorial autonomy in terms of design and content, and began to substitute, at least for some readers, for reading or tuning in to their parent publications. Innovators such as *BBC Online* and *Guardian Unlimited* were more than merely cyber versions of broadcast and print news; rather they became autonomous entities providing increasing quantities of web-only content, much of it free of charge. This meant that most web sites were still, as of this writing, losing money for their proprietors, who were engaged in an urgent search for a business model that could make online journalism not just an integral part of their media business, but a profitable part. Although a number of sites, such as *FT.com*, charged subscription fees for access to premium services such as valuable financial data, many more were finding it difficult to persuade online users that they should be willing to pay. Declining audiences for established media in both the USA and the UK, to name two of the largest markets for news, were rarely matched by additional revenues gained from online sites. In January 2005 *Business Week Online* observed that the *New York Times* – a pioneer and pacesetter in the field of online journalism – 'like all publications' in the USA, faced 'a quandary' born not least from the success of its internet diversification strategy. 'A majority of the paper's readership now views the paper online, but the company still derives 90 per cent of its revenues from newspapers'.[7] And while use of *NYT.com* was increasing, sales of the print edition of the *New York Times* had dropped to 1.1 million per day by late 2004, not least because of the increasing popularity of the online version.

If the long-term economic viability of online journalism has yet to be established at the time of writing, there can be little doubt of the cultural significance of the new medium. The online sites established by print and broadcast media in the 1990s transformed the pattern of flow of journalistic communication by allowing print and broadcast news outlets hitherto constrained within national boundaries to achieve global reach, extending their readerships to anywhere and anyone on the planet with access to a networked computer and the relevant linguistic ability. In this sense the internet established a bridge between the national public spheres within which all media (except transnational broadcasters and newspapers) had traditionally functioned, and an emerging globalised communication space. People in Sydney could read news produced in Dublin, and vice versa, and respond to it by email if they wished. The significance of this facility revealed itself to me in the days after 9/11 when, from my temporary base in far north Queensland, Australia, my discussions with others about the meaning of the event, and the appropriate response of the Australian and other governments, was informed by downloaded articles written by Robert Fisk of the UK's *Independent* newspaper, Andrew Sullivan, Noam Chomsky and many others. The immediate availability and accessibility of these materials to anyone in that remote community with a PC facilitated conversations which linked the local to the global with an unprecedented degree of closeness.

The birth of the blogosphere

Alongside the growth of professional online news sites after 1994 emerged a category of independent, more or less amateur online publication such as the *Drudge Report* and Harry Knowles' *ain't-it-cool-news* in the USA. These sites, like the more recently established *Popbitch* and *Holy Moly* in the UK, specialised in celebrity news, gossip and other niche content categories. Although primitive and unrefined when launched, if they achieved any degree of success they quickly developed in sophistication and professionalism, becoming lucrative income generators for their inventors, charging for access to premium services, taking advertisements, and entering into sponsorship deals. These sites were often identified with individuals such as Harry Knowles and Matt Drudge (the two best known in that first wave). Knowles specialised in honest, hard-hitting, often unauthorised reviews of Hollywood movies, while Drudge, as is well known, made his site essential reading with scurrilous gossip about politicians, some of it true.

Home pages were also being established in the late 1990s by growing numbers of individuals in the arts and academia, functioning not as journalism but as personal bulletin boards to the world, publicising books and articles, providing students with teaching materials and aids, or merely opinions for consideration. By the late 1990s many journalists had established their own websites to act as shopping windows for their work, and to invite dialogue with readers.

Though the term was not commonly in use until the early twenty-first century, these individual web sites displayed all the key features of what we know now as blogging. They were relatively inexpensive to launch and maintain, at least by comparison with any previous media platform. Where, as we have seen, satellite technology reduced the cost of 24-hour news to a fraction of what it had been a few years before, thereby eroding the dominance of the big transnational corporations such as News Corp in countries like India, the internet opened up publishing to any individual with the motivation, skills and comparatively modest resources required to do so. The resulting web logs, or blogs as they would eventually become known, had three characteristics that distinguished them from traditional media outlets, attributable in large part to the space they provided for driven, determined individuals to establish a media presence of their own.

Subjectivity

First, the web logs were personal, subjective and prone to discursive risk-taking. Free of the professional obligations of those who engaged in journalism for a living, bloggers could say more or less what they liked without fear of being sacked. Where the long-established normative principles of the fourth estate stressed the importance of objectivity, restraint and understatement, bloggers were aggressively opinionated, prepared to expose their own views to public scrutiny and engage others in the fierce heat of online debate.

Opinionated journalism has long been the prerogative of the newspaper columnist, of course, and radio shock jocks and talk-back hosts brought assertive subjectivity into broadcasting in the US and elsewhere in the 1980s. Now the internet provided a platform for the rest of us to join in. Shortly after he had broken the Clinton–Lewinsky scandal, Matt Drudge was described as 'a new kind of columnist, on a new medium for columnists – the Internet'.[8] Drudge saw himself as firmly in the tradition of critical scrutiny of elites preferred by British liberal journalism, although the fact that he seemed to care little for the latter's concern with accuracy and reliability distinguished him from the fourth estate as normatively understood. While Drudge was both accurate and first in his exposure of the Clinton–Lewinsky scandal, there have been subsequent stories where he has been wrong, as have many other bloggers. This fact has provided defenders of the established media with a weapon to attack the bloggers' journalistic credentials, and to seek to preserve a cultural distance between old and new media. Catherine

Seipp observes that there is 'a serious problem of quality control in the increasingly powerful blogging world'.[9]

Few would deny that observation, including the bloggers, although recent plagiarism and inaccuracy scandals affecting such paragons of the established American news media as the *New Republic*, the *New York Times*, *USA Today*, and NBC network news have reminded audiences that the attempt to distinguish old/quality from new/lack of quality is problematic (see below). To this extent, bloggers make transparent the capacity for exaggeration, error and even deliberate falsification which has always been true of all journalism, if rarely conceded in public.

Interactivity

The second distinctive feature of blogs was their interactivity, allowing communication in both directions to an extent unmatched by traditional media. There have always been readers' letters to newspapers, but these have been very much a minority pursuit, with space for publication limited to one page of a newspaper at most. The internet has, in practical terms, unlimited space for online dialogue. Given access to a computer, replying to something encountered on a web site was quick and easy by comparison with the demands of print, to the extent that by 2004 one survey noted that one-third of all users of web logs (millions of people in the US alone) were in the habit of replying to items read online.

The internet also permitted an unprecedented degree of what some observers have called 'citizen's journalism', as exemplified by the *www.backfence.com* site established by Mark Potts in Washington. The site challenged regional newspapers in the area it served, by allowing ordinary people to contribute reports, photographs and other information of local relevance. The site was

> taking reporting of local news, community events and debates down to the people . . . a leader in a new phenomenon called 'citizen's journalism': a sharing of information where the audience itself decides what's important and writes about it.[10]

'User-generated content', as it is described by BBC management, in the form of e-mails and digital photography and video was increasingly being integrated with professionally generated material in coverage of stories such as the 2004 Asian tsunami and Hurricane Katrina in the late summer of 2005.

Typical of the enhanced accessibility of the blogosphere, and illustrative too of the decentralising power of 'citizen reporting' is *Diary from Baghdad*, a web log operated by 'Rose', a 27-year old female civil engineer. As Rose describes herself on her home page:

> I write about the current events in Iraq in my point of view [*sic*] and as I hear from people living here around me and the way they see things here. Not as you hear from the news, but the way we feel and live with it and how it affects us.

In every country, and every conflict zone, more and more voices of this kind are making their way onto the blogosphere.

Connectivity

Third, these sites were often used as gateways, or portals, into other web sites, linking users to related information elsewhere on the internet. They were links in a chain, or a network of chains of similarly themed sites. A popular site such as Glenn Reynolds' *instapundit.com* or Danny Schechter's *Mediachannel.org* – 'the global network for democratic media' – would contain links to dozens, even hundreds of other online sites, all engaged in constant debate with one another and their readers. In both these aspects – their interactivity and their interconnectedness – blogs were a uniquely dialogic media form. One observer defined the blog as 'a Web journal that comments on the news – often by criticising the media and usually in rudely clever tones – with links to stories that back up the commentary with evidence'.[11] Some blogs were unmistakeably journalism, however, as well as journal, read avidly for the analytical insights and commentaries they contained on the events of the day.

The amazing, expanding blogosphere

The first blog, in Andrew Sullivan's opinion, was launched in 1994 by Justin Hall, under the rubric of *Links to the Underground*. The term 'blogosphere' was coined by William Quick in 1999, the same year that Sullivan's attention was brought to the phenomenon as a quick, cheap and user-friendly way of going online.[12] In the early years of the twenty-first century the blogosphere expanded rapidly, propelled like previous waves of NICT by a few explosive events. Key for the blogosphere was 9/11, when thousands of individuals went online to disseminate written and pictorial accounts of their own experiences in New York, or to express their opinions about the significance of the event. In a manner analogous to the expansion of real-time satellite news through a succession of major news events such as the Challenger disaster and the first Gulf War, 9/11 provided the blogosphere with a purpose and an urgency which accelerated its evolution. As Sullivan puts it, after 9/11 'the market for serious commentary took off'.[13] Not just policy wonks and party activists, but millions of more or less ordinary citizens found themselves with both motive and means to enter the global debate that accompanied the war on terror, free of the gatekeeping which protects traditional print and broadcast platforms.

This has led to a huge expansion in the range of views available in the public media domain. Andrew Sullivan is among those who welcomed the emergence of the blogosphere because of its 'democratisation' of the public sphere, and its capacity to give voice to outsiders.[14] From his perspective these outsiders were on the right, since the liberal left dominated (in his view) the mainstream. The same point was made by former Tory leader Ian Duncan Smith in a piece written for the *Guardian* in 2005.[15] In this he argued that 'the [liberal] dominance of America's mainstream media is coming to an end', as is the power of 'metropolitan elites'.

With the rise of the blogosphere, for Smith, 'the national conversation is being democratised'. As for the UK, where the Conservatives went down to their third successive electoral defeat in May 2005:

> The blogosphere will become a force in Britain, and it could ignite many new forces of conservatism. The internet's automatic level playing field gives conservative opportunities that the mainstream media have often denied them.
>
> (Ibid.)

Stuart Purvis observes of the Rony Abovitz case (see below) that the blogger 'is one of those conservative online activists who believes that the internet is an opportunity to balance what they see as media pro-liberal bias'.[16] Both right and left, in fact, recognise the democratising, decentralising potential of the internet, while disagreeing fundamentally on the nature of the problem with the mainstream media which it can usefully address. One side sees the media as 'liberal' in their bias; the other sees them as deeply conservative.

In the context of 9/11 and the subsequent invasion of Iraq, some of those who had been on the left but found themselves departing from the critical orthodoxy on matters of peace and war found blogging a timely vehicle for self-expression. Marxist academic Norman Geras, whose *norm.blog* attracted mainstream media attention in February 2005 because its pro-Iraqi war position[17] had been picked up by pro-war and neo-con bloggers in the USA, described his motivation to begin the blog in July 2003:

> I didn't agree with what was and has remained the left liberal consensus about the war in Iraq. It was everywhere around me, in the papers I read and the social milieu I inhabit, and I just wanted to state what I thought was a better point of view. The beauty of blogging is – anyone can start one. It costs nothing, or next to nothing. Blogging is an informal or democratic kind of journalism. You put up stuff – opinions, arguments, etc. – and you don't need to own a printing press or work for a big media owner. Anyone who's got access to the internet can do it.[18]

And millions of people did. The number of individual web logs active on the internet increased from approximately 200,000 in 2002 to some 3.3 million by the end of 2003. By the beginning of 2005 there were at least 5 million active US-based web logs on the internet, producing everything from personal diaries to professional journalism, and perhaps as many again deemed by online monitors to be inactive. Indeed, some two-thirds of all blogs are estimated to be dormant at any given time.[19] Across the world this pattern is repeated, with some 11 million web logs estimated to be active in Korea at the time of writing.[20] Even allowing for the high level of depletion, it was still possible for one observer to note in early 2005 that 'blogs have gone from web curiosity to mainstream media'.[21]

The vast majority of these sites are of only marginal interest to the present discussion, or to anyone beyond the producer him- or herself, since they comprise individual reflections on personal lives, interests and obsessions. They are online diaries, as ephemeral and self-centred as those written in pen and paper and hidden away in an attic. According to a 2004 survey of US blogs, more than half are started by teenagers aged between 13 and 19, and another 40 per cent by people between 20 and 29. A majority (56 per cent) are started by females, leading to the conclusion that 'the typical blog is written by a teenage girl who uses it twice a month to update her friends and classmates on happenings in her life. Underneath the iceberg, blogging is a social phenomenon: persistent messaging for young adults'.[22] This source estimated that on average personal blogs of this kind have readerships of perhaps 250 per day, on the assumption that each user in the US accesses 50 sites per day.

The blogs in which we are mainly interested here – a much smaller number – are those that present themselves as journalistic in nature, providing access to information in the form of self-authored news and commentary, or linking to other online sources of news and commentary. These include Andrew Sullivan's *Daily Dish*, Glenn Reynolds' *Instapundit*, and Danny Schechter's *Media Channel*, which supports the *Global News Index* and *Globalvision News Network*. This last, according to its home page, 'aggregates information from its worldwide network to give a stronger voice to previously unheard sources of news and information'.[23]

The most successful news blogs, which include the three aforementioned sites, have become sources of information and opinion not just for the casual reader, but for professional journalists in print and broadcast media, academics, and activists in the preparation of their work and campaigns. As the number of blogs increased, so did the influence of pioneering sites such as that run by journalist Andrew Sullivan. By his own account, visitors to his site increased from 4,000 to 100,000 between 2000 and 2004, including among that number many journalists from the old media. Sullivan noted that 'producers for cable news shows now consult the blogs as much as *The Times* for tips about upcoming stories. Throughout the day, news managers consult the blogosphere for updates, while the mainstream media tread water'.[24]

A very small number of these sites cross over to the mainstream and become known to the public in general, through being regularly cited as sources in newspapers or on TV news, or being reproduced as print journalism, as in the case of Salam Pax, the 'Baghdad Blogger'. Salam Pax achieved fame in the build-up to and execution of the 2003 invasion of Iraq. In the absence of a substantial foreign news corps on the ground, the Baghdad Blogger provided regular dispatches from the scene of the most dramatic events. The professionalism of his writing, the intimacy and colour of his pieces, and the inherent newsworthiness of his stories encouraged the *Guardian* newspaper to take him on as a columnist, and eventually to publish a collection of his pieces in book form.

Crossing over

The blogosphere, then, has a hierarchical, pyramidical structure. At the top of the pyramid are those very few sites (20 or so in the USA in 2004) that regularly register

more than 10 million page views per month. At the next level of usage are so
200 sites that regularly register more than 1 million page views per month, and so
on down to those millions of personal diary-type sites recording monthly hits of up
to about 250. What determines the success of an individual blog then?

As the career of the Baghdad Blogger suggests, perhaps the most important
criterion making cross over more likely is the scarcity or use-value of the information it makes available; its capacity to reveal information that no established media
have in their possession, or are able and willing to publish. In his case, the absence
of established news organisations gave his words value; his presence in the Iraqi
capital gave him a rare and inherently newsworthy insight into the conditions
of life there.

Print and broadcast media are governed by the libel and defamation laws of the
nation-state within which they are located, laws which usually prevent the publication of unsubstantiated allegations, far less rumours and gossip. Online sites,
on the other hand, are freer, if not entirely absolved of these constraints. The law
on internet publication is still vague and difficult to enforce. Many of the news blogs
have little or no reputation to protect, and feel free to publish and be damned.
Doing so, indeed, has proven an effective means of putting a particular site on
the map of the blogosphere. Matt Drudge, for example, whose website broke the
Clinton–Lewinsky scandal to the world, was able to do what *Newsweek* magazine
could not because he had, in a sense, nothing to lose and a whole world of free
publicity to gain. Many scandals affecting politicians and other elites have appeared
on the internet long before making it into print. Many, such as the allegations about
Prince Charles which circulated in November 2003, remain restricted to the
internet, unpublishable by print and broadcast news media.

Style and quality of content also matter. The Baghdad Blogger was not just
uniquely placed to provide a valuable source of news about events behind the lines
in Iraq; he was a skilled writer, whose columns were lively and readable. His blog
was neither pro- nor anti-Coalition, but satirical and irreverent, documenting
the mood of the people as their liberation and its chaotic aftermath unfolded.
In general, the success of a blog is related to the skill with which it is put together,
from the quality of the writing to the layout of the pages. Blogs by professional
writers such as Andrew Sullivan – in his case, a writer valued for his newspaper
columns and books long before he ever launched a blog – are more likely to succeed
with a general audience than the postings of a 15-year-old girl blogging about
her favourite boy band. Defending himself, and bloggers in general, against the
allegation that blogging is a form of vanity publishing (by implication, undertaken
by those for whom conventional forms of commercial publication are not possible),
Norman Geras made the obvious point that 'you have to write to a quality that will
interest people. It's the quality of what's done on the blog which determines
whether it will sink or swim. If the stuff is poor, fewer people will come back.'[25]

Even with competent writing and useful content, however, it remains a challenge
for a web log to rise to the tip of the vast iceberg of invisible, unnoticed sites which
comprise the greatest portion of the blogosphere. This can be done, as in the case
of Norman Geras's *norm.blog*, by posting something that challenges convention

wing' academic defends the Republican-led invasion of Iraq),
ɲe narrative others want to tell – in Geras's case, the neo-
rrative that even some on the left recognise the validity of the
ɪq from Saddam Hussein. Geras's authority as an intellectual voice,
ctiveness of what he had to say, propelled his blog to prominence in
ɪere, from whence it became an object of interest for the established
ɪsh press and broadcast media, especially those neo-conservatives who
founɖ ɪeful ammunition in advancing their own pro-war cause. At that point,
even casual users of the internet would have been alerted to log on to *norm.blog*,
to see what the fuss was about.

If being adopted as a source by journalists working for the off-line media is
one route to visibility in the blogosphere, so too is providing the service of linkage
to the global online network, connecting readers with bloggers, and bloggers with
one another for the purpose of conducting debate. To achieve this means establishing one's site as an information hub in the global network, a widely used node
in what one observer calls 'a vast heterarchy'[26] of blogs. An obvious problem
associated with the blogosphere is its sheer size and complexity. Even after
discounting the millions of abandoned, dormant or diary-type sites which make up
the bulk of the blogosphere, one is still left with thousands, if not tens of thousands
of potential sources of relevant news and commentary from which to choose.
Sites such as *Instapundit* – 'the Grand Central station of Bloggerville'[27] – act as
gatekeepers in this context, sifting and sorting the wheat from the chaff, and guiding
the online reader by the shortest route to the most relevant information. Once
established as reliable and trustworthy guides, their reputation for convenience
and reliability attracts more and more users, and other bloggers strive to get listed,
in a cycle of expanding visibility and influence.

Most blogs remain obscure throughout their lives, before becoming dormant or
extinct. But some – a very small proportion, much less than 0.1 per cent – survive,
and then cross over to the mainstream. Andrew O'Baoill observes that 'weblogs
have seen the emergence of a small loose group of A-list bloggers, whose traffic and
in-bound links are far in excess of those of most other bloggers, and around whom
much coverage of weblogs in traditional media is based.'[28] Such blogs – many of
them operated by professional journalists – become bridges between the alien,
impenetrable world of the internet and the mainstream world of traditional journalism. John Hiler argues that Glenn Reynold's 'dual status as a blogger/journalist
gives him the power to bring stories from the Blogosphere into the mainstream
press'.[29] The extent of this crossover has increased since those words were written
in 2002, confirming his argument that 'bloggers and journalists are in a symbiotic
relationship, working together to report, filter and break the news': 'Bloggers break
the news and hash it out . . . A journalist adds a layer of reporting, bringing that
news beyond the blogosphere.'

For this reason, one observer argues, 'the rise of blogs does not equal the death
of professional journalism. Increasingly, the Internet is turning the media world
into a symbiotic eco-system, in which the different parts feed off one another
and the whole thing grows'.[30] John Hiler uses similar language to characterise the

blogosphere as 'a media ecosystem. Surfing the blogosphere you can see evolutionary forces play out in real time, as weblogs vie for niche status, establish communities of like-minded sites, and jostle for links to their sites'.[31]

The need for gatekeeping and quality control is a direct consequence of the very characteristics which give the blogosphere its appeal: independence, interactivity and accessibility. Since the seventeenth century, journalists in capitalist societies have stressed the qualities of trust, credibility, reliability and objectivity in the information they produce. These standards are jealously guarded by professional codes and practices, training and editing. The online debate provoked by the Jayson Blair plagiarism scandal in 2003, and NBC's embarassment over its error in reporting George W. Bush's war record during the 2004 presidential election campaign, reveal how important they continue to be. Both scandals were broken and then inflamed by bloggers, as they disseminated and discussed the details online.

The two media are radically different in their approach to information, however. For the *New York Times* and NBC, like many media of record, news tends to be filtered by editors before publication, and errors of fact identified and corrected. In the blogosphere, publication comes first, and filtering only comes later as it becomes clear what is true and what is false in a story. By allowing almost anyone access, the blogosphere inevitably facilitates the circulation of information which is less reliable, on the whole, than that found in a rigorously edited broadsheet newspaper. For enthusiasts of blogging, however, this is a small price to pay for the vast richness of the new medium. As one advocate puts it:

> The ethos for news and information blogs is based on values such as immediacy, transparency, interconnectivity and proximity to events. As a heterarchy, diverse bloggers post, cross-link, blogroll, and backtrack to interact in a network, pulling ideas and knowledge from the edges.[32]

At times of global crisis the blogosphere comes into its own as a uniquely diverse and rich information pool, for which the occasional error or malicious rumour may be judged a small price to pay.

By way of illustration, the Asian tsunami of late 2004 marked a significant moment in the evolution of the blogosphere as a vehicle for what was earlier called 'citizen's journalism'. In the aftermath of the biggest natural disaster of the internet era, blogs displayed their communicative power by disseminating to a global audience the hundreds of eye-witness testimonies and documents which digital cameras and e-mail made available. For one observer:

> where once disaster eyewitness photographs and videos turned up for widespread viewing only on news programmes and in newspapers, today through e-mail, blogs, and a blogging infrastructure that spreads amateur news quickly and efficiently, they often find large audiences without the help or need of mainstream news outlets.[33]

For many observers, the Asian tsunami provided futher evidence that traditional journalistic structures and practice are losing their 'sovereignty'.

The good, the bad and the ugly of the blogosphere

There has always been a tendency in media analysis, both lay and scholarly, to assume the worst when considering the likely impact of new media on existing institutions. One manifestation of cultural pessimism, ever since the invention of print itself, has been that the rise of one media form heralds the demise of another. Cinema, radio, print, book reading – all have at various times been written off as finished in the face of home video, television, computer games and so on. The most recent of these narratives of decline occurred with the rise of the internet, and from 1994 as the medium began to spread to the mass market the death of print was regularly foretold. That has not happened yet, although there have been slow, steady declines in newspaper circulation and network news ratings in both Britain and the US in recent times, reflecting the fragmentation of the news market rather than the wholesale abandonment of one medium for another. Since 1994 the proportion of the American public that regards the traditional media of network TV news and newspapers as its main source of information has declined, while users of real-time news channels and online journalism sites have increased. As the Pew Internet and American Life Project (PIALP) puts it, on the basis of research conducted at the end of 2004, the American 'news universe has been completely transformed'[34] by this shift. In particular, 'no single source today is nearly as dominant as network news was in the early 1990s'. American daily newspapers have seen a decline in their average circulations of about 3.5 per cent since 1998. In the key category of campaign news coverage, the internet has become a source of growing importance. In the presidential election campaign of 2004 the internet was identified as the main source of its news by nearly one-fifth of the population as a whole, and by 38 per cent of those with broadband access. As PIALP put it, summarising their survey data:

> For the typical American, the internet is still a second-tier source of news about politics; television and the daily newspaper continue to lead the way. But for young Americans with . . . [broadband] at home, the internet has taken a distinctive role in how they get news about politics. Among this group, television is still the most widely used source, but the internet is now a strong second, while radio, newspapers and magazines lag well behind.

Inter-media competition has become more intense, particularly amongst the young, and there has been a general erosion of trust in network news and news-papers.

> More people are turning away from traditional media outlets, with their decorous, just-the-facts aspirations to objectivity, toward noisier hybrid formats that aggressively fuse news with opinion or entertainment, or both. Young

people in particular are bypassing mainstream sources in favour of alternatives they find on the internet or late-night television.

Since 1994, those declaring themselves regular users of network TV news have declined from 74 to 60 per cent; of newspapers from 49 to 42 per cent; and of radio from 47 to 42 per cent. While these figures are not alarming if they indicate a substitution of internet sources for traditional media, overall use of news is also found by PIALP to be down since 1994. These data suggest that mainstream US media are losing their traditionally privileged status, at the same time as audiences increasingly opt for news outlets that reflect their values and political affiliations, a demand more than satisfied by Fox News and the talk radio channels. Many US observers express concern that the long-standing aspiration towards objectivity as a professional ethic is eroding, although this is not solely due to the explosion of online journalism. Scandals among established news media of record such as the *New York Times* have eroded the quality gap which once existed between old and new media. As one observer puts it, 'the once-Olympian authority of the *New York Times* is being eroded not only by its own journalistic screw-ups, but also by profound changes in communications technology and in the US political climate'.[35]

In these respects 'professional journalism has entered a period of declining sovereignty in news, politics and the provision of facts to public debate'.[36] Illustrating that point the UK press reported in February 2005 the case of Rony Abovitz, a blogger who that month posted a story which 'claimed one of the most senior scalps in US journalism'.[37] The tale of how Abovitz forced the resignation of CNN news executive Eason Jordan for alleging during an off-the-record meeting that the US military had deliberately killed 12 journalists in Iraq was further evidence that the mainstream print and broadcast media no longer controlled the speed of flow of news, and were no longer the exclusive filters and gatekeepers between news makers and their audiences.

This trend can be viewed both positively and negatively. On the one hand, it implies the possibility of more information in circulation which is exaggerated, distorted, incorrect or downright deceitful. As one commentator observes:

> Blogging is especially amenable to introducing negative information into the news stream and for circulating rumours as fact. Blogging's fact-checking apparatus is just the built-in truth squad of those who read the blog and howl loudly if they wish to dispute some assertion. It is, in a sense, a place where everyone has his own truth.[38]

But, as noted above, rumour and negativity are hardly unknown to the established news media of record. And as the bloggers have shown in a series of high-profile exposés, falsehood and untruth are just as likely to be encountered in a respectable newspaper or periodical as online. The *New Republic*'s unhappy experience with staff reporter Stephen Glass, who invented and falsified a number of feature articles for the periodical before his discovery and dismissal, demonstrated that even the most scrupulously edited, quality-controlled journalism is potentially flawed. We had always known that, of course (and much critical media analysis has been dedicated to showing us in what ways bias and other flaws were built into content). But one consequence of the blogging revolution has been to make much more transparent the imperfections of the established media. If this punctures their pomposity (pomposity, not least, towards online journalism) at the same time as contributing to the construction of a critical reading public, that will be considered a valuable service by many. Blogging, and some of the stories it has broken about the arrogances and imperfections of more respectable news sources, has broken down the controlling distinctions that once existed between 'media of record' and alternative media, between mainstream and marginal, insiders and outsiders, professionals and amateurs. Objectivity remains a crucial value for journalists to uphold, and the best bloggers know this. But the notion that it resides only among the media behemoths of Manhattan and London has been challenged, to the point where some commentators in 2005 detected something 'between a crisis and a panic' in the established US news media.[39]

Following the plagiarism/fabrication scandal surrounding *New York Times* correspondent Jayson Blair in 2003, the paper's executive director Howell Raines was forced to resign under pressure from other media, not least the bloggers. As one report observed at the time, 'e-mails, magazine websites and blogs poured out gossip and venom against Raines at a speed that left the slow-footed, bureaucratic newspaper looking like a media dinosaur'.[40] For one observer, such incidents revealed that 'the tectonic plates of journalism are moving. There is awesome potential in the internet as a gatherer, distributor and checker of news. This does not mean that old media will die. But [they] will have to adapt quickly to what has so far been an asymmetrical relationship'.[41] A *Sunday Spectator* column quoted on *instapundit.com* observed that 'a revolution is happening right now; a revolution with huge political implications'.[42] 'In a newspaper or magazine', continues this observer, 'sources of information may be stated but must be taken by the reader on faith, unless the reader has the time, ability and personal connections to retrace them.' By contrast,

> [the blog] may be updated by the minute or the hour, it remains accessible and searchable through its archives, but most crucially, it contains Internet links. Through them, the Bloggers are universally networked. The almost infinitely extendable electronic field of text, allows whatever space is necessary to delve into its fine details.

As a result the practitioners of print journalism now have to watch their backs, and take extra care to avoid the editorial sloppiness displayed in the Jayson Blair scandal. The print establishment, like political elites in Britain and the US, now faces online scrutiny of a type not experienced before. Just as politicians increasingly lose control of the media agenda because of the internet, so does the media establishment. Paradoxically, and against the received wisdom that the babel-speak of the blogosphere will undermine the rationality of public debate, it has become a source of independent scrutiny of the establishment media. Professional journalism has indeed entered a period of 'declining sovereignty',[43] which some will view as no bad thing. John Hiler welcomes the fact that 'blogs feast daily upon articles written by journalists, linking to each article and adding their own comment and perspective. In doing so, weblogs provide yet another valuable function: filtering and fast checking articles by journalists'.[44]

In taking this interpretation on board, we again contrast the cultural pessimism of scholarly tradition with an alternative, more optimistic reading of the trends. The internet has permitted an expansion and a democratisation of opinion journalism, or 'news that reflects one's own beliefs and preferences and tends to filter out dissenting views'.[45] While this approach to journalism is hardly new in itself, but is 'actually as old as the pamphleteers of the early days of American [and British] journalism', it may be regarded as unwelcome in excess. At the same time, quality control arises from the inevitable competition for access and influence engaged in by bloggers. In the absence of a major scoop such as the Clinton–Lewinsky scandal, only the best written and most reliable become consistently influential in the mainstream of the public sphere. And these tend to be relatively professional in their approach. John Hiler suggests that 'a clear majority of the top fifty links every day are written by journalists and published in big media newspapers and magazines'.[46] Quality rises to the top of the blogosphere, distinguished from the millions of ephemeral, short-lived expressions of personality by their demonstrable usefulness to the broader public sphere.

Governments, NGOs and online activists

In addition to teenage diarists, websites run by professional journalists and established news organisations, and web logs, the internet has provided a whole new medium of political communication for use by governments and official agencies, party organisations, non-governmental organisations, lobby groups and all forms of political collectivity, including terrorist organisations and insurgent armies. Websites run by these groups have functioned as tools for campaigning, fund-raising, public relations and propaganda, information dissemination and, most spectacularly in recent times, psychological warfare against 'infidel' governments and populations. At times they have become significant political players.

Political communicators have always used the media available to them at any given time, and in this respect the growing employment of the internet for the purpose of engaging with various publics and actors does not represent a qualitatively new era in the history of political communication. As in the production of journalism, however, the internet exponentially increases the quantity of political communication, the speed of its flow, and the extent of its reach as it flows down a billion pathways to TV monitors and computer screens all over the networked world. As a consequence, ordinary people – i.e., those who are not activists, or involved in organisations, but maybe participate in elections – enjoy much easier access to much more information about politics than they have ever had before. All government departments in the UK and most comparable societies now maintain web sites for the dissemination of information in which the public have an interest. With newsworthy exceptions such as the Hutton Inquiry website, they are not widely used, as a rule,[47] but they are there, accessible to anyone who wants them.

Political parties and lobby groups, too, use the internet to fight campaigns and mobilise support, with growing efficacy. Observing the 2004 US presidential election, commentator Andrew Sullivan observed that the blogosphere had 'supplanted the network news, mainstream newspapers and political parties as the critical arbiters of the course of this election'.[48] Howard Dean's unsuccessful bid to become the Democratic Party's presidential candidate in 2004 was praised for its innovative use of the web in fund raising and mobilisation of party workers. Largely as a result of this success he was appointed Democratic national chairman in January 2005, and was being tipped as a potential Democratic presidential front-runner in the 2008 campaign. During the 2004 campaign – for the first time in an American presidential election, bloggers were given accreditation to cover the party conventions – blogging was recognised as an important new factor in public opinion-formation. Media scholars are increasingly focused on such issues as the implications of internet use – including government and other organisations' web sites as well as news and journalism – for public participation in democratic processes.[49]

Conclusion

The web has become a knowledge resource of unprecedented depth and richness, not just for journalists, but for the public in general, who now have access not merely to the thousands and millions of independent news sites and bloggers crowding the net, but to official documents of government, think tanks and campaigning and lobbying organisations such as the Project for a New American Century. Far from being secretive and conspiratorial, the Project's often controversial documents are open and accessible to all on the internet, as are those of their critics. Also available to the public at the press of a mouse are the deliberations of such official bodies as the Hutton Inquiry into relations between the BBC and the UK government in the run-up to the invasion of Iraq; the Starr Commission into the Clinton–Lewinsky scandal, and a number of major US reports on the events of 9/11, all of them critical of at least some of the actions and reactions of the Bush administration. Both in their real-time, gavel-to-gavel coverage on 24-hour news channels, and in their presence on the internet, these materials have become much more accessible than has ever been the case before. Hitherto they were available in relatively expensive printed form. Downloading them from the net is free of charge. Through these means the workings of government, the abuses of individual agencies of the state, and the intimate sexual transgressions of individuals up to the level of the president himself, have become newly transparent. We know more, as individuals and publics, than we ever did. Few of us have read the report of the Hutton Inquiry in all its mind-numbing detail, but we can if we want to, and that is a significant fact.

9 From blogosphere to public sphere?

Can the transnational and global media described in the preceding chapters be evaluated as an emerging, globalised public sphere; or, as many critical commentators argue, should they be viewed as the source of 'noise' rather than information which, if not necessarily always 'rational' (where rationality is a subjective term) is of some value in the processes of democratisation at both the nation-state and global levels? Part IV will examine how transnational and global media interact with and impact on nation-state public spheres to influence political processes in democratic and authoritarian states respectively. Here I evaluate the characteristics of satellite and online media against criteria defined by what a global public sphere, should such a thing indeed exist, might be expected to incorporate, as indicated in Habermas's *Structural Transformation of the Public Sphere* (1989) and subsequent refinements of the concept. The German sociologist's work has come to define the standard for a democratic media infrastructure, and while it has been extensively revised in the period since Habermas first outlined it in the 1960s, it remains the starting point for discussion of the relationship between media institutions and political processes. Can the model of the public sphere, developed to describe processes and structures of political communication within the nation-states of early modern capitalism, help us to assess the potential contribution of globalised news culture to the evolution of democratic politics world wide?

A global public sphere – why it matters

For Monroe Price, writing in 1995 as the internet was just coming into mass consciousness as a new communicative phenomenon, 'government and media are yoked in the democratic process' (1995: 21). Chambers and Costain have argued that 'healthy democracies need a healthy public sphere, where citizens (and elites) can exchange ideas, acquire knowledge and information, confront public problems, exercise public accountability, discuss policy options, challenge the powerful without fear of reprisal, and defend principles' (2000: xi). The connection between democracy and a media system capable of doing all these things is axiomatic in liberal political theory. As Paul Starr's *Creation of the Media* (2004) shows in relation to the US, and others have described in relation to Britain, France and other pioneering democracies (Raymond 1996; Conboy 2004),[1] media and political institutions have evolved in parallel since the beginnings of representative democracy in the seventeenth century, one reinforcing the independence and authority of the other. Without a properly functioning public sphere, it is fair to say, there can be no democracy worthy of the name.

What has been true of advanced capitalism has also come to be accepted as true for the developing world, and those countries now in transition from various forms of authoritarian government to more democratic polities, such as Russia and the former countries of the Soviet bloc, many Central and South American states, and much of Africa and Asia. The limitations on the development of a fully functioning public sphere in Zimbabwe, for example, are routinely interpreted outside the country as both a measure and a contributory cause of Zimbabwe's democratic deficit.[2] In post-Soviet Russia one index of the success of the ongoing transition to democracy is widely recognised to be the degree of freedom and independence enjoyed by that country's media institutions, which have varied considerably since the failure of the 1991 August coup. In the summer of 2005 the tenure of President Putin was being criticised in many quarters, both inside and outside of the country, because it had become associated with a more authoritarian approach to the Russian media, including the alleged intimidation of journalists and the violent removal of unruly editors from influential publications, both in Moscow and the regions (see next chapter).

Whether democratic or authoritarian, advanced or developing, consolidated or transitional, the nation-states of the twenty-first century have in common their shared occupancy of a world that is more interconnected than ever before, and in which for the first time in human history, it is possible to speak of a truly global community of media users and producers, linked by their shared consumption of movies, pop music, journalism and other cultural commodities, and by a common interest in issues of global resonance, such as the post-9/11 war on terror and climate change. Although there is no 'world government' as such, and no evidence that such a system would be desirable or practical in the foreseeable future, the trends described in previous chapters mean that it has become timely to ask if there can nonetheless be such a progressive entity as a global public sphere, functioning in a manner comparable to the public spheres which are universally recognised as important in the political lives of nation-states. Can such an entity facilitate the globalisation of democracy, if not necessarily *global democracy* in the institutional sense of representative world government?

Defining the public sphere

Definitions of the Habermasian public sphere crowd the media studies and political science literature. Bennett and Entman define it as 'any and all locations, physical or virtual, where ideas and feelings relevant to politics are transmitted or exchanged openly' (2001: 3). My own attempt at a textbook definition identifies the public sphere as 'in essence the communicative institutions of a society, through which facts and opinions circulate and by means of which a common stock of knowledge is built up as the basis for collective political action' (McNair 2003b: 21). The terminology used to talk about the public sphere varies among media sociologists, but most would agree that it encompasses the set of media outlets by means of which particular groups of individuals are provided with the information they need to participate in the political processes that affect their lives. This information should be of sufficient quality to form the foundation for the rational political decision-making required by liberal democratic theory.

'Rational' is a relative term, however, and we should recognise at this point that the public sphere is now, and always has been segmented into sub-spheres organised by demography, political viewpoint, lifestyle and ethnicity, to name just four categories of readership into which media are typically grouped.[3] As Erik Eriksen puts it, paraphrasing Habermas at a recent conference on this subject, 'the public sphere is not an institution, but rather a communicative network . . . There has never existed only one single authoritative public sphere . . . They were many and they were stratified' (Eriksen 2004). The public sphere, then, is not a single thing, defined by a single set of aesthetic and taste hierarchies, but comprises even in its most primitive form a virtual, cognitive multiverse of spheres within spheres; sets of cultural institutions serving overlapping, intersecting, interconnected communities of readers/listeners/viewers who are linked by their shared consumption of the information contained in particular media. These communities of readers – publics – are then linked to wider communities by their media's shared agenda of reportage, analysis and discussion. Readers of broadsheet newspapers will learn about a celebrity scandal such as 2005's Michael Jackson child abuse trial at the same time as viewers of Sky News and readers of the *National Enquirer*. Law and order may be an issue throughout the news media, although it will be treated differently in a conservative as opposed to a liberal organ. In their shared sense of what is important and newsworthy, however, these separate media, with their distinctive styles and audiences, combine to form a national public sphere within which the 'red top' tabloid reader is linked with the broadsheet-preferring teacher or lawyer. Come election time, or even during the periods between elections when politicians must be sensitive to public opinion, these different communities of readers have what is in theory an equal voice in influencing and shaping policy (or at least the public presentation of policy).

From these initial observations the characteristics of a normative public sphere can be summarised under three headings as *accessibility*, *independence* and *influence*.

Accessibility

Self-evidently, it must be possible for the information contained within the public sphere to be accessible to those who rely upon it. This is a statement about media *consumption*, implying two characteristics of media institutions: (a) that they supply economically affordable information for the individual reader; and (b) that they employ language that is understandable to the publics at whom content is targeted. In Britain and America one might say that this criterion has been manifest in the supply of cheap, popular newspapers following the introduction of new printing technologies and the abolition of stamp duties in the nineteenth century. Such a supply was premised on the gradual universalisation of education, granting the masses access to the linguistic skills necessary to read newspapers and periodicals, and to discuss what was in them. Today literacy in print and audio-visual media is a prerequisite of the public sphere's accessibility. By extension, so is the existence of educational provision which, if not universal, is at least capable of enabling sufficient numbers of people to form politically significant communities of readers.

The criterion of accessibility also refers to media *production*, in so far as a healthy public sphere must be able to accommodate a plurality of voices and perspectives broadly representative of the public it serves. The harsh economics of media production have historically placed practical constraints on this normative feature of the public sphere and brought forth justified criticism of the oligopolistic structures of media ownership which have always been a feature of advanced capitalist societies. That said, even in the darkest days of megaphonic media and propagandistic proprietors, democracies have always supported 'alternative' media, from the radical press in seventeenth- and eighteenth-century Britain to the documentaries of Michael Moore in the twenty-first. As previous chapters have argued, however, one consequence of the evolution of satellite and internet technologies has been an enhanced capacity for relatively resource-poor groups to participate at the transnational and global level in the kinds of public journalistic activities that were hitherto the province of established print and broadcast media organisations. The media of a developing country such as India are no longer dominated by Anglo-American corporations, while within states such as Britain and America the established media are increasingly subject to competition and challenge from online sources. Daniel Drezner observes that the internet 'dramatically lowers the cost of networked communication' (2005), to the benefit of all manner of citizen-activists, 'smart mobs' and other campaigners. If there have always been alternative newspapers, fanzines and other outlets for the expression of dissidence, their proliferating twenty-first-century online equivalents are the millions of bloggers and online news sites now jostling to be heard.

Accessibility of media production (and the diversity of views which should ideally result from that) implies the second key characteristic of the public sphere, *independence*.

Independence

Media in a healthy public sphere must be editorially independent of public and private interests. There are a few state-owned media outlets such as the publicly funded BBC, but in a capitalist system the majority of media are privately owned. But the system of regulation within which media operate should guarantee that neither politicians nor private interests in society can dictate or inappropriately distort to their advantage the content of the public sphere as a whole. Thus, the constitutional independence of the BBC from the UK government is guaranteed by legislation. It may be challenged, and an event such as the Andrew Gilligan affair may test the regulatory system to its limits, but the principle of independence was never questioned by any of the parties to that particular dispute, and any perceived threats were forensically covered by political journalists, effectively constraining the Blair government from extracting any revenge on the corporation post-Hutton. In an article defending both himself and the BBC against suggestions that they might be vulnerable to governmental pressure, leading presenter John Humphrys declared that 'independent journalism is our lifeblood. It is the main reason for the BBC's existence. It is by a mile the most important thing we do.'[4]

As for privately owned media, competition law in most advanced democracies provides for restrictions on how much of which media sectors a particular proprietor may control. Exceptionally high concentration of ownership, as enjoyed by Silvio Berlusconi in Italy, is generally regarded as a deviation from the normative standard. The freedom and independence of media are the subject of frequent challenge, but that they should exist, and that a government's duty is to defend them in the public interest, has been a taken-for-granted marker of a mature democracy for centuries. Where they are absent, or fragile, as in Putin's Russia, the integrity of democracy in that country is itself questioned.

This independence is the cornerstone of the public sphere's function of exercising the key Habermasian notion of *critical scrutiny* over political elites. To the extent that the media have a fourth estate or watchdog role, they must have sufficient political and economic independence to be able to monitor the activities of elite groups in government and other institutions, and to criticise where necessary. This does not preclude bias in the editorial stance of any given organisation, and indeed most privately owned newspapers and online media publicly declare an ideological preference. But a healthy public sphere does imply a diversity of bias, and a balance of critical opinion within a political culture.

Influence

Critical scrutiny is meaningless if it has no impact on the elites being criticised. Third in our criterion of fitness, therefore, is the extent to which the public sphere *matters* politically. To approach the Habermasian ideal, media should have a demonstrable *influence* on political decision-making, by enabling the formation and expression of public opinion, and thus collective pressure or action on government. This quality of political efficacy may be observed in the context of voting for parties at a general election, where individuals form their preferences on the basis of what they have encountered in their media about the issues around which competing parties ask for support. Elections are relatively rare, and in between times political efficacy may also be manifest in the construction of public opinion as measured by polling agencies. In this case, the 'collective action' of a public is the impact of the aggregated weight of their views on organisational political actors.[5]

To say that a fully functioning public sphere should have influence is merely to say that in a democracy political elites should reflect and be responsive to what publics articulate; that expressions of popular will and public opinion disseminated through media should, to the extent that they can be gauged, be capable of having real impacts on political institutions, of making a difference to people's lives. It does not imply or require the existence of fully-fledged democracy, although the debate and pressure for change it enables may be expected to lead to such an outcome, as occurred in Ukraine after the initial fraudulent round of presidential elections in 2004. The coffee-house cultures of early modern Europe which inspired Habermas's model of the public sphere predated the established, settled democratic systems of Britain, France and America, but were crucial elements in the revolutionary processes which produced democracy in those countries (Hartley 1996).

The evolution of a public sphere is, in other words, part of the process by which democracy evolves within nation-states. The public sphere can come into being without democracy (and the emergence of lively, diverse, critical media may well be a response to the absence of effective representative institutions) but democracy cannot come into being without a public sphere. When we come to look at the transnational level of political debate, this means that we do not require the existence of 'global democracy', or of democracy in any particular country, to be able to talk about the possibility of public spheres emerging to link communities or audiences whose members transcend the borders of the democratic (or indeed the authoritarian) nation-state. What we must show is the existence of *accessible, independent, influential* media of transnational or global reach, capable of disseminating relevant information from a plurality of voices, and impacting on global political processes.

The global public sphere – extending Habermas

In a recent essay addressing the role of the media in European politics, Erik Eriksen poses the question of 'how to conceptualise the public sphere in sites beyond the nation-state? Is it merely a communicative space or can it develop into a democratic sovereign – a collective entity able to act?' (2004). Applying that outlook to the world beyond the European Union leads to another question, perhaps more realistic given the difficulties of different countries acting collectively on any but a few issues of common concern. Can the global comunication system facilitate or enable the processes of public debate and political action which lead to the erosion of authoritarianism and the acceleration of democratisation? Does the transnational public sphere allow individuals and organisations to exercise effective communicative power on national, transnational and global decision-making bodies? For Eriksen and Weigard, the answer to these questions is a cautious yes. In the modern era, they note, 'deliberative and decision-making bodies emerge transnationally, in between societies and beyond the state' (2003: 250). With that in mind we can group the media that form what I will characterise as an emerging global*ised* public sphere into three categories: national public spheres, transnational satellite news and the internet.

National public spheres

In every nation-state, even in the globalised communication environment of the twenty-first century, the primary media of reportage, analysis and commentary continue to be, not least for pragmatic reasons of accessibility and literacy, locally produced print and broadcast outlets in indigenous languages: those newspapers, periodicals, TV and radio organisations which operate at local, regional and national levels within a country. National media (including local and regional) remain the dominant providers of information within nation-state boundaries, and will do so for some time to come.

Grouped not into one but many intersecting, overlapping spheres roughly corresponding to the terms 'broadsheet', 'mid-market' and 'popular', they can be further categorised into *static* and *flow* media, or *freeze-frame* and *real-time* media. The former are all those media that seek to tell us, in the traditional manner of journalism through the ages, what has happened (reportage), and what it means (analysis and commentary). These media are distinguished by the application of more or less rigorous editorial processes such as fact-checking, intended to ensure objectivity. The media that have done so most convincingly – the great media of record such as the *New York Times*, the *Financial Times*, or the news and current affairs output of the BBC – have been accepted as key sources of information on which people within nation-states form their views about politics. Their interventions into national public spheres may have resonance and influence beyond a country's borders (the whole world followed the *New York Times* difficulties at the time of the Jayson Blair scandal, for example), but their primary impact is national.

Flow or real-time media, on the other hand, comprise those 'always on', 24-hour news services on TV and radio which, though they punctuate their flows of journalistic information with freeze-frame bulletins, are distinguished by their capacity to cover events as they happen, and in many cases before anyone (including those in government) can know what they mean. Because of their instantaneity and 'live-ness' they are subject to relatively little editorial processing, and are marketed instead on the basis of their unique perspective on something that is happening, as it is being reported. The attacks on the World Trade Center were such an event, as was the siege and massacre of schoolchildren at Beslan in Russia in September 2004, and the invasions of Iraq and Afghanistan in 2003 and 2001 respectively.

Both types of public sphere institution – freeze-frame and flow media – have come to perform different functions in domestic political debate and opinion formation. The latter report events immediately and viscerally, making us feel part of the action to an extent never before possible, while limited in their ability to explain and interpret meanings. Those who watched the live coverage of the destruction of the World Trade Center will recall the confusion on the part of CNN and other broadcast news organisations as their reporters struggled to interpret the meaning of the events they were reporting. Even as the second airliner slammed into the North Tower, CNN anchors were not sure if they were dealing with an accident, an attack by a foreign government (one presenter speculated that the cylindrical shape which millions watched come into view and crash into the tower was a cruise missile), or terrorism by a non-state actor.

Freeze-frame media, on the other hand, lack the intimacy and adrenalin-fuelled excitement provided by real-time news on a day like 9/11, but allow us to pause and make sense of events, as journalists qualified for the task apply the time and resources required to analyse, interpret and comment on their meaning. These are the media of record, in the technical sense, operating on a different timescale and with different professional goals to produce definitive accounts of what has happened. These definitions, and the editorials, commentaries and analyses they feed, can have a major impact on the political process, articulating 'public opinion', advising and warning politicians to act in a certain way, advising the public to act in a certain way towards their politicians. Where flow media may generate immediate and barely considered political responses to events (see Chapter 11), media of record assess events, reflect on their meaning and recommend action. These recommendations may or may not have political impacts, depending on actors' perceptions of their importance (British politicians have taken careful note of 'What the *Sun* says', for example, especially at election times).

Transnational satellite news

The second tier of the globalised public sphere is that inhabited by the transnational broadcaster, on TV and radio: CNNI, BBC World, Star TV, Bloomberg, CNBC, Al Jazeera, Al Arabiya. These are mainly flow media as I have defined them above, crossing national boundaries and enveloping the public spheres of nation-states with 24-hour supplies of real-time information from around the world. These media do not form a network, and are relatively few in number. Rather, they are conveyor belts of always-on information, running in parallel. They are like plumbing pipes, to be turned on when we want news, and turned off again when we have had enough.

Satellite news organisations are large scale, structured and hierarchical like TV broadcasters everywhere, capital intensive and bearing relatively high costs of entry (though falling sharply in recent years, as Chapter 7 showed). Their brands – CNN, BBC, Al Jazeera – can be said to be global, although their services are often tailored to the political and cultural conditions prevailing in the regional markets where they operate (CNN Asia, CNBC Pakistan, etc.). Where domestic real-time news channels such as Fox News or BBC News 24 are produced locally for local audiences (although they may be accessible overseas on digital satellite), the transnational broadcasters set out to address audiences in more than one country or region. To the extent that they do so, they may impact on national public spheres, as when an Al Jazeera report on US troop abuses of Iraqi prisoners becomes the basis of a story for Fox News, or when Channel 4 News editors in the UK agonise over how much Arabsat footage of a hostage beheading can be transmitted on their bulletins.

The internet

A third tier of news media in this globalised environment – and the only truly *global* tier, in that it is accessible anywhere on the planet where the necessary skills and technological resources are in place – is formed by the internet. Comprising neither flow nor freeze-frame media but both, often within the same web site, online news and journalism may be conceived as a network, or membrane of connected information outlets, including the web sites of pre-Net print and broadcast media, and the millions of independent home pages and blogs that make up the blogo-sphere. While production of these outlets is rooted in the nation-states of the world, their outputs connect the communication environments, or public spheres of those locations, to the world wide web, which encloses everything within it in a network of independent voices. In visualising this membrane one might imagine something like an orange skin, dimpled and lumpy, its nodes connected to each other and to the transnational and national spheres.

A public sphere can be said to be globalised when the national, transnational and global tiers are connected to and can interact with one another. This three-dimensional public sphere comprises networks of commonly accessible media (24-hour news and TV; online news media; a handful of print organs) with transnational or global reach, which co-exist and constantly interact with local and national media within countries. It is segmented geographically (from global to local), politically (communities of like-minded bloggers debating with each other and opposing communities), and demographically. Anti-globalisation campaigners use the blogosphere to network and organise at both local and global levels, while transnational satellite media cover local events for heterogeneous audiences across the world. This network, or network of networks, enables a global/transnational debate to take place between individuals using the internet as a means of com-municating with their media, and with each other. Thus, the debate about the war in Iraq is informed by a rich variety of media of diverse viewpoints, and a global community of bloggers, online columnists and online portals.

The early (national) public sphere was bounded temporally and geographically to a particular country, with some external input woven into the national debate by foreign correspondents. The twenty-first century public sphere is much more complex and interconnected, and it is global, interacting with the local, and using NICTs to involve global publics in debating the key issues of the time (which are global in nature, such as the management of the environment and the war on terror). Politics has been globalised, and so has the means of debating it.

Evaluating the globalised public sphere

For these three tiers of media outlet to qualify as a globalised public sphere, and for that description to be more than a nice-sounding phrase, we must be able to show that it has the characteristics identified above, of *accessibility* (to transnational and global audiences, through reasonably equitable distribution of NICT hardware, linguistic and educational competence); *independence* (from public and private interests operating at the transnational and global level); and *influence* (on decision-making around international political issues). The pessimists are sceptical. In August 2004 the UK editor of the *Die Zeit* newspaper complained that 'the dream that the new information age would be one of greater enlightenment, of a rational discourse and greater participation has not come true'.[6] Before commenting on that assessment, let us take on board its identification of three important criteria against which a normative evaluation of the content of what the global media provide can be made.

- First is the degree of *enlightenment* it permits.
- Second is the extent of *rational* discourse, or reasoned debate, which those media allow, as for example between differing interpretations of the roots of the conflict in the Middle East, or competing theories of environmental change.
- And third is the extent of *participation* of global publics and their representatives in the output of those media. This latter depends on the *accessibility* and *interactivity* afforded those publics by media institutions, a variable which has technological as well as political and cultural determinants. It can be measured by the extent to which individuals and resource-poor groups are enabled to enter into the production of information through the media.

Democratisation and decentralisation

To these criteria of evaluation we should add two more, which have always been crucial to the analysis of the public sphere at the level of the nation-state: democratisation and decentralisation or, to put it another way, representativeness in respect of the structure of public feeling on issues, and freedom in respect of the state on the one hand, and commercial pressures on the other. The absence or presence of these qualities determines the degree of independence which individual media outlets possess, and the level of ideological (or editorial) diversity displayed by the global media system as a whole. This in turn determines the capacity of the public sphere for critical scrutiny of elites, considered at both the nation-state level and that of global politics as a whole.

Fortunately, the degree of democratisation and decentralisation which characterises a given 'public sphere', and is expressed in the degree of pluralism and diversity it supports, is a measurable quantity. Much has been written, for example, of the emerging Arab public sphere which has been a consequence of the rise of the Arab-language satellite news channels. As Chapter 7 showed, the rise of MBC after the first Gulf War, then of Al Jazeera from 1996, has produced a culture of political debate in the region which, for the first time in its history, recognises the legitimacy of diverse opinions about key issues affecting its people. Live talk shows such as Al Jazeera's *The Opposite Direction (Al Ittijah Al Muaakis)* have broken with the heavily restricted conventions of authoritarian political discourse by hosting debates on everything from women's rights in Islam to the corruption and competence of local regimes (Al Kasim 2005).

Chapter 7 located the origins of Al Jazeera's independence from state and commerce in the particular status of Qatar as an Arab state seeking to maintain its position against more powerful neighbours such as Saudi Arabia, while being allied to the United States, all in an environment of rising Islamic fundamentalism. Whatever the reason, and without prejudice to the possibility that the channel would in the future be privatised, Al Jazeera's independence introduced a 'culture of accountability' (Zayani, 2005: 2) into the Arab-language media, and expanded 'what people in the Arab world can talk about' (ibid.: 4). This is precisely the function of a public sphere, and a key contributing element of the 'ongoing process of democratisation' which has been unfolding in the Arab world since 9/11 (Da Lage 2005).

Huntington's *Clash of Civilisations* (1996) expressed scepticism that the globalisation of media, and news in particular, would lead to a corresponding globalisation of democratic and liberal values. What we see with Al Jazeera, and many other non-western media operating at the transnational and global level, is the adoption of precisely these values, at least as they define the relationship between journalism and local power elites.

As for decentralisation, the network structure of the world wide web and the blogosphere is decentralised by definition, not least because that is how the US military sought to guarantee its security when the internet was being constructed. Online media are not organised hierarchically, with a controlling centre of operations. Each online entity has a centre, clearly, but each is located somewhere on the world wide web of nodes and hubs, neither more nor less central to the global audience now using the web in their millions.

Critical scrutiny

Does international policy on matters such as global warming or debt relief change? Do unpopular and heavily criticised regimes reform? Do democratic revolutions happen? And if so, can any of these impacts be attributed to the activities of transnational and global media? If not (and direct cause–effect linkage will always be difficult to prove), can there nonetheless be seen to be a media contribution to the process of change?

The Abu Ghraib example is instructive here, presenting as it does an instance where global media coverage of a particular series of events (the torture of Iraqi prisoners by US soldiers) led to a US president's public display of contrition before an Arab audience, and to a more rigorous investigation and punishment of the abuses by the American legal system than might otherwise have been the case. In addition to facilitating global debate (a key characteristic of any public sphere), the global media network is an environment in which, like the normative public sphere, critical scrutiny of power is being exercised over political elites. The widespread criticism of the Bush administration around the scandal of Abu Ghraib, or of authoritarian Arab governments by Al Jazeera, typify the adversarial, watchdog journalism now constantly circulating around the global media system, impacting on national public debates like discursive tornadoes touching down on smooth midwestern plains. Naomi Sakr observes that before Al Jazeera's emergence in the mid-1990s, 'the vast majority of journalists employed by Arab-owned media were either working for government-controlled broadcasting monopolies or for newspapers closely allied to governments or political interest groups' (2005c: 145). The critical, pluralistic tradition of liberal western journalism had been embraced by Al Jazeera and others as the model to follow.

The impacts of this scrutiny are unpredictable, as we shall see, but that there are impacts, even if only on the need for governments and ruling elites to be seen to respond, is beyond dispute. Al Jazeera has been bombed by the Americans, banned by the Saudis, rubbished by both the Palestinians and the Israelis, and censored by just about every state in the Middle East at one time or another, accused among other things of 'sowing seeds of dissent and disintegration in Arab communities' (Ayish 2005: 108).[7] Overall, the extent and breadth of the hostility displayed towards Al Jazeera is the best evidence one could cite that the channel exerts a significant, indeed unique critical scrutiny and has become, as a consequence, a key foundation of an increasingly robust Arab public sphere.

The adversarial, often aggressive media which comprise globalised news culture can be compared in their elite-critical posture to the pamphleteers and essayists of the early modern era. The bloggers and online journalists form a cyber-press, a virtual coffee house culture which, though it transcends nation-state borders, can easily be compared to the image conjured up by Habermas of engaged, literate readers debating the current issues of the day and forming opinions. These media are more difficult to censor than those of the past, and can thus be argued to have an enhanced capacity for critical scrutiny of elites.

As the previous chapter discussed, this scrutiny has been turned against the established 'liberal' media in ways which have generated what Todd Gitlin describes as a sense of 'crisis'.[8] Alternative media though they certainly are, blogs are not necessarily left of the mainstream in terms of their political orientation. On the contrary, the most visible and effective users of the blogosphere, at least in its early years, have been those commentators – academic, journalistic and activist – often described as 'neo-conservative'. Individuals such as Andrew Sullivan, best known for his mix of conservative (i.e., generally pro-Republican) party politics, and progressive sexual and social politics, present themselves as dissenters against mainstream media culture, and what Sullivan himself describes as 'the suffocating liberalism of the pseudo-objective networks'.[9] More recently, left-wing commentators have become more visible, to the extent that 'the range of voices in the blogosphere suggests that dissatisfaction with mainstream media is no longer an exclusive entitlement of the right'.[10] The public humiliation of US senator Trent Lott after he made racist remarks in 2003 was facilitated by left-wing bloggers.

Ideological predisposition aside, Alistair Alexander observes that the internet has given voice to 'dissent that would previously have gone unheard. And for [many] the diversity of information highlighted the narrow priorities of the main-stream news agenda' (2004: 278). This has resulted in 'an emerging global pattern of people using the web to find alternative news sources to their traditional media channels . . . web users can now compare their local news agenda to virtually anywhere on the planet.'

Can, certainly, but do they? And if they do, how can they be sure that the vast range of alternative news sources available to them on the web is reliable, given that there is generally conceded to be 'a serious problem of quality control in the increasingly powerful blogging world'.[11] That there is a problem of reliability in any medium that is free from the traditional codes, conventions and constraints of established professional journalism goes without saying, although there is evidence that it is exaggerated, not least by supporters of the 'old' media which the blogosphere is often perceived to threaten. As we have seen, one of the factors pushing the blogosphere into the domain of the mainstream media has been the propensity of bloggers to blow the whistle on the errors – intentional or otherwise – of print and broadcast journalists. Not just the powerful in politics, but the established media have increasingly found their status and output being challenged and contested by this culture, as when CBS had to retract a story alleging that George W. Bush had dodged the draft, or when Fox News had to retract a piece accusing John Kerry of 'metrosexuality', or when blogger Rony Abovitz forced the resignation of a CNN executive. In all these cases (and there have been many more) the enhanced critical scrutiny of elites, be they in politics or the established media, provided by the global public sphere is evident.

Transnational media and national identity

One marker of the existence of a public sphere is the extent to which the media which comprise it facilitate the formation of a sense of *collective identity* amongst its users, whether founded on ethnic, ideological, or lifestyle-oriented elements. The post-Stonewall gay community, for example, has its identity reinforced and serviced by a proliferation of lifestyle and consumer magazines. There is, in this sense, a 'gay' public sphere, which is a subset of the leisure and lifestyle media sphere, and of the national public sphere more broadly. Drawing on Benedict Anderson's assertion of the role of media in the building of 'imagined communities' (1982), we can ask whether, despite the obvious linguistic, cultural and other divisions that exist among the world's population, 'transnational' or 'global' can be a basis of a unifying collective identity, or imagined community, and even of some kind of global governance. Can there be international consensus on issues such as the environment or terrorism, the formation of which might be facilitated by a global public sphere?

This question has already been asked in the context of Europeanisation, and the possibilities for a common media space linking the countries of the European Union. Here the issue is of more than academic interest, since the European Union does in fact have a government with European-wide powers that often take priority over national governments. Although this government is made up of sovereign, democratic nation-states with rights of veto and opt-out in a variety of areas, it is mandated to develop and enact legislation applicable across EU territory. In doing so, European intellectuals argue, it needs the support of a public sphere, or common media space, within which relevant information can be made available and where policy matters can be discussed.

There is general agreement that such a space has not yet evolved in Europe, largely because of the constraints associated with linguistic and cultural variation, and the strong, competing national identities which often obstruct the formation of a 'European' identity. The majority of European countries are united in their adherence to the EU model of shared political, economic and security goals but are distinct, if not necessarily divided, in their linguistic and cultural profiles. The obvious practicality of using a common lingua franca for EU business – English, since this is the language most Europeans understand well enough to use in cross-border communication – is rejected in favour of a politically correct and inefficient multilingualism. The national identities of the French and others constrain the evolution of a European public sphere which can replicate at the continental level the structures of public debate within nation-states.

Globally, however, there is less resistance to the adoption of English as a lingua franca. More of the world's people speak Mandarin or Spanish as their first language than English, but the latter's ascendancy, however imperialistic that process may be judged to have been, is now a fact of global cultural life which those of the world's population who wish to communicate across borders must accept. This is the main reason news brands such as CNN and the BBC can be viewed as genuinely global in their reach, acting as platforms for global conversations. As with air traffic control, there *is* a common language of global communication, to a greater extent than in the European context. Whether this gives rise to a form of global identity in the future remains to be seen, but it is probably a prerequisite of any such development.

By no means all the transnational and global media use English, however. Thomas Friedman notes that two-thirds of all online media use languages other than English (2005). In the Middle East, it is the rise of Arab-language media which has been the most noteworthy feature of the NICT revolution in recent times. And in so far as there is an Arab national identity, it appears to be being facilitated and strengthened by the increased availability of transnational media. In the words of one Arab commentator, 'Arab satellites are creating the infrastructure for the dream of Arab unity'.[12] Al Jazeera's Faisal Al-Kasim asserts that his and other transnational Arab-language outlets are 'reviving pan-Arabism and pan-Islamism by raising Arab self-consciousness, sense of identity, and feelings of solidarity'.[13] For Mohamed El Oifi, 'Arab nationalism is very prominent as a unifying sentiment on [Al Jazeera]' (2005: 72).

From imagined community to democratic empowerment

As already noted, the liveliest, most irreverent and diverse media environment imaginable would mean little if it had no discernible impact on the decisions of governments and rulers. Authoritarian governments have made no pretence of taking notice of critical media content in their decision-making processes, but a defining feature of democratic government is its acceptance of free and independent media – a fourth estate – scrutinising and legitimising power. No democratic government exists which did not arise from the cut and thrust of political debate, as mediated through newspapers, periodicals, radio and TV. And if this is true of nation-states seen in isolation, can it be argued that an emerging globalised public sphere may facilitate global democratisation? And what would global democratisation look like, in the Middle East for example?

For Habermas, the public sphere should be considered as 'a power-free space outside of the state', in which 'equal citizens assemble into a public and set their own agenda through open communication . . . this public sphere is power-free, secular and rational' (Eriksen and Weigard 2003: 179). This is clearly too limiting to accommodate a channel such as Al Jazeera, which disseminates information heavily infused with Islamic religiosity and is not necessarily rational (as in its assertions of a Zionist conspiracy behind 9/11) to audiences that are not 'global' citizens in the liberal democratic sense. Muhammad Ayish attacks Al Jazeera for its 'failure to deliver rational, sensible, and balanced debates that represent existing intellectual and political trends in the Arab world' (2005: 107). Democracy, however, and a democratic public sphere in the full sense of the term, means giving voice not just to those whom one finds personally convenient or appealing, but to the other side as well, and if that means a programme such as *The Opposite Direction* giving airtime to veiled women defending Islam's record on women's rights, so be it. In the end, it will be for Arab women to sort out the 'rationality' of their submission to this particular religious law. At least they are visible, however, on a channel which, for all that it is anti-American and anti-western in its editorial policy, has pioneered in the Middle East context 'the notion of a free marketplace of ideas, providing for critical, free and balanced exchanges of information between politically diverse actors' (ibid.).[14]

Another qualification which can be made of the Arab public sphere is that some of the parties seeking to be heard within it freely concede that were they to win a democratic election, the first thing they would do is ban democratic elections. This is one of the uncomfortable paradoxes of the globalisation of the public sphere, especially as the process evolves in the Middle East. It is difficult to see what can be done to resolve it, beyond seeking to support those Arabs – 'civilists', as they describe themselves, committed to separation of church and state – who would choose not to elect parties who would outlaw elections. Encouragingly, since 9/11 the trends in the Middle East appear to be towards forms of representative democracy, wherever one looks from Iraq to Iran, Lebanon to Palestine, Syria and Saudi Arabia (see next chapter). What remains unclear is the sustainability and ultimate destination of these movements.

That is less important to the present discussion, however, than the fact that just as the print media of early modern Europe shaped the formation of national identities within states, transnational Arab-language media are performing the normative public sphere function of creating a common space for knowledge formation and debate in political environments where such debate was hitherto prohibited or suppressed. If the Habermasian ideal public sphere cannot exist where democratic institutions are absent or undeveloped, it is not unreasonable to predict that the emergence of the latter will be assisted rather than constrained by the existence of the embryonic public sphere made up of Al Jazeera and other independent Middle East media. For some regional observers, the new generation of Arab-language media have played a greater role in creating the conditions for democratisation in the Middle East than have organised political movements. In the words of Al Jazeera's managing director, the channel 'has introduced a new culture and a new paradigm into the Arab world . . . that rest upon the free exercise of journalism and public affairs broadcasting'.[15] Writing in *Foreign Affairs*, Marc Lynch has welcomed Al Jazeera and its Arab-language competitors as 'a genuinely new kind of Arab public sphere', bringing together within a common media space disparate views, and forming 'an alternative location of vibrant and open political debate' (2003).[16] That such a space now exists in the Middle East is a significant evolution in the political culture of the region, even if fully democratic polities are still some way off.

Accessibility and interactivity

Notwithstanding the exponential increase in publicly accessible information which the internet has made possible, for many years in the 1990s critical theorists were predicting that it would contribute not to human progress, but to the consolidation of the divide between the haves and the have-nots, between the information-rich and information-poor. The internet would bring with it, as had been predicted with satellite TV before it, a digital divide rather than democratisation. This pre-diction has been proven wrong. Chapter 7 described the growth of real-time news in India, the Middle East and other areas of the developing world as costs of entry to satellite TV production fall. As with satellite news, so too with online journalism. Confounding pessimistic forecasts, the growth of online media has been pronounced in many parts of the developing world, where geographical distance and low levels of conventional literacy may be a handicap to the introduction of more traditional media.

The cultural pessimist disputes that the internet can solve the problems of global socio-economic development, and on its own it clearly cannot. But it is simply untrue to argue that the information gap is widening because of the internet. Armand Mattelart cites figures showing that in India, as of 2001, there were only 26 million phone lines servicing a population of one billion. At that time internet penetration had reached only 0.2 per cent (Mattelart 2003: 148). As this book went to press, India's population was officially estimated at 1.2 billion, of whom about 5 per cent (upwards of 50 million) were regular users of the internet. Next door in China were several hundred million more net users. One might ask why China has progressed so much faster in this respect, and find answers in the competence and commitment of local governments, but it is clear that both countries, account-ing between them for nearly half of the world's population, are in the vanguard of the global internet explosion.

For one observer, writing about *aljazeera.net* in particular, but nicely summarising the difference between the satellite news channel and the online version:

> The website goes beyond the television channel; its public is no longer regional. It is now accessible in the most remote locations worldwide, and those who choose to visit the site can react instantaneously to the posted messages.
>
> (Awad 2005: 84)

As a result, argue Hamilton and Jenner:

> the audience – now fragmented and active – is far better able to choose and even shape the news . . . Consumers of internet news are taking on functions once the province of editors. Consumers now increasingly select the international news that they want to read, view, or listen to.
>
> (Hamilton and Jenner 2003: 132, 135)

Web sites allow self-editing and customising of news consumption, and globalise the audience to an extent never before seen. As of August 2004, 45 per cent of the UK *Guardian*'s 9.6 million regular users were resident in the US. As one observer puts it:

> today's on-line readers are part of an experience that goes way beyond the passivity of reclining in your easy chair to read the weekend book review. They have more control over content, access to a wider range of opinions, and in many cases contribute themselves.[17]

The internet, like no other communication medium, allows the formation of 'diverse networks of opinion, and active participation' by non-professional, non-proprietorial voices. In the words of the dean of journalism at the University of California, 'the Roman Empire that was mass media is breaking up, and we are entering an almost feudal period where there will be many more centres of power and influence.'[18]

To its advocates, one great strength of the blogosphere is the support it gives to a culture of 'dialogue and fairness'. In addition to its potential for checking and monitoring the performance of the traditional news media, the blogosphere encourages users to cross-reference and access competing positions on current debate. It promotes diversity, adding to the pluralising impact of existing media. As Andrew Sullivan argues, there has been a 'fracturing of the media in which cable, the internet and talk radio have given every constituency its own echo chamber'.[19] Elsewhere, he has argued that 'this [the blogosphere] is democratic journalism at its purest. Eventually, you can envision a world in which most successful writers will use this medium as a form of self-declared independence'.[20] The rise of the blogosphere represents 'a publishing revolution more profound than anything since the printing press'. Glenn Reynolds, using language of relevance to this chapter, describes the blogosphere as 'very much like the network of European coffee shops in the eighteenth century'.[21]

Supporters of this optimistic assessment point to the rise of 'citizen journalism', as contained on a site such as *ohmynews.com*, 'where every citizen is a reporter', or *backfence.com*, established in San Francisco in May 2005 as a platform for ordinary people to write their own news (see previous chapter). Is so-called 'citizen journalism' a licence for character assassination, however, as was also suggested in Chapter 8? Yes and no. When blogs spread false information, they become mere rumour-mongers. When their stories are true, they disrupt and subvert elite authority in significant ways, through their impact on mainstream media and public perceptions. The Clinton–Lewinsky scandal proved that in 1998 and 1999, and there have been many more examples since. Both the left and right of the political spectrum have used the blogosphere to expose what they view as unacceptable speech or behaviour. According to Rony Abovitz, who disseminated the allegations about CNN executive Eason Jordan and forced a retraction:

> This is not a left- or right-wing phenomenon. The story is much, much bigger than [one individual]. This is John Lennon's Power to the People, but turbo-charged and amplified. The people want a voice, and now they really have it. Their own voice, unedited, and unfiltered.[22]

Conclusion

The question, then, is not 'Is there a global public sphere?', but 'what kind of public sphere is emerging at the global level?' I have argued in this chapter that the *globalised public sphere* of the twenty-first century is real, both in terms of the normative standards of the Habermasian tradition, and by its facilitation of transnational and global debate, especially in the Middle East, where Arab observers are agreed that satellite television and other media have established a new culture of political debate characterised by unprecedented diversity, independence and critical scrutiny of local elites hitherto protected from it.

Although the globalisation of the public sphere has clearly started, in the Middle East and elsewhere, further progress down this road, like the 'Europeanisation' of the EU's communication environment referred to earlier, is a process that depends on three elements:

- the continuing availability and expansion of free and independent transnational/global media;
- the global adoption of a common language of communication (easier at the global level than at the European, as we have seen, where resistance to cultural homogenisation is a major structural constraint – at the global level, there clearly has to be a common lingua franca, if there is to be any commmunication at all);
- the continuing emergence of political issues which have global resonance.

Since 9/11 the war on terror has provided just such an issue, linking the world in common contemplation of the Middle East conflict, the future of Iraq, religious fundamentalism, multiculturalism and a number of other issues which have no obvious left–right division, nor are restricted to one country (although each country has its own foci and priorities, shaped by local conditions). 9/11 has, in this sense, accelerated the evolution of the globalised public sphere.

Looking beyond the war on terror and the 'clash of civilisations' which some see as underpinning it, environmental change is another issue of global resonance which cannot be avoided, as are the consequences of global networks for the dissemination of viruses (biological or computer-based) and the migration of peoples. World poverty has long been an issue of concern for many, but is today part of the mainstream political agenda, with pop stars, popes and presidents engaging in public debate about issues such as famine in Africa. While no one can say, on the basis of past form, that any of these issues is more likely to be resolved than they were before the invention of satellite and internet technologies, it is the case that for the first time in human history the communicative infrastructure is in place for genuinely global resolutions to the problems that afflict the planet as a whole; not resolutions imposed by one imperial power or another, but by governments compelled by democratic institutions to reflect the views of their people, formed and articulated through a globalised public sphere.

Although this emerging system is different in many ways from the coffee-house cultures of early modern Europe which inspired the normative public sphere of the Habermasian ideal type, its impact on global democracy may be comparably profound. Which is to say that while these transnational and global media cannot of themselves *create* democracy in the regions where they impact, they are part of the conditions that need to exist for democratic political cultures to come into being. And just as there are no guarantees that cultural globalisation will solve famine in Africa or foment world peace, the heightened visibility of such issues in the public spheres of advanced capitalist societies renders the political costs for democratically accountable governments of doing nothing, and being seen to do nothing, much higher than they were previously.

There are serious limitations on the fitness for purpose of the globalised public sphere, to do with access, the quality of information, and the capacity of the public to absorb ever-increasing amounts of information. But these are not new issues to the current period, and should not be cited to deny the great advances in the information environment confronted by the majority of people. Media assets have never been equally distributed. Since the invention of print their distribution has been getting steadily more equitable, through a gradual extension of media literacy and usage to broader and broader swathes of the population, culminating in the current expansion of satellite and computer-based media. Paul Starr observes that as late as 1790 in the United States, the 'political reading public' comprised only 5 per cent of the population (2004: 39). Although there are still billions of individuals excluded from communicative resources, or with limited access to them, their numbers are falling rapidly.

As a consequence, all over the world, from China and India to Iran and Saudi Arabia, we are witnessing a qualitative leap forward in the capacity of journalistic media to facilitate and reinforce those communicative processes which are at the heart of democratisation. Through the broadcasting of phone-ins and e-mails to CNN and BBC World, for example, viewers from around the world are enabled to comment on the issues raised in the news, and to engage in dialogue. The internet, and the blogosphere in particular, nurtures thousands of expert and authoritative voices, and millions more who are neither expert nor authoritative, but still have an unprecedented capacity to speak, all expressing their opinions on the entire range of topics occupying global decision-makers and publics at any given time. It is the electronic analogue of the coffee houses and salons of early modern Europe, except that it is immeasurably larger in scale, and much more accessible. One does not have to be an educated, propertied, white gentleman to have access to the internet, either as a reader or a speaker.

This leads to a potential cacophony of voices, to the 'Babel-speak' observed by Paul Virilio (1997), which has to be sifted and subjected to quality control. But the seriousness with which individual speakers are taken by the blogosphere and internet users, and then by print and broadcast media within national public spheres, is a factor not of class privilege or status, or of which university the speaker attended, but of the quality of their speech. Well-written, perceptive, regularly produced blogs such as those of Andrew Sullivan or the Baghdad Blogger become influential and widely read, straddling the online and printed worlds. Ignorant rants, unsubstantiated propaganda, and boring or irrelevant posts usually disappear into the hidden reaches of the virtual universe. They may perform a valuable psychotherapeutic function as an online diary for their authors, or satisfy the reasonable desire to express a view in public, but have little impact on anyone else.

The globalised public sphere is a highly competitive environment, where criteria of entry and acceptance tend to erode the elitism of the ideal normative model, and where debate is extensive. To dispute the rationality of its content, or to dismiss its democratic impact, is to apply the same criteria of evaluation which defines tabloid journalism as less worthy than broadsheet, or daytime talk shows about domestic violence as less worthy than men in suits discussing economics. It is also to assume that the founding media of the early public sphere – the newspapers and periodicals of early modern Europe – never contained fallacious, tendentious or ignorant opinions. Are the exaggerations and rants of a Matt Drudge really more heinous than the 1930s columns of Walter Winchell, or the fabrications and plagiarisms indulged in by Jayson Blair and Stephen Glass? The globalised public sphere is crowded and noisy, to be sure, and in an era of declining print circulations, the journalists of the old media may find in that chaos an enhanced role as gate-keepers and sense-makers.

Part IV

The consequences of cultural chaos

10 Global news culture and authoritarianism

In 1993 the chairman of News Corp, Rupert Murdoch, declared that

> advances in the technology of telecommunications have proved an unambiguous threat to totalitarian regimes everywhere. Fax machines [then cutting edge technology, now quaintly old-fashioned] enable dissidents to by-pass state controlled print media; direct dial telephones [and even more so today, cell phones] make it difficult for a state to control interpersonal voice communications; and satellite broadcasting makes it possible for information-hungry societies to bypass state-controlled television channels. The Bosnian Serbs cannot hide their atrocities from the probing eyes of BBC, CNN and Sky News cameras . . . the extraordinary living standards provided by free-enterprise capitalism cannot be kept secret.
>
> (cited in Atkins 2002: 49)

A confident statement of technology's democratising potential by the head of one of the world's leading media organisations, if undermined somewhat by the experience of Murdoch's own TV services in China, which have been obliged to accept political constraints on the content of news, including removing the BBC from its Star package. If the emerging globalised public sphere would appear to increase the scope for mass participation in media production, enhanced critical scrutiny of political elites, public debate and thus for democratisation of societies such as China, is there evidence that such trends are actually under way? Murdoch's 1993 speech was made in the triumphalist afterglow produced by the fall of the Berlin Wall and the dissolution of the Soviet Union, events in which the media clearly played a role. But was he overstating the threat posed by NICTs to authoritarian societies?

NICTs and the fall of the Soviets

As a young media sociologist studying in Moscow in the late 1980s, I observed what I described then as 'the potentially dislocating effects of a global information revolution' on the USSR (McNair 1989: 345). In the era before the internet, when e-mail was in its infancy and satellite TV far from being a mass medium, the increasingly leaky information environment of the USSR was having profound consequences for the Soviet Communist Party (CPSU), eroding its efforts to maintain a monopoly on news and commentary and slowly undermining the ideological basis of its despotic rule. The campaigns for openness (*glasnost*) and restructuring (*perestroika*) inaugurated by Mikhail Gorbachev in the mid-1980s were a response not least to the reality of increasingly porous Soviet borders, and the eroding capacity of the Soviet state to police information coming in and out of the country.

Gorbachev's policy response was to sanction the dissemination of information within the USSR which was critical, on the one hand, of the current performance of the Soviet economy, and on the other, of the founding myths of Soviet society. This was unprecedented in the history of Marxism-Leninism, and set in motion an unpredictable series of events which exemplify cultural chaos as I have defined it in this book. Up until 1985 or thereabouts, the official ideologues of the Soviet Union presented the country to its inhabitants as the best of all possible worlds. In the global competition with capitalism, and the USA in particular, the Soviet Union was always portrayed as the superior system, with lower unemployment, better health services and education, cheaper transport and housing, and a more humane culture in which, for example, crime was virtually unknown. In relation to the founding myth of Bolshevism and its evolution, the Soviet people were presented with an image of Vladimir Lenin as a beneficent, all-knowing figure, endowed with superhuman powers. An abiding memory of my time in the country was finding a comic book for children, in which Lenin appeared as a Santa Claus-like figure, bestowing gifts and good cheer on the children gathered around him with awe-struck expressions on their faces. The Soviet communists, of course, did not recognise Christmas, nor encourage its celebration. Instead, they secularised it, with the founder of the Soviet state occupying the Father Christmas role. The figure whose stuffed, waxed body lay in the Mausoleum in Red Square had become a divine icon; a god, literally, with precisely the same ideological function as the more familiar gods of the great religions.

Gorbachev rejected this deification, sensing that it had become untenable in the era of fax, VCR and e-mail. Tentatively at first, then with gathering boldness, the CPSU reformers encouraged a more accurate, and thus more critical history of the Soviet Union to emerge, including hints at the true scale of the horrors inflicted on its people by Lenin's successor, Stalin. The historian Roy Medvedev, for example, in an interview for the mould-breaking journal *Argumenty i Fakti* published in 1989 estimated that, taking into account the numbers of those shot, imprisoned, resettled, or who died of hunger during the famines of the 1930s caused by Stalin's collectivisation policy, the overall number of victims of Stalinism reaches approximately 40 million people.[1] In the decades before *glasnost* such claims had been dismissed by the Soviet communists as western propaganda, a strategy which appeared to work in so far as the Soviet population showed no signs of losing patience with the party which had permitted such a holocaust to occur. After 1989, though, the mere fact of their circulation in legal form within the country reinforced their credibility, and contributed to a broader process of demystification of popular belief in the myths of Soviet history. Stalin was exposed as a criminal, and his successors as, if not as murderous as he, at the very least complicit in his brutality. Although Nikita Kruschev's efforts at reform in the years after Stalin's death were recognised in the *glasnost*-era Soviet Union (not least because Gorbachev wished to present his own party with a precedent for the *perestroika* and *glasnost* policies), the regimes of Brezhnev, Andropov and Chernenko were increasingly exposed as corrupt and incompetent, and the country as requiring radical restructuring if it was to fulfil its socialist potential.

Criticism of the past and the present were part of the same strategy of stripping away the official myths of Soviet reality in order, or so Gorbachev hoped, to put state socialism back on the correct path. *Glasnost* and *perestroika* were, respectively, the informational and organisational components of an attempt at orderly renewal of the Soviet system. Increased openness would increase the flows of creative, constructive energy coming in and out of the Soviet system. Gorbachev combined this strategy for internal reform with a sophisticated source strategy for improving the USSR's image overseas. In the era of the Great Communicator (Ronald Reagan) and the Iron Lady (Margaret Thatcher), Gorbachev became the Man We Can Do Business With, the first Soviet leader to understand and apply the lessons of the information age to domestic and foreign policy.

I have previously suggested that there is a sense in which public relations can be said to have ended the Cold War (McNair 2003b). Gorbachev's sophisticated and effective use of political communication techniques such as news conferences and image management transformed the international political environment in the late 1980s. The decade began with US presidential talk of an Evil Empire, the escalation of the nuclear arms race with the introduction of Cruise missiles and other provocative new weapons of mass destruction into western Europe, the Korean airlines disaster and the Soviet occupation of Afghanistan. Peace movements of unprecedented size developed throughout the advanced capitalist world because people of all political views genuinely feared that nuclear war was becoming more likely. By the end of the 1980s, however, Gorbachev's ability to charm global audiences with slick public relations (founded on plain speaking and what was, by Soviet standards, disarming honesty), combined with real changes in policy, had generated an environment in which George Bush senior could declare that the Cold War was over. The practical implementations of this transformation were seen in the first Gulf War, when the American-led invasion of Kuwait and Iraq was supported by the Soviet Union, and a New World Order appeared to have come into existence.

These were the successes of Gorbachev's information-led reforms, if seen from the perspective of humanity as a whole, since they meant the end of the post-Second World War logjam in global development, and the beginning of the ideological dissolution and realignment described in Chapter 5. Without them the Berlin Wall would not have come down when it did, and the velvet revolutions, had they occurred at all, might have been much less velvety. At home, however, within the borders of the USSR itself, the reform process was more chaotic, shaped by unforeseen events with unintended consequences.

In late April 1986, just as *glasnost* was getting going, the nuclear reactor at Chernobyl in the Ukraine exploded, showering the surrounding towns with lethal radiation and contaminating much of Western Europe for decades to come. The incident contributed substantially to the ongoing demystification of the myths of Soviet society, with its stark demonstration of the inferiority of its technological base. At Chernobyl the Soviet nuclear industry was revealed, at precisely the time when the environment was becoming a global political issue, to be dangerously unsafe. The accident also exposed the callousness of pre-Gorbachev information policy, the policy of 'say nothing, but if you must say something, say as little as possible', which briefly reasserted itself after the explosion.[2]

During the international outrage provoked by the Korean Airlines disaster in 1983 the Soviet state had adopted a policy first of denial, then of strict control of information which was, in any case, widely perceived to be lacking in credibility (McNair 1988). This approach, which Gorbachev had observed with impatience from his senior, but still subordinate position within the Soviet Politburo, contributed substantially to the ease with which it was possible for Ronald Reagan to cite KAL 007 as evidence of Soviet 'barbarism', and to mobilise international support for his definition of the USSR as a 'terrorist' state, as if the shooting down had been an intentional act of mass murder. The public relations disaster of KAL 007 (which substantially eased the obstacles in the path to Reagan's escalation of the nuclear arms race) was noted by Gorbachev and his reformist allies, and influenced their adoption of *glasnost* as an alternative information policy when he came to power.

Chernobyl, however, saw a temporary reassertion of the old style of information control, with the disaster reported in a sparse two-line statement, followed by a news blackout and surreal May Day coverage on the state TV news programme of happy Soviets dancing on the banks of the Dnieper (meaning, in the read-between-the-lines language of old-style Soviet media – Chernobyl is no big deal, despite what you might be hearing on the rumour mill). Chernobyl *was* a big deal, of course, a fact which by the 1980s could not be hidden even by the most authoritarian of media control regimes. Chernobyl was a transnational disaster, polluting nearby countries as much as the immediate vicinity of the reactor. I was living in Moscow throughout the crisis and witnessed the circulation of rumours, many of them started by the large corps of western correspondents who had set up in the city to exploit Gorbachev's openness. There were tourists, and students like me, and Finnish businessmen, all providing information about what was really going on. The BBC World Service was available to many Soviets, and CNN was up and running. Against this background of information leakiness, with much of the information in circulation wrong or exaggerated (British TV news, for example, at one point reported as credible the rumour that mass graves containing thousands of bodies had been dug in the countryside around Chernobyl), the Soviet government had to open up. TV news began to cover the rescue operation at the site, much as a western news organisation would. Accurate information about the degree of risk was provided. The scale of the disaster was conceded.

Gorbachev later stated that he had wanted to adopt such an approach all along, but that at this point in 1986 he was insufficiently secure in power to override more conservative elements who preferred the old ways. Indeed, and for all that it was a hugely destructive event, the Chernobyl incident performed a service for the reform process in so far as it provided, by example of how *not* to handle official information, the rationale for a degree of information openness which would not otherwise have occurred at that time.

After Chernobyl *glasnost* was consolidated. Rather than generate the communication environment for a renewal of socialism, however, as Gorbachev had hoped, the expanding, accelerating flow of information steadily eroded the CPSU's hegemonic control over the Soviet people. The possibilities for a peaceful transition to some form of democratic socialism were complicated by ethnic unrest (suppressed for decades, it now came violently to the surface in places like Nagorno-Karabakh and Georgia) and conservative reaction, culminating in the failed coup of August 1991 which sounded the death knell of the Soviet state. In a mere six years, seven decades of Soviet statehood were swept away, to be replaced with a mix of democratic, semi-democratic and authoritarian states in various stages of transition.

Around the same time the authoritarian Yugoslav state also collapsed, with tragic consequences for the people of Sarajevo, Srebrenica and elsewhere. Once-solid Soviet allies such as East Germany and Bulgaria abandoned state socialism. In Hungary, what Maria Heller calls the 'restricted public sphere' of the era of Soviet control had already given way by the late 1980s to an 'extremely open and liberated domain of public discussion' (2004: 9). A kind of cultural chaos ensued, 'a sudden explosion of rather violent and intolerant debates, where all former taboo questions burst into the public discussion'. In the end, a democratic political culture and associated institutions became established.

The precise role of the media in these processes has not been quantified. John Downing notes that while De Sola Pool and others have assumed the 'inherently liberatory character' of communication, there have been 'few systematic attempts to try to collate detailed evidence for the importance of communication in the dissolution of Soviet power' (Downing 1996: 89). Peter Gross has argued, in the context of the post-Warsaw Pact environment in Central and Eastern Europe, that 'there are no models or theories to explain how the media change in the transition from an authoritarian regime to a democratic one, and what or how they contribute to these processes' (2002: xi). There is a theory of the public sphere, as we have seen, but it is in the chaotic nature of communication processes that no directly linear cause-and-effect relationships between media content and political outcomes can be proven. No experiment can isolate the effects of communication as against the effects of all the other factors which come into play. No experiment can determine what might have happened to the Soviet Union had Gorbachev, or *glasnost*, never happened. All we can say for sure is that they did happen, and that flows of diverse and independent communication expanded and accelerated at the same time as, by various routes, more or less peaceful, more or less smoothly, democracies came to the USSR and most of its allies. There are a handful of former Soviet states, such as Belarus and Uzbekistan, which continue to be dominated by authoritarian governments, and events in Andizhan in May 2005 demonstrated that, for some, democracy may not be along for a while. For the most part, however, from the

Baltic countries to the Caucasus, pressure for democratisation has followed on from media liberalisation and the easing of totalitarian controls on communication. Observing the popular uprising which removed the ruling elite of Kyrgyzstan in April 2005, the *New York Times* suggested that here, as in some other authoritarian states, tolerance for independent news outlets had provided 'the nuclei around which dissatisfaction crystallised and grew'.[3] The remainder of this chapter asks if the same processes of dissolution are currently underway in the small number of remaining socialist states such as China and Cuba and, more urgently in the context of global jihad, the authoritarian states of the Middle East.

Cultural chaos and the decline of authoritarianism

The theory of the public sphere elaborated in Chapter 9 allocates to a free and independent media the function of facilitating public political debate and the formation of civil society, leading to pluralism, democratic elections and the rest. The experience of post-1989 Europe indicates that this function can be effective. What of the current period, in which the majority of authoritarian regimes under pressure are not communist but Islamic?

There is clearly a correlation between the evolution of NICTs and the decline of authoritarianism across the world. Chapter 4 noted that the twentieth century saw an unprecedented growth of democratic institutions, and that in many of those societies currently defined as authoritarian the trends appear to be in the direction of democratisation. After the fall of the Taliban in Afghanistan, and Saddam Hussein in Iraq, only about 20 per cent of the world's states can any longer be classified as authoritarian or totalitarian (a reduction of 150 per cent since 1980), with most of these clustered in the Middle East and Asia. In the few remaining socialist states it seems likely, as the impact of the collapse of Marxism-Leninism as a viable ideological system works its way through sclerotic communist elites, that democratic systems will eventually emerge. In Cuba, the continuing hold on power of a charismatic leader appears to be the main factor holding a stagnant and corrupt central economy together. China, while embracing a hyperactive market economic system, will persist for some years yet in its adherence to a nominally socialist path, although the introduction of NICTs into the country is radically altering the terms and conditions of Communist Party rule. North Korea is stuck in an absurd and increasingly anachronistic parody of socialism.

In January 2005 free elections were held in Iraq for the first time since the demise of the pre-Baathist monarchy 50 years before, with turnout recorded at 58 per cent. The December 2005 elections recorded a turnout of 80 per cent. At the time of writing, it remains to be seen if those elections, and by extension the 2003 invasion of Iraq which made them possible, will enable the establishment of a stable democracy in the country, as well as encouraging democratisation in the other Arab countries. Notwithstanding insurgent attempts to provoke civil war in Iraq, there are some grounds for believing that they might. Successful elections in Palestine after the death of Yasser Arafat, and in Saudi Arabia in February 2005, for all their flaws, suggested that the trend towards democratisation continues even amidst the turmoil of conflict in the Middle East. Around the same time the assassination of the Lebanese prime minister, allegedly by Syrian-supported elements, provoked popular protests and mounting pressure on the Syrian Baathist regime to withdraw its troops from the country. In former autocracies such as Bahrain and Qatar, democratic reforms were proceeding, though not without resistance.

That the 'Arab spring' or 'cedar revolution' about which commentators were writing in early 2005 was one consequence of the removal of Saddam Hussein has been accepted by most commentators. Less clear is the contribution of the media to the process, though that there has been and continues to be one is assumed by conservatives and reformers alike. In March 2005 the *Sunday Times* reported that in Bahrain, where the pace of democratic reform is constrained by deep-rooted conservatism, 'without a fully free press the internet has emerged as a forum for dissent through weblogs'.[4] According to one blogger quoted in this report, 'every village in Bahrain has one [a blogger] – even the most remote villages. You get a lot of different opinions on there and you really feel the pulse of the street.' In response, dissenting web sites have been hounded by the authorities, although with declining conviction. As the *Sunday Times* put it, the Bahrain bloggers have 'transgressed in a relatively benign climate'.

In May 2001, even before the events of 9/11 thrust his channel into the epicentre of global politics, Al Jazeera executive Mohammed Jassim Al Ali stated in an interview with an American journalist that:

> In this age, the powerful can no longer control the people. Democracy is coming to the Middle East because of the communication revolution. You can no longer hide information, and must now tell people the truth.
>
> (Cited in Zayani 2005: 33)

In a documentary about the house of Saud broadcast by the BBC in 2004, a Saudi defence expert identified the post-Gulf War environment of live 24-hour, Arabic-language news channels as the end of the era of authoritarian control in the Middle East, and the beginning of 'a new paradigm' for understanding political development in the region.[5]

How, then, do we get from a 'new paradigm' to a region-wide process of democratisation? The globalised news culture of transnational satellite and online news media, spearheaded by (but not restricted to) Al Jazeera has exposed Arab audiences to images of popular protest and pressure for democratic change. Taken together, 'these new Arab media increasingly construct the dominant narrative frames through which [Arabs] understand events'.[6] For one Arab observer, writing in late 2003,

> The Arab world has finally joined the contemporary communications revolution. The road to Arab public opinion will never be via the shabby government channels, but via the private channels with their high degree of freedom and, more importantly, their high degree of professionalism.[7]

Even if it is only in demonstrating what is possible, both journalistically and in the political reform process, the emergence of these channels has become a major factor in the evolving politics of the Middle East. Al Jazeera, as we have seen, pioneered the form, familiar to western audiences but hitherto unknown in the Middle East, of political debate shows featuring sharply contrasted opinions, some of them critical of local regimes. Without regard to the content of these opinions, the mere fact that they are heard, and recognised as the independent, non-state-sponsored voices which they are, communicates a new model of mediated politics which can only be beneficial to the broader project of democratisation. Al Jazeera and the other Arab-language channels are demonstrating by example the possibilities of what one Arab writer calls 'the free exercise of journalism and public affairs broadcasting'.[8]

There is also, as Rupert Murdoch suggested in 1993, the possibility of an economically derived demonstration effect, as hitherto insulated populations are exposed to the realities of life in other, more open societies. Miguel Centeno puts it well when he identifies one consequence of cultural globalisation as 'the ability of the poorest to witness the life-styles of the richest and, conversely, inability of the rich to isolate themselves' (2005: 48). This is applicable to the relationship between rich and poor countries, and to that between rich and poor within both advanced and developing countries. Newly configured, globalised public spheres highlight inequality and social division within nation-states hitherto insulated from socially destabilising information. On the March 4 2005 edition of BBC2's *Newsnight* current affairs programme, the British foreign secretary Jack Straw suggested a 'ripple effect' on Egypt and Syria as populations in these countries watched coverage of elections in Iraq and Palestine. McKenzie Wark suggests that 'technologies do not create utopias all by themselves. Rather, they offer the potential for proposing new images and ideas of the good life with which people might choose to think and act of their own accord' (1999: 3).

Apart from the issues of democratisation and economic modernisation, though not unrelated to them, the post-Al Jazeera generation of Arab media have also been credited with opening up space for debate on women's rights and other previously taboo topics in the Arab world. Naomi Sakr writes that, through programmes such as *For Women Only* (*Lil Nissa Faqat*), Al Jazeera 'has expanded the space for critical and contestatory discursive interaction over issues related to women's empowerment' (2005a: 145).

Beyond the sphere of news journalism, one outcome of the spread of internet and satellite media has been the exporting of reality TV genres pioneered in the west to the Middle East, often with dramatic consequences. When the Dutch production company Endemol launched *Arab Big Brother* in March 2004, for example, it brought to a notoriously conservative cultural environment all the qualities which had made *Big Brother* controversial even in the liberal capitalist world. In the Islamic countries of the Middle East, however, at the epicentre of fundamentalism, the format was truly transgressive. Men and women shared the same living space. Women were shown without veils, and there was public acknowledgement of both male and female sexuality. Out of respect for local sensitivities, and conscious of the violence triggered by the misguided attempt to stage the Miss World contest in Nigeria in 2002, *Arab Big Brother* eschewed many of the more raunchy elements of the programme as it had developed in the secular, feminised west. Contestants were not shown in states of undress, or in the toilet area of the house, and male and female housemates occupied separate bedrooms, as well as separate living spaces. A prayer room was provided, and the possibility – routine in British and other versions of *Big Brother* – that participants might actually have sex, was firmly excluded. From the *Big Brother* house in Bahrain, the programme was broadcast to a potential audience of 150 million Arabs.

The spectacle of men and women living together in conditions approximating to sexual equality, and engaging in modest sexual flirtation, was branded by fundamentalists as a 'threat to Islam' and 'entertainment for animals'.[9] In Bahrain and other Gulf states street protests were organised, with the clear threat of violence if the programme was not taken off air, which it duly was. The fear amongst local male elites of the programme's destabilising effect on their tightly controlled societies was sufficient to force the cancellation of the experiment. Even in its failure, however, the experience illustrated the potential of popular culture to challenge authoritarian structures.

Later that year a less controversial exercise in reality TV was received in the Middle East with less overt hostility. *Superstar*, the Middle East's variant on the successful UK series *Pop Idol*, was produced in Lebanon, and featured male and female contestants from several Arab states. As one (western) observer described the positive impact of the show: 'thanks to the proliferation of the internet, mobile phones, and satellite television stations operating beyond the sphere of government control, Arabs from every nation can watch a single Lebanese television show and take responsibility for its outcome'.[10] There are, of course, those who would interpret the infiltration of reality TV into the Middle East as another victory for 'the global missionaries of capitalism'. From within a chaos paradigm, however, it represents visible evidence of the energising impact of forms of entertainment media which, however modestly, introduce notions of public participation and democratic decision-making into societies where they have hitherto been alien.

Mohamed Zayani, writing before the wave of democratisation which swept through the Middle East in late 2004 and early 2005, took a cautious approach to the thesis that Al Jazeera and other examples of a newly free Arab media could presage 'real change' in Arab authoritarian regimes:

> One should be sceptical about the often ambitious transformative claims for new media as well as the claims made about its democratising potential and its ability not just to increase and widen participation amongst the various social strata in the Arab world, but to transform social and political organisation. Real change cannot be expected solely or mainly from the media sector.
>
> (Zayani 2005: 34)

One can share this view and still accept that political change in the Middle East is premised on the existence of free and independent media, of a public sphere which can articulate Arab opinion and support the emergence of democratic political cultures within individual Arab states. Just as *glasnost* was the necessary first step towards democratisation in the Soviet Union and its client states, the 'culture of accountability', the debate and the dissent visibly championed by Al Jazeera to its expanding Arab audience is a condition, if not sufficient in itself, for reform of political institutions. This is the lesson of Eastern Europe in the late 1980s and early 1990s, and of the Middle East in the current era.

Of Iran, which in June 2005 conducted a flawed democratic election for president, Daniel Drezner observes that 'weblogs allow young Iranians, secular or religious, to interact, partially taking the place of reformist newspapers that have been censored or shut down. Government efforts to impose filters on the Internet have been sporadic and only partially successful' (2005: 88). Iran is an anomaly in the context of this chapter, since its authoritarian regime has a measure of democratic legitimacy. As this book went to press, the Iranian theocracy continued to be under pressure, not just from the international community over the issue of nuclear technology, but from internal reformists, who were finding the internet and the blogosphere a powerful tool. In December 2004 reformist Abdollah Momeni launched a web site to gather signatories for a referendum on the Iranian constitution. One observer noted that, beyond its political applications:

> The spread of the internet has changed the lives of young Iranians by allowing them not only to download files of forbidden music, but also to indulge in digital dating. In a phenomenon that has taken the country by storm, hundreds of web logs have been created in both Farsi and English.[11]

At the time of writing, Iran remains a country where women are banned from singing on record, and from appearing in public without head scarves; where public dancing by men or women is banned. The election of fundamentalist Mahmoud Ahmadinejad as president in June 2005 indicated that powerful theocratic tendencies remained in control of Iran. But that there was a widespread desire for progressive social movement was beyond dispute. The internet appeared to be acting as a vehicle for that expression, and as an organisational tool.

The limits of change

NICTs alone, then, are not sufficient to propel change. In addition to a technological infrastructure which allows free and independent expression, democracy requires a *political culture* of debate and discussion. For Michael Gurevitch (1991: 188), 'the relationship between the press and broadcasting systems and the political system is governed, in every country, by the nature of its political system and the norms that characterise its political culture'. Thus we see many examples of societies in which, although the level of development of NICTs is high, democracy struggles to emerge. William Atkins' study of several countries of the southeast Asia region concludes that 'media information can only contribute to change if other social, political and economic conditions are at a particular stage and are receptive to the information and able to act upon it' (2002: 68).

Atkins examines the cases of Thailand, Malaysia and Singapore, all of whose governments enthusiastically developed NICTs for economic reasons in the 1990s, while resisting political liberalisation. That they largely succeeded in this dual strategy, if not without increased pressures for democratic reform, he interprets as a reflection of the traditionally closed and deferential political cultures of southeast Asia, set against the deradicalising impact of high economic growth. In the case of Singapore, for example, the population appears to be prepared to accept an authoritarian regime, including its censorial attitude to media content, on condition that the government delivers a successful economy. In Thailand, on the other hand, where the economic environment has been rather more volatile in recent years, the pro-reform protests of 1992 were fuelled by what Atkins calls a 'global feedback loop' comprising BBC and CNN coverage of the protests. This provided Thais with externally produced information which may have 'influenced' the action. In Indonesia, NICTs have contributed to the process of nation-building in one of the world's most ethnically and religiously diverse countries, a process which has included a substantial measure of democratisation, and occasional media-fuelled crises.

Although Atkins stresses that the relationship between NICTs and democratisation processes 'remains an area of uncertainty and contention' (ibid.: 58), his account of the contrasting experiences of several ASEAN countries, alongside the evidence of China since 1989, allows the conclusion that contingency and context are key determining factors in this discussion. Information of itself will not spark a revolution or a democratisation campaign, but it will form a 'component of the political dynamic', interacting with economic, cultural and other environmental factors to create (or prevent) the conditions for progressive change. The only universal trend is for increased social pressure on authoritarian elites, as they steadily lose control over media imports, and what their populations do with those imports. The Tiananmen Square option of violent repression is always there, but without the impact of the already fast-moving evolution of NICTs on late 1980s China, and indeed the example of Gorbachev's Soviet Union (the Soviet leader visited Beijing in the days before the massacre) it would probably not have been necessary.

A similar conclusion emerges from the work of Kalathil and Boas, who examined the impact of the internet on eight authoritarian countries, including China, Vietnam, Cuba and several Arab states. 'Overall', they found, 'the internet is challenging and helping to transform authoritarianism. Yet information technology alone is unlikely to bring about its demise' (2003: x). In China, for example, 'commercialisation, globalisation and pluralisation have all combined to break down the state's ability to shape the ideological environment' (ibid.: 18). Writing of China in 2004, the *New York Times* reported that 'text messages have generated popular outrage about corruption and abuse cases which had received little attention in the state-controlled media'.[12]

There have been many other manifestations of an emerging culture of technology-fuelled dissent. But the regime remains solid, at least on the surface. This may be attributed to the fact that democracy was unknown in China, even before the communists took power, and that several generations have known nothing but state control of cultural and intellectual life. Some attribute it to China's rapid economic growth in recent times, achieved by the adoption of a market economic base beneath a Marxist ideological superstructure ('capitalism with Chinese characteristics'). The great unanswered question for today's sinologists is the extent to which the apparent post-Tiananmen acquiescence of the population to the politico-ideological status quo is consensual or coerced (the memory of Tiananmen must be a factor for young Chinese as they consider their futures), masking a deeper restiveness which might, as the possibilities of life after communism become ever clearer through expanding access to cultural imports, lead to some kind of political upheaval.

Political change in a given country will not be the product of NICTS alone, then, but of technology in combination with political and cultural factors which are specific to each country. There is no single template for a communication-led transition from authoritarianism to democracy. The Soviet Union went one way, China has pursued another path. Iran, Cuba and North Korea maintain varying degrees of communicative isolation, while China is rapidly opening itself and its people up to outside influences. As a British academic who has taught some of the 50,000 Chinese students registered for courses at UK universities, I am struck by the evident ease with which these students, in stark contrast to the experience of young Soviets even in the late 1980s, are permitted to leave their home country, and seem happy to return.

In Hungary, as in other authoritarian countries, freeing up the political media loosened the bounds on a repressed culture of debate and democracy. Whether this leads quickly to full democratisation, as in Hungary, or to a slower process of democratisation as in Ukraine, which finally achieved free and fair elections only in 2004 (and not before the widely reported poisoning of the main opposition candidate), depends on the historical, political and cultural contexts. Is a country's political elite and population open to western influence and technology (for example, Hungary, the Baltic countries of the former Soviet Union, Russia itself), or are they suspicious and eastward leaning (eastern Ukraine, Kazakhstan)? Is democratisation welcomed as overdue modernisation, or the unwelcome imperialist imposition of an alien tradition? In short, a revolution in the political culture will have constitutional consequences which vary according to the environment within which they are shaped, which are in turn contingent upon that environment and the historical context it embodies.

To examine the authoritarian world as a whole is to recognise that the internet does not create a climate for progressive democratic change where none has existed, nor can it by itself force reform on an unwilling regime prepared to use violence and repression as its tools. By connecting internal dissent to external forces and resources which can provide information, advice and support, the internet allows pressure for change to be focused, intensified and maximised. Like the party newspapers of an earlier era, NICTs provide new organisational and agitational tools for activists, but they are not magic bullets. The degree of change which results from their adoption within a particular country will depend on other factors, not least the attitude of foreign governments, and the US government in particular. Military intervention in Iran would probably strengthen the democratically legitimised theocracy and marginalise the moderates and reformers. Progress on women's rights and other areas, if and when it comes, will be rooted in Iranian desires. For better or worse, the US and British governments decided that Iraq required invasion and occupation to depose a dictator. Iran, on the other hand, needs the patience associated with the application of what Robert Nye has called 'soft power', in the knowledge that the theocrats are confronted by their greatest ever challenge – not the Great Satan, but the world wide web, before which they are as powerless as every other nation on earth.

Conclusion

There is a correlation between global democratisation and the trends I have identified towards more and faster information, less and less subject to effective censorship. This information environment galvanises, focuses and intensifies pressure for democratic reform in countries where the objective conditions make reform popular. And this effect is demonstrative and cumulative – as one Middle Eastern autocracy falls, so its neighbour, many of whose people are watching coverage of events on Al Jazeera, begins to consider the possibilities for reform in its own country. The 'ripple effect' spreads through the region, and it becomes harder for any individual regime to resist the pressure. The tipping point is reached.

   This need not mean the emergence of governments that are more amenable to western interests than before. On the contrary, democratisation can mean, as in Iran, the emergence of anti-western governments. Where the fall of the Soviet Union and the 'velvet revolutions' that followed it in Central and Eastern Europe were anti-communist rather than anti-capitalist movements, the Arab spring and 'cedar revolutions' are rooted not just in popular dissatisfaction with corrupt autocracies, but in anti-western, anti-capitalist, anti-American belief systems of the type espoused in its most extreme variant by Al Qaida. Democratisation in the Middle East, therefore, is unlikely to have the same political outcome as democratisation in the former Warsaw Pact countries. Elections in Iraq have facilitated the ascendancy of a more extreme Islamic strand than Saddam Hussein ever tolerated. In late January 2006 Hamas won a majority of votes in the first Palestinian election in which it took part. David Hirst observes correctly that there is a sting in the tale of democratisation, not least in the Middle East where it has been promoted with the most zeal. 'Imperial America', he writes, 'will not like the democratic Arabia that missionary America will have helped to spawn.'[13] The UN-sponsored *Arab Human Development Report*, published in 2005, noted the opportunity which had been created for a 'historic, peaceful redistribution of power within Arab societies', but warned that 'chaotic upheavals' could also be a product of democratising trends.[14] Cultural chaos can have negative and positive outcomes, from the point of view of social progress.

11 Democracy and hyper-democracy

The sociological implications of the trends described in Parts II and III, and of the general dissolution of temporal-spatial, geographical, politico-ideological, epistemological and aesthetic-generic distinctions which have hitherto structured the media environment are, as Chapter 1 noted, a matter of dispute, with interpretations falling broadly into two schools – optimistic and pessimistic. Pessimistic pespectives have tended to take the form of narratives of decline of various kinds, tales of doom in which an increasingly crowded communication environment is implicated in the collapse of civilised ethical and aesthetic standards, or the imposition of some vaguely felt state of siege, or the rapacious global expansion of Messianic capitalism. The alternative, more optimistic interpretation permitted by a chaos paradigm focuses on the new possibilities provided by the emerging climate of communicative turbulence for demystifying, democratising and decentralising power in societies where, no one will deny, it is still open to excessive accumulation and abuse. Where the media have been expected to play a watchdog role over power in capitalism for centuries, the emerging environment provides enhanced means and opportunities for the exercise of that role. In democratic societies liberated from the ideological straitjacket of the Cold War, the positive impacts of more media outlets, faster information flow, less censorship, and a more competitive cultural market-place are (if viewed from the normative perspective) fourfold:

1   enhanced critical scrutiny of elites;
2   enhanced critical scrutiny of media;
3   decentralisation and diversification of media production;
4   globalisation of public spheres.

Even an optimist will not deny, however, that the globalised news culture described in Parts II and III brings with it costs as well as benefits to democratic societies, so let me now address the former.

Panics, frenzies and scares

One of the most pronounced consequences of an environment of accelerated communication flow, and an expanded, globally connected network of news outlets, is the apparent growth in the number and intensity of media panics, including moral panics of the traditional kind,[1] as well as food panics and health scares, and apocalyptic narratives such as the Y2K story which filled media around the world at the end of the millennium. This trend has generated a cultural environment in which perceptions of risk are heightened beyond the point at which they could be described as rational, or in the public interest. For example, recent years in the UK have seen news stories about a range of health threats, including those allegedly caused by meningitis, oral contraceptives, flesh-eating necrosis and forms of food poisoning such as salmonella. Every individual case of harm is of huge significance to the victim, of course, and on occasion the risks of a more general harm to public health will justify extensive coverage (for example, bird flu, which generated global media coverage in the summer of 2005). Just because there is a panic, in other words, does not mean that there is nothing to worry about. But in many cases the threat to public health has been exaggerated by a media which, for economic, professional and technological reasons beyond the control or whim of any individual journalist, editor or proprietor, acts to produce an inflated perception of the real risk.

Stories of alarming new threats are inherently newsworthy, and once picked up by one or a few media are likely to spread through the system as a whole. In the globalised public sphere of the twenty-first century stories about risk cascade through the system, spreading anxiety around the world like the contagions and viruses they are often reporting. This may lead to serious harm to those members of the public who may feel, for whatever reason (to protect their children, for example), compelled to act on information provided by the news media. Extensive UK media coverage of the MMR vaccine in 2002 caused public attitudes to exaggerate the risk of autism associated with the vaccine. According to a survey undertaken by Justin Lewis and others of Cardiff University School of Journalism, Media and Cultural Studies:

> Although almost all scientific experts rejected the claim of a link between MMR and autism, 53 per cent of those [members of the public] surveyed at the height of the media coverage assumed that because both sides of the debate received equal media coverage, there must be equal evidence for each. Only 23 per cent of the population were aware that the bulk of evidence favoured supporters of the vaccine.[2]

In the aftermath of the story, many parents chose to withdraw their children from the MMR vaccination programme, thereby exposing them to an increased risk of measles epidemic. A similar sequence of events occurred in October 1995 when thousands of women ceased using an oral contraceptive, having heard on several BBC news bulletins that it carried an enhanced risk of inducing coronary thrombosis. As Anna Ford announced on BBC 1's main news bulletin: 'A million and a half women are told their contraceptive carries a higher health risk than previously thought.'[3] In fact, the 'higher risk' represented only a marginal increase in the degree of risk overall, which was far outweighed by the health risks associated with pregnancy and childbirth. Without this context, the story persuaded thousands of women to stop taking the pill, and hundreds of unwanted pregnancies were reported to have resulted, with serious implications for the health of at least some of the women thus affected. In relation to media coverage of public health in general, a recent study concludes that:

> The news media tend to focus on stories about health services. Only rarely do they publish stories about public health – that is, measures to improve health, prevent illness or reduce health inequalities. Public health specialists find it infinitely more difficult to cultivate media interest in serious, proven health risks, such as smoking, alcohol and obesity, than in, for example, 'crises' in the NHS. Meanwhile, unusual hazards such as the severe acute respiratory syndrome (SARS) virus, which pose relatively little danger, can occupy the headlines for weeks on end.[4]

Journalist Polly Toynbee read the report's findings as evidence that

> health coverage is in direct inverse proportion to real risk. What kills most people gets less coverage . . . Politicians have often been forced to change policy priorities and health spending according to what the media highlights, regardless of public good or even public opinion.[5]

In the *Sunday Times* Allan Massie expressed feelings that most of us have shared as we read about the latest research into the potentially deadly effects of too many potato crisps or artificial sweeteners.

> We live at a time when people are healthier and live longer than at any previous period of history. And yet we are persuaded to worry about our health to an unprecedented degree. Scarcely a week goes by without some new scare hitting the headlines. It doesn't matter that the experts themselves are inconsistent . . . The theme is constant: we must live in a state of heightened anxiety.[6]

As for health, so too with species-threatening asteroids (Figure 1), super-volcanoes, climate change and other harbingers of imminent apocalypse.

Oliver Bennett notes that mass anxiety about the end of the world as we know it is a long established sub-category of cultural pessimism (2001). The demand of an expanded media for dramatic and spectacular news (or even the possibility that such news will be forthcoming) has made such outbreaks more common, while the globalised news culture of the twenty-first century spreads them further and faster than in the past.[7] The consequences of this for good government follow on from the changed political culture described in Chapter 4. In a world where public opinion matters to elected politicians more than ever before, the temptation of governments to respond to public rather than professional scientific perceptions of risk is greater. Whether this pressure will result in poor official decision-making

Nightmare scenario ... if the asteroid hit Earth it could cause the same destruction as a nuclear war Illustration: Robert Harding

March 2014 brings small risk of huge disaster

Tim Radford Science editor

The world can breathe again. Probably. Asteroid 2003 QQ47, a lump of rock the size of Ben Nevis, could hit Earth at a speed of about 13 miles a second on March 21 2014, to cause the kind of destruction expected in thermonuclear war, experts warned yesterday.

But they gave the 2,600m tonne monster a danger rating of just one on the Torino scale. That means its chances of actually slamming into Earth are 909,000 to 1 against.

The Torino scale goes up to 10, at which point collision is a certainty. That the object rates as a danger at all is because earthlings know so little about their nearer neighbours. At present astronomers have counted 523 potentially hazardous objects — bits of rubble left over from the building of the solar system 4.5bn years ago — that may be

on collision course with Earth. Asteroid 2003 QQ47, three-quarters of a mile in diameter, first spotted on August 24 and observed so far only 51 times, could be another.

"The near-Earth object will be observable from Earth for the next two months, and astronomers will continue to track it over this period," said Alan Fitzsimmons, of Queen's University, Belfast.

Kevin Yates, manager of the UK near-Earth object information centre, based at the National Space Centre in Leicester, said: "As additional observations are made, and uncertainties decrease, aster-

oid 2003 QQ47 is likely to drop down the Torino scale."

Earth's nearest neighbour, the moon, is pockmarked by aeons of cosmic collisions. There have been many impacts on Earth during geological history, but for the most part the dents have been smeared away by wind, rain and plant growth.

The last epic impact was probably 65m years ago, at the close of the Cretaceous period, when an asteroid or comet may have wiped out the dinosaurs and most other life on Earth. But there have been many smaller impacts, including the equivalent of a powerful atomic bomb over the Tungus region of Siberia in 1908.

The cosmos, astronomers warn, remains a potentially dangerous place. Amateur astronomers at a BBC "star party" 10 days ago, to celebrate national astronomy week, may

have identified 20 more potential killers.

The planet is showered by small objects every day — many of them burn up harmlessly as shooting stars — but larger lumps of rock hit the ground as meteorites.

The bigger fragments have the potential to wipe out whole cities. One of them sped harmlessly past Earth on August 16, missing it by about 2.4m miles. Others have come to within almost the distance of the moon.

Links

ll.mit.edu/LINEAR/ Lincoln Near
Earth Asteroid Research
impact.arc.nasa.gov/index.html
Nasa asteroids page
impact.arc.nasa.gov/torino/
Torino scale
spaceguarduk.com Spaceguard UK
guardian.co.uk/
spacedocumentary

Goodbye, cruel world

Astronomers and Earth scientists have proposed a number of potential endpoints for humanity
● The runaway greenhouse effect. Could Earth end up like Venus, with ground temperatures at the melting point of lead?
● Snowball Earth, or at least the return of the ice age, with vast glaciers ploughing as far south as Middlesex. The last

ice age ended only 10,000 years ago
● The swelling of the sun. In about 5bn years, the sun will expand to red giant stage, incinerating all the rocky inner planets, and any life on them
● Cosmic collapse: a random quantum fluctuation in space could destroy mass and trigger a bubble of destruction that would advance at the speed of light

Figure 1 Guardian, September 3 2003

or not depends on other factors, such as the stage of the electoral cycle at which the issue arises in the public domain, the vulnerability of a government to shifts in public opinion, and so on. In the case of MMR media panic did not lead the government to do what many editors and commentators (claiming to represent an alarmed public) advocated and introduce a much more expensive and complicated 'triple vaccine' system on the NHS. Following the Dunblane shootings of 1996, on the other hand, understandable public anger at the murder of 16 schoolchildren and their teacher was built by media pressure into a campaign to ban hand guns which the Labour government felt unable to resist. Many categories of hitherto legal firearms were banned under the Firearms Act 1997. The rate of gun crime nonetheless rose by 10 per cent in the following year, and has remained high ever since.[8]

Feeding frenzies and the destabilisation of elites

If panics and scares are alarming for most of us, feeding frenzies of the type that nearly toppled Bill Clinton and did much to bring down the Conservative government of John Major in the 1990s raise the issue of how much media freedom is consistent with good government in a democracy. In the case of the Clinton–Lewinsky scandal, events were driven from the outset by the then-emerging technology of the internet, which allowed Matt Drudge to break the story over the heads of the mainstream media, and then pushed the late entrants into a prolonged period of private exposure and sexual revelation which no previous US president had ever experienced. CNN broadcast the videotape recordings of Clinton's intimate testimony before the Starr Committee to the world, unedited. Every graphic detail of the unfolding story became public, analysed and commented upon, satirised and condemned. That Clinton survived in office was evidence not just of his personal popularity and resilience, but of the American people's readiness to accept a leader's private frailties if his public works are of a sufficiently high calibre.

Throughout Clinton's presidency hostile media voices flooded the US and UK public spheres with damaging stories of more or less accuracy. According to David Brock, a repentant source of much of this material, there was an active 'Arkansas Project' designed to undermine the Clinton presidency by casting him as sexually deviant and financially corrupt: 'Spurious AP material was pumped into the *Spectator* and then flowed through the right's extensive network of propaganda mills, from talk radio, to internet sites, and some right-leaning mainstream newspapers including the *Sunday Telegraph*.'[9]

The same pattern of online dissemination was seen in coverage of Prince Charles's alleged sexual proclivities in November 2003. As his media advisers sought to contain the damage caused by the story, it came to exemplify the chaotic, uncontrollable nature of the globalised public sphere, and the fact that

> Blogs, with their soundbite commentary, round-the-clock updates, and open-door policy to posters – make an ideal breeding ground for character assassins . . . a couple of choice links and an axe to grind are all that is required to spread innuendo around the web with lightning speed.[10]

Declining deference towards elites, competitive pressures on media organisations, and the infrastructure of cultural chaos thus combine to produce what I have elsewhere called a *striptease culture* (McNair 2002), in which the traditional distinction between public and private affairs is dissolved in journalism (political journalism in particular), and elite deviance becomes fair game.

A recent study of domestic UK news asserts that 'conservatism over the theme of monarchy typifies the British press' (Blain and O'Donnell 2003: 3), and that 'royal and monarchical media accounts' are 'an obvious stratagem of distraction and ideological reinforcement' (ibid.: 59). This study was published before the scandal of November 2003, during which the alleged sexual practices of HRH Prince Charles were the subject of global media speculation for days on end. It also appeared before the *Mirror* newspaper's successful infiltration that same year of the royal household at Buckingham Palace with an undercover reporter, Ryan Parry, whose reports subsequently became the basis for an extended period of royal coverage which was, even by the standards of the twenty-first century, less than respectful. Such coverage may legitimately be judged to be a 'distraction', but 'ideological reinforcement' seems problematic, unless one believes that the survival of British capitalism is strengthened by the depiction of its present head of state as a figure of fun, and its future king as a sexual deviant. To the consternation of royalist commentators, royal coverage in most of the British print and broadcast media, and especially the right-wing tabloids (and especially the newspapers of the arch-republican Rupert Murdoch) has, since the marriage of Charles and Diana in 1981, been consistently subversive of the respect and deference in which the monarchy had been held in the United Kingdom throughout most of the twentieth century.

Further confirmation of this trend came on January 13 2005, when the UK's *Sun* newspaper published a photograph of Prince Harry, third in line to the British throne, dressed in a Nazi uniform complete with swastika armband. The offending apparel was the prince's choice for a private fancy dress party, and thus not on the face of it evidence of any predisposition to Nazism. However, media criticism was intense, quickly extending beyond the UK to the global public sphere, where the hapless Harry was roundly condemned by the Israelis, the Germans, the European Union and an emergency resolution of the UN Security Council (I exaggerate, but only a little). In Britain the incident revived calls for a republic, as such scandals have been doing since the 1980s. In the same pattern as previous royal stories, Harry's private misdemeanour became an occasion for public anger and dissent, directed not merely at the young royal but at the institution of the monarchy itself. Where once such behaviour would have remained hidden from media scrutiny and public view, now it was thrust to the top of the global news agenda.

Observing hostile UK media coverage of the wedding of Prince Charles and Camilla Parker-Bowles in April 2005, American journalist Sarah Lyall noted that 'the British news media has seized on each misstep, each gaffe, each potential impediment with glee'.[11] This 'casual meanness' contrasted sharply with the 1950s, when historian John Grigg's description of the Queen as 'elitist and complacent' was deemed by most of the British media to be 'shocking, almost treasonous'. Since that time UK coverage of the monarchy had become 'steadily more contemptuous . . . a problem', she concluded, 'of too much information'.

I will not waste time defending the honour of inherited wealth and privilege, and republicans will see the above story as strong evidence that a chaotic communications environment can indeed have progressive political outcomes (in this case, the further erosion of the legitimacy of the British monarchy). But there is a sense in which Blain and O'Donnell's argument that royal coverage in the British press is a 'distraction' from more important issues can be supported, though not for the reasons they suggest. Far from being, in their words, a conservative ideological reinforcement of the status quo, the kind of coverage from which Harry suffered in 2005, and his father Charles experienced on many occasions before that, can be criticised from the purely ethical perspective. If it is wrong for the news media to gorge on the private flaws and pecadilloes of politicians such as Bill Clinton or Cherie Blair, especially when these have no bearing on the public duties of the individual concerned, why should it be right for members of the royal family, born into their privileged place purely by accident of fate, to be similarly pilloried? Some argued at the time that Harry's wearing of a swastika was insensitive and childish, coinciding as it did with the sixtieth anniversary of the liberation of Auschwitz. And so it was, just as at times are the antics of 20 year olds everywhere on the planet. The rush into print, the fervour with which other media leapt on the bandwagon, the 'manufactured outrage' identified by British satirist Armando Ianucci[12] when asked to comment on the story, were all products not of considered anti-monarchical ideology but the speed of news transmission within the UK and then globally, economic competitiveness between media outlets, not to mention a ruthless disregard for the feelings of this particular young man at a time in his life when transgression and taboo-breaking are practically obligatory, and thus when some allowances might be expected to have been made.

The world will not stop turning because a member of the British royal family comes in for criticism in the world's media, and compared to the much greater injustices routinely inflicted on many less powerful individuals by a hyperactive, always hungry press, few people shed tears at the story. But it typifies what some commentators have likened to a bear pit atmosphere in contemporary journalism, the default stance of 'corrosive cynicism' discussed in Chapter 4. If the decline of journalistic deference towards elites, the rise of irreverence and a readiness to expose anything and everything, can be counted as being among the positive democratising effects of cultural chaos, then the voyeuristic gleefulness of stories like this suggests a downside – the universalisation, or globalisation, of the worst of British tabloid news values and editorial practices. If the fact that members of power elites can now be treated with as little sensitivity and common decency as we ordinary members of the public unfortunate enough to become the subject of press interest may be regarded as a kind of progress, it is a progress in which there can be little pleasure for any but the most mean-minded.

Celebrities of stage, screen and sporting arena are just as likely to be the victims of this elite media mugging, as when David Beckham's sexual relations with various women not called Posh Spice were the subject of global media coverage in 2004. Most readers will experience difficulty in feeling sorry for a multimillionaire married couple who lived by media publicity and were then brought low by it, but who could witness their fellow human beings' most intimate affairs being publicised so widely across the world and not feel a modicum of sympathy? To welcome the elite-demystifying effects of an increasingly chaotic media environment does not require the abandonment of moral and ethical principles. Indeed, the question of journalistic ethics acquires greater importance in the era of cultural chaos precisely because, in this era, much more is possible journalistically.

Al Qaida – global terror network or media panic?

As Chapter 4 noted, a chaotic media environment expands the opportunities for terrorist organisations (often poorly resourced by comparison with the states against which they are fighting) to intervene in and shape the news agenda. The introduction of new information and communication technologies allows spectacular acts of terrorism to have impacts much more broadly, and much faster, than ever before. In this context the global terrorism of Al Qaida can best be understood as one long campaign of political communication, with targets selected and attacks designed to have the maximum impact, through media coverage, on key global publics. John Gray's 2003 essay on globalisation and terrorism noted that 'the attack on the Twin Towers demonstrates that Al Qaida understands that twenty-first century wars are spectacular encounters in which the dissemination of media images is a core strategy' (2003: 76). Indeed, and as weapons of war, media images are far less predictable and controllable in their effects than more conventional arms. On September 11 2001 a co-ordinated series of acts of violence, conducted by 18 men in total and estimated to have cost less than $1 million to their organisers, set off a chain of events that led Coalition troops to Aghanistan and Iraq, impacted severely on Muslim nations such as Pakistan, Indonesia and Saudi Arabia, and on the Muslim citizens of western societies such as Britain, France and the United States. They impacted on the conduct of the Russian military in Chechnya, in the direction of politics in oil-rich Venezuela and the Philippines. It is no exaggeration to say that the future of the human race has been irrevocably changed by that single day of spectacular terrorist actions, and that this is possible because of the availability of a global media network along which the news could travel terrifyingly fast.

Following 9/11, as the war on terror commenced and the invasions of Afghanistan and Iraq proceeded, Al Qaida's use of the media to command the news agenda continued. Bomb attacks in Bali and Madrid against Australians and Spanish civilians respectively, were not on the scale of 9/11, but had comparable impact on those countries. The Madrid bombing of March 11 2004, timed to coincide both with the symbolic 9/11 and an imminent Spanish general election involving pro- and anti-war parties, successfully altered the outcome of the election in so far as the government of Jose Maria Aznar was unexpectedly defeated. The reason for its defeat was widely speculated to have been its opportunistic efforts to blame the indigenous terror group ETA for what soon emerged as an Islamic fundamentalist operation. Opportunism or not, however, it seems likely that in the absence of the Madrid bombs, Aznar's party would have remained in power and that here, as elsewhere, terrorists proved themselves 'adept at influencing domestic politics'.[13] In Bali Al Qaida's capture of the global news agenda by blowing 200 innocent clubbers to bits while they partied was similarly impactful on the Australian public and political agenda, although it did not lead to defeat for the Howard government at the following general election.

In 2004, as the US-led coalition struggled to maintain order and security in occupied Iraq, the insurgents there adopted a tactic of kidnapping foreign workers, then beheading them in the most gruesome manner. In a unique twist to the semiotics of terror, these beheadings were filmed on video, before being sent to media organisations and websites where they became available to the global public. Beheadings were powerful symbols of both the visceral ferocity and the ruthlessness of the insurgents in Iraq, given added communicative power by the availability of global news media to disseminate them. Indeed, just as the growth of the mass media in the 1960s was a crucial explanatory factor in the rise of urban terror in the west, the emergence of real-time satellite news and the internet was the catalyst for the development of the kidnapping/beheading tactic – an effective source tactic if ever there was one, guaranteed to command headlines and space on the global news agenda. As one American commentator put it, 'the ability to broadcast messages over the Internet and on Arabic-language satellite television networks like Al-Jazeera creates a whole new forum to display horrifying acts.'[14] The technology created the conditions for a new form of psychological warfare. According to Ed Blanche of Jane's Information Group, 'this is a breakthrough in communication that has transformed the whole ethos of terrorism. What has changed is that the Arab world, the Muslim world, the Third World, now has access to this communication.'[15]

Faced with these episodes throughout the summer and autumn of 2004, the British and American governments, indeed all governments whose nationals were caught up in the kidnapping wave,[16] were required to deal with chaotic information flows and their impact on public opinion. Recognising this, as well as in pragmatic acknowledgement of the sheer horror of the images, the BBC, ITN and other mainstream broadcasters refrained from transmitting the most graphic sections of footage. These videos typically showed hostages kidnapped by insurgent groups such as the Al Jallawi faction, then made to plead for their lives before the camera, then shot or beheaded on film. They were made possible by communication technology, and employed as tools to shape the global news agenda by terrorist organisations well schooled in the strategies and tactics of public relations. Videotape footage of beheadings and other atrocities by Islamic terrorist organisations in Iraq were intended to influence British public opinion and ultimately UK government policy in Iraq. The videotaped address by Osama Bin Laden released to Arabsat channels in the run-up to the November 2004 US presidential election promised blood in the streets if George W. Bush were re-elected.[17]

Chapter 5 argued that, while real, the global threat posed by Al Qaida has been misrepresented, even exaggerated. I argued too that the mythologising of a loose collection of modern-day medievalists into a 'global terror network' has not been the product of conspiratorial propaganda emanating from the White House or Downing Street, but of a more chaotic process of media–society interaction triggered by the spectacular images of 9/11. Since then, routine journalistic news values have combined with genuine public and elite horror to create a heightened perception of risk, and a readiness to accept draconian legal and security measures. Adam Curtis' film, *The Power of Nightmares*, performed an important service in showing that Al Qaida is neither as organised nor as dangerous as some politicians claim and many in the general public believe. But as I argued in Chapter 5, those claims and those beliefs have not been the planned outcome of elite propaganda by a national security state or some other committee of the powerful. On the contrary, as many critical official reports have pointed out, the 9/11 attacks caught the US government as much by surprise as anyone else, prompting a reaction which can be compared to that of a moral panic or a health scare.

We know, for example, that the January 2001 publication of the Hart–Rudman Commission's report on the growing threat of Islamic fundamentalist terror to the USA, including its recommendation for the establishment of a National Homeland Security Agency, was dismissed by the vast majority of the US media as a nonstory. The *New York Times* reporter who attended a publicity-generating briefing session on the report left early, declaring 'there's no story here' (quoted in Hess and Kalb, 2003: 114). Despite the African embassy bombings of 1998, the attack on the *USS Cole* and other incidents, routine journalistic news values decided that, with a presidential inauguration only a few days away, this particular report was not sufficiently important or interesting to command a place on the main news agenda. To point this out is not to criticise US journalists and editors, because few in the western world thought of Al Qaida before 9/11 as anything but an anachronistic throwback to pre-modernity. It is to suggest that the sudden emergence of a 'global terror network' after 9/11 was a phenomenon driven by round-the-clock media coverage of terrorist spectaculars which though horrifying, were never as threatening to western civilisation as they became in the political, journalistic and public imaginations.[18] And if the global terror network is a kind of myth, like the threat of flesh-eating necrotisis or imminent apocalypse from a passing asteroid, what of government policies founded on it, such as the war on terror, the passing of the Patriot Act or the introduction of identity cards in the UK?

Cultural chaos and the CNN effect

The sociology of journalism has been interested for some time in the long-term impacts of news on public opinion, and on governmental policy-making. In 1990 Gurevitch and Levy noted that

> among the various consequences of instant global communication, the opportunity afforded to television viewers around the world to become immediate witnesses of major events in far-away places is among the more significant. It is likely to have major shaping influences both on the cognitive maps of the world that these viewers carry in their heads, and perhaps also on the events themselves.
>
> (Gurevitch and Levy 1990: 27)

Since then, journalists, politicians and scholars have addressed 'the CNN effect' (Robinson 2002), and related phenomena such as 'compassion fatigue' (Moeller 1999), or what happens to our capacity to care about faraway events of which we know relatively little until they are broadcast into our living rooms.

In the mid-1990s broadcast journalist Nik Gowing published a study of the impact of real-time news on western policy-makers, concluding at that time that any such effects were minimal. He noted that politicians 'fear that emotive pictures provided by real-time TV coverage forces them into an impulsive policy response when the reality on the ground is different' (Gowing 1994: 76). Based on his interviews with western policy-makers and military professionals, Gowing's study of the CNN effect pointed out that live coverage of atrocities and human rights abuses in Rwanda, Bosnia and Burundi did not appear to have influenced the American or British responses to these events. On the other hand, live coverage of events in Somalia, Srebrenica and Kurdish Iraq did appear to have shaped at least the appearance of a western response. For Gowing in 1994, it appeared that the link between media coverage and policy was conditioned by context. Coverage of the bodies of American soldiers being dragged through the streets of Mogadishu in 1992 had considerably more impact on American policy in this part of Africa than the televised deaths of hundreds of thousands of Tutsis in Rwanda; as indeed did the murder and mutilation of US construction workers near Fallujah in 2004, which led to the virtual razing of that city.

Why did the deaths of a few dozen in one country generate a media and public response so different to that provoked by the slaughter of nearly a million people in another country? Because, I would suggest, the images from Mogadishu and Fallujah, in addition to making great television, connected with potent collective memories of the Vietnam War, and the persistent unease of the American population about combat deaths. Because they were broadcast for all to see, the deaths of ten American soldiers, or four construction workers, meant more to US public opinion, and thus had a greater impact on US government policy, to put the calculation at its crudest, than the deaths of hundreds of thousands or even millions of anonymous Africans in a vaguely understood tribal conflict. In the years between the two incidents, however, the political environment, and the context within which coverage of events has impacts, changed entirely. In Somalia in 1992, TV images produced a humiliating reversal in US foreign policy, and a victory for the Somali insurgents (who included supporters of a still largely unknown Osama Bin Laden). In the case of the Fallujah deaths a decade later, a hard-line Bush administration successfully used the footage of Americans being murdered and mutilated as justification for an escalation of Coalition violence to end that city's status as a rebel stronghold.

Television coverage, Gowing concluded in 1994, 'is a powerful influence in problem recognition, which in turn helps to shape the foreign policy agenda. But television does not necessarily dictate policy responses' (ibid.: 18). On some occasions, as in the former Yugoslavia, media coverage of ethnic cleansing has played a key role in creating a climate of public opinion where military intervention can be contemplated. The invasions of Kosovo and the subsequent bombing of

Serbia would not have occurred, we might reasonably speculate, had publics in the UK and USA not witnessed on their television screens the crimes being committed by Milosevic's forces. On the other hand, strategic considerations might have required a military intervention irrespective of public opinion, as occurred in Iraq in 2003.

On some occasions, such as the international pressure on the Sudanese government which accompanied the atrocities of the Janjaweed militiamen in 2004, media coverage produces the appearance of a response, though little in the way of meaningful action. As Gowing observed in 1994, 'governments frequently go out of their way to appear to modify policy when little or nothing of substance has changed' (ibid.: 11). Context and meaning are crucial here, as in other aspects of the media effects debate. Since the days of the First World War, media coverage has always shaped the political environment within which democratically elected governments make decisions, but has never been the only consideration and is not so today. Media coverage of atrocities (including potential atrocities, as in the case of the UK government's 'sexed up' dossier on WMD) may be convenient for a government which seeks intervention in any case, and wishes to have public opinion on its side. Or it may be an inconvenient complication in an already complex situation in which realpolitik militates against the compassionate or humanitarian intervention, as was the case in Rwanda, and again in Darfur in 2004.

The increased pressure on political elites to be seen to act in response to media images of tragedy and trauma sets up a feedback loop between events, their coverage in news, and policy responses. Such a connection always existed, but the time between events happening, being reported and then responded to by politicians was more or less extended. Today those distances have dissolved, intensifying the pressures on politicians to respond in a manner and within a timescale acceptable to the media and their audiences. The dissolution of time and space means the acceleration of information flow from one point to another, and the reduction of the time available for politicians to make decisions. Like all other types of media impact, the specific content of these decisions will be contingent upon a variety of contextualising factors. Consider, for example, President Bush's appearance on Arab satellite news channels in early May 2004, when he attempted to deflect criticisms of the US military which had been provoked by the publication of photographs of torture and prisoner abuse a few days before.[19]

> **Interviewer:** Mr. President, thank you for agreeing to do this interview with us. Evidence of torture of Iraqi prisoners by US personnel has left many Iraqis and people in the Middle East and the Arab world with the impression that the United States is no better than the Saddam Hussein regime. Especially when this alleged torture took place in the Abu Ghraib prison, a symbol of torture. What can the US do, or what can you do to get out of this?
>
> **Bush:** First, people in Iraq must understand that I view those practices as abhorrent. They must also understand that what took place in that prison does not represent America that I know. The America I know is a compas-

sionate country that believes in freedom. The America I know cares about every individual. The America I know has sent troops into Iraq to promote freedom, good, honorable citizens that are helping the Iraqis every day.

It's also important for the people of Iraq to know that in a democracy, everything is not perfect, that mistakes are made. But in a democracy those mistakes will be investigated and people will be brought to justice. We're an open society. We're a society that is willing to investigate, fully investigate in this case, what took place in that prison.

That stands in stark contrast to life under Saddam Hussein. His trained torturers were never brought to justice under his regime. There were no investigations about mistreatment of people. There will be investigations. People will be brought to justice . . .

We've discovered these abuses; they're abhorrent abuses. They do not reflect – the actions of these few people do not reflect the hearts of the American people. The American people are just as appalled at what they have seen on TV as the Iraqi citizens. The Iraqi citizens must understand that. And, therefore, there will be a full investigation, and justice will be served. And we will do to ourselves what we expect of others.

Without digital cameras, and the rapid global dissemination of the Abu Ghraib photographs made possible by new media technologies, and the availability of satellite channels for presenting the US administration's propaganda counter-offensive, the story would not have evolved in that way, leading to convictions of several soldiers implicated by the photographic evidence at trials in 2005. The My Lai massacre took years to become public knowledge and be recognised as the outrage it was. The Iraqi prisoner abuse scandal was the subject of angry global debate, necessitating a rare public display of presidential contrition within days, and a period of genuine soul-searching within the United States. This happened not because Mr Bush was running a particularly open and media-friendly execu-tive, but because he knew to give at least the appearance of regret, in the interests of winning the global campaign for public opinion within which the Iraqi invasion was conducted. To an extent unprecedented in military history, the Gulf War of 2003 was conducted in full view of the world's people. In that context, and regardless of what he might have preferred to do, the president had to give an account of himself and his country. Bush survived the revelations about what had gone on in Abu Ghraib prison, winning a second presidential term in November 2004, but not because the American people were ignorant of what had transpired in Abu Ghraib.

The extent to which publics and media professionals become actors in the evolution of events was demonstrated in the aftermath of the destruction of New Orleans by Hurricane Katrina in September 2005. The US media on that occasion identified presidential and other official responses to the disaster as inadequate, setting up debates about excessive bureaucracy, racism and the president's competency. Coverage of these debates, and their rapid dissemination through the globalised public sphere, and the perceived impact of that coverage on both the Republican party at home and America's reputation overseas, drove a much more urgent response to the humanitarian crisis after an initial period of delay and confusion.

Observing the impact of satellite TV in the early 1990s, Michael Gurevitch argued that:

> The role television now plays in the conduct of international relations is merely an extension into the international level of the actively participatory role that the media have always played in the life of societies. But the dramatic expansion of the stage upon which television now performs this role – from a national/societal into a global one, has endowed it with a qualitatively new and sharper edge. This is especially the case in times of social and political turmoil, of rapid and revolutionary social change, or in periods of international crisis. The capacity of television, utilising satellite technology, to tell the story of an event as it happens, simultaneously with its unfolding, can have direct consequences for the direction that the event might take.
>
> (Gurevitch 1991: 183)

A decade later, historian Eric Hobsbawm could observe that:

> There can be no doubt that the new role of public opinion has had a decisive role in changing the nature of war. The 'CNN effect', as we might define it. Selective news of what is happening becomes immediately available. This is another result of the end of the Cold War, because government control and censorship of information is much less than in the past, and on occasions even impossible. This was not the case during the Vietnam War, and still less during the years immediately after it. Television's extraordinary domination has made it impossible now for governments to manage international crises in the manner they were accustomed to. But it is also an instrument for mobilising public opinion with a rapidity unthinkable in the past. The effect of television is immediate, but it is also no longer controllable.
>
> (Hobsbawm 2000: 16)[20]

Reflecting on the implications of the new media environment for public opinion, a UK Ministry of Defence paper entitled 'The Future Strategic Context for Defence' noted the need for government 'to be aware of the ways in which public attitudes might shape and constrain military activity'. In an age of 24-hour real-time news, the paper went on, 'increasing emotional attachment to the outside world, fuelled by immediate and graphic media coverage, and a public desire to see the UK act as a force for good, is likely to lead to public support, and possibly public demand, for operations prompted by humanitarian motives' (quoted in Curtice 2004: 70). An obvious illustration of the growing complexity of public opinion management in conflict contexts is provided by the war on terror and the occupation of Iraq, neither of which could have been prosecuted without consideration of electoral outcomes, as the Spanish government discovered to its cost in March 2004, and the Bush and Blair governments were required to remember as their own re-election campaigns loomed into view in 2004 and 2005. While the war took place against the background of massive street protests, its justification, and the conduct of the invasion itself, were managed with an eye on public attitudes. In the case of Iraq's possession of weapons of mass destruction and the '45 minute' claim made by the New Labour government to bolster its case for war, attention to public opinion set in motion several years of constant back-tracking and defensive official wrestling with a critical media.[21]

The volume and rate of flow of the information that circulates in the globalised public sphere, the immediacy and unpredictability of its content, and its cognitive impact (dependent on individuals' belief in the truth and reliability of their news), are obvious causal factors in the cultural chaos observed on such occasions as the 9/11 attacks, the Clinton–Lewinsky scandal, or the occupation of Iraq. Just as the regular drip-drip of a household tap differs from the turbulent flow of a rain-swollen river, such a crowded, pressurised media environment is more volatile, less easy to get the measure of, than that of a few years ago. The global availability of real-time satellite news, from Al Jazeera and Al Arabiya as well as BBC, Sky and CNN, alongside a sprawling virtual universe of online media, means that political elites in democratic societies (and also in authoritarian states such as China, when confronted with a crisis such as the SARS outbreak of 2003) must respond to events at speeds which might conflict with the demands of good government.

In his response to the critical findings of the Butler inquiry in July 2004, the British foreign secretary attributed his government's controversial approach to the use of intelligence on Iraqi weapons of mass destruction (WMD) to change in the media environment. As one newspaper reported it, 'the pressure of a 24/7 news agenda and the need to react quickly made traditional decision-making obsolete'.[22] That said, no expression of public opinion can be sufficiently well organised or focused to compel a government to send troops overseas against its better judgement, or indeed to prevent intervention which a government has decided to undertake. The participation of Tony Blair's Labour administration in the attack on Iraq in 2003 took place despite the largest anti-war demonstrations ever seen in Britain. The protests of more than a million marchers in London, and close to 100,000 in Glasgow, set the news agenda for weeks, and commanded headlines on the day. The government invaded Iraq anyway, having secured a parliamentary majority in support of its policy. On this occasion the government acted in what it believed, rightly or wrongly, to be the national interest, taking the risk of ignoring the anti-war movement, and the media criticism which accompanied that stance. There are clearly occasions, however, when it suits politicians to be less principled. Which approach will be adopted in a particular context depends on the answers to three questions, directed at three sets of social actors:

1   Who sets the news agenda (or what makes the media interested in, directs their attention to, a particular event)?

2 What makes the public interested in a particular news story, and what are the influences shaping the outcomes of that interest – in particular, public opinion about what government should do in response to reported events?
3 What makes political elites responsive to public opinion?

We also have to consider what responses in terms of policy and presentation are possible at a given moment in the political cycle. In the language of non-linear dynamics, this is a complex 3-body problem, to which there are a virtually infinite variety of solutions, and which only research into the specifics of a particular interaction can generate. Outcomes are inherently unpredictable, because they are sensitively dependent on initial conditions. In this sense, the 'CNN effect' can never be precisely specified.[23]

Conclusion

Hamilton and Jenner ask if elites will 'become more powerful because of their access to advanced media technologies? Or will the increasing variety of news formats, which offer more entry points for the public, increase non-elite interest and participation in foreign affairs?' (2003: 138). The answers to such questions can never be conclusive, but I will venture to suggest that on the evidence thus far, they are 'no' and 'yes' respectively.

The four elections affecting the leading Coalition powers since the invasion of Iraq provided little evidence that elites were stronger in power. It is true that Bush, Blair and John Howard in Australia were all re-elected in 2004/2005, against backdrops of substantial media criticism of their policies in Afghanistan and the Middle East. Jose Maria Aznar, on the other hand, was defeated, for the reasons suggested in Chapter 4, rather than the fact of the Madrid bombing in itself. In Australia, the Bali atrocity solidified support around a pro-war premier. In Spain, a pro-war premier's attempt to use an Al Qaida bombing to attack a local terrorist movement (one with some popular support amongst Basque nationalists) backfired. Each case was contingent on local circumstances. All had in common the fact that in the democratic world – countries where democratic conditions and political culture are established and deep rooted – cultural chaos produces a kind of *hyper-democracy*.

Where in the not too distant past advanced capitalist societies were characterised by relatively high levels of official secrecy and governmental closure, consumer ignorance and elite control of everything from aesthetics to public agendas for political debate, today we see increased incidence of panics of all kinds (moral, food, health), scandals and feeding frenzies, usually centred on elites, and volatility of the political agenda as reflected in the public sphere. Public discussion on all kinds of issues has become fast and frantic, the media agenda unstable and predictable. In feeding frenzies of the type that engulfed Bill Clinton in 1998, or the British Tories for much of the 1990s, we see loss of governmental, official and corporate control over information flows, leading to heightened competition for control of the media and public agendas.

Where control, or primary definition, was once the default position for elites in government, business and social administration, now they must fight for it, with no certainty of outcome. Official resources are deployed on public relations and spin, but the resulting communication strategies themselves become part of the media agenda, and public evaluation of everything from car advertisements to political campaign posters moves to a set of criteria premised on a sophisticated knowledge of the fact that persuasion is their aim. With all that in mind, the next chapter considers the options available to governments for restoring some order and control to this anarchy.

12 Controlling chaos

It would be simplistic to view the trends described in this book as positive or negative in any absolute sense. As we have seen, not all the dissolutions associated with cultural chaos are to be viewed as positive in their socio-cultural impacts, and to adopt a pragmatic optimism in assessing their implications is not, I hope, to fall into what James W. Carey calls 'the rhetoric of the technological sublime' (2005).[1] I have argued that cultural pessimism should no longer be the default stance of the critical scholar, because the expansion of the internet, the blogosphere and real-time satellite news outlets have been accompanied or paralleled by significant economic and political progress at the global level, not least in the developing countries of what used to be known as the Third World.

In India, China, Latin America and substantial parts of Africa, the application of NICTs such as mobile telephony[2] and the world wide web has opened new doors to educational and economic improvement. NICTs do not on their own resolve long-standing problems of exploitation, incompetence or corruption, but they do make them more transparent, as well as providing the tools for new approaches to modernisation and networked political activism. In India, the 2 million mobile phones now coming on to the market each month have transformed basic industries such as fishing and are contributing materially to the remarkable fact that the country will emerge as an economic superpower within a few years. In China, Cuba and the Middle East, the blogosphere steadily eats away at authoritarian control regimes.

I have also noted the downside of cultural chaos, however. It may facilitate the rise of religious reaction and theocracy, at least in the short term, as much as demo-cratic reform and social liberalisation. The election of Mahmoud Ahmadinejad as Iranian president in June 2005 demonstrated the truth of Daniel Drezner's observation:

> If repressive societies become more open [as a result of NICTs], this does not mean they automatically become more liberal. Religious fundamentalists have embraced the information society just as fervently as classical liberals. Revolution in Iran and genocide in Rwanda show that information tech-nologies are conduits for any kind of information transmission – not just 'desirable' forms'.
>
> (Drezner 2005: 95)

Democratic elections in Iraq may lead to more women in veils, and more homo-sexuals executed in public squares.[3] Skilled politicians and activists of every hue may use NICTs to advance their prospects.

In democratic societies, meanwhile, the accelerating flow of news and journalism that confronts political elites may complicate the practice of good governance by fuelling an environment in which media panics, scares and frenzies intensify, and where popular opinion (or elite perceptions of what popular opinion is, which may not be the same thing) rather than considered judgement drives decision-making by governments and other agencies.

The emerging global communication network erodes intellectual copyright control, which may be a good thing for teenagers downloading digital copies of their favourite music and films, but not necessarily for the global creative community which depends on royalties for its income. States have an interest in protecting intellectual property rights and other forms of trade in electronic data, as well as in the policing of child pornography, 'spam' e-mail and e-fraud. John Palfrey calls for the 'unfettered global flow of information',[4] but this is probably unrealistic, as well as undesirable. The internet can only be as humane and pro-gressive as the people who use it, and since the latter may include religious fundamentalists beheading hostages on camera, as well as paedophiles, white supremacists, and all manner of sociopaths, the continuation of a control regime of some kind is inevitable. Boundaries have positive functions for the maintenance of an ethical and just social order, as well as negative functions of control and domination.

The issue, of course, is who decides where the boundaries lie, and which means of control are appropriate for the globalised public sphere? And which, assuming one can ever answer those questions to a degree which makes a global control regime possible in principle, are likely to be effective?

Controlling chaos

Scientists have three methods of restoring order to chaotic systems. They may try to alter the parameters within which a system behaves chaotically, in the hope of returning it to some kind of stability. Or they may introduce external influences of various kinds to counteract the chaotic behaviour. Or, they may seek to push a chaotic system back onto a more orderly and predictable path. By analogy, the communication control strategies available to political elites in the early twenty-first century can be grouped into three categories:

1   *coercive* strategies designed to destroy or neutralise offending media;
2   *regulatory* strategies designed to manage the global flow of information;
3   *persuasive* strategies of media and opinion management.

Coercive control strategies

Coercive control of global information flows remains an option for political elites in both democratic and authoritarian societies. The invasion and subsequent occupation of Iraq, like the post-9/11 intervention in Afghanistan before it, was accompanied by unprecedented levels of violence by US military forces against journalists, including many from Coalition countries. The resignation of Eason Jordan from his position as managing editor at CNN (see Chapter 8) followed his off-the-record assertion that a number of 'friendly fire' incidents involving journalists from Coalition countries had been deliberate. While Coalition policy-makers have strenuously denied the use of violence and coercion against journalists from their own countries, they have been less concerned to negate the perception that Al Jazeera is a legitimate target. According to Hans Wechsel, regional director of the US State Department's Middle East Partnership initiative, 'we have issues with them giving a platform to people who are calling for violence. It's not a matter of government interference, it's strictly an issue of ethics. After all, we raise ethical concerns with journalists in the US too.'[5] Yes, but not usually with smart bombs.

As Chapter 7 described, Al Jazeera's independent editorial stance has infuriated governments in both the authoritarian and democratic worlds. The channel has upset political elites from Washington to Jeddah with its pro-fundamentalist approach to coverage of the Middle East since 9/11 (using the word 'martyr', for example, to describe suicide bombers and insurgents). The Iranian government closed its Tehran office in April 2005 for allegedly failing 'to respect Iran's national integrity and security'.[6] Al Jazeera had reported ethnic unrest in the Khuzestan province of the country, and publicised the contents of an inflammatory letter by a senior Iranian official. In August 2004 a commission appointed by the Coalition Provisional Authority in Iraq closed Al Jazeera's Baghdad office for a period of one month, on the grounds that the channel's coverage of the fighting in the country was inflammatory and threatened national security. The ban came just days before Coalition forces moved into the city of Najaf to engage the Shia militiamen of Mohammad Al Sadr, and was widely interpreted as an attempt to prevent coverage sympathetic to the insurrectionists, and harmful to the Coalition, from emerging into the global public domain.

The ban was defended on security grounds, and the suggestion that Al Jazeera's presence might jeapordise Coalition and Iraqi security forces on the ground. The decision disappointed many observers, however, who saw it as a depressing example of the Coalition's readiness to adopt the same controlling tactics as authoritarian Arab regimes, not least Saddam Hussein himself, and thus to undermine the publicly declared basis of the Iraqi intervention – i.e., the establishment of democracy in the Middle East. Maher Abdullah, international relations officer for Al Jazeera, wrote in the *Guardian* that 'we have grown used to harassment from authoritarian regimes in the Middle East, but since the Afghanistan war in 2001, we have had more harassment from US officials than from their Arab counterparts.'[7] Abdullah reminded readers that Al Jazeera's offices had been closed in similar fashion by many authoritarian Arab regimes, always on the grounds that its coverage was in some way damaging to the regime concerned. The same thing was happening in Iraq, he argued, despite the democratising rhetoric of the Coalition. 'Blaming the messenger for bad news', he concluded, 'might help in hiding these from the public for the while. But it doesn't make them go away.'

Abdullah is right, in more than one sense. Not only does banning Al Jazeera not make the bad news from Iraq go away; it doesn't make Al Jazeera go away. In response to the ban, commentators all over the world leapt to the channel's defence, arguing that the principles of press freedom and independence were more important than the short-term inconvenience of having Al Jazeera reporters bearing witness to what Coalition forces were doing. The film *Control Room* (Jehane Noujaim, 2004), which documented the efforts of Al Jazeera staff to cover the Iraqi War, conveyed to audiences all over the world both the strengths and weaknesses of the channel, but reinforced the notion that in a world where Fox News could be accepted as a serious news organisation, why not Al Jazeera? As one commentator puts it:

> Al-Jazeera is not perfect; it can be lurid and over-heated. Some say it sits somewhere between the BBC and the heavily-slanted Fox News. Still, it is the nearest the Arab world has to an independent media organisation of heft.[8]

This commentator quoted the former US ambassador to Qatar, Kenton Keith:

> For the long-range importance of press freedom in the Middle East and the advantages that will ultimately have for the west, you have to be a supporter of al-Jazeera, even if you have to hold your nose sometimes.

The repeated bans on Al Jazeera in Iraq and elsewhere sparked similar media coverage all over the world, demonstrating the difficulty of containing dissident voices in an ever-more closely connected communication environment. The desire for control on the part of the US and its Iraqi allies, as well as by authoritarian regimes in the region, is clearly there, but the capacity for achieving it is limited. The attempt to control has a tendency to become part of the story, reflecting especially negatively on democratic governments which have claimed the moral high ground. Satellite and online media quickly turn the ban into a story of global reach and resonance, engaging audiences from the Middle East to Milwaukee in debate about the meaning of media freedom. Al Jazeera, whether biased towards Islamic fundamentalism or not, emerges from the story as victim, and the demo--cratic governments which attack its staff and bureaus as hypocritical.

In his introduction to *The Al Jazeera Phenomenon*, Mohamed Zayani warns that any attempt 'to silence Al Jazeera [by the US] shatters the widely held perception about the freedom of the American press and plays havoc with the liberal discourse on democracy' (2005: 27). For Al Jazeera's communications director, Jihad Ballout, questioning the basis of western governmental hostility to the channel:

The Americans call for reform [of the Arab world]. They call for freedom of expression. For democratisation, liberalisation. We have been part of that process, helping create real and lasting change in society, giving people a voice. We are part of the march towards reform in the Middle East.[9]

These words were given added weight by the fact that the person to whom Ballout addressed them was Alistair Campbell, former Downing Street communications director and fierce critic of any and all criticism of his governmental masters. Here, just one year after his resignation at the height of the Hutton Inquiry, Campbell acknowledged that 'Al-Jazeera represents an opportunity as well as a potential threat'.

Control through censorship

If bombs and bullets might 'work' against an organisation such as Al Jazeera (and its rival Al Arabiya, which was attacked by suicide bombers in Baghdad in 2004), they are less difficult to apply to net-based media. States do have a range of options available to them in policing the internet, however. Monroe Price observes that 'new technologies can enhance as well as diminish forms of control' (2002: 17). NICTs empower as well as subvert state authority, in so far as techniques such as geo-locational filtering enhance state enforcement capabilities and permit the continued policing of nation-state boundaries.

The networked nature of the internet is also its weakness. The world wide web is comprised of structural choke points which are vulnerable to attack. States can exploit these vulnerabilities to police various forms of offending communication, and are developing their disruptive tools all the time. Post-9/11, preventing use of the internet to disseminate terror manuals and Islamic fundamentalist hate speech has become a pressing national security issue for western governments likely to be the target of jihadist activity. In the aftermath of the July 2005 suicide bombings in London, reported one newspaper, 'one by one, Al-Qaeda's affiliated websites have vanished until only a handful remain'.[10]

In China, after text messaging helped to expose governmental cover-up of the 2003 SARS epidemic, officials began to filter the 220 billion text messages sent in the country each year, and to reassert their control over a rapidly expanding zone of 'cyber dissidence' by increased inspection of service providers and more arrests. In January 2004 Chinese authorities arrested the editor and six other journalists working for the *Southern Metropolis Daily*, after the newspaper reported a fresh outbreak of SARS.[11] This and similar incidents, such as the closure of the ideologically unruly *21st Century World Herald* were interpreted by observers as evidence that China was reasserting its authoritarian control over information flows within the country, even as it opened up its economy to the global market.

Hundreds of ideologically unruly bloggers have been arrested by the Iranian authorities, and web sites blocked, including that run by former vice-president and leading reformer Mohammad Ali Abtahi. In Bahrain in early 2005, dissenting bloggers were being arrested and accused of defaming the monarch Hamad bin

Isa al-Khalifa, a crime which could attract a ten-year jail sentences on conviction. Repressive action of this kind suggests that the authorities in many countries are concerned about the impact of the internet on pro-democracy movements. These authorities retain the power to shut down offending web sites, or to prosecute those who operate them, and will continue to do so for a variety of reasons. But they cannot entirely or forever shut down offending voices, which may simply relocate beyond the zone of control. Thus, Chinese dissidents will set up web sites in Taiwan. Child pornographers will find relatively unpoliced countries in the Caribbean and elsewhere from which to establish their criminal businesses. Jihadist web sites will route around the national security agencies working to keep them offline.

At the point of use, whether in Iran or America, individual demand combined with the economic imperatives of cultural capital to export its commodities tends to erode state constraints on the free flow of global information, although efforts to maintain control continue. In September 2005 the British government announced a consultation to determine ways of criminalising the consumption of violent pornography on the internet. Recognising the difficulties of eliminating the offending overseas web sites, the government was seeking to deter individuals from accessing the material, in the same way that consumption of child pornography has been tackled in the UK through high-profile policing initiatives such as Operation Ore. Sceptics doubted, however, that even if consensus could be reached about what constitutes 'violent' pornography, and the capacity of particular images to 'deprave and corrupt', the practical difficulties of policing a law which hundreds of thousands of people would routinely flout could be overcome.

Some states, such as France, intervene to prevent domestic consumption of various forms of content on grounds of defending national identity and resisting cultural imperialism, imposing limits, for example, on the percentage of foreign-produced music or film which should be released in the French marketplace. Authoritarian states in the Middle East and elsewhere, as we have seen, have cited 'cultural imperialism' as a reason for prohibiting mass access to foreign-produced TV channels, sexually explicit magazines and the like. But such policies are increasingly difficult to sustain. One consequence of free information flow in countries where the authorities have traditionally resisted it is to generate and facilitate opposition to continued state control of the media. As with the bomb dropped on an Al Jazeera bureau in Kabul or Baghdad, the repressive act in a globalised media environment is a transparent one which generates media attention and criticism. Once exposed to such materials, be it Al Jazeera, CNN or Disney, and once aware that exposure is being restricted by political elites, demand for them increases. People want more of what they know they haven't got, whether it be Beatles records in pre-*glasnost* Moscow, or internet porn in puritan Iran.[12] Economic forces and basic human curiosity drive anti-authoritarian tendencies. In the chaotic communication environment of the twenty-first century, the cultural marketplace tends to self-adjust and work around state control apparatuses faster than those apparatuses can adapt to a rapidly evolving environment.

Control of the internet continues to be a strategy adopted by a variety of states nonetheless, and the various technical approaches to net filtering have been documented by researchers working on the OpenNet Initiative. They note that 'these filtering regimes can be understood only in the political, legal, religious and social context in which they arise' (Palfrey 2005). China, for example, filters potentially subversive political material, while Singapore focuses on pornography. Other countries filter out web sites relating to gay and lesbian sexualities. These researchers distinguish between opaque and transparent control regimes, and between consistent and periodic control. Thus, Saudi Arabia's restrictions on internet use are transparent, i.e. clearly communicated to the population, while China's are opaque (no one knows exactly what is and what is not permitted). Saudi restrictions are consistent, while those applied in Iraq in the run-up to the December 2004 election were periodic. All such efforts produce diminishing returns, however. As this source suggests, 'technically savvy users [in Saudi Arabia or elsewhere] can simply not be stopped from accessing blocked content'.

Regulatory strategies

If repression and coercion are limited in their effectiveness as control strategies, what of regulation? Lawyer Joel Reidenberg argues that 'democratic states can and should intervene in network design',[13] and some regulatory tools are available. The domain name licensing system for the world wide web is controlled by the USA, for example, giving it a degree of influence over the evolution of the system. For as long as it perceives itself to be involved in a war with groups that use the internet as an organisational and propaganda tool, the US government is likely to wish to use that influence as a regulatory tool.

The difficulty with regulation of content, however, is that there are few areas of global consensus on what constitutes illegitimate online activity, and on which illegitimate activity should be regulated or forcibly prohibited. Western standards of sexual display, for example, are unacceptable to states governed by Sharia law. A global regulatory regime assumes global cultural norms which do not, and probably never will, exist.

Policing through commercialisation

Chapter 6 noted concerns about the impact on Al Jazeera's independent editorial stance of its being privatised. I suggested there that such concerns were premature, given that the channel's audience – the very thing that gave it commercial value – had been attracted precisely by its perceived independence, and was therefore unlikely to remain loyal to an organisation seen as tainted or corrupted by commercial values (if indeed such corruption were to happen). But in general, and if measures are taken early enough, as in the southeast Asian states discussed in Chapter 10, commercialisation and mainstreaming of dissident media can be a potentially effective approach to the control of unwelcome communication. Societies such as Singapore, Malaysia and Thailand (and indeed China) have with some success pre-empted the potentially problematic political use of NICTs by harnessing their development to strategies of nation building and economic modernisation.

Monroe Price observed in 1995 that 'if states have less control over accounts that come across borders, they will seek to exercise more control over journalists and the reports they export' (Price 1995: 77). Rupert Murdoch's Star TV, for example, is understood to have removed the BBC from its China service because of political pressure from a government concerned by the British broadcaster's independence and unpredictability. In the run-up to the 2008 Olympics in Beijing, Chinese authorities began to put pressure on all foreign media channels operating in the country (including those owned by News Corp), citing the maintenance of what they called 'national cultural security'.[14] In January 2006 Google announced that it would censor its service for the Chinese market. Price adds that in circumstances where control of media is increasingly uncertain, states may instead resort to what he describes as 'enhanced acceptance of commercialisation, and the depoliticisation of the media' (ibid.: 78). This is one interpretation of what has happened in China since 1989, where a dynamic market economy has been allowed to import western brands of consumer goods and services, including cultural commodities, amidst strict censorship of political media. Chinese scholar Li Xiguang notes with distaste that 'in the age of globalisation, the Chinese television audience is increasingly becoming the passive subject of manipulation and control by thirteen state TV channels and nine Murdoch channels'.[15]

The suggestion that commercialisation equates to depoliticisation assumes an overly narrow definition of what constitutes politics, however. As Chapter 6 argued, many commercial cultural products embody assumptions (sexual liberalism, freedom to travel, the right to rebel against the parental culture) that are deeply threatening to authoritarian societies, and thus profoundly political. In Iran, as in the former Soviet Union and now in many Middle Eastern Arab states, the presence of 'outside' cultural influences, far from narcoticising the easily-led masses, has been an essential element in the volatile mix which has led to pressure for political change. There are countries, it is true, where access to advanced capitalist standards of consumer affluence, including the consumption of cultural commodities, can be argued to have had a stabilising impact, and perhaps to have prevented social unrest and revolution. Singapore is one. China may turn out to be another. But the story of China's 'miracle' is only a few years old, and no one really knows for how long the uneasy compromise between a capitalistic economy and a communistic polity can be maintained. The lack of Tiananmen-style protests today does not mean that they will not suddenly explode tomorrow (assuming that the Chinese government does not itself see the benefits of permitting democratisation and the ultimate surrender of its power monopoly to a democratic system). In 2004 more than 70,000 protests against corruption and other failures of local and national government in China were recorded. Shanghai was reported to be a site of growing popular impatience and unrest.

If pressure for reform is growing, who can say that it has not been amplified by a misjudged shut-down of an unlicensed news web site, or a film about poor safety standards in the Chinese mining industry, banned in China but disseminated through pirated DVDs? China cannot prevent such leakages merely by the use of such techniques as persuading News Corp to remove the BBC from its Star TV service, or broadcasting CNN with a time delay (as was the practice at the time of this writing), or cracking down on foreign-owned media. The globalised public sphere is simply too leaky for that.

Persuasive strategies

Apart from strategies of coercion and commercialisation, a third strategy for exercising at least some control over a chaotic media environment is available: management of media content and thus of opinion, exercised not through bombs dropped on or bans of offending media, nor through regulation of the infrastructure of globalised news, but through the design and deployment of persuasive communication which can shape that news in favourable ways.

To communicate effectively in an environment characterised by a heightened cultural chaos (which will include the unpredictable eruptions associated with democratic politics, free market economics, and diffuse, accessible, interactive technologies) requires paying more attention than ever before to the content, presentation and distribution of the message; to the design, in other words, of effective source strategies, or public relations. As we have seen, bombs can be dropped on unwelcome Arabsat bureaux, organisations banned and journalists assassinated, but in contemporary conditions these tactics result only in more critical scrutiny for the perpetrators. The murder and intimidation of journalists by corrupt officials and businessmen in Togliatti, Russia, may have had some short-term impact on that region, but is common knowledge to the entire world thanks to a documentary broadcast on Channel 4 in 2004.[16] Very little happens, not least to the media, which is not witnessed and made public sooner or later. In these conditions openness, honesty and transparency in communication become the most effective tools for any official organisation that wishes to preserve its credibility and legitimacy, along-side professional public relations of the type capable of reactive crisis management as well as proactive agenda setting. In the age of online journalism and 24-hour real-time news, 'propaganda in the historical sense is not an option. The prolifer-ation of alternative news sources on the web goes hand in hand with an increasingly media-savvy audience'.[17] Propaganda *is* an option, still. Just not a very sensible one.

Coalition forces recognised this fact in the preparation for the 2003 invasion of Iraq. In January that year the Bush administration set up its Office of Global Communication 'to ensure consistency in messages' overseas (Snow 2004: 60). On another front, the policy of *embedding*, which saw 500 American and 100 British journalists integrated into fighting units as the invasion began, was a deliberate attempt to make military public relations 'fit for purpose' in an information environ-ment which had changed radically even since the first Gulf War of 1991 (only 30 journalists covered the Normandy landings during the Second World War).[18] In 1991, and again during the UK–US intervention in Kosovo in 1998, media organisations had been critical of official secrecy and reticence in providing accurate and timely information. In both of those conflicts the unintended deaths of civilians produced negative coverage throughout the world. In 2003 communication officials in both the UK and US armed forces stated:

What you have got to do is to be more honest about your mistakes. Ideally what we want to do is tell the press that something has gone wrong before they find out through other sources.

(Ministry of Defence spokesperson, March 2003)

The flow of information must be timely, accurate and useful.

(Victoria Clarke, Assistant US Secretary of Defence for Public Affairs)

Notwithstanding the widely discussed problems that inevitably arise with embedding, such as the tendency for journalists to become dependent on and over-identify with their units, the policy was judged to have been a success by most observers after the invasion (Katovsky and Carlson 2003). 'The Pentagon was happy, the press was satisfied, and the American [and British] people got coverage that was more close-up, personal and immediate than they had ever gotten' (Hess and Kalb 2003: 94). All this was true, although it would be an error to think that the policy was motivated by the official desire for openness as an end in itself. The objective of embedding was to manage, and thus control, an information environment more chaotic than any ever encountered by military planners before. Both the US and UK governments have moved towards strategies of information dominance in conflict situations, as part of the military doctrine of *full spectrum dominance*. This approach recognises the fact that, as the media environment has become more complex and unpredictable over time, so must governmental information management become more sophisticated and scientific.

Cultural diplomacy and international communication

Beyond the battlefields of Afghanistan and Iraq, and in response to the growing reach and influence of Al Jazeera and other Arab-language media, the United States adopted a policy to information management familiar to observers of the Cold War, and criticised then for its ineffectiveness. During the Cold War years the US government's Information Agency (USIA) supported Radio Free Europe and Radio Liberty, overtly anti-communist propaganda outlets, in their efforts to penetrate the Warsaw Pact countries with pro-western, anti-communist propaganda. As Chapter 7 noted, the efforts of these channels were always tainted with the 'propaganda' brush, and few observers would argue that they had very much to do with the end of the Cold War and the collapse of the Soviet Union in 1991.

Having closed the USIA as a response to the fall of the Berlin Wall and the dissolution of the USSR, after the 9/11 attacks the Bush administration set up its Office of Global Communication with a budget of $1 billion. Some of the money was used to establish the Arab-language Radio Sawa in 2002, broadcasting to around 20 Middle Eastern countries. In July 2004 the US launched the 24-hour TV channel Alhurra ('the free one'), largely to counter the success of Al Jazeera. Conceived by Norman Pattiz, the founder of America's largest radio empire, Westwood One, to counter what he described as 'anti-American hate speak on radio and television', the channel's stated aim was to provide a source of 'reliable news'. Like Radio Free Europe and Voice of America, however, such overt US government involvement in news-making risked failure, in so far as it was 'routinely dismissed as a US propaganda mouthpiece' from the start.[19] One Arab observer noted that Alhurra was 'stubbornly bent on hammering home the [US] government agenda, preaching to Arabs about the frailties of their society.'[20]

Whether such criticism was justified or not, the mere perception that Alhurra was motivated by propagandist objectives would inevitably limit its reach and influence. Broadcasting from Washington to 70 million people in 22 countries of the Middle East, a key aim of Alhurra was to prepare the Iraqi public for the elections of January 2005, though few observers predicted much success in this objective (on election day in January 2005, 58 per cent of Iraqis voted, although it was not clear how many had been persuaded to do so by Alhurra). With its $62 million of US taxpayers' funding, one journalist described Alhurra as 'the most sophisticated and expensive US attempt to influence international opinion since the creation of the Voice of America radio network during the Second World War'.[21] Like that earlier example of US propaganda, went the implication, Alhurra would fail to gain credibility and audience loyalty. According to the Lebanon's *Daily Star* newspaper, 'like the US government's Radio Sawa before it', Alhurra would be regarded by Arab audiences as 'an entertaining, expensive and irrelevant hoax'.[22] After the invasion of Iraq, the United States government spent $96 million to set up the Iraqi Media Network (IMN), comprising an 'Alliance friendly' satellite news channel and a newspaper (*Al Sabah*). In May 2004 it was reported that the editor of *Al Sabah*, Ismail Zayer, had resigned from his post, citing political interference. The largely accurate perception that the IMN was little more than a US propaganda tool has prevented it from achieving anything like the credibility of the BBC, far less Al Jazeera and the other Arab-language channels.

In July 2004, and in response to the launch of Alhurra, the BBC's global news division set up a new Arabic-language news channel, supported with $50 million of Foreign and Commonwealth Office money. Though benefiting from the BBC's well-established reputation, many observers were sceptical of the new channel's chances of gaining widespread public trust against a background of UK military involvement in Iraq.[23] For the BBC, as for the US-based organisations seeking to make an impact in the Middle East, the only path to such credibility, and thus to the persuasive power of credible information, is through journalism that is perceived to be independent of political elites.

Conclusion

Away from the war zone, within which at least some forms of control may well be justified in the interests of protecting life and national security, the clamour for a re-assertion of twentieth-century standards of media control can occasionally be heard above the noise of cultural chaos. In 1997, responding to a particularly irreverent live TV debate about the royal family which had been broadcast on the UK's mainstream ITV channel, David Goodhart had asked if it was not time to consider if 'an untrammelled, populist media' could be 'too free for an intelligent democracy?'[24] Nearly a decade later a former editor of the *Financial Times*, Richard Lambert, suggested that the media were now so subversive, so cavalier towards their obligations to rationality and the maintenance of deliberative democracy, that it was time to revise the historic belief in press freedom. Lambert asked:

> Is it [media freedom] adequate for a world in which global media con- glomerates publish and broadcast across frontiers, using a battery of new communications technologies, and in which states have limited powers to influence what citizens read, hear or see? Powerful institutions that secure unlimited rights to self-expression may dominate and distort communications and the agenda for public debate. In the end, they may actually constrain freedom of expression.[25]

Caution is needed to ensure that such statements, reasonable though they may seem when confronted with the evil of child pornography, or the brutality of racist hate speech, are not used to justify censorship of the globalised public sphere on political grounds. Not only is censorship counterproductive, because of the enhanced transparency of the act in a globally connected world (even when it succeeds in closing down some offending outlet or other), but *effective* censorship that actually works assumes that there can be such a thing as global standards of decency and good taste in matters of political journalism, sex and morality, or religious expression. Twenty-first-century governments may strive to exercise control over the media consumed within their own nation-state borders, while local conditions – not least the degree of democratic participation involved in deciding what is to be controlled – will determine how effective such efforts can be in the short term. In the long term, and in the context of cultural globalisation, sustainable strategies for the control of media output can only be based on persuasion, and the building of global public consensus around specific content categories. Where such consensus can be reached, as for example in the revulsion felt by the great majority of countries at the spread of child pornography on the internet, coercive control mechanisms may have some prospect of success. Such agreement is rare, however, and opposition to censorship – be it political, moral or religious – must continue to be the default position of all those who aspire to the promotion of human freedom and dignity. The experiences of murdered film director Theo Van Gogh, his colleague Muslim MP Asi Al Firsi in Holland (threatened by Islamic funda- mentalists in her country for being both a woman and a feminist), or Gurpreet Kaur Bhatti, the British author of the play *Bezhti* in Britain (driven into hiding by male Sikhs who found her work offensive), remind us that freedom of thought and expression continue to need defending, even in the most liberal countries of the advanced capitalist world.

13 Conclusion and postscript: cultural chaos and the critical project

Let me now summarise by identifying the main constituents of the shift from the control to a chaos paradigm in the contemporary communication environment.

Control		Chaos
Information scarcity	—	Information surplus
Sealed (closed)	—	Leaky (open)
Opacity	—	Transparency
Exclusivity	—	Accessibility
Homogeneity	—	Heterogeneity (diversity)
Hierarchy	—	Network
Passivity	—	(Inter)activity
Dominance	—	Competition

Figure 2 The constituents of chaos

Information scarcity – Information surplus

In the era of cultural chaos, people have access to more information than ever before. If information is the prerequisite of knowledge, and if knowledge is power, other things remaining equal, this trend corresponds to a power-shift from the traditionally information-rich elite to the no-longer so information-poor mass. Which is not to prejudge the quality of information available, nor to assume that everyone has equal access to it, nor that all who have access to it use that access to develop their intellectual resources in ways that might have positive political impacts on their own lives or on the management of the society in which they live. Throughout history, all communication technologies have been put to destructive as well as constructive uses. What has changed is the vastly expanded supply and availability of information, and with it the potential depth and range of individual and collective knowledge.

Sealed (closed) – Leaky (open)

Information no longer flows along sealed pathways, prevented from escape and contamination of the masses by state censorship regimes. It was never entirely leakage-free, of course, but the possibilities for maintaining information closure were clearly much greater in the days of mass media illiteracy and relative elite monopoly on information production and dissemination than they are in the era of proliferating satellite, online and digital media.

Information leaks not just because of the connective, networked features of these media, but also because of the economic imperatives of the media market-place, which rewards scoops and exclusivity, irrespective of who and what are damaged in the leaking. The pattern of political scandals of recent years reflects not merely the decline of deference discussed in Chapter 4, but commercial pressures on the media to break news about elite deviance whether or not it conflicts with editorial or proprietorial allegiance. As one observer puts it: 'New forces are creating powerful and sometimes irresistible pressures on editors. Information technologies are changing the way news is reported and circulated' (Sabato *et al.* 2000: 38).

The chaos paradigm views power, like the information on which so much power is based, as a fluid. It ebbs and flows between locations and centres, spreading amongst societies along the channels and pathways provided by communication media. Power *pools*. It evaporates, dilutes and drains away as environmental conditions change. Communication is the medium through which power resources are disseminated, and leaky channels of communication therefore mean less secure power centres.

Opacity – Transparency

As information leaks, the sources and mechanisms of power become more transparent. There remains, of course, much that is hidden and secret, even in the leaky information environment of the twenty-first century. Much of the information that really matters is never made public. But in the contemporary political culture of disclosure, which sees everything from the pornographic detail of the Starr Report to the forensic burrowing of the Hutton Inquiry go online, much more of it is than in the past, and not necessarily because political elites wish it so. Since at least 1985 and the launch of Mikhail Gorbachev's *glasnost* campaign, perceived at the time as a specifically Soviet phenomenon but thereafter achieving the status of a universal principle of good government, the maximum extent of information openness has become a political necessity for regimes which wish to retain legitimacy in the public domain, because whether they permit it or not, bad news will out and the mechanisms of power will be made transparent.

The struggle between opacity and transparency is constant and subject to roll back at any time. Elites may seek to give the appearance of openness by legislative or presentational means, and the apparatuses of spin and public relations are extensively employed to achieve these as well as other, less sinister objectives. But a public predisposition to transparency in the processes of power acquisition and management has become a given for serious political actors in a democracy. This is a feature of the contemporary political environment with real consequences for what the limits on power can be.

Exclusivity – Accessibility

This surge in the quantity and quality of revelatory information, be it in the form of the Hutton Inquiry website or the Drudge report, stems largely from the eroding exclusivity of the global media. Until recently, resource-poor groups had relatively restricted access to media production, and were more or less dependent on mainstream and established outlets. By the late twentieth century Ithiel de Sola Pool could observe of the electronic media that 'they allow for more knowledge, easier access, and freer speech than were ever enjoyed before' (1983: 251). A quarter of a century later, with the establishment of the internet as a mass medium, there will soon be hundreds of millions of online producers.

Chapter 8 examined those factors that might be said to undermine the quality of the information which results from this heightened access, but that it is possible at all is an unprecedented cultural phenomenon, as recognised by US Justice Stewart Dalzell when he opposed the censorial tendencies of the Communications Decency Act of 1996:

> The internet has achieved the most participatory marketplace of mass speech that the world has yet seen. Individual citizens of limited means can speak to a world-wide audience on issues of concern to them.
>
> (Dalzell quoted in Katz 1997: 44)

Homogeneity – Heterogeneity (diversity)

From accessibility derives heterogeneity, or editorial diversity. Yes, the great majority of words posted on those millions of blogs are disposable; personal diaries and other whimsy of interest to few beyond their immediate authors (which is not to downplay their significance to those authors). But even the few hundreds or thousands that make it through the informal quality control mechanisms described in Chapter 8 represent a significant augmentation of the degree of diversity of viewpoint available to users of the globalised public sphere. The rise of Al Jazeera and other satellite news media has substantially eroded the historic western monopoly on transnational news, and provides even a radical dissenter such as Osama Bin Laden with what one observer calls 'a delivery system in a competitive media environment' (Bessaiso 2005: 153). What he says is less important for our purposes here than the fact that he is *able* to say it, irrespective of the wishes of the world's leading superpower.

Hierarchy – Network

The impacts of information leakage, of elite transparency, and enhanced diversity of opinion are amplified by the network structure of so much of the global media system. While national and transnational media remain largely as they always have been, hierarchical and centralised, albeit more driven to leakage and editorial subversiveness than in earlier times, the network structure of the world wide web, in combination with the 24-hour presence of real-time satellite news, produces an environment where information cascades become more unpredictable, more frequent, and more difficult for elites to contain when they begin.[1] News storms develop without warning, placing power elites on permanently reactive, defensive mode.

Passivity – (Inter)activity

Once informed, there is in this environment unprecedented opportunity for mass interactivity with the media system, and through it, engagement with power elites. Audiences have never been as passive as the cultural pessimists have assumed, always having had the capacity for negotiated, differential or aberrant decoding of the messages they have received (Hall 1980). In the past, though, the great majority had no choice but to confront those messages in sullen silence, having little or no access to the means of feeding back. One might write a letter to a newspaper, with no certainty of publication, while the big top-down media of the twentieth century – radio, film and TV – by their nature allowed few opportunities for public participation. Now there are daytime talk shows, political debate programmes, and digital means of instantaneous commentary on programme content. There are millions of personal websites and blogs, through which more people than ever before routinely engage with and express views on the issues of the day.

Dominance – Competition

Thus, an information environment once characterised by dominance and hierarchy has become one of much greater competitiveness and uncertainty; more like a market of competing ideas than a planned economy of dominant ones; more like information anarchy than information control, and with a greater capacity for the disruption of political authority than at any time in human history. Even before the internet had become a mass medium, Arquilla and Ronfeldt observed that the information revolution made governments of every stripe 'less able to control the dissemination of information', and that

> it disrupts and erodes the hierarchies around which institutions are nor-
> mally designed; it diffuses and redistributes power, often to the benefit of

what may be considered weaker, smaller actors; it crosses borders and redraws boundaries; it generally compels closed systems to open up.

(Arquilla and Ronfeldt 1997: 26)

For Robins and Aksoy, as a result of these trends, 'the nation-state is an abode of order now increasingly threatened by global turbulence' (2005: 18).

Journalism and power in a globalised world

At any given time particular societies will be describable in terms of the degree to which their communication environments exhibit the constituents of chaos listed above, and thus the extent to which they are clothed in an unpredictable and volatile information environment, as opposed to a controlled and apparently stable one. In combination with an analysis of the structure of the communication environment in the given society, and the extent to which it accommodates a functioning public sphere, this provides a means of evaluating the current state of its political culture, and the direction of political trends (if not outcomes). Paradoxically, if consistent with the evolutionary principle that adaptable systems are better at coping with environmental change than rigid and inflexible ones, a high measure of cultural chaos within a particular society will equate with a relatively high capacity for progressive reform, and a low propensity for systemic collapse. Systems which enforce top-down closure and homogeneity – *closed systems* – are conservative by definition. They may maintain the appearance of stability for longer or shorter periods, all the while stagnating and ossifying until they fracture under the pressures produced by the increasing encroachment of external information sources.

In a society such as the US, on the other hand, with its vibrant and crowded media system (including a hyperactive blogosphere), its constitutional emphasis on freedom of speech, its argumentative journalistic culture and its highly developed counter-cultural marketplace, the pressures for catastrophic upheaval or collapse are weak. Dissent and dissidence have places to go and be heard, including the mainstream multiplex, the glossy pages of *Vanity Fair*, or the bestseller shelves in Borders' book store. You may not like the government, but you can't say that you're not allowed to criticise it relentlessly and without mercy, and to consume with glee the criticisms of others, be they journalists, documentary-makers, academics or stand-up comedians. To the extent that capitalist societies are *open systems*, in which communication and information flow freely in and out, they are more likely to evolve in a progressive and sustainable manner, notwithstanding the tendencies to hyper-democracy and 'mediated mob rule' discussed in Chapter 11. As the sociological effects of democratisation, cultural commodification and technological evolution have been felt on capitalist social organisation, the power relationships which hitherto existed between, say, boss and worker, man and woman, gay and straight, or black and white, have dissolved into a more fluid, volatile, continually evolving state in which the control of economic resources no longer equates to the control of cultural resources and political power. Power flows up, down and along the extended networks of communication which straddle the globe and render boundaries increasingly porous. Media barons can no longer act in the baronial manner of old, though they may wish to, and sometimes try.

Not only does the chaos model imply that political dominance through control of media output is relatively difficult to establish and maintain in contemporary conditions. It also implies that social progress in a variety of forms can emerge from the chaotic flow of information which characterises the contemporary period. Progressive sexual and ethnic politics in the advanced capitalist world, economic modernisation and democratisation in the developing countries are spreading faster in the new conditions than they might otherwise have done. If cultural change is a process of memetic evolution in which meanings transform over time (the meanings of ethnicity, homosexuality, women's equality, etc.), that process tends to accelerate under the conditions I have described in this book.

Postscript: cultural chaos and the critical project

In making these arguments, I have frequently been challenged on their implications for the critical role of the communication scholar. What is left for us to do, I am asked, if my qualified cultural optimism is indeed justified? Scott Lash argues that in the 'new, non-linear regime of power' associated with the information age, 'critique is no longer possible' (2002: xi). Is he right?

Of course not. Critique *is* possible, but not the critique of something defined as 'dominant ideology' or 'bias', nor of 'dumbing-down' and all the variants on that concept which have prevailed in media scholarship for so long. In a multi-channel media-verse proving the bias of one channel, even such an esteemed source as the BBC is meaningless when set against the content of the system as a whole. No one, least of all the journalist, knows what 'dominant ideology' is any more. The ideological environment comprises a chaotic whirl of competing ideas and belief-systems, sitting atop a crowded cultural-commodity marketplace of unprecedented depth, diversity and adversarialism towards elites in all walks of life. The concept of 'dumbing-down', meanwhile, is a recurring critical trope founded on subjective aesthetic and moral judgements with which one can agree or disagree, but which have little place in the sociology of journalism except as a reminder of how elitist intellectual discourse on culture used to be.

There continue to be competitive economic pressures on journalistic organisations to cut their costs and to take inappropriate editorial shortcuts. It is important to maintain a critical overview of how these pressures are acting on content, and to monitor the degree to which the privileged information status of journalism may be compromised by decisions that are financial rather than editorial in nature. But this monitoring requires neither the aesthetic presumptions of the dumbing-down discourse, nor the conspiratorial dogma of the propaganda model.

If dominant ideology, bias and dumbing-down are, with due acknowledgement to Tom Wolfe, the 'three stooges'[2] of critical media scholarship, now due for a dignified retirement, let me propose a critical agenda for the twenty-first century focused on three sets of empirically researchable problems:

- the evolving information content of journalism;
- the sociological impacts, and the communicative dynamics, of an increasingly chaotic news cycle;
- the ethics and mechanics of communication control.

The information content of news

This book has identified a number of challenges to what we can call the 'quality' of the information available in the globalised public sphere. Journalists have more and better news-gathering technology to work with, but less time to develop their stories, and more space to fill. In these circumstances there is value in examining the substance of what it is that journalists in the twenty-first century are saying. What is 24-hour news telling us, and how do its stories compare in content, structure and meaning with more traditional print and broadcast modes of journalistic delivery? What kind of narratives are supported by the flow medium of 24-hour news (as opposed to the freeze-frames of older print and broadcast platforms) and does it add to the stock of human knowledge in significant ways? If news cycles are faster, and there is more space and time to fill with stories, is the content of news becoming less 'hard' and more 'soft'? Does the quantity of speculation, extrapolation and inaccuracy increase in real-time news, and does this devalue its information content?

Online journalism poses a further problem of quality control, arising from its decentralised, democratised, accessible nature. Of the millions of bloggers active at any given time, only a few hundred become credible, *trusted* sources of news and comment in the globalised public sphere. The rest comprise a communicative Tower of Babel, fleeting and insubstantial, perhaps mischievous, sometimes dangerous. Although it has already begun, there is much more work to be done on understanding the processes by which some online sources 'infect' and become absorbed into the mainstream of globalised news culture. Chapter 8 discussed the crossover of *norm.blog* in February 2005, and suggested some explanations as to why it happened. It should be part of the research agenda of the sociology of cultural chaos to plot and monitor these memetic contagions as they spread virus-like around the world. What processes and factors come into play in determining the 'success' of a blog: content, style, coincidence and contingency, or combinations of these and other factors?

There is also an emerging educational agenda for media studies. While dissolving boundaries between journalism and not-journalism, amateur and professional, objective and subjective, the blogosphere has also exposed the weaknesses and incompetences of many 'respectable' media outlets, generating what some characterise as a crisis of credibility and authority for journalism as a cultural form. Media scholars can contribute to the resolution of this problem not only by critiquing the quality of journalism, but by educating journalists in what John Hartley has described as 'the conditions for journalism's existence: where it comes from, what it is for, and how it works' (1996: 35). More recently Hartley (2005) has argued that journalism education in universities must take a lead in the teaching of what good journalism is, and that this knowledge is of value as much to professional journalists at the *New York Times* as to amateurs on the blogosphere. For Hartley, we have entered a 'redactional' society of writing publics, where everyone is potentially a journalist. And if everyone has the potential, through blogs and other online means, to be read (if not necessarily read *as journalism*), then journalism studies has an enhanced educational role to play in ensuring that those opportunities and potentials can be realised to the full.

The socio-psychological impacts of an increasingly chaotic news cycle

Chapter 11 discussed the growth of media panics, frenzies and scares associated with cultural chaos, and the possibility that public anxiety may be heightened, lives and reputations damaged and good government undermined by the information trends discussed in this book. These effects are not deliberate, necessarily, but can be harmful to individuals, organisations and societies. As such, they are an appropriate topic for empirical research. How do people experience a media event such as the 9/11 or Beslan attacks, and what does it tell them about the world in which they live? What drives the emergence of panics and scares? Can they be predicted, and their effects mitigated? These are questions to be answered with audience research, content and context analysis, interviews with journalists, editors and political actors designed to identify the multiple factors involved in the rise and fall of news stories into and out of news agenda, and their impacts on political decision-making. Work of this kind already exists, such as the Cardiff university study on MMR coverage cited in Chapter 11, but in the era of cultural chaos, and with new sources of global anxiety such as bird flu and global warming in the air, it is rising up the agenda of research priorities.

Another way of formulating this set of problems is to ask – where is the boundary between order and chaos in journalistic communication? Where does the constructively critical coverage and scrutiny of politics and public affairs become the destructive dissemination of panic, frenzy and scare? How does legitimate journalistic coverage of the threat of terrorism become panic about Al Qaida's 'global terror network' sufficient to produce something like the Patriot Act in the USA or identity cards in the UK? How does legitimate coverage of food and lifestyle issues become a health scare? How does socially useful coverage of a problematic reality such as crime become a moral panic about gypsies, as occurred in the UK in 2004? Does the damage done to good government by the latter outweigh the good done in the public interest by the former? In this version of what chaos scientists call the 'Boundary Problem' the sociological task is to locate the moment of phase transition, to identify or anticipate the tipping point between order and chaos, and contribute to the management or prevention of media-fuelled panics.

The ethics and mechanics of communication control

As control of media output becomes harder, and the news cycle becomes more chaotic, in the technical sense of the term, what are the limits of control? What degree of control of information by political authorities is legitimate? And what kinds of tactics and strategies work? In asking these questions, the chaos paradigm reasserts the importance of the sociology of sources. Paul Manning has identified 'the task of a sociology of news and news sources' as being 'to trace the sources of order and control' (2001: 48) in the construction of journalism. The sociology of sources is also the analysis of how – indeed, if – order can be maintained in the emerging chaos of global communication, while preserving its decentralising, democratising effects at both national and global levels.

Final thoughts

Beyond these foci, the traditional critical task of monitoring the media's performance of their democratic role is as valid as ever. Just because the relationship between media ownership (an expression of economic power) and cultural and political power is loosening does not mean that the desire of some to reassert undemocratic control, be they big proprietors of a particular ideological bent, or governments selfishly interested in survival, is diminished. If critical scrutiny of political power by the journalistic fourth estate is key to democracy, and if it is made more intense and probing by the trends explored in this book, the critical scrutiny of both media and political power, and the always-evolving relationship between the two, is a further mechanism for maintaining democratic accountability, and one which neither the politician nor the journalist can be relied on to perform in the interests of society as a whole. Things may, on balance, be getting better in the globalised public sphere of the twenty-first century, but further progress is not inevitable. On that point, developments in the global economic, geo-political and ideological environments (as well as the catastrophic deterioration of the natural environment itself)[3] could require revision of my pragmatically optimistic conclusions, and constrain or reverse the positive trends described in this book.

The coming crisis of capitalism?

First, they could be thrown off course by a global economic crisis of capitalism, bigger than any of the stock exchange and currency or oil crises of the previous three decades; this would undermine the ability of the system to continue to provide increases in average living standards. The chaos paradigm applies as much to economics as to cultural evolution, and there can be no guarantee that patterns of the recent past will continue into the future. The coming crisis of global capitalism, occasionally glimpsed but never realised, may indeed be waiting just around the corner, triggered perhaps by an event such as Hurricane Katrina, which struck the Gulf Coast of the USA in late August 2005, wrecking that region and disabling the US oil industry. From such events, and they are becoming more frequent and intense, unpredictable consequences for global economic, political and cultural trends follow.

The rise of China

In the economic evolution of global capital the future development of China is clearly crucial. As we have seen, China's economic modernisation has been conducted thus far in the absence of political democratisation. China will one day, and in the not too distant future, be the world's leading economic power. In the absence of wise political leadership both in the east and west, it is entirely possible that China could emerge not just as an economic but as a military competitor to any or all of the USA, Russia, India, the European Union or Japan, leading to conflict based not on the capitalist–communist divide of the Cold War, but the more familiar competition for scarce resources which produced the First World War. Unlike the disturbing, but ultimately hollow threat posed by Islamic fundamentalism to capitalist modernity, China's challenge will be based on the hard power of economics, setting up a competition between two variants of capitalism – the authoritarian model favoured by China and other countries in Asia, versus the liberal democratic model of the USA.

That this competition will ever lead to war seems unlikely, given the west's nuclear capacity and the declared view of many Chinese that the country's national interests lie in peaceful economic competition rather than military conflict (Friedman 2005). On the other hand, the dispute with a US-backed Taiwan remains unresolved, and there are significant elements in the Chinese military who see this issue as more important to the country's national prestige than economic success. In July 2005 Major General Zhu Chenghu of China's National Defence University was reported to have declared in a public speech that Beijing 'would repulse a US military intervention over Taiwan by attacking US cities with nuclear weapons . . . hundreds of cities will be destroyed by the Chinese'.[4] While the Chinese government distanced itself from his remarks, describing them as a 'minority opinion', the possibility that they could become more representative of the majority cannot be ruled out. And military conflict on this scale, should it ever occur, would negate the democratising and liberalising trends described in this book, just as the war on terror has already been used as justification for illiberal measures in both the USA and Britain.

The rise of religion

Media sociology would have little impact on either of these scenarios, but there is a third source of renewed ideological control, in the prevention of which scholarly scrutiny can play a role. Chapter 5 discussed the relationship between ideological dissolution and an expanded media sphere of debate and dissent. That expansion could be reversed by western governments committed to the notion that the war on terror is akin to a strategic struggle of the Cold War type. In the USA, for example, such a regime would be founded on a reactionary combination of neo-conservatism and Christian fundamentalism, and be a response to the Islamic fundamentalism of Al Qaida and the 'clash of civilisations' (Huntington 1996) which it threatens to unleash. There were concerted moves to roll back sexual liberalism in the USA during both of the Bush terms of office. The application of a 'God on our side' approach to global politics could conceivably lead to an assertion of much stricter control over the world's news media (and to media in general) than we have seen in recent times. We have already witnessed upsurges in religious protests against cultural expression in America, Britain, France and other countries. While it would be premature and alarmist to view this trend as a harbinger of the kind of western society depicted in Margaret Atwood's dystopian novel *The Handmaid's Tale*, it has been an unpredicted and unwelcome by-product of an emerging political environment in which fundamentalist tendencies within all religious denominations were growing in confidence and assertiveness as this book went to press.

The modern media's ability to disseminate messages of modernity and liberalism to cultures alien or resistant to them has been a key causal factor in the rise of Al Qaida and similar groups. The danger for progressives in the years ahead is not that these forces will 'win' their jihad but that in unleashing the forces of religious reaction to the sexual, intellectual and political freedoms which capitalism delivered in the late twentieth century, they at the same time revitalise the forces of Christian conservatism in the west. Since 2001 the Islamist assault on western values has produced a domestic backlash to the liberalised sexual and political cultures of our time, and it is not yet clear how far this backlash will be able to roll back the freedoms won by women, gays and other communities. The very openness, volatility and uncensorability of the media in a chaotic information environment will continue to militate against the attempted imposition of successful control. That said, the possibility that the period we are now living in is the beginning of the end of a brief era of communicative accessibility and diversity associated with the phase transition from Cold War to an intensifying clash of civilisations, rather than a permanent feature of a democratised global capitalism in the twenty-first century, cannot be ruled out.

The chaos paradigm views the journalistic media in contemporary conditions as agents of democratisation and progressive social change, not conservative stasis or reaction. They can of course be both, and could become conservative again as the forces of religious fundamentalism gather. For those of us who choose not to be directly involved in that clash – atheists, humanists, liberals, multiculturalists, 'civilists' in the Islamic world, moderate religionists everywhere – for whom the preservation of tolerance, diversity, intellectual freedom and secularism are paramount, the new critical paradigm is focused on resisting the assault on free and independent media, from whatever direction it comes. Be it in the razing of the twin towers by one side, the bombing of Al Jazeera in Baghdad by the other, the banning of gay marriage in Massachusetts or the religiously sanctioned murder of rape victims in Pakistan, the battle lines have shifted from where they were in the late twentieth century. The old divisions have dissolved, and new ones formed around questions of ethnicity, nationalism, religion and personal morality. The defence of lifestyle and sexual freedoms is now in the front line of twenty-first-century politics.

In this context the role of the media scholar must be to work for the maximum degree of media freedom within and between nation-states, and against censorship and other constraints on content, whoever promotes them and for whatever reason, unless these are clearly justified on grounds of harm reduction and the defence of individual rights (as in the policing of child pornography, for example, or racist hate speech, or digital piracy and computer hacking). The critical priorities of the twenty-first century are clear: not futile and misguided battles against capitalism in general, and American capitalism in particular, but sustained, coherent, morally consistent criticism of the forces of authoritarianism everywhere (especially religious authoritarianism), and in support of democracy, modernity and freedom (intellectual, political, lifestyle, cultural). This is not class war on the twentieth-century model, but *mass war* for the defence of the rights of all human beings, wherever they are on the planet.

Notes

Preface

1 Paradigm shifts are said to occur in science when accounts of phenomena which once made intuitive or common sense begin to jar with the empirical evidence available to the objective observer, often one armed with new technologies of observation, measurement and analysis provided by the previous paradigmatically challenged generation. Galileo's telescopically enhanced observations of celestial movements made the earth-centred universe untenable. The discovery of million-year old fossils rendered the biblical version of Creation mythical, where before it had been viewed as scientific.

2 Oliver Bennett's book-length study of *Cultural Pessimism* (2001) analyses the sources of what appears to be an essential element of the intellectual make-up of cultural criticism. He observes that 'the idea of cultural decline has been a recurrent feature of the history of the West' (ibid.: 12).

3 The assertion of a dominant, controlling media is not monopolised by critical media scholars. Many non-academic commentators mirror critical theory by blaming the media for all manner of socio-cultural phenomena defined *a priori* as negative (such as the mainstreaming of homosexuality, sexual permissiveness, violence and anti-social behaviour). Adherence to a control paradigm in which the media are perceived to be doing bad things *to* people, rather than good things *for* them, and to a cultural pessimism which sees everything going to the dogs, is not a function of a particular ideological or political allegiance, but of a way of seeing the world and the people who live in it as passive objects forever vulnerable to malign external influences which oppress them, and which degrade their capacity to think and act for themselves. Conversely, a chaos paradigm should not be viewed as the province of a left- or a right-wing sociology, but of a revised materialism which transcends the ideological bi-polarity of the twentieth century to focus on the very different political and cultural environment of the twenty-first.

4 As opposed to religion, which Marx famously described as the 'old' opium of the masses.

5 See my *Mediated Sex* (1996) and *Striptease Culture* (2002).

Foreword: a note on chaos

1 Contained in *Dialectic of Enlightenment*, London, Allen Lane, 1973.

2 From this we can infer their view of cultural chaos as a kind of social and moral anarchy, or disorder, arising from the dissolution of hitherto existing moral standards and certainties. From their subsequent discussion of the evils of cultural uniformity, the reader senses that they would rather this disorder than the mass culture they identify as a feature of 'late' capitalism.

3 Reported by Tim Ellsworth, CNS News, http://www.cnsnews.com/Culture/Archive/1998-2000/CUL19990831c.html.

4 The science of chaos postulates that beneath the apparent disorder and randomness of many natural phenomena, universal laws of motion are still active; and that a significant degree of predictability for these systems can thus be aspired to, given the availability of sufficient data-gathering and processing capacity. Only in the late twentieth century, however, with the exponential growth of computing power, was it possible to begin to assemble the quantity and quality of information required to achieve that goal. Armed with the microchip, this science was about restoring order to chaos, discovering how and why one state became another, and where the boundaries (phase transitions) between those states lay. The relative success of this endeavour would later assist engineers to prevent or ameliorate cascading electrical blackouts such as those that afflicted North America in 2002, and Italy in 2003, and the feared (but never realised) consequences of the Y2K computer bug. It would assist in the prevention of weather-related accidents and disasters, including the prediction of earthquakes and tornadoes (though only to a point; the mathematics of chaos may suggest that an earthquake is likely in a particular zone, never that it is certain). It would increase understanding of the chaotic workings of the human body, and the forces which, for example, tip a previously healthy heart into cardiac arrest without warning. To this extent, chaos was about bringing hitherto 'unknowable' phenomena within the purview of scientific enquiry, assisted by the evolution of supercomputers such as that which came on stream in July 2004 with a reported capacity of 40 trillion operations per second.

5 For a collection of images of chaos in nature, see Gleick and Porter (1990).

6 In the song 'The Certainty of Chance', from the album *Fin de Siecle* (2000) written by Neil Hannon and Jody Talbot.

7 Sokal and Bricmont's argument is that a number of (mainly) French intellectuals in the humanities have 'repeatedly abused scientific concepts and terminology: either using scientific ideas totally out of context, without giving the slightest justification, or throwing around scientific jargon in front of their non-scientist readers without any regard for its relevance or even its meaning' (1998: x). Their argument is given weight by the fact that in 1996 Alan Sokal produced a fake essay entitled 'Transgressing the boundaries: Toward a transformative hermeneutics of quantum gravity', which committed precisely these sins, and submitted it for publication to the prestigious cultural studies journal, *Social Text*. The essay was published, appropriately, in a special edition of the journal devoted to rebutting the critics of such usage.

8 As many scholars of English literature, philosophy, history, public relations and management theory already have. For the application of a chaos paradigm to history, see Manuel de Landa's *A Thousand Years of Nonlinear History* (2001). Helen Hawkins's *Strange Attractors: Literature, culture and chaos theory* (1995) adapts chaos science to literary criticism, while Priscilla Murphy's work seeks to apply chaos and complexity theory to the practice of public relations (1996, 2000).

9 See too 'The demolition merchants of reality' in Francis Wheen's *How Mumbo-Jumbo Conquered the World* (2004).

10 In his essay 'Digibabble, fairy dust, and the human anthill', Tom Wolfe, observes that:

> memes [are] viruses in the form of ideas, slogans, tunes, styles, images, doctrines, anything with sufficient attractiveness or catchiness to infect the brain . . . after which they operate like genes, passing along what had been naively thought of as the creations of culture . . . [T]here turns out to be one serious problem with memes, however. They don't exist. A neurophysiologist can use the most powerful and sophisticated brain imaging now available – and still not find a meme.
>
> (Wolfe 2000: 84)

The same point could be made of communication in general, however. Would Wolfe deny on that basis that communication is real?

11 Dawkins's concept of the meme has been ridiculed in much the same way as the

suggestion that the science of chaos has anything to offer social theory. Ideas do not 'think' or develop by themselves, it is argued by his opponents, but are the product of real people acting in real situations. Similar arguments have been used against the concept of *The Selfish Gene*, on the basis of a fundamental misunderstanding of what Dawkins was saying in that book. Genes don't think, nor do they have conscious intentionality, selfish or otherwise, and Dawkins does not suggest that they have. Contrary to the caricature of his argument which some have presented, Dawkins allows for the possibility of altruism, and shows how it can be a rational evolutionary strategy. The selfish gene does not imply a selfish human being, in other words. Genes replicate, interact and spread according to natural laws which have been identified and described in a scientific manner, and which are ultimately determined by the needs of their own reproduction. In this respect only are they selfish.

Memes, in an analogous manner, have no agency of their own, being purely communicative abstractions. Memes, like genes, don't think, but they do spread, independently of individual action and often without conscious or co-ordinated human agency. Advertising and marketing companies do their best to intervene in and facilitate the process of memetic replication, or social contagion, with varying degrees of success, as Malcolm Gladwell's *Tipping Point* shows (2000). Gladwell attempts to explain what it is that makes some ideologies, belief systems, fashion fads, brands of walking shoe (all categories of meme) spread faster and further than others, just as evolutionary biology seeks to understand why some genes survive and prosper while others become extinct. Memetics, in this sense, is about understanding how ideas are disseminated and become 'dominant', or 'consensual', or 'trendy', or 'old-fashioned'. From the point of view of media studies, memetics improves on traditional theories of ideology by introducing the elements of contingency and chance, adaptability and fitness to the analysis of why some ideas are more successful at mass dissemination than others. Religion, for example, spreads and survives because of its promise of a heavenly afterlife for those who behave appropriately in this one. As materialists have always argued, man makes God in his own image, not least as a means of coming to psychological terms with his mortality, and with the disappointments and deprivations of mortal life. Media sociologists have tended to think of ideas as dominant because they represent elite interests, which are then imposed on society as a whole through control of media institutions. Memetics allows that the successful spread of ideas can be much more accidental and unpredictable than that.

12 See Dawkins's collection of essays, *A Devil's Chaplain* (2004).

13 Defined by Kapitaniak and Wojewoda as 'objects in phase space towards which trajectories are drawn as time approaches infinity' (1993: 9). One can conceive strange attractors as points of stability to which complex systems would gravitate if left long enough, like water down a sink hole. Mathematical formulae have been developed to describe, without prejudice to variation and divergence over repeated iterations of a particular sequence, the predispositions of a system towards a particular evolutionary outcome.

14 The pioneers of chaos science were among the first to advocate interdisciplinarity and an end to the rigid demarcation lines which have traditionally structured the study of both nature and society. Through the work of the Santa Fe institute and others, physicists of chaos and its related sub-fields began to work with astronomers and meteorologists, mathematicians with biologists, as practitioners of previously divided disciplines discovered that the objects of their scientific enquiry – complex, non-linear systems – had some important features in common, be they planets in complex orbits or tectonic plates in motion.

15 Although to read Derrida and the like as wannabee scientists is perhaps to miss the point. What they are engaged in is perhaps best read as a kind of creative writing, an aesthetic philosophy which, while it has no scientific validity, can appeal to a readership for whom the discourse of science is reassuring in its apparent certainty and precision.

16 See, for example, Althusser's *Lenin and Philosophy and Other Essays* (1971) and *Reading Capital* (Althusser and Balibar 1970).
17 This would happen because of its tendency to pauperise the toiling masses, or proletariat, reducing them to wage slavery and abject poverty of the type dramatised in the works of Dickens, whose greatest and most poignant novels were already hugely popular before Marx began his exile in London, and may well have driven his moral outrage and anger at the excesses of a capitalism still red in tooth and claw. Marx arrived in Dover in 1849, three years before the publication of Dickens' final novel, *Bleak House*.
18 See for example, his *Materialism and Empirio-criticism* (1920).
19 Wilson, D., 'Between fantasy and action', *Guardian*, August 31 2005.
20 In 1961 Lorenz was testing weather models on his crude computer, and rounding off values to three rather than six decimal points, on the assumption that such rounding up would have no impact on the behaviour of the model. On inspecting his results, however, he found that making this minor change to the inputs in his model resulted in large-scale variation in outputs, to the degree that they quickly became unpredictable.
21 For a discussion of *Jurassic Park* and other works of literary fiction, see Hawkins (1995).
22 For a relatively accessible introduction to the science of chaos, see Gleick (1996).

1 Cultural chaos and the globalisation of journalism

1 Channel 5 came on air in April 1997, with a news service provided by Independent Television News (ITN).
2 For information on the size of the internet see the Sims Berkeley project website (www.sims.berkeley.edu/research/ projects). A terabyte is 10 to the power of 12, or a trillion bytes.
3 To this extent the chaos paradigm adopted here differs from the approaches of such as Deleuze, Guattari and de Landa, who seek to 'model the structure-generating processes involved in the genesis of social forms', and to 'explain these in an entirely bottom-up way. That is, not simply to assume that society forms a system, but to account for this systematicity as an emergent property of some dynamical process' (De Landa 2000: 270). While welcome in so far as they break with the 'top-down method that orthodox sociologists use', they lose sight altogether of the role of social actors, elite and non-elite, as they seek to shape the direction of social evolution, and to conserve or replace a system. The chaos model suggests that systematicity is not imposed from above, because it cannot be, and need not be, while acknowledging that there are those actors who will always strive to command and control the societies within which they operate.
4 Giddens himself, in this work, distances himself from the discourse of postmodernity, arguing that the term is 'best kept to refer to styles or movements within literature, painting, the plastic arts and architecture. It concerns aspects of aesthetic reflection upon the nature of modernity' (1990: 45).
5 It is true, as critics of technological utopianism such as James W. Carey (2005) and Armand Mattelart (2003) point out, that there have been many communication 'revolutions' in human history. But none has spread so far, so rapidly, as that of the current era.
6 Paul Virilio observes that 'we live in a world no longer based on geographical expanse but on a temporal distance constantly being decreased by our transportation, transmission and teleaction capacities' (1997). For Zygmunt Bauman, 'geographical discontinuity no longer matters, as speed-space, enveloping the totality of the globe's surface, brings every place into nearly the same speed-distance from each other and makes all places mutually contiguous' (2002: 12). He adds:

> With the velocity of transmission approaching its limit – the speed of light – the near instantaneity of the cause-and-effect succession transforms even the largest distance

into proximity, and in the end puts paid to the cause–effect distinction itself. For all practical intents and purposes, we are all now in the close, indeed intimate proximity of each other.

(Ibid.: 13)

7 See Jacques, M., 'Strength in numbers', *Guardian*, October 23 2004, for a discussion of the particular nationalisms of China and India, which he predicts will drive global politics in the twenty-first century.

8 Eco, U., 'See China, learn what Europe must become', *Sunday Times*, August 8 2004.

9 Corner and Pels note in their introduction to a recent study of *Media and the Restyling of Politics* that 'the proliferation of differences within institutions (such as political parties) and social categories (such as class) spills over and tends to blur the boundaries *between* them, while individuals themselves travel more freely across these institutional and classificatory boundaries' (2003: 7).

10 For studies of scandal and the role of journalism in mediating it, see Tiffen (1999), Lull and Hinerman (1997) and Thompson (2000). Foreman's *Georgiana, Duchess of Devonshire* (1998) is an entertaining reminder that, long before the trials of Princess Diana in the late twentieth century, salacious and intrusive press coverage was a problem for elites in British society.

11 An exception was the coverage extended in the summer of 2005 to the alleged romantic liaisons of Cecilia Sarkozy, wife of the former French prime minister.

12 To this extent, as Sabato *et al.* argue, 'the line political reporters draw between private and public life is perhaps more blurry than ever before' (2000: xi). McKenzie Wark has identified a 'chaotic dance of information passing between public life and private worlds' (1999: 33).

13 The second series of *Big Brother* in the UK, which involved the participation of a diverse group of young people (in terms of sexual orientation, social class, ethnicity and religious affiliation) coincided with riots between white and non-white residents of Burnley. The image presented on prime-time TV of a multi-ethnic, socially and sexually diverse Britain contrasted starkly with the racial hatred fuelling the riots.

14 Reality-based programming has become what Jon Dovey calls 'a main course in the diet of North American television viewers (2000: 17), as it has in the diet of TV viewers all over the world. From the early observational (or 'fly-on-the-wall') documentaries of the 1970s, to daytime talk shows in the 1980s and 1990s, to the reality TV and docusoap strands of the present day, the rise of this kind of factual programming has brought with it 'a foregrounding of the individual subjective experience as guarantor of knowledge' (ibid.: 21), and 'an emphasis on individual tragedies which would once have remained private but which are now restaged for public consumption'.

15 In 2004 Jonathan Caouette's *Tarnation* became the first mainstream cinema release to have been edited entirely on Apple Mac's software, bundled free with its home computers. The film was shot on video.

16 McChesney concedes that 'global [media] conglomerates can at times have a progressive impact on culture, especially when they enter nations that had been tightly controlled by corrupt, crony-controlled media systems (as in much of Latin America) or nations that had significant state censorship over media (as in parts of Asia' (2003: 34).

17 The term comes from George Ritzer's work on the rationalisation and standardisation of journalism alleged to be a feature of the current era (1993, 1998).

18 I use it there to refer to the view that the quantitative expansion of political journalism in the media, combined with changes in the form, content and style of that journalism, have reduced its quality as a democratic resource. Although those observations applied to academic and journalistic critics writing in the 1990s, this strand of pessimism continued to surface in the new century. In August 2004, for example, the UK editor of the German *Die Zeit* newspaper complained that 'the dream that the new information age would be one of greater enlightenment, of a rational discourse and greater

participation has not come true' (Kronig, J., 'A crisis in the fourth estate', *Guardian*, August 16 2004). In language typical of the cultural pessimist's mindset, this critic accuses commercialisation of the media of 'dumbing down political journalism'.

19 From an interview on American radio about his book, *Media Unlimited: How the torrent of images and sounds overwhelms our lives* (2002).

20 From comments made at the Information Society Project conference, Yale University, April 2005.

21 Žižek, S., 'Revolution must strike twice', *London Review of Books*, July 25 2002.

22 Andrews, A., 'Thatcher's legacy: no more Us and Them', *Guardian*, March 5 2004.

23 Wark suggests that 'if there is a reason why the left often appears to be struggling to keep up with the pace of change, it may be that the forces traditionally identified as "left" no longer represent the frontline in the class conflict that determines the forward movement of history' (1999: 278).

24 He adds: 'I have seen so much misled sacrifice, so many dead ends induced by ideology'.

2 Materialism and the media

1 As Kevin Williams sums it up: 'While it is possible to identify several traditions within neo-Marxism, they all emphasised the role of the media as ideological, agencies or apparatuses in maintaining and legitimating the power of the bourgeoisie or the dominant group' (2003: 52).

2 Hardt does not define 'working class', or say whether this includes the vast majority of affluent wage labourers who populate advanced capitalism. The existence of a 'captive audience' is presumed, as is the idea that 'commercial gain' and 'public enlightenment' are mutually exclusive properties of a media message.

3 Lewis, J., 'Images of citizenship on television news', www.goldsmiths.ac.uk/ departments/media-communications/pdfs/justinlewis-paper.pdf.

4 Decades later, in the unpublished volume 3 of *Capital*, discussing the capitalist production process which had been the subject of his life's work, Marx writes:

> If the analysis of the actual intrinsic relations of the capitalist process of production is a very complicated matter and very extensive; if it is a work of science to resolve the visible, merely external movement into the true intrinsic movement, it is self-evident that conceptions which arise about the laws of production in the minds of agents of capitalist production and circulation will *diverge drastically from these real laws and will merely be the conscious expression of those visible movements*.
>
> (Marx 1974: 313; my emphasis)

'Vulgar economy', he adds (as opposed to his own, scientific analysis), 'actually does no more than interpret, systematise and defend in doctrinaire fashion the conceptions of the agents of bourgeois production who are entrapped in bourgeois production relations' (ibid.: 817).

5 Francis Wheen's biography of Marx argues that he and Darwin 'were the two most revolutionary and influential thinkers of the nineteenth century' (Wheen 1999: 364). Wheen quotes a letter from Marx to Engels in which he writes that Darwin's *On the Origin of Species* 'is the book which contains the basis in natural history for our view'. He also quotes Engels' graveside oration at Marx's funeral that 'just as Darwin discovered the law of evolution in human nature, so Marx discovered the law of evolution in human history.'

6 State socialism may be viewed in evolutionary terms as a systemic mutation, artificially created and imposed on social formations (tsarist Russia, Chiang Kai-Shek's China, 1950s Cuba) which were unable to exploit its theoretical benefits. State socialism was not fit for the purpose, and quickly degenerated into authoritarianism wherever it was implemented. Capitalism, on the other hand, proved capable of adapting to changing

political and cultural conditions, harnessing individual effort and ability, and producing surpluses sufficient to maintain more or less constantly rising living standards for the workers as well as the bosses. The survival of capitalism, and now its emergence as the dominant global socio-economic model, is not mysterious, but the product of the market mechanism. Cultural commodities have acted as the vehicle for its successful adaptation to changing political and socio-economic environments.

7 Ormerod, P., 'Darwinian selection: the way to do business', *Sunday Times*, March 13 2005.

8 Sullivan, A., 'It's a wonderful life', *Sunday Times*, August 14 2005.

9 American biologist William Emerson Ritter (1856–1944) wrote several books on the theme of the parallels between natural history and social science, viewing human society as a 'superorganism' in which the whole is greater than the sum of its parts.

10 Socialist revolutions which were initially successful (in so far as they led to the establishment of socialist regimes), such as Castro's or Mao's, quickly degenerated into totalitarian parodies, non-viable mutations of the capitalist mode of production against which their leaders pitted themselves in competition. Their fragility was masked for much of the twentieth century, first by the global threat of fascism which united capitalist and communist states against the Germans and the Japanese, and then by the enforced stability of the Cold War, which defined the post-war settlement until the late 1980s, when the internal pressures for change within socialist societies became irresistible (not least because of the increasing influence of international communication). Where these pressures led the USSR to collapse under the weight of its own contradictions, the Chinese adopted a hybrid form of capitalism, which allowed that country to achieve its current levels of economic success. The Chinese economic miracle, however, is based on the application of market forces and the exploitation of global trade advantages such as cheap labour – in short, the pragmatic repudiation rather than dogmatic application of Marxist ideology.

11 Wolfe, T., 'Daydream Believers', *Guardian*, November 11 2000. His essay, 'Hooking up: what life was like at the turn of the second millennium', observes that:

> The average electrician, air-conditioning mechanic, or burglar-alarm repairman lived a life that would have made the Sun King blink. He spent his vacations in Puerto Vallarta, Barbados, or St. Kitts. Before dinner he would be out on the terrace of some resort hotel with his third wife, wearing his Ricky Martin cane-cutter shirt open down to the sternum, the better to allow his gold chains to twinkle in his chest hairs. The two of them would have just ordered a round of Quibel sparkling water, from the state of West Virginia, because by 2000 the once-favoured European sparkling waters Perrier and San Pellegrino seemed so tacky.
>
> (Wolfe 2000: 3)

12 The obviousness of this point is addressed in Jonathan Franzen's *The Corrections* (2002). The novel contains an irreverent stab at critical media studies when one of its main characters, Chip, a 'radical' lecturer in a provincial college, seeks to persuade his students of the evils of consumer capitalism. One of them questions his pessimism:

> 'What's wrong with making a living?' Melissa said. 'Why is it *inherently* evil to make money?'
>
> 'Baudrillard might argue', Chips said, 'that the evil of a campaign like "You go, Girl" consists in the detachment of the signifier from the signified. That a woman weeping no longer just signifies sadness. It now also signifies: "Desire office equipment". It signifies: "Our bosses care about us deeply."'
>
> 'Excuse me', Melissa said, 'but that is just such bullshit.'
>
> 'What is bullshit?' Chip said.
>
> 'This whole class', she said. 'It's just bullshit every week. It's one critic after another

wringing their hands about the state of criticism. Nobody can ever quite say what's wrong exactly. But they all know it's evil. They all know "corporate" is a dirty word. And if somebody's having fun or getting rich – disgusting! Evil! And it's always the death of this and the death of that. And people who think they're free aren't "really" free. And people who think they're happy aren't "really" happy. And it's impossible to radically critique society anymore, although what's so radically wrong with society that we need such a radical critique, nobody can say exactly. It is so typical and perfect that you hate those ads!' she said to Chip as, throughout Wroth Hall, bells finally rang. 'Here things are getting better and better for women and people of colour, and gay men and lesbians, more and more integrated and open, and all you can think about is some stupid, lame problem with signifiers and signifieds . . .'

(Franzen 2002: 51)

13 Monbiot, G., 'Goodbye, kind world', *Guardian*, August 10 2004. It is only fair to point out that Monbiot makes this uncharacteristically optimistic point in an article otherwise devoted to a resolutely pessimistic analysis of the global future. While accepting the reality of progressive economic change, he goes on to argue that the successes of western capitalism are fragile, its prosperity short-lived. The reasons for this are argued to be environmental (global warming), social (one example given is the rising 'social cost' of crime) and economic:

> We are living off the political capital accumulated by previous generations, and this capital is almost spent. The massive redistribution which raised the living standards of the working class after the New Deal and the Second World War is over. Inequality is rising almost everywhere, and the result is a global resource grab by the rich. The entire land mass of Britain, Europe and the United States is being re-engineered to accommodate the upper middle classes. They are buying second and third homes where others have none. Playing fields are being replaced with health clubs, public transport budgets with subsidies for roads and airports. Inequality of outcome, in other words, leads inexorably to inequality of opportunity.

(Ibid.)

3 From control to chaos

1 We certainly continue to need an ideological theory of the media, in so far as news and other forms of culture remain artefacts which reflect the values and ideas of the society within which they are produced. Leading media sociologists such as James Curran have argued correctly that the media are indeed 'powerful ideological agencies' (2002: 165). The question is: on behalf of whom, and with what consequences for social order and elite control within capitalism?
2 For the full report and other documents relating to the Hutton Inquiry, see http://www.the-hutton-inquiry.org.uk/.
3 From research conducted by Professor Justin Lewis, Dr Rod Brookes and Kirsten Brander and reported in Wells, M., 'Study deals a blow to claims of anti-war bias in BBC news', *Guardian*, July 4 2003. See also www.cf.ac.uk/news/02-03/030708.html for a summary of the research.
4 McNair, B., 'Accidents don't just happen', *New Statesman and Society*, July 15 1988.
5 Philo, G., 'What you get in 20 seconds', *Guardian*, July 14 2004.
6 Mosey, R., 'The BBC was no cheerleader for war', *Guardian*, July 27 2004.
7 Herman and Broadhead state that 'A propaganda system is one which uses – and sometimes manufactures – a politically serviceable fact or claim, gives it aggressive and one-sided coverage, and excludes from discussion all critical facts and analyses. An imperfect propaganda system will allow a small quantum of leakage, but not enough to prevent the effective mobilisation of bias and the establishment of the convenient story as a patriotic truth in the minds of the general public' (1988: 174).

8 Cited in Tumber and Palmer (2004).

9 Sullivan, A., 'Left, left, left: media bias on the march', *Sunday Times*, January 13 2002.

10 In the early phases of the invasion and occupation of Iraq, the Australian government's communication minister published a lengthy dossier documenting what he alleged to be examples of anti-government and anti-Coalition bias on the part of the Australian Broadcasting Corporation. While the Blair government in the UK did not go to such lengths, its communication managers regularly attacked the BBC for hostile and negative coverage (see Chapter 4).

11 In the age of 'information globalisation', as Mohamed Zayani puts it, 'relatively small players [such as Al Jazeera] introduce an element of contingency in a traditionally structured and well defined environment where media and politics are entangled' (2005: 27).

12 In Luhmann's terms, 'world society has reached a higher level of complexity with higher structural contingencies; more unexpected and unpredictable changes and, above all, more interlinked dependencies and interdependencies. This means that causal constructions (calculations, plannings) are no longer possible from a central and therefore "objective" point of view. We have to live with a polycentric, polycontextual society' (Luhmann 1997).

4 The politics of chaos: democracy, media and the decline of deference

1 For more detailed figures on the rise of global democracy, see the Freedom House website Democracy's Century (www.freedomhouse.org/reports/century.html).

2 Naomi Sakr observes that 'Al-Jazeera, left mostly to the direction of journalists as opposed to politicians, became a driving force in Arab print and broadcast journalism from around 1998 onwards, mainly because its distinctive and largely uncensored approach attracted audiences from across the Arab-speaking world' (2005c: 149).

3 *An Independent Review of Government Communications*, January 2004. Available online at www.gcreview.gov.uk.

4 Quoted in *Transnational Broadcasting Studies*, no. 12, Spring 2004.

5 *An Independent Review of Government Communications*, January 2004. Available online at www.gcreview.gov.uk.

6 Kronig, J., 'A crisis in the fourth estate', *Guardian*, August 16 2004.

7 http://www.the-hutton-inquiry.org.uk/.

8 Research by this writer and others (Hargreaves and Thomas 2002; Kevill 2002) has shown that, notwithstanding the condemnations of intellectual elites, these forms of mediated access are valued by UK citizens as a counterpoint to what they perceive as the aloofness and unaccountability of their elected leaders. At the same time, they are judged to be significant indicators of public opinion by political elites, requiring readiness to participate, as well as competence in media performance (McNair *et al.* 2003).

9 For the full text of the report see www.richardalston.dcita.gov.au.

10 Quoted in Tumber and Palmer 2004: 135.

11 Sheehan's son was killed on active duty in Iraq.

12 Patterson, J., 'Clooney's tune', *Guardian*, September 16 2005.

13 Hyper-adversarialism, he argued then, involved 'a relentless emphasis on the cynical game of politics', and the implication by journalists, 'day after day, that the political sphere is mainly an arena in which ambitious politicians struggle for dominance' (p. 31).

14 Barnett, S., 'The age of contempt', *Guardian*, October 28 2002.

15 Toynbee, P., 'Breaking news', *Guardian*, September 5 2003.

16 Barnett, S., 'The age of contempt', *Guardian*, October 28 2002.

17 Sampson, A., 'The fourth estate under fire', *Guardian*, January 10 2005.

18 Toynbee, P., 'Breaking news', *Guardian*, September 5 2003.

19 Humphrys defended his work in the 2005 campaign on the grounds that 'the biggest responsibility on an interviewer is to take a complex subject and make it simple, or to take a political comment or statement or claim, and test it' (quoted in Gibson, O., 'Here today, gone tomorrow', *Guardian*, May 2 2005.

5 Cultural chaos and the end of ideology

1 There were of course many varieties of 'socialism' on offer in the twentieth century, some violently opposed to each other. Thus, followers of the Trotskyite Fourth International rejected the USSR and other Marxist-Leninist regimes as 'state capitalism'. Supporters of the Maoist model in China rejected the Stalinism of the USSR, as did Tito's Yugoslavia and the Eurocommunists of the 1980s. The Albanians and North Koreans, on the other hand, regarded the USSR as having gone soft on socialism. Pol Pot in Cambodia interpreted socialism as a return to rural simplicities, and the rejection of all modernising influences, such as education and consumerism. All had one thing in common, however: the assertion that capitalism would eventually, indeed had to, evolve into a superior form of social organisation.

2 Jacques, M., 'The only show in town', *Guardian*, November 20 2004. No one, east or west of the Berlin Wall, left or right of the ideological divide which it symbolised, predicted these events. If the fall of the Soviet Union was foreseen, it was usually in the context of a global catastrophe involving nuclear war and the end of civilisation as we know it.

3 Jacques, M., 'The only show in town', *Guardian*, November 20 2004.

4 Friedman, T., *New York Times*, April 3 2005.

5 It cannot succeed, we may reasonably predict, since there is no conceivable reason why the interests of any but a tiny minority of the world's peoples would be served by abandoning the productive power of capital and retreating to a system not seen in the west since before the Industrial Revolution. Even among the world's billion or so Muslims, the vast majority live in capitalist societies of growing prosperity, and seem happy to continue doing so. That said, Al Qaida will persist for some time in its global jihad, and through skilful manipulation of the global political agenda with such spectaculars as 9/11, the Bali bombing, and the London Underground attacks of July 2005, may well have more impact than its extreme ideas and small core of activists would suggest.

6 For an account of the development of Islamic fundamentalism, see Dilip Hiro's *War without End* (2002). On August 20 2005, the BBC's *Panorama* examined the revolutionary ideas of UK-based Islamic organisations such as the Muslim Council of Britain and the Muslim Association of Britain ('A Question of Leadership', BBC1), exploring among other manifestations of alleged anti-semitism the MCB's boycott of Holocaust Memorial Day in 2004, and its association with Muslim ideologists such as Sayyid Qutb.

7 Although I share Huntington's assertion that the bi-polar conflict of the Cold War has been replaced by a multipolar 'clash of civilisations', and his argument that the main strategic challenges to the west in the coming years will come from Islamic fundamentalism, on the one hand, and what he calls 'Sinic assertiveness', or an ascendant China, on the other, I reject his premise that culture and cultural identity are the driving forces of human history. This idealist position neglects the role of economics as the driver of human evolution (the materialist position), and neglects the importance of capitalism as a unifying, globalising force. Islamic fundamentalism can terrorise civilians with ease, given the open nature of a globalised world, but cannot compete with the productive capacity of capitalism, and offers no credible economic alternative. As such, and notwithstanding the slogans of jihad, it is an untenable, unsustainable worldview which must fail on all but the most primitive, terroristic level. China, on the other hand, which has adopted capitalism and is now in a rapid economic and political ascent, can and will challenge the west one day, in some form or other. The success of this challenge

will depend on which version of capitalism proves to be the most efficient and productive not just of economic wealth but human satisfaction in general.

8 Jacques, M., 'The only show in town', *Guardian*, November 20 2004.

9 Even if a dominant ideology *had* been required to keep the masses in line post-Cold War, it was by then possible to argue that there was no clearly identifiable ruling class around which it might take shape, and who might act collectively to disseminate it down through the means of intellectual production. There are governing elites in capitalist societies, of course, as in every other kind of society, but these rotate between parties of different and often competing ideological persuasions, and have a variety of often conflicting relationships to the means of economic and cultural production. To the extent that there is a capitalist class defined in the Marxian sense by its ownership of capital, that class is itself divided between different factions with many competing interests (financial as against manufacturing capital, for example, or both of the above as against leisure and media capital), many of which are fought out in public, through the media. An article in the June 2004 edition of *Vanity Fair* examined the wave of media criticism of US business leaders since the Enron scandal of 2002, and concluded that 'the power elite, it turns out, does have deep, unresolved conflicts: political and media power did turn furiously against the business class' (Wolff, M., 'Wing tips and leg irons', *Vanity Fair*, June 2004).

10 Ibrahim, S.E., 'Democracy's not a devil for Islamists', *The Australian*, May 23 2005.

11 Quoted in Swain, J. and Baxter, S., 'The Arabian spring', *Sunday Times*, March 6 2005.

12 Freedland, J., 'The war's silver lining', *Guardian*, March 2 2005.

13 Quoted in Swain, J. and Baxter, S., 'The Arabian Spring', *Sunday Times*, March 6 2005.

14 In the article quoted above, Ibrahim lists the source of anxieties surrounding Islamist success in the polls. 'Can they be trusted? If they rise to power, will they respect the rights of minorities and women and leave office when voted out? Will they tolerate dissent? Or will such elections be based on "one man, one vote, one time"?' Ibrahim believes that many Islamist parties can be trusted to respect democracy, if and when they are elected to power, and that they can be 'incorporated' into democratic systems.

15 Hirst, D., 'Dangerous democracy', *Guardian*, April 20 2005.

16 Australian journalist and academic David McKnight has argued the need for the left in his country to regroup around the 'dog whistle' issues of identity and morality which have energised the right-of-centre Liberal Party and helped secure its electoral dominance (2005). Ultimately, however, the left has to recognise that there is no longer a left as traditionally understood; that the centre of ideological gravity has moved – not to the right, as sometimes argued – but to a location in which neither left nor right has much meaning.

17 See, for example, Andrews, A., 'Thatcher's legacy: no more Us and Them', *Guardian*, May 5 2004.

18 From comments made during an interview for *The Message*, BBC Radio 4, February 11 2005.

19 See *A Long Short War* (Hitchens 2003) for a collection of his articles and essays on the subject of the Iraqi war.

20 My own post-doctoral research included a comparative study of media coverage of two superficially similar aircraft disasters – the shooting down of Korean Airlines 007 in 1983, and the shooting down in similar circumstances of an Iranian Airlines passenger jet in 1989. In both cases, the armed forces of a major superpower claimed to have destroyed civilian aircraft in error. In both cases, hundreds of innocent people died. The Soviets' destruction of KAL 007 produced a global wave of media outrage, with the media uncritically reporting international calls for boycotts of the USSR, as well as accusations of terrorism, barbarity and atrocity from the US president (McNair 1988). By comparison, the American navy's destruction of an Iranian jet over the Persian Gulf a few years later was given much less coverage, in strictly quantitative terms, than the KAL 007 incident, and generally reported as an unfortunate accident, for which the

Iranians were themselves largely to blame by virtue of their Islam-inspired anti-Americanism (McNair, B., 'Accidents don't just happen', *New Statesman and Society*, July 15 1988).

21 Woolcott, J., 'To live and die in Iraq', *Vanity Fair*, August 2005.

22 Kronig, J., 'A crisis in the fourth estate', *Guardian*, August 16 2004.

23 Woolcott, J., 'To live and die in Iraq', *Vanity Fair*, August 2005.

24 Before hostilities commenced, I myself wrote an op-ed commentary for the Scottish broadsheet *Scotland On Sunday*, questioning the WMD argument then being presented by the British government as a rationale for war. I argued that 'You don't have to be George Galloway to believe that an attack on Iraq won't really be about weapons of mass destruction, or even about Saddam's long record of human rights abuses. The West has lived with both for decades, and if he hadn't invaded Kuwait he would probably still be the Americans' preferred partner in the region' (McNair, B., 'This is no time to shrink from war', *Scotland On Sunday*, March 2 2003.

25 Ahmed, K. and Hinsliff, G., 'No. 10 regret on war dossier', *Observer*, June 8 2003.

26 See his article, 'We dreamed up "Al-Qaida". Let's not do it again with "evil ideology"', *Guardian*, August 30 2005.

27 The United States spent some $300 million supporting Mujahidin fighters in their war against the Soviet occupation of Afghanistan. Saudi Arabia and Pakistan provided the majority of the rest of their financial support, as well as training camps and other resources.

6 Cultural capitalism and the commodification of dissent

1 By then, indeed, some men were publicly complaining about a trend in which, as esteemed BBC journalist Michael Buerk put it in August 2005, 'women increasingly set the agenda in business, politics, the media and in society at large . . . Women's values are now considered superior to men's values' (reported in Flintoff, J., 'Of course women don't rule the world', *Sunday Times*, August 21 2005.

2 Sullivan, A., 'It's a wonderful life', *Sunday Times*, August 14 2005.

3 This also applies to dissenting, reactionary ideas. One of the consequences of Islamic fundamentalist terrorism in London and elsewhere has been to highlight the free availability of hate speech delivered through video, internet and other media. Only after the London underground bombings of July 2005 did the UK government move to restrict the circulation of such media.

4 Walker, Rob, 'The alienation market', *New York Times*, June 13 2004.

5 Quoted in Bachrach, J., 'Moore's war', *Vanity Fair*, March 2005.

6 For a detailed account of the background to the release of *Fahrenheit 9/11*, see Bachrach, J., 'Moore's war', *Vanity Fair*, March 2005.

7 All around the world in 2004 and 2005 feature-length documentaries were making unprecedented sums at the box office. In Australia, *Rolling Stone*'s Yearbook for 2004–05 described 2004 as 'the year of the doco' (Boland, M., 'Year of the doco', *Rolling Stone*, no. 636, January 2005). Author Michaela Boland listed *Fog of War* (Errol Morris), *Metallica: Some kind of monster* (Joe Berlinger), *Capturing the Friedmans* (Andrew Jarecki) and *Control Room* (Jehane Noujaim) as among the many full-length documentaries making the big screen in 2004. In September 2005 *Sight & Sound* noted that documentaries had made more money at the UK box office in 2004 than in any previous year (Gant, C., 'Does truth pay?', *Sight & Sound*, September 2005).

8 Quoted in Walker, Rob, 'The alienation market', *New York Times*, June 13 2004.

9 Made for less than $400,000, the film was not released in mainstream cinemas, but topped Amazon.com's DVD bestsellers' chart.

10 For the full text of the article, see http://www.guardian.co.uk/comment/story/0,3604,551036,00.html.

11 Beard, M., 'Reflections on the present crisis', *London Review of Books*, September 20 2001.

12 She asked ('A Mature Democracy', *New Yorker*, September 24 2001):

> Where is the acknowledgment that this was not a 'cowardly' attack on 'civilization'
> or 'liberty' or 'humanity' or 'the free world' but an attack on the world's self-
> proclaimed superpower, undertaken as a consequence of specific American alliances
> and actions? . . . [I]f the word 'cowardly' is to be used, it might be more aptly applied
> to those who kill from beyond the range of retaliation, high in the sky, than to those
> willing to die themselves in order to kill others. In the matter of courage (a morally
> neutral virtue): Whatever may be said of the perpetrators of Tuesday's slaughter,
> they were not cowards.

13 Quoted in Walker, Rob, 'The alienation market', *New York Times*, June 13 2004.
14 Boland, M., 'The year of the doco', *Rolling Stone* (Australian edition), no. 636, January
    2005.
15 Quoted in Bachrach, J., 'Moore's war', *Vanity Fair*, March 2005.
16 Steve Grossman, former chairman of the Democratic National Committee and chair
    of the unsuccessful 2004 campaign by Howard Dean, quoted in Bachrach, J., 'Moore's
    war', *Vanity Fair*, March 2005.
17 Paul Seib adds that such reporting 'is uncommon in much of mainstream American
    journalism', although to those who have witnessed the competing approaches of Fox
    News, CNN and MSNBC, not to mention the thousands of bloggers on the internet,
    such a conclusion might seem outdated.
18 The Glass case was dramatised in the movie *Shattered Glass* (2003).
19 For the full report and other documents relating to the Hutton Inquiry, see
    http://www.the-hutton-inquiry.org.uk/.
20 In reality, Fox News serves a predominantly domestic market with an unashamedly
    unbalanced 'pro-American' editorial slant, in overt competition with 'liberal' media
    such as the *New York Times* and CNN, and makes no serious effort to engage with the
    world beyond US borders, where its output is generally seen as jingoistic propaganda.
    Within the US satirical TV programmes such as Jon Stewart's *The News Show* mock it
    mercilessly. But even Fox must operate in a pluralistic editorial environment, in which
    aggressively right-wing commentators, such as Hannity and Colmes, exist in a market
    where audiences can choose to read Michael Moore or watch *Fahrenheit 9/11*, and do
    so in their millions. All preach mainly to the converted, and all rely on the existence of
    equally vociferous opponents to give their polemical journalism edge. The battle of ideas
    has become part of the infotainment that is contemporary news in the US.
21 For a discussion of the biases of Rupert Murdoch's news media in Australia, see
    McKnight, D., 'Rupert Murdoch and the culture war', *Australian Review of Books*,
    February 2004.
22 Shibley Telhami, quoted in *Transnational Broadcasting Studies*, no. 13, fall 2004.
23 See Cornwell, R., 'US accused of plan to muzzle al-Jazeera through privatisation', *The
    Independent*, February 15 2005. Cornwell reports the anxieties of some Al Jazeera staff
    that privatisation plans by the Qatari government will lead to tighter editorial controls
    on the channel.
24 Kinninmont, J., 'Qatar draws up plan to sell off al-Jazeera', *Guardian*, April 27 2005.
25 For Michael Schudson, writing in 1995, media proprietors are governed by markets as
    much as by personal political preferences, and the demands and expectations of the
    former may overtake the latter.
26 For an account of the Berlusconi case, see the European Federation of Journalists report,
    Crisis in Italian Media: How poor politics and flawed legislation put journalism under pressure,
    November 2003.
27 Teather, D., 'Paying the Republican piper', *Guardian*, February 2 2005.

7 Mapping the global public sphere I: transnational satellite news

1 'New' is a relative term in this context, used to distinguish the media of the late twentieth and early twenty-first centuries from those – print and broadcasting – which had hitherto existed. To children, the internet is not new but something they have always known.

2 For an accessible account of the origins of the internet, see Naughton (1999).

3 As of December 2004 the *Financial Times* was selling 100,000 copies in the UK and another 300,000 overseas. Separate front pages are produced in London for the UK, US, European and Asian markets. According to its editor, 'lots of people in Wall Street, in banks and global corporations read us first because we're more global, concise and smart' (quoted in Greenslade, R., 'We have sailed through a perfect storm', *Guardian*, December 6 2004).

4 Greenslade, op. cit.

5 A new edition of MacBride's report was published by Rowman & Littlefield to mark the 25th anniversary in 2005.

6 Herman and McChesney do concede some positive consequences of cultural globalisation: 'the global media's competitive pressure on, and threat to, state-controlled broadcasting systems that are sometimes complacent, stodgy and performing poorly . . . the rapid dissemination of the popular culture developed in the dominant commercial centres to the four corners of the earth; the carrying across borders of some of the fundamental values of the West, such as individualism, skepticism of authority, and the rights of women and minorities' (1997: 8).

7 Eric Louw's recent study of political communication, generally framed by adherence to the control paradigm, describes the situation well: '[D]uring the 1970s–1980s NWIO theorists argued that problems facing Third World governments were so serious that journalists needed to avoid "negative" stories which might destabilise those governments, and instead actively collaborate with their governments by producing "development" journalism . . . [which] deliberately focused on positive news. Much development journalism mutated into propaganda, while sunshine journalism [*sic*] allowed corruption and mal-administration to flourish' (Louw 2006).

8 Terhi Rantanen's *The Global and the National* argues that 'in the Soviet and post-Soviet context, media imperialism scholars must confront the unthinkable – Russian audiences actually wanted to have Western programmes, to which they were denied access for decades' (2002: 11).

9 For the standard history of CNN's first decade, see Flournoy (1992).

10 From a personal interview with the author conducted in 1991, and quoted in McNair (2003c: 137).

11 By the end of 2004 Fox News had overtaken CNN for the domestic cable news audience, with 25 per cent of total share as compared to CNN's 22 per cent (Pew Internet and American Life Project, Trends 2005).

12 Wise, L., 'Between theory and practice', *Transnational Broadcasting Studies*, no. 13, fall 2004.

13 O'Carroll, L., 'Leader of the pack', *Guardian*, August 16 2004.

14 Wise, L., 'Between theory and practice', *Transnational Broadcasting Studies*, no. 13, fall 2004.

15 Schleifer, S.A., 'Al Jazeera update', *Transnational Broadcasting Studies*, no. 13, fall 2004.

16 Ibid.

17 Ibid.

18 Saeed, A.M., 'The Arab satellites – some necessary observations', *Transnational Broadcasting Studies*, no. 11, fall 2003.

19 Schleifer, S.A., 'Al Jazeera update', *Transnational Broadcasting Studies*, no. 13, fall 2004.

20 The BBC's Arabic TV Centre suffered not just from censorship, but also from a shortage of skilled Arab journalists, and what S. Abdullah Schleifer calls 'the relative indifference

of many BBC executives' ('Media explosion in the Arab world: the Pan-Arab satellite broadcasters', *Transnational Broadcasting Studies*, no. 1, fall 1998).

21 Sharabi, H., 'The Arab satellite channels and their political impact after the Iraq war', *Al Hayat*, July 18 2003.

22 Jihad, F., 'Reaching the Arabs through Al Hurra: US chooses easy way out?', *Transnational Broadcasting Studies*, no. 12, spring 2004.

23 Cochrane, P., 'Proposed Arabic BBC channel regarded with scepticism in the Middle East', *Worldpress.org*, August 1 2004.

24 Schleifer, S. Abdallah, 'MMDs and the new satellite television technologies: a media explosion in the Arab world', *Transnational Broadcasting Studies*, no. 13, fall 2004.

25 Quoted in Randeep, R. and Jha, S., 'NDTV makes Murdoch's Star wane in India', *Guardian*, September 22 2004.

8 Mapping the global public sphere II: online journalism and the blogosphere

1 'Internet: the mainstreaming of online life', *Trends 2005*, Pew Internet & American Life Project.

2 UK Office of National Statistics.

3 Of the former, *www.xinhuanet.com* (run by the Xinhuan News Agency) and *www.cctv.com* (operated by the Chinese Central TV Station) are the most authoritative.

4 Hargrave, S., 'Sino the times', *Guardian*, January 24 2005. For further information on the internet in China, see the China Internet Network Information Centre.

5 Reported in Greenslade, R., 'Murdoch sets out internet challenge', *Guardian*, April 18 2005. For a full text of the speech see http://media.guardian.co.uk/city/story/0,7497,1459456,00.html.

6 Schulze, J., 'News clicks on to next big thing', *The Australian*, July 20 2005.

7 Bianco, A., 'The future of the *New York Times*', *Business Week Online*, January 17 2005.

8 Cash, W., 'Inspired by Britain', *The Spectator*, February 7 1998.

9 Seipp, C., 'Online uprising', *American Journalism Review*, June 2002.

10 Day, M., 'Building a sense of community across the Backfence', *The Australian*, June 16 2005.

11 Ibid.

12 Sullivan, A., 'Blogger manifesto', *Sunday Times*, February 24 2002. Another source attributes the term to Peter Merholz (Burkeman, O., 'The new commentariat', *Guardian*, November 17 2005).

13 Sullivan, A., 'A blogger manifesto', *Sunday Times*, February 24 2002.

14 Sullivan, A., 'Left, left, left: media bias on the march', *Sunday Times*, January 13 2002.

15 Smith, I.D., 'Bloggers will reserve the right', *Guardian*, Febuary 20 2005.

16 Purvis, S., 'The rise of the right in the blogosphere', *Guardian*, February 21 2005.

17 Norm.blog was the subject of reportage in the US *Spectator* and then the UK-based *Sunday Times*.

18 Interview conducted on *The Message*, BBC Radio 4, February 11 2005.

19 McGann, R., 'The blogosphere by numbers', *Click2Stats*, November 22 2004.

20 Given its size, complexity and rate of evolution, the blogosphere is an inherently difficult thing to measure. The figures provided in this chapter are estimates only, although there is little to suggest that they are not reasonably accurate. Commercial and academic agencies such as Technocrati and Perseus are developing the sophistication of their measurements all the time, while services such as Blogodex and Nielsen/NetRating provide data on patterns of online usage.

21 Hudson, R., ' March of the mutant blogger', *Sunday Times*, January 2 2005.

22 Henning, J., 'The blogging iceberg', Perseus Development Corporation survey, perseus.com.

23 See too the *Daily World* – 'diverse perspectives drawn from our global network of more than 340 local and regional news organisations . . . Critical news coverage from the inside out'; the *Global Feed* – 'a real-time news wire moving 4,000 stories each day'; and the *Crisis Capsule*, 'daily intelligence on the "War on Terrorism" from our editors'.

24 Sullivan, A., 'Now blog this', *Sunday Times*, September 12 2004.

25 Interview conducted on *The Message*, BBC Radio 4, February 11 2005.

26 Carroll, B., 'Culture clash: journalism and the communal ethos of the blogosphere', *Into the Blogosphere* (http://blog.lib.umn.edu/blogosphere).

27 As described by Catherine Seipp in Online uprising', *American Journalism Review*, June 2002, http://www.ajr.org/Article.asp?id=2555.

28 O'Baoill, A., 'Weblogs and the public sphere', *Into the Blogosphere* (http://blog.lib.umn.edu/blogosphere).

29 Hiler, J., 'Blogosphere: the emerging media ecosystem', *Microcontent News*, May 28 2002.

30 Bianco, A., 'The future of the New York Times', *Business Week Online*, January 17 2005.

31 Hiler, J., 'Blogosphere: the emerging media ecosystem', *Microcontent News*, May 28 2002.

32 Carroll, B., 'Culture clash: journalism and the communal ethos of the blogosphere', *Into the Blogosphere* (http://blog.lib.umn.edu/blogosphere).

33 Outing, S., 'Taking tsunami coverage into their own hands', *Poynteronline*, January 6 2005.

34 'Media: more voices, less credibility', *Trends 2005*.

35 Windsor, D., 'Bloggers vs. journalists is over', paper to *Blogging, Journalism and Credibility* conference, Harvard University, January 21–22 2005.

36 Ibid.

37 Younge, G., 'Net gains', *Guardian*, February 16 2005.

38 Warren, J., 'Point and think', *Globe and Mail*, March 2 2002.

39 Todd Gitlin, quoted in Younge, G., '"Between a crisis and a panic"', *Guardian*, March 21 2005. Younge's article reported on the resignation of Dan Rather, and the passing of his generation of US news anchors (including Tom Brokaw and Peter Jennings) at a time when growing commercial pressures and the challenge of online journalism had 'converged to create a state of siege'.

40 Baxter, S., 'Editor falls to bloggers' rapid passion', *Sunday Times*, June 8 2003.

41 Keegan, V., 'Blogging on', *Guardian*, September 28 2004.

42 *David Warren Online*.

43 Windsor, D., 'Bloggers vs. journalists is over', paper to *Blogging, Journalism and Credibility* conference, Harvard University, January 21–22 2005.

The phenomenon of the online encyclopedia Wikipedia presents a similar clash of 'old' and 'new'. Wikipedia was established in 2000, and by October 2004 had expanded to include more than one million entries (360,000 in English), written in 100 languages, at a total cost after four years of £300,000. The 2004 edition of the *Oxford Dictionary of National Biography*, by contrast, cost £25 million and contained only 65,000 entries. Critics have condemned its 'lack of authority' and the fact that, as the executive editor of the *Encyclopaedia Britannica* puts it, 'with many of the pieces you don't know who it's written by, and who the administrators are' (quoted in Waldman, S., 'Who knows?', *Guardian*, October 26 2004). On the other hand, regular users of Wikipedia insist that its errors are few and far between, and quickly corrected (incorrect or malicious entries rarely stay on the net for more than five minutes).

Wikipedia's emergence might be seen as a paradigm for the global media in an age of communication chaos, occurring as it has without conscious direction or capital investment. Wikipedia has grown 'organically' from the bazaar-like interactions of its contributors, rather than from a top-down process of managed expansion. Where the established media (in the world of encyclopaedias, Britannica and the rest) are, in Eric Raymond's terms, Cathedrals, Wikipedia 'resembles a great babbling bazaar of differing agendas and approaches . . . out of which a coherent and stable system [emerges] only by a succession of [seeming] miracles'. Applying this language to news media, Alistair Alexander argues that:

> On the internet, the mass media cathedrals have to jostle for attention in a burgeon-ing information bazaar. While control of the mass media might be increasingly concentrated in a handful of corporations, on the internet a diverse and vibrant alternative news culture is developing with bewildering speed.
>
> (2004: 280)

44 Hiler, J., 'Blogosphere: the emerging media ecosystem', *Microcontent News*, May 28 2002.
45 Pew Internet and American Life Project, *Trends 2005*, 'Media: more voices, less credibility'.
46 Hiler, J., 'Blogosphere: the emerging media ecosystem', *Microcontent News*, May 28 2002.
47 The Hutton website was attracting 80,000 hits per week at the height of the controversy in August 2003.
48 Sullivan, A., 'Now blog this', *Sunday Times*, September 12 2004.
49 See Hudson, R., 'E-politics wins a vote of confidence', *Sunday Times*, March 13 2005, for recent UK research on e-democracy.

9 From blogosphere to public sphere?

1 Conboy, like other historians, demonstrates the contributory role played by early independent media in the battles of the English Civil War and the establishment of representative democracy in what would become the United Kingdom.
2 For an evaluation of the media–state relationship in Zimbabwe, see Ronning (2005).
3 The existence of these segments has fuelled long-standing debate, not least within media studies, about the degeneration of the public sphere, its loss of rationality, and related side-effects such as 'the crisis of public communication' (Blumler and Gurevitch 1995). Statements of crisis nearly always turn out to mean that the content of the public sphere has been deemed by someone, somewhere, to be deficient from the Habermasian ideal. Politics is not covered rationally, goes the lament, but 'packaged' in an inauthentic manner (Franklin 2004). Critical scrutiny by journalists is not healthy adversarialism in action but, as Chapter 4 noted, 'corrosive cynicism'. Daytime talk shows in which ordinary people address their concerns are viewed not as legitimate discussion, but as 'freakshows' (Dovey 2000) dominated by 'cultural fallout' (Ast and Mustazza 1997), arenas for mediated mob rule with no place in an authentic democracy. However, and despite ongoing anxieties about what is perceived by many critical commentators as 'dumbing down', 'tabloidisation' and the rise of 'infotainment' in the journalistic institutions of the public sphere (a recurring narrative of decline within the master narrative of cultural pessimism), there is growing acceptance of the idea that traditional taste distinctions between 'serious' and 'tabloid' (in relation to the British press, for example, and also in discussion of phenomena such as talk radio and daytime talk shows), or between the broadsheet and the popular – distinctions which have been used to shore up intellectual elitism and devalue popular political culture since at least the late nineteenth century (Carey 1992) – are redundant in the twenty-first.

In previous writing I have defended the emergence into the public sphere of what some call 'value issues' such as sexual politics, personal morality and lifestyle choice, not as the degeneration of 'serious' political journalism but its democratisation after centuries in which it remained the domain of wealthy, educated, white men. In the post-feminist era the argument that discussion of domestic violence and child abuse on daytime talks shows such as *Oprah* or *Tricia* is less worthy than men in suits talking economics on a news magazine programme like the BBC's *Newsnight* is rightly perceived as patriarchal elitism rather than defence of the public sphere's integrity. Habermas himself, whose original conception of the public sphere, developed in the 1960s, was patriarchal and exclusive (and criticised as such by feminist media scholars) had by the 1990s revised his model to more accurately reflect the plurality and complexity of public media space.

4   Leading BBC presenter John Humphrys, writing in September 2005, stated that his Radio 4 programme (on which Andrew Gilligan's offending report of May 2003 had been broadcast) had never been put under political pressure by the Blair government. As he put it, 'I have never been leaned on by anyone at the BBC to take a particular line' (Humphrys, J., 'Objectivity is our lifeblood', *Guardian*, September 9 2005).

5   Public opinion is a tricky thing to measure, of course, and it is an important function of the public sphere to regularly alert citizens to that fact.

6   Kronig, J., 'A crisis in the fourth estate', *Guardian*, August 16 2004.

7   Ayish quotes the view of one commentator that Al Jazeera is responsible for airing the 'vulgarity that is cheerfully migrating from the West to the Arab east . . . while theoretically opening up new channels of public discourse on previously taboo subjects of social import' (2005: 124).

8   Quoted in Younge, G., 'Between a crisis and a panic', *Guardian*, March 21 2005.

9   Sullivan, A., 'Let's hear it for the prejudiced television news', *Sunday Times*, November 17 2002. See too his 'Left, left, left: media bias on the march', *Sunday Times*, January 13 2002. As Chapter 8 showed, the motivation of these participants in the new media is in large part the perception that the mainstream media are biased in favour of liberalism, and against conservatism. In June 2002, as the blogosphere was emerging into public consciousness, one observer asked:

> Why do they do it? In the US, conservative groups have been quicker than their liberal counterparts to colonise alternative media, using it to vent their frustration with a left-leaning mainstream press . . . The Web fits easily into the conservative movement's alternative media universe.
>
> (Mareth, J., 'The blog brings freedom to the Net', *The Age*, June 2002)

10 Mareth, op. cit.

11 Berger, N., *American Prospect*, March 2002.

12 Ibrahim, Saeed Eddin, quoted in *Transnational Broadcasting Studies*, no. 13, fall 2004.

13 Quoted in Wise, L., 'Between theory and practice', *Transnational Broadcasting Studies*, no. 13, fall 2004.

14 For a detailed discussion of Al Jazeera's representation of women, see Sakr (2005a).

15 Khanfar, W., 'The future of Al Jazeera', *Transnational Broadcasting Studies*, no. 13, fall 2004.

16 Reproduced in *Transnational Broadcasting Studies*, no. 11, fall 2003.

17 Warren, J., 'Point and think', *Globe and Mail*, March 2 2002.

18 Orville Schell, quoted in Rosen, J., 'Journalism is itself a religion', *Pressthink*, January 7 2004.

19 Sullivan, A., 'Battlelines deepen in the US', *Sunday Times*, November 9 2003.

20 Sullivan, A., 'The blogging revolution', *Wired*, vol. 10, no. 5, May 2002.

21 Quoted in Hiler, J., 'Blogosphere: the emerging media ecosystem', *Microcontent News*, May 28 2002.

22 'Thoughts on being on O'Reilly – power to the people', posted at Abovitz's blog, *fixtheworld.blogs.com*, February 15 2005.

10 Global news culture and authoritarianism

1   *Argumenty I Fakti*, no. 5, February 7 1989.

2   See my *Glasnost, Perestroika and the Soviet Media* (McNair 1991) for a detailed account of the media dimension of the Chernobyl crisis.

3 Myers, S., 'What would happen if Russia exploded in protest?', *New York Times*, April 3 2005.

4 Swain, J. and Baxter, S., 'The Arabian spring', *Sunday Times*, March 6 2005.

5 *The House of Saud*, broadcast on BBC2 as part of the *Storyville* series, September 2 2004.

6 Lynch, M., 'Taking Arabs seriously', *Foreign Affairs*, vol. 82, no. 5, September–October 2003.

7 Saeed, A.M., 'The Arab satellites – some necessary observations', *Transnational Broadcasting Studies*, no. 11, fall 2003.

8 Khanfar, W., 'The future of Al Jazeera', *Transnational Broadcasting Studies*, no. 12, spring 2004.

9 For a journalistic commentary on *Arab Big Brother* see McNair, B., 'Arab Big Brother's demise should be mourned', *Scotland On Sunday*, March 7 2004 (http://scotland onsunday.scotsman.com/artsandbooks.cfm?id=264832004).

10 Mackenzie, T., 'The best hope for democracy in the Arab world', *Transnational Broadcasting Studies*, no. 13, fall 2004.

11 Walt, V., 'Iran's young lose faith in reform', *Sunday Times*, February 20 2004.

12 Kahn, J., 'China is filtering phone text messages', *New York Times*, July 3 2004.

13 Hirst, D., 'Dangerous democracy', *Guardian*, April 20 2005.

14 For the text of the report, see www.undp.org/rbas/ahdr.

11 Democracy and hyper-democracy

1 For the classic sociological work on moral panics, see Cohen (2002).

2 From press release published at http://www.cardiff.ac.uk/newsevents/media/ mediarel/mr0503/mr030519.html. The full text of the report, *Towards a Better Map: Science, the public and the media*, by Justin Lewis, Ian Hargreaves and Tammy Lewis, is available at www.esrc.ac.uk.

3 Extract shown on the documentary *Anxiety Attack*, broadcast on BBC2 in 1996.

4 Harrabin, R., Coote, A. and Allen, J., *Health in the News*, King's Fund Publications, 2003. For a downloadable PDF of the report, see www.kingsfund.org.uk/publications.

5 Toynbee, P., 'The BBC must not be led by the shock tactics of the Mail', *Guardian*, August 11 2004.

6 Massie, A., 'Let's not lose our bottle over pleasures', *Sunday Times*, April 18 2004.

7 Malcolm Gladwell's *The Tipping Point* shows how social and cultural epidemics, including the ideas that make up global political debate, diffuse until they reach a point – the tipping point – at which they spread exponentially. This process of diffusion is fundamentally chaotic, in so far as 'epidemics are sensitive to the conditions and circumstances of the times and places in which they occur' (2000: 139).

8 I am not suggesting that the legislation caused a rise in crime, merely that it failed to reduce it, and can thus be deemed an example of bad government driven by media coverage of public pressure.

9 Brock, D, 'How I almost brought down the president', *Guardian*, March 12 2002.

10 Seipp, C., 'Online uprising', *American Journalism Review*, June 2002.

11 Lyall, S., 'Toasting the happy couple with hemlock', *New York Times*, April 3 2005.

12 Comment made during his appearance on the BBC's *Question Time*, January 13 2005.

13 *Sunday Herald*, September 26 2004.

14 Workin, D., 'Assessing a gruesome toll after a rash of beheadings', *New York Times*, June 24 2004.

15 Ibid.

16 As this book went to press, over 200 foreign nationals had been kidnapped, and over 100 killed in the post-invasion period.

17 In September 2004 the tactic of the media spectacular was taken yet further down the road of nihilistic degeneracy by the taking hostage and subsequent murder of more than 300 men, women and children by Chechnyan Islamists at a school in Beslan, Ingushetia.

In this case, reflecting the transitional nature of the post-Soviet Russian government, and its continuing tendency to fall back on pre-*glasnost* information policies, while the world's media were present and actively reporting at the scene, Russian audiences were prevented from seeing live coverage on their own TV channels.

18 Of course the threat of Al Qaida, once established in the public imagination, can be manipulated and exaggerated for short-term policy and propaganda goals, by Osama Bin Laden as much as by the Bush and Blair governments. That fact does not make it an imaginary threat. September 11 did happen, as did Bali, Madrid and the London bombings. Whether these events justify the declaration of a global state of war comparable to that necessitated by the 1939–45 struggle against fascism is doubtful, but so is the notion that 'the threat' is the conscious creation of a ruling elite conspiracy in Washington and London.

19 For the text and video footage of one of the interviews, given to the US-funded Alhurra channel, see http://www.whitehouse.gov/news/releases/2004/05/20040505-5.html.

20 From comments made in conversation with Antonio Polito.

21 Had the prime minister and his government been more honest about the real reasons for attacking Saddam's Iraq in March 2003, it is likely that he would not have obtained the necessary legal and political authority to undertake it.

22 Views attributed to the foreign secretary Jack Straw and Blair government 'loyalists' in the *Guardian*, July 16 2004.

23 Factors in generating media attention will include the ability of political actors to manufacture relevance (which is a problem of political communication and source strategies), as well as the suitability of an event for narrativisation as news (i.e., the extent to which it 'fits' with historical context, and can be narrated within a recognised sense-making framework).

12 Controlling chaos

1 Carey adds that 'while technology overcomes many borders (of space, time, politics and economics) other social borders may be created at the same time' (ibid.: 443).

2 One recent study noted that in the five years between 1999 and 2004, mobile phone subscriptions grew each year on average by 59 per cent in Africa and 34 per cent in Asia. Reviewing the positive impact of this growth on Africa in particular, it is observed that 'in a culture where people travel long distances to find work, the mobile has become the most useful and ubiquitous piece of technology since the bicycle' (Vasagar, J., 'Talk is cheap, and getting cheaper', *Guardian*, September 14 2005).

3 Two gay teenagers were executed by hanging in the Iranian city of Masshad on July 19 2005. A 16-year-old girl, Atefeh Rajabi, was hanged in July 2004 for having sex outside of marriage.

4 Comments made at the 'Global Flow of Information' conference, Yale Law School, April 2005.

5 Quoted in Kinninmont, J., 'Qatar draws up plan to sell off al-Jazeera', *Guardian*, April 27 2005.

6 Reported in Whitaker, B., 'Iran bans Arab TV station after riots', *Guardian*, April 20 2005.

7 Abdullah, M., 'A fear of free speech', *Guardian*, August 11 2004.

8 Freedland, J., 'The failed occupation', *Guardian*, August 11 2004.

9 Quoted in Campbell, A., 'I was wrong about al-Jazeera', *Guardian*, September 15 2004.

10 *Sunday Times*, July 31 2005. According to this report the Pakistan-based site www.mojihedun.com, which contained a section titled 'How to Strike a European City', was one of the jihadist sites disabled by the intelligence services of the UK or some other country.

11 *New York Times*, January 7 2004.

12 For a report on life in Iran compiled just before the 2005 presidential election, see Hitchens, C., 'Iran's waiting game', *Vanity Fair*, July 2005. Hitchens observes that beneath the theocratic appearance of things in the country, and 'under the noses of the moral enforcers, Iranians are buying and selling videos, making and consuming alcohol, tuning into satellite TV stations, producing subversive films and plays and books, and defying the dress code . . . People live as if they were free, as if they were in the West, as if they had the right to an opinion, or a private life'.

13 Comments made at the 'Global Flow of Information' conference, Yale Law School, April 2005.

14 McDonald, H., 'Murdoch out of step in New China', *Fairfax Digital Business*, August 30 2005. (http://www.smh.com.au/news/business/murdoch-out-of-step-in-new-china/2005/08/29/1125302506746.html?oneclick=true)

15 Xiguang, L., 'Live coverage of lies or truth?', paper delivered to conference on 'Arab and Western Media Coverage of the War in Iraq: The Continuing Debate', University of Cambridge, March 17–21 2004, reproduced in *Transnational Broadcasting Studies*, no. 12, spring 2004. The argument that China's governing elite might permit a limited degree of cultural freedom and exposure to international media as a way of pacifying their population takes us back to Adorno and Horkheimer's view of mass culture as a narcotic, or opiate of the masses. The assumption of a passive, easily controlled audience is explicit.

16 *The Russian Newspaper Murders*, July 8 2004. The programme press notes observe that:

> During the last five years, more than a dozen journalists have been killed in Russia, yet none of their murderers has been brought to justice. Facing fierce political and economic pressure, Russia's few remaining independent journalists risk their lives to expose organized crime and government corruption. *Wide Angle* examines the industrial city of Togliatti, whose main automobile factory is allegedly run by corrupt oligarchs and where killings attributed to organized crime occur nearly every week. In 2002, Valery Ivanov, editor-in-chief of the *Togliatti Observer*, the city's only independent newspaper, was shot to death after reporting on local corruption. Eighteen months later, Alexei Sidorov, Ivanov's successor at the newspaper, was stabbed to death. This film reports on the risks that journalists run in modern-day Russia and explores the tangled web of wealth, power and politics that defines Russia today.

17 Gibson, O., 'Spin caught in a web trap', *Guardian*, February 17 2004.

18 See Katovsky and Carlson's *Embedded: The media at war in Iraq* (2003) for recollections by some of the 700 embedded correspondents.

19 Wilmsen, D., 'Alhurra – a dialogue with the deaf', *Transnational Broadcasting Studies*, no. 12, spring 2004.

20 Ibid.

21 Allen-Mills, T., 'America fights for Iraqi hearts with TV onslaught', *Sunday Times*, January 16 2005.

22 As this book went to press, Alhurra was reported to be gaining in credibility with the Iraqi audience, although such claims could not be confirmed.

23 Other Anglo-American initiatives have included the business-oriented CNBC Arabiya in July 2003 (joining CNBC Pakistan and others), competing with the Dubai-based Business Channel for the Arab-language financial news market. The BBC was also criticised for its parallel decision announced in November 2005, to cut back on several of its foreign language World Service channels.

24 Goodhart, D, 'Who are the masters now?', *Prospect*, May 1997.

25 Lambert, R., 'The path back to trust, truth and integrity', *Guardian*, January 17 2005.

13 Conclusion and postscript: cultural chaos and the critical project

1 For a discussion of network theory and its application to the internet, see Watts (2003).

2 The term is borrowed from Tom Wolfe's essay 'My three stooges', in *Hooking Up* (2000).

3 Geo-strategic competition aside, humanity's forward march (as I have characterised it) could also be destroyed or seriously retarded by a natural disaster of species-threatening proportions, caused by catastrophic climate change, a super volcano, a colliding asteroid or some other event for which we are as yet unprepared but which our media constantly remind us is a possibility. The millennial turn was characterised by an upsurge in anxieties about impending catastrophe, played out in documentaries, news journalism, feature films such as *The Day after Tomorrow* and best-selling books. Much of this coverage can be understood as examples of media panic, frenzy and scare (see Chapter 11), while containing a kernel of truth. Such narratives usually include some acknowledgement of the statistical improbability of global disasters, but rely for their appeal on the knowledge that apocalypse tomorrow, or the day after tomorrow, is theoretically possible. Should it happen on our watch, humanity if it survives at all would undoubtedly be transported back to more brutal, controlling times.

4 Shanahan, D. and Elliott, G., 'Chinese general irresponsible: PM', *The Australian*, July 18 2005.

Bibliography

Abercrombie, N., Hill, S. and Turner, B., (eds), *Dominant Ideologies*, London, Unwin Hyman, 1990.

Al Kasim, F., '*The Opposite Direction*: A program which changed the face of Arab television', in Zayani, M. (ed.), *The Al Jazeera Phenomenon*, Boulder, Col., Paradigm Publishers, 2005: 93–105.

Alexander, A., 'Disruptive technology: Iraq and the Internet' in Miller, D. (ed.), *Tell Me Lies: Propaganda and media distortion in the attack on Iraq*, London, Pluto, 2004: 277–85.

Alexander, J., 'The mass news media in systemic, historical and comparative perspective', in Katz, E. and Szecsko, T. (eds), *Mass Media and Social Change*, London, Sage, 1981: 18–39.

Allan, S. (ed.), *Journalism: Critical Issues*, London, Routledge, 2005.

Althusser, L., *Lenin and Philosophy and Other Essays*, London, New Left Books, 1971.

Althusser, L. and Balibar, E., *Reading Capital*, London, New Left Books, 1970.

Alves, R.C., 'From lapdog to watchdog: the role of the press in Latin America's democratisation', in De Burgh, H. (ed.), *Making Journalists*, London, Routledge, 2005: 181–202.

Anderson, B., *Imagined Communities*, London, Verso, 1982.

Arquilla, J. and Ronfeldt, D., *In Athena's Camp: Preparing for conflict in the information age*, Santa Monica, Cal., Rand, 1997.

Ast, V. and Mustazza, L., *Coming after Oprah: Cultural fallout in the age of the TV talk show*, Bowling Green, OH, Bowling Green State University Press, 1997.

Atkins, W., *The Politics of Southeast Asia's New Media*, London, RoutledgeCurzon, 2002.

Awad, G., 'Aljazeera.net: identity choices and the logic of the media', in Zayani M. (ed.), The *Al Jazeera Phenomenon*, Boulder, Col., Paradigm Publishers, 2005: 80–9.

Ayish, M.I., 'Media brinkmanship in the Arab world: Al Jazeera's *The Opposite Direction* as a fighting arena', in Zayani, M. (ed.), *The Al Jazeera Phenomenon*, Boulder, Col., Paradigm Publishers, 2005: 106–26.

Bakan, J., *The Corporation*, New York, Free Press, 2004.

Bauman, Z., *Society under Siege*, Cambridge, Polity Press, 2002.

Bell, D., *The End of Ideology*, Cambridge, Mass., Harvard University Press, 2000.

Bennett, O., *Cultural Pessimism: Narratives of decline in the postmodern world*, Edinburgh, Edinburgh University Press, 2001.

Bennett, W.L. 'Communicating Global Activism: Strengths and Vulnerabilities of Networked Politics', *Information, Communication and Society*, vol. 6, no. 2, 2003: 143–68.

Bennett, W.L. and Entman, R.M.: *Mediated Politics: Communication in the future of democracy*, Cambridge, Cambridge University Press, 2001.

Bessaiso, E.Y., 'Al Jazeera and the war in Afghanistan: delivery system or a mouthpiece?', in Zayani, M. (ed.), *The Al Jazeera Phenomenon*, Boulder, Col., Paradigm Publishers, 2005: 153–70.

Blain, N. and O'Donnell, H., *Media, Monarchy and Power*, Bristol, Intellect, 2003.

Blumler, J. and Gurevitch, M., *The Crisis of Public Communication*, London, Routledge, 1995.

Bourdieu, P., *On Television and Journalism*, London, Pluto, 1998.

Boyd-Barrett, O. and Rantanen, T. (eds), *The Globalization of News*, London, Sage, 1998.

Carey, J., *The Intellectuals and the Masses*, London, Penguin, 1992.

Carey, J.W., 'Historical pragmatism and the internet', *New Media & Society*, vol. 7, no. 4, 2005: 443–55.

Carroll, B., 'Culture clash: journalism and the communal ethos of the blogosphere', *Into the Blogosphere*, http://blog.lib.umn.edu/blogosphere/.

Castells, M., *End of Millennium*, Oxford, Blackwell, 2000.

Centeno, M., paper delivered to 'The Global Flow of Information' conference, Yale Law School, April 1–3 2005.

Chalaby, J.K. (ed.), *Transnational Television Worldwide: Towards a new media order*, London, Tauris, 2005.

Chambers, D., Steiner, L. and Fleming, C., *Women and Journalism*, London, Routledge, 2004.

Chambers, S. and Costain, A. (eds), *Deliberation, Democracy, and the Media*, Lanham, MD, Rowman & Littlefield, 2000.

Chomsky, D., 'The mechanisms of management control at the *New York Times*', *Media, Culture & Society*, vol. 21, no. 5, 1999: 579–99.

Chomsky, N., *Manufacturing Consent*, New York, Pantheon, 1988.

—— *Necessary Illusions*, Boston, Mass., South End Press, 1989.

Chomsky, N. and Herman, E., *The Political Economy of Human Rights, vols 1&2*, Boston, Mass., South End Press, 1979.

Cohen, J. and Stewart, I., *The Collapse of Chaos*, London, Penguin, 1995.

Cohen, S., *Moral Panics and Folk Devils*, 2nd edition, London, Routledge, 2002.

Conboy, M., *Journalism and Popular Culture*, London, Sage, 2000.

—— *Journalism: A critical history*, London, Sage, 2004.

Connell, I., 'Monopoly capitalism and the media', in Hibsen, S. (ed.), *Politics, Ideology and the State*, London, Lawrence & Wishart, 1983.

Corner, J. and Pels, D. (eds), *Media and the Restyling of Politics*, London, Sage, 2003.

Cottle, S., 'Mapping the field', in Cottle, S. (ed.), *News, Public Relations and Power*, London, Sage, 2003: 3–24.

Cottle, S. (ed.), *News, Public Relations and Power*, London, Sage, 2003.

Curran, J., *Media and Power*, London, Routledge, 2002.

Curran, J. and Gurevitch, M. (eds), *Mass Media and Society*, London, Edward Arnold, 1991.

Curtice, M., 'Psychological warfare against the public: Iraq and beyond', in Miller, D. (ed.), *Tell Me Lies*, London, Pluto, 2004: 70–9.

Da Lage, O., 'The politics of Al Jazeera or the diplomacy of Doha', in Zayani, M. (ed.), *The Al Jazeera Phenomenon*, Boulder, Col., Paradigm Publishers, 2005: 49–65.

Dawkins, R., *The Selfish Gene*, Oxford, Oxford University Press, 1989.

—— *A Devil's Chaplain*, London, Phoenix, 2004.

De Burgh, H. (ed.), *Making Journalists*, London, Routledge, 2005.

De la Haye, Y. (ed.), *Marx and Engels on the Means of Communication*, New York, International General, 1983.

De Landa, M., *A Thousand Years of Nonlinear History*, New York, Zone Books, 2001.

De Sola Pool, I., *Technologies of Freedom*, Cambridge, Mass., Harvard Bellknap, 1983.

Dovey, L., *Freakshow: First person media and factual television*, London, Pluto Press, 2000.

Downing, J., *Internationalising Media Theory*, London, Sage, 1996.

Drezner, D., 'Weighing the scales: the internet's effect on state–society relations', paper delivered to 'The Global Flow of Information' conference, Yale Law School, April 1–3 2005.

Eco, U., *Travels in Hyper-reality*, London, Picador, 1986.

Eisenstein, E., *The Printing Revolution in Early Modern Europe*, Cambridge, Cambridge University Press, 1983.

El Oifi, M., 'Influence without power: Al Jazeera and the Arab public sphere', in Zayani, M. (ed.), *The Al Jazeera Phenomenon*, Boulder, Col., Paradigm Publishers, 2005: 66–80.

Eng, I., 'The performance of the sponge: mass communication theory enters the postmodern world', in Brants *et al.* (eds), *The Media in Question*, London, Sage, 1998: 77–88.

Eriksen, E., 'Conceptualising European public spheres', unpublished paper given to the 'One EU – Many Publics' workshop, Stirling University, February 5–6 2004.

Eriksen, E. and Weigard, J., *Understanding Habermas*, London, Continuum, 2003.

Fallows, J., *Breaking the News*, New York, Pantheon Books, 1996.

Ferguson, P. (ed.), *Public Communication*, London, Sage, 1989.

Fiske, J., *Media Matters*, Minneapolis, University of Minnesota Press, 1996.

Flournoy, D., *CNN World Report: Ted Turner's International News Coup*, London, John Libbey, 1992.

Foreman, A., *Georgiana: Duchess of Devonshire*, New York, Random House, 1998.

Franklin, B., *Packaging Politics*, London, Arnold, 2004.

Franzen, J., *The Corrections*, London, Fourth Estate, 2002.

Friedman, T.L., *The World Is Flat: A brief history of the twenty-first century*, New York, Farrar, Straus & Giroux, 2005.

Fukuyama, F., *The End of History and the Last Man*, London, Hamish Hamilton, 1992.

Giddens, A., *The Consequences of Modernity*, Cambridge, Polity Press, 1990.

Gitlin, T., *Media Unlimited: How the torrent of sounds and images overwhelms our lives*, New York, Henry Holt & Company, 2002.

Gladwell, M., *The Tipping Point*, London, Little Brown, 2000.

Gleick, J., *Chaos: The amazing science of the unpredictable*, London, Minerva, 1996.

Gleick, J. and Porter, E., *Nature's Chaos*, Boston, Mass., Little, Brown & Company, 1990.

Gowing, N., *Real-time Television Coverage of Armed Conflicts and Diplomatic Crises*, Cambridge, Mass., Harvard University Press, 1994.

Gray, J., *Al Qaeda and What It Means to Be Modern*, London, Faber & Faber, 2003.

Gross, P., *Entangled Evolutions*, Baltimore, Johns Hopkins University Press, 2002.

Gurevitch, M., 'The globalization of electronic journalism', in Curran J. and Gurevitch, M. (eds), *Society*, London, Edward Arnold, 1990: 178–93.

Gurevitch, M. and Levy, M., 'The global newsroom', *British Journalism Review*, vol. 2, no. 1, 1990: 27–37.

Habermas, J., *The Structural Transformation of the Public Sphere*, Cambridge, Polity Press, 1989.

Hall, S., 'Culture, the media and the "ideological effect"', in Curran, J., Gurevitch, M. and Wollacott, J. (eds), *Mass Communication and Society*, London, Edward Arnold, 1977: 315–48.

Hall, S., Connell, I. and Curti, I., 'The "unity" of current affairs television', *Working Papers in Cultural Studies*, 9, 1976: 51–93.

Hall, S., Hobson, D., Lowe, A. and Willis, P. (eds), *Culture, Media, Language*, London, Hutchinson, 1980.

Hallin, D., *The 'Uncensored War': The media and Vietnam*, New York, Oxford University Press, 1986.

Hamelink, C.J., 'World communication: conflicting aspirations for the twenty-first century', in Brants *et al.* (eds), *The Media in Question*, London, Sage, 1998: 64–76.

Hamilton, J.M. and Jenner, E., 'The new foreign correspondence', *Foreign Affairs*, September/October 2003: 131–38.

Hardt, H., *Myths for the Masses*, Oxford, Blackwell, 2004.

Hargreaves, I. and Thomas, J., *New News, Old News*, London, Independent Television Commission/ Broadcasting Standards Commission, 2002.

Hartley, J., *Popular Reality*, London, Arnold, 1996.

—— 'Journalism as a human right: a cultural approach to journalism', paper delivered to the 'International Communication Association' conference, New York, June 2005.

Hawkins, H., *Strange Attractors: Literature, culture and chaos theory*, New York, Harvester Wheatsheaf, 1995.

Heller, M., 'Enlargement of the European Union, citizenship, identity and the Hungarian public sphere', paper delivered at the 'One EU – Many Publics' workshop, University of Stirling, February 5–6 2004.

Herman, E. and Broadhead, F., *Demonstration Elections*, New York, Sheridan Square Publications, 1988.

Herman, E. and McChesney, R., *The Global Media: The new missionaries of global capitalism*, London, Cassell, 1997.

Hersh, S., *The Dark Side of Camelot*, New York, Little Brown, 1997.

Hess, S. and Kalb, M., (eds), *The Media and the War on Terrorism*, Washington, Brookings Institution Press, 2003.

Hiro, D., *War Without End: The rise of Islamist terrorism and global response*, London, Routledge, 2002.

Hitchens, C., *A Long Short War: The postponed liberation of Iraq*, New York, Slate, 2003.

Hobsbawm, E., *The New Century*, London, Abacus, 2000.

Horkheimer, M. and Adorno, T., *Dialectic of Enlightenment*, London, Allen Lane, 1973.

Huntington, S., *The Clash of Civilisations and the Remaking of World Order*, New York, Simon & Schuster, 1996.

Jameson, F., *Postmodernism, or the Cultural Logic of Late Capitalism*, London, Verso, 1991.

Johnson, S., *Everything Bad is Good for You: How popular culture is making us smarter*, London, Penguin, 2005.

Kalathil, S. and Boas, T.C., *Open Networks, Closed Regimes: The impact of the internet on authoritarian rule*, Washington, DC, Carnegie Endowment for International Peace, 2003.

Kapitaniak, T. and Wojewoda, J., *Attractors of Quasiperiodically Forced Systems*, Singapore, World Scientific, 1993.

Katovsky, B. and Carlson, T., *Embedded: The media at war in Iraq*, Guilford, The Lyons Press, 2003.

Katz, J., *Media Rants: Postpolitics in the digital nation*, San Francisco, Hardwired, 1997.

Keane, J., *Media and Democracy*, Cambridge, Polity Press, 1991.

Kevill, S., *Beyond the Soundbite*, London, BBC, 2002.

Klein, N., *No Logo*, London, HarperCollins, 2000.

Lash, S., *Critique of Information*, London, Sage, 2002.

Le Pottier, G., 'The emergence of a pan-Arab market in modern media industries', in Al-

Rasheed, M. (ed.), *Transnational connections and the Arab Gulf*, London, Routledge, 2005: 111–28.

Lenin, V.I., *Materialism and Empirio-criticism: Critical notes concerning a reactionary philosophy*, London, Martin Lawrence Ltd, 1920.

—— *Imperialism: The highest stage of capitalism*, Moscow, Progress Publishers, 1978.

Lewin, R., *Complexity: Life at the edge of chaos*, New York, Macmillan, 1992.

Lloyd, J., *What the Media Are Doing to Our Politics*, London, Constable, 2004.

Lorenz, E., *The Essence of Chaos*, Seattle, University of Washington Press, 1993.

Louw, E., *The Media and Political Process*, London, Sage, 2005.

Luhmann, N., 'Speaking or silence', *New German Critique*, Winter 1994, no. 61: 25–39.

—— 'Globalisation or world society: how to conceive of modern society?', *International Review of Sociology*, March 1997, vol. 7, no. 1: 67–80.

—— *The Reality of the Mass Media*, Cambridge, Polity Press, 2000.

Lull, J. and Hinerman, S. (eds), *Media Scandals*, Cambridge, Polity Press, 1997.

Lumby, C., *Gotcha: Life in a tabloid world*, St Leonard's, Allen & Unwin, 1999.

Lynch, M., 'Taking Arabs seriously', *Foreign Affairs*, vol. 82, no. 5, September–October 2003.

MacBride, S., *Many Voices, One World: Towards a new, more just, and more efficient world information and communication order*, Lanham, MD, Rowman & Littlefield, 2005.

McChesney, R., 'Corporate Media, Global Capitalism', in Cottle, S. (ed.) *News, Public Relations and Power*, London, Sage, 2003: 27–39.

McKnight, D., *Beyond Right and Left*, Sydney, Allen & Unwin, 2005.

McLuhan, E. and Zingrone, F. (eds), *The Essential McLuhan*, London, Routledge, 1997.

McNair, B., *Images of the Enemy*, London, Routledge, 1988.

—— 'Glasnost and restructuring in the Soviet media', *Media, Culture & Society*, vol. 11, no. 3: 1989: 327–51.

—— *Glasnost, Perestroika and the Soviet Media*, London, Routledge, 1991.

—— 'Media in Post-Soviet Russia: An Overview', *European Journal of Communication*, vol. 9, no. 2: 1994: 115–35.

—— *Mediated Sex: Pornography and postmodern culture*, London, Arnold, 1996.

—— *The Sociology of Journalism*, London, Arnold, 1998.

—— *Journalism and Democracy*, London, Routledge, 2000.

—— *Striptease Culture*, London, Routledge, 2002.

—— *An Introduction to Political Communication*, London, Routledge, 2003b.

—— *News and Journalism in the UK*, London, Routledge, 2003c.

—— 'PR must die: spin, anti-spin and political public relations in the UK, 1997–2004', *Journalism Studies*, vol. 5, no. 3, 2004: 325–38.

McNair, B., Hibberd, M. and Schlesinger, P., *Mediated Access*, Luton, University of Luton Press, 2003.

Manning, P., *News and News Sources: A critical introduction*, London, Sage, 2001.

Marx, K., *Theories of Surplus Value, vols. 1–3*, London, Lawrence & Wishart, 1969.

—— *Capital, vol. 1*, London, Penguin, 1973.

—— *Capital, vol. 3*, London, Penguin, 1974.

Marx, K. and Engels, F., *The German Ideology*, London, Lawrence & Wishart, 1976.

—— *The Communist Manifesto*, London, Verso, 1998.

Mattelart, A., *The Information Society*, London, Sage, 2003.

Miliband, R., *The State in Capitalist Society*, London, Quartet, 1972.

Miller, D. (ed.), *Tell Me Lies: Propaganda and media distortion in the attack on Iraq*, London, Pluto, 2004.

Moeller, S., *Compassion Fatigue: How the media sell disease, famine, war and death*, London, Routledge, 1999.

Mowlana, H., Gerbner, G. and Schiller, H.I. (eds) *Triumph of the Image: The media's war in the Persian Gulf – a global perspective*, Boulder, Col., Westview Press, 1992.

Murphy, P., 'Chaos theory as a model for managing issues and crises', *Public Relations Review*, vol. 22, no. 2, 1996: 95–113.

—— 'Symmetry, contingency, complexity: accommodating uncertainty in public relations theory', *Public Relations Review*, vol. 26, no. 4, 2000: 447–62.

Naughton, J., *A Brief History of the Future: The origins of the internet*, London, Weidenfeld & Nicolson, 1999.

O'Baoill, A., 'Weblogs and the public sphere', *Into the Blogosphere* (http://blog.lib.umn.edu/blogosphere/.)

Ormerod, P., *Why Most Things Fail*, London, Faber, 2005.

Palfrey, J.G., 'Local News: filtering and the internet governance problem', paper delivered to 'The Global Flow of Information' conference, Yale Law School, April 1–3 2005.

Paterson, C., 'Global battlefields', in Boyd-Barratt, O. and Rantanen, T. (eds), *The Globalization of News*, London, Sage, 1998: 79–103.

Pavlik, J., 'New media and news: implications for the future of journalism', *New Media and Society*, vol. 1, no. 1, 1999: 54–9.

Philo, G. and Berry, M., *Bad News From Israel*, London, Pluto, 2004.

Pitcher, G., *The Death of Spin*, Chichester, John Wiley & Sons, 2003.

Pool, I. de Sola: *Technologies of Freedom: On free speech in an electronic age*, Cambridge, Mass., Harvard University Press, 1983.

Price, M. *Television, the Public Sphere, and National Identity*, Oxford, Clarendon Press, 1995.

—— *Media and Sovereignty: The global information revolution and the challenge to state power*, New York, Peter Lang Publishing, 2002.

Rantanen, T., *The Global and the National*, Lanham, MD, Rowman & Littlefield, 2002.

Raymond, J., *The Invention of the Newspaper*, Oxford, Clarendon Press, 1996.

Rifkin, J., *Age of Access*, New York, Putnam, 2000.

Ritzer, G., *The McDonaldization of Society*, London, Sage, 1993.

—— *The McDonaldization Thesis*, London, Sage, 1998.

Robins, K. and Aksoy, A., 'Whoever looks always finds: transnational viewing and knowledge-experience', in Chalaby, J.K. (ed.), *Transnational Television Worldwide*, London, Tauris, 2005: 14–42.

Robinson, P., *The CNN Effect: The myth of news, foreign policy and intervention*, London and New York, Routledge, 2002.

Ronning, H., 'African journalism and the struggle for democratic media', in De Burgh, H. (ed.), *Making Journalists*, London, Routledge, 2005: 157–80.

Rushkoff, D., *Coercion*, New York, Riverhead, 1998.

Sabato, L.J., Stencel, M. and Lichter, S.R., *Peepshow: Media and politics in an age of scandal*, Lanham, MD, Rowman & Littlefield, 2000.

Sakr, N. 'Women, development and Al Jazeera: a balance sheet', in Zayani, M. (ed.), *The Al Jazeera Phenomenon*, Boulder, Col., Paradigm Publishers, 2005a: 127–49.

—— 'Maverick or model? Al Jazeera's impact on Arab satellite television', in Chalaby, J.K. (ed.), *Transnational Television Worldwide*, London, Tauris, 2005b: 66–95.

—— 'The changing dynamics of Arab journalism' in De Burgh, H. (ed.), *Making Journalists*, London, Routledge, 2005c: 142–56.

Schiller, D., 'Transformation of news in the US information market', in Golding P. *et al.* (eds) *Communicating Politics*, Leicester, University of Leicester Press, 1986: 19–36.

Schlesinger, P., *Putting Reality Together*, London, Constable, 1978.

—— 'Rethinking the sociology of journalism', in Ferguson, P. (ed.), *Public Communication*, London, Sage, 1989a: 61–83.

—— 'From production to propaganda', *Media, Culture & Society*, vol. 11, no. 3, 1989b: 283–306.

Schlesinger, P., Murdock, G. and Elliott, P., *Televising Terrorism*, London, Comedia, 1983.

Schudson, M., 'The sociology of news production', *Media, Culture & Society*, vol. 11, no. 3, 1989: 263–82.

—— *The Power of News*, Cambridge, Mass., Harvard University Press, 1995.

Seib, P., *Beyond the Front Lines: How the news media cover a world shaped by war*, New York, Palgrave Macmillan, 2004.

Simons, J., 'Popular culture and mediated politics: intellectuals, elites and democracy', in Corner, J. and Pels, D. (eds), *Media and the Restyling of Politics*, London, Sage, 2003: 171–89.

Snow, N., 'Brainscrubbing: the failures of US public diplomacy after 9/11', in Miller, D. (ed.), *Tell Me Lies*, London, Pluto, 2004: 52–62.

Sokal, A. and Bricmont, J., *Intellectual Impostures*, London, Profile Books, 1998.

Starr, P., *The Creation of the Media*, New York, Basic Books, 2004.

Thompson, J.B., *Political Scandal: Power and visibility in the media age*, Cambridge, Polity Press, 2000.

Thussu, D., 'The transnationalisation of television: the Indian experience', in Chalaby, J.K. (ed.), *Transnational Television Worldwide*, London, Tauris, 2005: 156–72.

Thussu, D. and Freedman, D. (eds) *War and the Media: reporting conflict 24/7*, London, Sage, 2003.

Tiffen, R., *Scandals: Media, politics and corruption in contemporary Australia*, Sydney, University of New South Wales, 1999.

Tumber, H. and Palmer, J., *The Media at War*, London, Palgrave, 2004.

Tunstall, J. and Machin, D., *The Anglo-American Media Connection*, Oxford, Oxford University Press, 1999.

Virilio, P., *Open Sky*, London, Verso, 1997.

Waldrop, M.M., *Complexity: The emerging science at the edge of order and chaos*, London, Penguin, 1992.

Wark, M., *Celebrities, Culture and Cyberspace: The light on the hill in a postmodern world*, Sydney, Pluto Press, 1999.

Watts, D. *Six Degrees: The science of a connected world*, London, Heinemann, 2003.

Wheen, F., *Karl Marx*, London, Fourth Estate, 1999.

—— *How Mumbo-Jumbo Conquered the World*, London, Abacus, 2004.

Wilkins, P. and Lacy, M. (eds), *Global Journalism*, Manchester, Manchester University Press, 2006.

Williams, K., *Understanding Media Theory*, London, Arnold, 2003.

Wolfe, T., *Hooking Up*, London, Jonathan Cape, 2000.

Zassoursky, I., *Media and Power in Post-Soviet Russia*, New York, M.E. Sharpe, 2003.

Zayani, M. (ed.) *The Al Jazeera Phenomenon: Critical perspectives on new Arab media*, Boulder, Col., Paradigm Publishers, 2005.

Zelizer, B. and Allan, S. (eds) *Journalism after September 11*, London and New York, Routledge, 2002.

Index

Related titles from Routledge

Cultural Studies: A Critical Introduction
Simon During

Cultural Studies: A Critical Introduction is a wide-ranging and stimulating introduction to the history and theory of Cultural Studies from Leavisism, through the era of the Centre for Contemporary Cultural Studies, to the global nature of contemporary Cultural Studies. *Cultural Studies: A Critical Introduction* begins with an introduction to the field and its theoretical history and then presents a series of short essays on key areas of Cultural Studies, designed to provoke discussion and raise questions. Each thematic section examines and explains a key topic within Cultural Studies.

ISBN10: 0-415-24656-3 (hbk)
ISBN10: 0-415-24657-1 (pbk)

ISBN13: 978-0-415-24656-9 (hbk)
ISBN13: 978-0-415-24657-6 (pbk)

Available at all good bookshops
For ordering and further information please visit:
www.routledge.com